DETERMINED TO PERSIST

General Earle Wheeler, the
Joint Chiefs of Staff, and the Military's
Foiled Pursuit of Victory in Vietnam

COLONEL MARK A. VINEY

UNITED STATES ARMY (RET.)

FOREWORD BY BRIGADIER GENERAL JOHN S. BROWN,
UNITED STATES ARMY (RET.)

Viney Development Solutions, LLC

101 Wando Reach Rd.

Charleston, SC 29492

Ordering Information:

For details, contact mviney503@gmail.com

Print ISBN: 978-1-66780-039-4

eBook ISBN: 978-1-66780-040-0

Printed in the United States of America on SFI Certified paper.

First Edition

TABLE OF CONTENTS

FOREWORD

To understand history, we should understand the thinking of the men who made it. For far too long, General Earle G. ("Bus") Wheeler has lacked an actual and accessible biography. This is despite the critical role he played as Chief of Staff of the Army and then Chairman of the Joint Chiefs of Staff from 1962 through 1970, the years most central to our Vietnam experience. Over time, a diminished understanding of Wheeler has contributed to a diminished understanding of much else. Now, Colonel Mark A. Viney has remedied the deficiency with this remarkable portrait. Drawing on untapped sources, largely from within the Wheeler family, as well as on sources previously exploited, he has drawn into focus General Wheeler and his role in the history of his time.

Determined to Persist: General Earle Wheeler, the Joint Chiefs of Staff, and the Military's Foiled Pursuit of Victory in Vietnam focuses on the Vietnam Era and defense deliberations that pertained to it. Far from passive, Wheeler and the Joint Chiefs pressed for their approach to winning the war with energy and conviction. Rebuffed within the Administration, they considered resigning *en masse* and "going public". Imbued with a sense of duty and deference to civil authority, they did not. They thought the nation would be better served if they stayed. As it was, most believed the United States "won the war and then pissed it away…" even with its flawed policies.

Viney's narrative offers a textbook case study in civil-military relationships spanning three Administrations. What is the proper margin between forthrightness and insubordination? What alternatives do experts have when their expertise is ignored? Can and should the pulse of battle be determined by electoral cycles rather than events in the field? Are we in wars to win them, or not to visibly lose them? As a corollary of that, does not losing on one's "watch" constitute a victory? How best can our nation define its strategic objectives, and do they change over time? These are perennial questions for students of national security. *Determined to Persist* offers us much to illuminate them.

The previously untapped sources Viney draws upon include numerous personal letters provided by the family, perhaps most notably those of Wheeler's wife Betty. These, reinforced by reminisces from Wheeler's son Dr. Gilmore S. Wheeler, will ultimately contribute to a social history of our Army from the 1930s through the 1970s. Even the greatest soldiers have families, loved ones, and lives out of uniform. Viney weaves these materials into his narrative, providing an engaging if sometimes jarring juxtaposition of the official and the unofficial, the exalted and the mundane.

Colonel Mark A. Viney is uniquely qualified to write this book. He is a fourth-generation soldier imbued with a sense of the Army's history, and himself the veteran of five overseas deployments. He has served as Director of the U.S. Army Heritage and Education Center, one of our most significant historical and archival facilities. As Fate would have it, his grandfather, Colonel George C. Viney, was the man tasked by General Wheeler to plan the invasion of North Vietnam intended to achieve decisive results. This bit of family lore lends itself to a unique appreciation of the arguments and issues at hand. Despite this connection, the younger Viney remains objective and analytic throughout. I recommend that the reader sit back, relax, and find out who General Earle G. Wheeler was and why he matters.

— Brigadier General (Retired) John S. Brown, United States Army

INTRODUCTION

If you believe that as a professional Soldier I am in any way proud of my association with the Vietnam War, you are damn wrong!
— General Earle G. Wheeler, c. 1972 [1]

One morning in February 1967, General Earle Gilmore "Bus" Wheeler, the Chairman of the Joint Chiefs of Staff, strode into the Pentagon's subterranean National Military Command Center (NMCC). He had an agenda on his mind, known only to himself.

The 59-year old Army General was six feet, two inches tall, broad shouldered, and slightly stooped. His dress green uniform was simply adorned with a pair of U.S. collar insignia, seven ribbons, the Army Staff Identification Badge, and four silver stars on each epaulet.

Having served as Chairman for two and half years, Wheeler was haggard and slightly overweight. He had put in long hours on the job, even on weekends and holidays. Since his previous assignment as the Chief of Staff of the Army began in July 1962, Wheeler had found practically no time for relaxation or exercise. His evening hours were often consumed with hosting or attending official social functions with his beautiful and devoted wife of 34 years, the former Frances "Betty" Rogers Howell.

Wheeler assumed the duties of Chairman at a critical point in our nation's history. He would ultimately serve a grueling, unprecedented, and never-duplicated six-year term. During these years, he carried a heavy responsibility of providing military advice to the President, the Secretary of Defense, and the National Security Council. Although not always heeded, Wheeler's advice was invariably wise, clear, and most often prescient.

During Wheeler's tenure, the voice of each Service was clearly heard in the forum of the Chiefs, with the assurance that all viewpoints were fully considered. Under his leadership, the role of the Joint Chiefs of Staff would expand to make that body's considered advice more readily available to the highest authorities.

As Chairman, Wheeler would provide military advice to two Presidents and three Secretaries of Defense. He would serve unprecedented additional terms as Chairman at the personal request of two Presidents. These presidential initiatives were the soundest measures of his leadership, the wisdom of his counsel, and the great value placed on his services. [2]

The NMCC was Wheeler's home turf. During his 32-year rise to Chairman, he had served nearly eight of the past fourteen years in the Pentagon in key positions on the Army and .

Wheeler ran a hand back over his short, dark hair worn slicked back in the usual style of his generation. He adjusted his dark-framed glasses, smiled, and returned the duty officers' greetings in a deep, assertive, yet approachable voice. [3]

Standing at attention for Wheeler in a secure conference room was Army Colonel George C. Viney, an energetic paratrooper now serving as an action officer in the Joint Staff's J-3, Pacific Division.

Wheeler returned Viney's greeting, sat down, and motioned for him to do the same. Candidly, he got straight to the point.

"Colonel, what I'm about to say is extremely close hold. The highest authority has become increasingly frustrated with Mr. McNamara's advice on how to run the war in Vietnam. At some point, he will ask me for a recommendation on how to get us out of this mess."

Wheeler continued, "You and I both know we've been fighting this goddamn war all wrong. Higher authorities have not permitted us to take the fight to the enemy, not effectively. Not in his territory. Not employing the full advantage of our superior combat power. Not as our warfighting doctrine proscribes."

Viney, who had served in Vietnam, nodded. "Sir, I agree wholeheartedly." [4]

American combat troops had been fighting and dying in Vietnam — almost 12,000 to date — for nearly two years without appreciable effect.

President Lyndon B. Johnson was growing desperate as Congress and the American public were becoming increasingly more skeptical and vocal about his Administration's decision to commit the United States to another land war in Asia. Vietnam was well on its way to becoming the most socially divisive American military conflict since the Civil War. The "hawks" demanded that Johnson do more, to pull off the gloves and fight toward a traditional military victory. The "doves," on the other hand, urged the Administration to cut its losses and pursue a negotiated peace. For disparate reasons, Johnson's senior foreign policy advisors were becoming increasingly frustrated. [5]

"I foresee an opportunity to get this war off the dime," Wheeler continued. "When the time comes, I will require a plan, ready to execute, to say to the highest authority, 'This is how we'll do it. This is how we'll begin to win this war.'"

Viney nodded expectantly.

"Colonel, I want you to plan an invasion of North Vietnam." [6]

* * * *

This book spans Wheeler's tenure as Chairman (1964-1970). It surveys the Johnson and Nixon Administrations' strategic direction of the Vietnam War that Wheeler and the Chiefs informed and endeavored to influence.

In disgust over the Vietnam War, Wheeler destroyed the manuscript of his autobiography on which he had labored in retirement for two years. At peace with his actions and the advice he offered, Wheeler died three years later.

As a student of military history with a passion for the American Civil War, Wheeler knew full-well that he was robbing future generations from ever truly understanding his perspective as one of Washington's most important figures of the Vietnam Era. Perhaps he thought he would have the last word and would prevent others less informed from speculating and second-guessing his thoughts and intentions. If so, he spurred that which he hoped to preclude. This, then, is a book the protagonist never wanted written.

Wheeler was, however, proud of the accomplishments of the American service men and women who served in Vietnam. He thought they deserved the better judgment of history. "Despite the torrents of words and pictures that have come from Vietnam, this war remains the least understood in our history," Wheeler stated in June 1968. "Americans, as they more fully understand the magnificent record of our Armed Forces in Vietnam, will accord these young men that full measure of respect and honor which is their due." [7]

Military historian Andrew J. Birtle noted in 2014, "Fifty years after the deployment of the first U.S. combat troops to Vietnam, Americans still have much to learn about the Vietnam War. Half-truths and misunderstandings clutter the historical literature, making it difficult to obtain an accurate picture of this controversial event." [8]

"History is important," Birtle suggests, "not just for its own sake, but because conceptions of the past — be they accurate or not — often shaped the decisions of later generations. This certainly has been true of Vietnam, as people have dredged up the alleged 'lessons' of the war every time America has contemplated using force since 1975." [9]

"[It is] imperative", Birtle asserts, "that Americans today comprehend one of the most traumatic events in our national history and understand the collective failures and shortcomings of national policy and leadership that joined, fought, and ultimately lost the Vietnam War". [10]

In 1984, Retired Army General Bruce Palmer, Jr., who had served as Vice Chief of Staff of the Army (1968 – 1972) and Acting Chief of Staff of the Army (1972), criticized his contemporaries' response to President Johnson's temporizing on Vietnam:

Senior U.S. military leaders recognized the weaknesses of the U.S. strategy being pursued, but unfortunately seemed unable to articulate their misgivings and communicate them effectively to their civilian superiors. ... Our military leaders failed to get across the message that the U.S. strategy was not working and over time would probably fail to achieve stated U.S. objectives. Indeed, the [Chiefs] apparently did not clearly and unequivocally tell the President and Secretary of Defense that the strategy was fatally flawed and that U.S. objectives were not achievable unless the strategy was changed. [11]

Palmer's accusations were shocking and intuitively hard to believe. By the late 1980s, Wheeler was still considered within the military as one of the most important and influential officers in Joint Chiefs of Staff history. Wheeler's reputation did not diminish until after 1997, when a mid-level Army officer and military historian Major (now retired Lieutenant General) H.R. McMaster labeled Wheeler and the Chiefs "five silent men." McMaster accused them, President Johnson, and his civilian advisors of "arrogance, weakness, lying in pursuit of self-interest, and, above all, the abdication of responsibility to the American people" during the first year of Wheeler's tour as Chairman. [12]

For lack of evidence to the contrary, Palmer's and McMaster's mischaracterizations have perpetuated. In 2018, best-selling military historian Dr. Max Hastings summarily dismissed Wheeler as "weak". That same year, military historian and retired Army Colonel Harry Rothmann omitted Wheeler from his list of Vietnam key players. This list included Johnson, McNamara, Westmoreland, Nixon, Kissinger, and Abrams, but not Wheeler, the instrumental middleman between the two Administrations and their senior military commanders. [13]

Other historians and senior military officers have felt that Palmer's and McMaster's accusations did not ring true, that there had to have been more to the story. Indeed, there was, as this book reveals.

In 2009, military historian Dr. John Prados challenged Palmer's and McMaster's portrayals of Wheeler and the Chiefs as parochial, unimaginative yes-men, complicit with, and unable to effectively articulate recommendations and consequences to the unreceptive Johnson Administration. [14]

This book reinforces Prados and demonstrates conclusively that Wheeler and the Chiefs were *not* derelict, passive accomplices to civilian mismanagement of the war in 1964-65. On the contrary, during that period and the subsequent and preponderant five years of Wheeler's tenure as Chairman, he and the Chiefs "determined to persist" in aggressively and proactively providing consistent, doctrinally grounded strategic recommendations *and potential consequences* to the Johnson Administration and then to the more receptive but politically constrained Nixon Administration.

This book shows that between August 1964 and July 1970, Wheeler, the Chiefs, and senior military commanders offered 143 documented recommendations to the two Administrations for pursuing the war toward a traditional military victory. In addition to these documented instances, senior military advisors to the President offered far more undocumented recommendations during phone calls, off-the-record meetings, informal hallway discussions, and during social events and ceremonies, etc. Assuming a conservative number of five such undocumented instances occurred for each one for which documentary evidence exists, senior military leaders offered more than 700 consistent, doctrinal recommendations during this period.

During the same 6-year period, the Chiefs also cautioned the Johnson and Nixon Administrations 70 documented times about the potential, negative military consequences of pending, non-doctrinal decisions that the Administrations were contemplating. Applying the same formula as above, senior military leaders warned at least 350 times that the Administrations' non-doctrinal decisions would undermine rather than promote attainment of U.S. objectives in Vietnam.

Thus, there is no doubt that senior military advisors to the President made their opinions known. Johnson and Nixon had a broad range of information provided to them from multiple advisory sources, however, and rendered decisions in accordance with their own prerogatives and priorities.

Concerned by the Vietnam War's debilitating effect on America's worldwide military posture, Wheeler persistently but unsuccessfully sought from May 1965 through February 1968 to convince President Johnson to authorize mobilization to reconstitute the strategic reserve.

Between June 1965 and March 1969, Wheeler also persisted in recommending a more aggressive, offensive strategy toward victory over North Vietnam. The centerpiece of Wheeler's strategy was Operation MULE SHOE, the invasion plan that my grandfather developed for Wheeler. MULE SHOE was a top secret, limited distribution plan for a limited invasion, or lodgment, into southern North Vietnam to destroy enemy sanctuary areas above the demilitarized zone. Wheeler intended it as a "foot in the door," a precursor to extended ground operations in North Vietnam. "The mother of all plans" to invade North Vietnam, MULE SHOE was the most thoroughly developed, and it informed all other U.S. Pacific Command (PACOM) and U.S. Military Assistance Command, Vietnam (MACV) invasion plans. The depth of Wheeler's conviction for his offensive strategy was evidenced by his determined efforts to secure unanimity among the Chiefs for MULE SHOE, as well as his subsequent actions to sustain the plan's viability should fortuitous events present an opportunity for him to suggest it to the President.

The operative question this book answers is, *why* did Wheeler and the Chiefs offer consistent, doctrinal recommendations in the face of tremendous and equally consistent opposition from most of the President's civilian national security advisors? *What* underpinned the Chiefs' logic?

This book does not contend that the Chiefs had a magic bullet that, had they been allowed to use it, the U.S. military could have won the war. Vietnam historiography is clear that U.S. combat involvement in Vietnam was doomed from the start. Adoption of the military's recommendations would not have substantially altered the war's ultimate negative outcome for the U.S. but may have hastened it and certainly would have increased the level of destruction and loss of life.

While researching and writing this book, I reserved judgment on Wheeler, a figure of considerable controversy during the Vietnam Era. I described my progress to colleagues as akin to piecing together a puzzle whose complete image I could not foresee. I have endeavored to provide a fair and balanced interpretation of the persistent but unsuccessful attempts by Wheeler and the Chiefs to influence Vietnam policy toward the pursuit of victory. I confess that my professional and personal admiration for Wheeler grew over the course of my research.

I have come to appreciate in Wheeler many fine attributes. He was eminently decent, hard-working, self-sacrificing, diplomatic, articulate, suave, no-nonsense yet personable, congenial, gregarious, and humorous. A devoted family man, a patriotic American, and an exceptional officer, it is no wonder then that Wheeler rose to the pinnacle of the military profession.

The prequel to this book, *General & Mrs. Earle Wheeler, Their Rise to Chairman of the Joint Chiefs of Staff Amid America's Descent Into Vietnam*, traces his distinguished, 46-year military career and family life against the backdrop of growing U.S. involvement in Southeast Asia.

The views expressed herein are my own and do not reflect the official policy or position of the Department of the Army or the U.S. Government. As this book was written while I was still serving on active duty as a U.S. Army Officer, it required clearance from the Defense Office of Pre-publication and Security Review. For that, I am grateful to Mr. Paul J. Jacobsmeyer.

I am particularly grateful for the encouragement and support provided by Wheeler's only son, Dr. Gilmore S. "Bim" Wheeler and his wife Judy.

I also wish to thank the following individuals for their reviews and constructive inputs on the draft of this book: General (Retired) George W. Casey, Jr. , Brigadier General (Retired) John S. Brown, Mr. Joseph Craig, Dr. Nick Phelan, and Dr. William T. Allison.

Special thanks to Mr. Randy Rakers and Mrs. Pam Cheney of the U.S. Army Military History Institute (USAMHI), who were instrumental to my official research at the National Archives in College Park, MD, as well as with the papers of General William C. Westmoreland at USAMHI.

This book is dedicated to my recently deceased grandfather, Colonel (Retired) George C. Viney, and to his devoted wife of more than 75 years, my grandmother, Margaret "Peg" Viney. I am very proud of them both.

More so, this book dedicated to the Lord, from whom all my blessings have flowed.

—Colonel (Retired) Mark A. Viney, United States Army

CHAPTER 1

NEW CHAIRMAN OF THE JOINT CHIEFS OF STAFF (JULY - DECEMBER 1964)

At the apex of the military pyramid whose base is the multitudes of men
and women in uniform is the Chairman of the Joint Chiefs of Staff,
usually the most respected military member of the inner circle of presidential
advisors. The strength of this link between the broader political process and the
military depends to a great extent upon the relationship between the Chairman
and his two civilian superiors, the Secretary of Defense and the President.
— Charles R. Scribner, 1980 [1]

Swearing-In

*Secretary of Defense Robert S. McNamara officiates a private ceremony in his Pentagon
office upon Wheeler's assumption as Chairman of the Joint Chiefs of Staff, Washington, DC,
3 July 1964. (Office of the Chairman of the Joint Chiefs of Staff)*

On 3 July 1964, General Earle G. "Bus" Wheeler was sworn-in as Chairman of the Joint Chiefs of Staff by the Secretary of Defense Robert S. McNamara. Wheeler's wife Betty beamed at his side. [2]

Wheeler presents the Chief of Staff of the Army flag to General Harold K. Johnson during Johnson's assumption ceremony, The Pentagon, Washington, DC, 3 July 1964. (Office of the Chairman of the Joint Chiefs of Staff)

Later that day, General Harold K. "Johnny" Johnson was sworn-in as Chief of Staff of the Army. Attending both ceremonies were the two Army generals' colleagues on the Joint Chiefs of Staff (JCS): the Chief of Staff of the Air Force, General Curtis E. "Curt" LeMay; the Chief of Naval Operations, Admiral David L. "Mac" McDonald; and the Commandant of the Marine Corps, General Wallace M. "Wally" Greene, Jr. [3]

Wheeler was already physically spent. The success of his two-year tenure as Chief of Staff of the Army had come at great personal cost. His relentlessly long work hours, frequent consumption of alcohol and rich party food, his lack of exercise, and his lifelong smoking habit had left him with a heart problem, high blood pressure, and a paunch waistline. Wheeler should have been medically retired from the Army, but instead transitioned straight into the Chairman's job with hardly a weekend break.

Sidelined

About two weeks after assuming duties as U.S. Ambassador in Saigon, Wheeler's predecessor as Chairman, retired Army General Maxwell D. Taylor, sent a message to Secretary of State Dean D. Rusk detailing a request for about 2,000 additional troops from the Commander, U.S. Military Assistance Command, Vietnam (COMUSMACV), General William C. Westmoreland. Combined with previous requests, the American military advisory and support force in Vietnam would grow from 16,000 to 22,000 troops over the next 6-12 months. Taylor fully supported the proposal, estimating that the increases would satisfy pacification requirements for the next year.

The Joint Chiefs of Staff were unable to influence the President's consideration of the Taylor-Westmoreland request in part because Taylor had a direct line to the White House and because interservice rivalry prevented the Chiefs from reaching an agreement on the issue in time to affect the decision. In fact, they never reached a consensus. Wheeler finally sent a split recommendation to McNamara on 4 August, two weeks after the President had already decided the issue. To Wheeler's chagrin, the Chiefs' chronic inability to transcend interservice rivalry continued to render them irrelevant to the policymaking process.

While the Chiefs bickered over the roles and missions of their respective Services, Taylor worked to establish his primacy as a military advisor on Vietnam policy. He intended to direct military planning from the U.S. Embassy in Saigon. The Office of the Secretary of Defense (OSD) complemented his effort by often bypassing the Chiefs to solicit Taylor's advice. [4]

On 27 July, the Chiefs responded to President Lyndon B. Johnson's request to develop contingencies for military action in Vietnam. Through McNamara, Johnson had ordered the Chiefs to consider only those military actions that would contribute militarily to the success of the counterinsurgency effort in South Vietnam; reduce the frustration and defeatism of South Vietnamese leaders by undertaking punitive measures against the enemy outside South Vietnamese borders; entail minimum risk of escalatory measures by the enemy; and require minimum U.S. participation in a combat role.

The Chiefs replied that "of the many courses of actions [*sic*] examined, only three fall within the established parameters." These included airstrikes against infiltration routes through Laos and South Vietnam, ground operations into Laos against the Communist infiltration effort, and airstrikes against military targets in North Vietnam. The Chiefs also cautioned that although these "limited actions... could prove militarily and psychologically beneficial to the war effort" in South Vietnam, they "would not significantly affect Communist support of Viet Cong operations in South Vietnam and might have counterproductive results in Laos." [5]

Wheeler's newness as Chairman, Taylor's circumvention of the Chiefs, the Chiefs' infighting, McNamara's restrictions on the military options that the Chiefs could consider, as well as the exclusiveness of the President's Tuesday luncheons with his closest inner circle had thus far removed the Chiefs entirely from policy deliberations on Vietnam.

Johnson's exclusion of the Chiefs had not gone unnoticed. Arizona Senator and Republican presidential candidate Barry M. Goldwater charged the President with ignoring his military advisors. On 14 July, much of Johnson's Tuesday luncheon focused on rebutting Republican charges that the Administration had "weakened the bonds of confidence between civilian leaders and the nation's top military professionals" and had "bypassed seasoned military judgment in vital national security issues." [6]

Because Johnson combined discussions about his presidential election campaign strategy with Vietnam policy deliberations during his Tuesday luncheons, he did not include the Chiefs, whose interests and priorities focused on national security issues. Furthermore, Johnson did not consider Vietnam primarily a national security issue but rather the issue that could cost him the election. The Chiefs obviously did not view Vietnam that way, and as such, were useless, and perhaps even threatening to Johnson's Vietnam policy deliberations. His principal objective remained keeping Vietnam out of the campaign. Whereas Johnson's closest civilian advisors tried to protect his campaign image as a peacemaker, his principal military advisors were not privy to his election strategy. [7]

Gulf of Tonkin

On 2 August, North Vietnamese gunboats engaged a U.S. Navy destroyer in international waters of the Gulf of Tonkin. Two days later, two U.S. warships reported being similarly attacked. [8]

Aware that Johnson wished to retaliate, McNamara took charge of formulating policy options. He queried the Chiefs for specific information with which he could develop his own options for retaliation. McNamara charged them with nominating targets for an immediate reprisal and recommending additional actions for twenty-four, forty-eight, and sixty hours ahead. [9]

The Chiefs insisted that the U.S. must "clobber" the attackers. As the naval episodes played out, the Joint Staff developed a series of retaliatory options ranging from limited airstrikes against North Vietnamese naval bases to mining parts of the coastline. [10]

Although the Chiefs endorsed the general idea of a "sharp limited response option," they also recommended a "heavy effort" to establish an "outer parameter" of how far the U.S. was willing to go should North Vietnam continue to undertake actions hostile to the United States." [11]

Wheeler feared that initial U.S. retaliatory attacks would fail to convince Hanoi that the U.S. had resolved to defend the South and would fail to end North Vietnamese support to the Viet Cong insurgency in the South. Eventually, he thought, more and larger air attacks would be needed, and in the end, U.S. troops might have to be deployed to Southeast Asia to meet the threat. In fact, Wheeler was certain that the U.S. should expand its attacks on the North, pummeling its modest industrial plant and strategic military assets with an air offensive that would compel its leaders to negotiate an end to the insurgency. The Chiefs agreed. Within days of the successful airstrikes, they convened to develop an expanded target list. [12]

*President Lyndon B. Johnson (third from left) confers with McNamara and the
Joint Chiefs of Staff following the Tonkin Gulf incidents, Johnson's ranch
in Johnson City, Texas, early August 1964. (LBJ Library)*

In a Tuesday luncheon with McNamara, Rusk, Deputy Secretary of
Defense Cyrus R. Vance, National Security Advisor McGeorge Bundy, and
Central Intelligence Agency Director John A. McCone, the President agreed
with McNamara's recommendation that the reprisal be both "sharp" and
"limited." He rejected the Chiefs' advice that the airstrikes establish an "outer
parameter" of how far the U.S. was willing to go. [13]

While Johnson shared Rusk's concern that the U.S. must stand firm in
Vietnam to contain an aggressively expansionist China, he feared even more
a political backlash from right-wing Republicans and Southern Democrats
should he falter in Vietnam. Johnson continued to worry that a retreat on
Vietnam would jeopardize his Great Society agenda of domestic social initiatives. [14]

The Tonkin Gulf incidents afforded the President an opportunity
to bolster his image as a defender against Communism and focused his
Administration on what many believed to be North Vietnam's central role in
directing and providing support for the insurgency in the South. [15]

Johnson seized the opportunity to secure congressional support for his
Southeast Asia policy, thereby signaling American unity and determination to

the North Vietnamese. Johnson felt that President Harry S. Truman's failure to obtain a similar mandate for military action in Korea in 1950 had been a mistake that he would avoid. Only after conferring with House and Senate leaders did Johnson order retaliatory airstrikes against North Vietnamese torpedo boat bases. [16]

The Tonkin Gulf Resolution permitted Johnson "to take all necessary measures to repel any armed attack against the forces of the United States and to prevent further aggression." With near unanimity, Congress gave Johnson a green light to send Hanoi a signal of national resolve to deter further hostile acts. Retaliatory airstrikes would be "limited but fitting," although the threat of further retaliation would have to be open-ended to be credible. Congress had granted blanket authority to the Administration to apply military sanctions against North Vietnam, and given adequate provocation, to commit the U.S. to war in South Vietnam. [17]

Johnson would soon invoke the Tonkin Gulf Resolution, considered by some in his Administration as the equivalent to a declaration of war, to justify the expansion of American military efforts within South Vietnam, against North Vietnam, and in Southeast Asia at large. [18]

Johnson's firm but restrained response to the Tonkin Gulf incident won broad popular support. His rating in the Louis Harris poll skyrocketed from 42% to 72% overnight. He satisfied his domestic political need by effectively neutralizing Goldwater's vigorous calls for escalation, a fact that would contribute to his overwhelming electoral victory in November. Moreover, the first formal Congressional debate on Vietnam had brought a near unanimous endorsement of the President's policies and provided him an apparently solid foundation on which to construct future policy.

In time, however, Johnson would pay a heavy price for his easy victory. American prestige was now publicly and more firmly committed, not merely to defending South Vietnam, but also to responding to North Vietnamese provocations. By attacking North Vietnamese targets, the President temporarily silenced his hawkish critics inside and outside of government, but in so doing, he had broken a long-standing barrier against taking the war to the North. The first steps having been taken, the next steps would be easier. Johnson's victory in Congress encouraged him to take the legislators lightly in making future policy Vietnam decisions. When the Administration's case for reprisals later turned out to be less than compelling, many members of Congress would conclude correctly that they had been deceived. Johnson's resounding domestic triumph brought enormous, if still hidden costs. [19]

Hanoi Gambles

Unbeknownst to the United States, the Tonkin Gulf incident had also raised the stakes for the Communists. Rather than deterring North Vietnam, Johnson's forceful response led it to step-up its efforts in the South. Encouraged by signs of continued deterioration in South Vietnam and persuaded that the U.S. was on the verge of expanding the war, Hanoi decided in September to send to the South the first units of its own regular army (NVA) to support a push for victory before the spring of 1965. In what would prove a major miscalculation, the North Vietnamese hoped to accomplish their goal before the U.S. could intervene directly in the war, thus avoiding a major conflict with a great power.

Shortly thereafter, North Vietnamese leaders sought additional support from Moscow and Peking. The Soviet Union was still cautious but found itself under increasing pressure to do something or lose its leadership position to China. While urging the North Vietnamese to prepare for a long war, China was more forthcoming, mobilizing forces along its border with North Vietnam and significantly expanding its military and economic assistance. [20]

Policy Formulation

Although Johnson had assured the American public that his Administration sought "no wider war," others within the Administration, most notably Taylor and the Chiefs, wanted to keep the pressure on Hanoi. Intelligence reports indicated a deteriorating situation in South Vietnam or one devoid of improvement. Taylor and the Chiefs regarded 4 August as a turning point in U.S. policy on direct action against North Vietnam, although they disagreed about both the form and intensity of subsequent operations. Taylor hoped to signal U.S. resolve to Hanoi in an unambiguous manner. Likewise, the Commander-in-Chief, Pacific (CINCPAC), Admiral Ulysses S. G. "Oley" Sharp, Jr. — who viewed the war in Vietnam against the broader perspective of U.S. national interests in the entire Pacific and Asian area — believed the initial reprisal airstrikes had "created a momentum which can lead to the attainment of our objectives in S.E. Asia." The Chiefs warned that "failure to resume and maintain a program of pressure through military actions ... could signal a lack of resolve." However, no new initiatives would be authorized against North Vietnam for the remainder of 1964. [21]

The Administration's deliberations about Vietnam had solidified three critical assumptions: first, that the principal difficulty in South Vietnam stemmed from North Vietnamese support for the Viet Cong; second, that overt military pressures against North Vietnam would probably be required; and third, that the gradual application of military and diplomatic pressures on North Vietnam would persuade Hanoi to terminate its support for the Viet Cong. Barring any critical developments, the President's civilian foreign policy advisors generally conceded that these actions should not begin until after Johnson's inauguration in January 1965. Planning for the application of such pressures would accelerate after the November election. [22]

Taylor echoed the Chiefs in urging direct U.S. military action against North Vietnam. His perspective on Vietnam policy had evolved since becoming U.S. Ambassador. Now exposed daily to the frustrations of organizing a counterinsurgency effort against an elusive and determined enemy, he began to sympathize with the Saigon government's call for action against the North.

South Vietnamese Head of State General Nguyen Khanh urged the U.S. and South Vietnam to "open the war up" with a decisive campaign to secure the objective of "total victory in order to liberate all the national territory." Khanh's recommendation was consistent with the warfighting doctrine that underpinned the Chiefs' recommendations, but the Administration was not about to let U.S. generals dictate the scope and tempo of the war, let alone South Vietnamese generals. [23]

French President Charles de Gaulle had warned in April that the U.S. was repeating "the experience that the French had earlier." He saw two options for the United States: pursue immediate neutralization of Indochina and the withdrawal of all foreign forces, or else demonstrate the "willingness of the U.S. to really carry the war to the North and if necessary against China." He strongly recommended the former. [24]

The Administration's interest in employing airpower as a solution reflected lingering sentiment in the U.S. against involving its ground forces in another land war on the Asian continent. Many of the President's advisors, including Taylor, believed that a carefully calibrated air campaign would be the most effective means of exerting pressure against the North and, at the same time, the method least likely to provoke Chinese intervention. Taylor considered conventional U.S. Army ground forces ill-suited for day-to-day counterinsurgency operations against Viet Cong insurgents in rural areas. Ground forces might, however, be used to protect vital air bases in the South and to repel any North Vietnamese attack across the demilitarized zone (DMZ) that separated North from South Vietnam. Together, a more vigorous counterinsurgency effort in the South and military pressure against the North might buy time for the South Vietnamese government to get its political house in order, boost flagging military and civilian morale, and strengthen its military position in the event of a negotiated peace. Taylor, Sharp, Westmoreland, Wheeler, and the Chiefs agreed that Hanoi was unlikely to change its course unless convinced that it could not succeed in the South. The Chiefs, however, were split over airstrikes as a panacea or substitute for military efforts in the South. [25]

Immediately after signing the Tonkin Gulf Resolution into law on 10 August, Johnson requested his advisors develop a plan of action for Vietnam that would allow the U.S. to retain the initiative gained during the reprisal airstrikes "with maximum results and minimum danger." [26]

The task of developing such a Vietnam policy fell to Assistant Secretary of State for Far Eastern Affairs William P. Bundy, brother of McGeorge Bundy. Despite Bundy's limited experience in the planning and application of military force, he was supremely confident in his own analytical ability and endeavored to reconcile calls for further action against North Vietnam with Johnson's "minimum danger" mandate. Bundy found it unnecessary to consult with the Chiefs and instead coordinated his effort closely with McNamara and Rusk.

Bundy's policy recommendations would set the Administration's agenda for policy deliberation until January 1965. [27]

Bundy circulated his draft policy paper before the Chiefs reached a consensus on recommendations. Yet again, they found themselves in the familiar position of responding to a paper that carried the weight of an agreed position between the Secretaries of Defense and State. [28]

Bundy recommended a "short holding phase" of 10-14 days, during which the U.S. would avoid any actions that might divert international attention from Hanoi's provocation in the Gulf of Tonkin. After this period of "military silence," U.S. and South Vietnamese forces would undertake a program of "limited pressures" against North Vietnam from September through December 1964. [29]

The Chiefs were reluctant to accept the implicit objective behind Bundy's "limited pressures" against North Vietnam, which aimed to send a "signal" of resolve to the Communists and boost the morale of the South Vietnamese while minimizing the possibility of escalation before the November election. Arguing against the "holding strategy," the Chiefs reiterated their doctrinal position that they had advocated for almost seven months: military action against North Vietnam should be decisive and aim to destroy the Hanoi government's "will and capability" to continue support for the insurgency in South Vietnam. They argued that the "sudden advantage" gained following the Gulf of Tonkin incident "must be retained" through the application of "more serious pressures" against North Vietnam "as necessary." However, still lacking consensus among themselves for specific military actions against North Vietnam, the Chiefs informed McNamara on 14 August that they would develop more detailed recommendations as soon as possible. [30]

The President had posed several questions to Wheeler: What, if any, action should be undertaken in the Laotian panhandle? Should the tempo of maritime sabotage operations against North Vietnam be increased? Should the U.S. initiate a tit-for-tat program of retaliation, or should it do something more, against North Vietnam? If so, what and when?

The Chiefs proved adept at providing technical information but were still unable to respond to questions with broad policy implications, principally due to their internal debate over the effectiveness of airpower as a solution to the problem in Vietnam. LeMay was convinced that airstrikes against North Vietnam "had every prospect for success" and that an effective air campaign against the North would lessen or remove altogether the possibility that U.S. ground forces would be needed in South Vietnam. If the U.S. displayed a willingness to apply overwhelming destructive force, it could prevent Chinese Communist intervention. "Johnny" Johnson, on the other hand, believed that LeMay and Greene had misdiagnosed the nature of the war itself. They thought that North Vietnam caused the war, whereas Johnson asserted that the insurgency in the South was essentially indigenous. Skeptical about the effectiveness of aerial interdiction and concerned that military action alone would do little to enhance political stability in South Vietnam, Johnson also feared that bombing North Vietnam would escalate the war.

The Chiefs were still at an impasse on 8 September when they recommended to McNamara and Taylor unconnected proposals for air operations against North Vietnam, air and ground operations into Cambodia and Laos, and intensified ground operations within South Vietnam. [31]

The Chiefs did not propose a comprehensive, integrated strategy or estimate of the situation because the President and Secretary of Defense expected them to perform a relatively limited function as technical advisors for Office of the Secretary of Defense (OSD) planners rather than as strategic thinkers and advisors in their own right. The Joint Staff merely categorized targets and determined the number of bombs and gallons of fuel required to hit them, while development of strategic options was the purview of former attorneys Bundy and Assistant Secretary of Defense for International Security Affairs John T. McNaughton. Vexed, Wheeler determined that he and the Chiefs would play a more proactive, substantive, and assertive role in Vietnam policymaking. [32]

The Chiefs did not believe that military power alone would solve South Vietnam's problems. Their recommendations to McNamara discussed the "lack of a viable politico/economic structure in [South Vietnam]" and the need to

"improve the combat effectiveness of the [South Vietnamese Armed Forces]."
While they clearly sought to expand the war into North Vietnam despite difficulties in the South, they acknowledged the need to "deter Communist China
from direct intervention." The Chiefs also recognized "that the lack of stability
in the central government, the low state of morale in the leadership, and the
poorly trained civil service in the Republic of Vietnam (RVN) militate against
early success and that the solutions, primarily political, to these problems are
also critical to the eventual termination of the insurgency." The Chiefs' dis-
jointed advice arose from their struggle to find ways to effectively employ U.S.
combat power in such a complex environment. [33]

Although convinced that the concept of graduated pressure was inconsistent with the "nature of war," the Chiefs dropped their fundamental objections to McNamara's assumption that sharply limited military action against
North Vietnam would reverse the deteriorating situation. Under Wheeler's
growing influence, the Chiefs would plan for the war within the parameters of
that concept, suppress their differences, and press for authorization for stronger military action in the future. Essentially, it would be a matter of "eating the
elephant one bite at a time." [34]

"Neither our civilian nor our military leaders dreamed that a tenth-rate
undeveloped country like North Vietnam could possibly defeat the United
States, the world's dominant military and industrial power," recalled future
Acting Chief of Staff of the Army, General Bruce Palmer, Jr. "Our military
leaders evidently assumed that although their strategies were preferable, the
United States would prevail regardless of what strategy was adopted." [35]

For weeks, the Administration did not follow-up the Tonkin Gulf
reprisals with additional attacks against North Vietnam. The President was
not about to jeopardize his political fortunes by escalating the war. Having
established his determination to defend U.S. interests with force if necessary,
he emphasized in the final months of the campaign his wish to limit U.S.
involvement if possible. "We seek no wider war," Johnson repeated in numerous speeches. [36]

At the same time, political turmoil in South Vietnam made caution
essential. Khanh resigned after massive protests against his regime. As open

warfare waged in the streets, politicians and generals jockeyed for power behind the scenes.

In early September, LeMay and Greene vigorously pressed for extended air attacks against North Vietnam. Taylor, backed by Wheeler, conceded that such steps would have to be taken in time, but argued that it would be too risky to "overstrain the currently weakened [South Vietnamese Government] by drastic action in the immediate future." The President concurred, stating that he did not wish to "enter the patient in a 10-round bout, when he was in no shape to hold out for one round." [37]

Committed to preventing dissent from his principal military advisors, the President informed the Chiefs on 10 September that he "would be ready to do more" later. He vowed that when "larger decisions are required at any time by a change of the situation, they will be taken." While keeping other options open, Johnson decided merely to continue covert operations against North Vietnam and to be ready to respond to North Vietnamese provocations on a "tit-for-tat basis." [38]

Aware of similarities between the Korean War and the U.S. involvement in Vietnam, Johnson feared massive Chinese intervention. "We know there are 200 million in the Chinese Army ... think about 200 million Chinese coming down those trails. No, sir! I don't want to fight them." Other domestic and international considerations, particularly American-Soviet relations, gave Johnson reason to hesitate; but a Chinese intervention that could turn a limited Vietnam conflict into a Korean-style stalemate was his paramount concern. He would, therefore, subsequently evaluate all potential military actions against North Vietnam on their likelihood to provoke Soviet or Chinese intervention. [39]

The contrived consensus between the President and his civilian and military advisors would enable planning for the Americanization of the war without full consideration of the potential costs and consequences. Momentum continued to build behind McNamara's concept of graduated pressure, while other options, such as a negotiated withdrawal, were discounted without due consideration. [40]

SIGMA II

During 8-17 September, the Department of Defense conducted a Southeast Asia wargame dubbed SIGMA II to "consider the major political and military questions that should be answered prior to making a decision to commit ... U.S. armed forces to combat in Southeast Asia." Military officers and civilians from both inside and outside the government attempted to replicate as closely as possible the outcome of an air campaign against North Vietnam. [41]

By the wargame's conclusion, the U.S. had deployed more than ten ground combat divisions to Southeast Asia and was contemplating an amphibious invasion of North Vietnam.

SIGMA II accurately predicted that the escalation of U.S. military involvement would ultimately erode public support for the war in the United States. Continued political instability in Saigon drew into question the worthiness and dependability of America's ally, and the subtlety of the Communist strategy made it difficult for the U.S. government to sustain its case for military intervention. The wargame concluded that the American public would rather pull out of South Vietnam than commit to a protracted war.

SIGMA II questioned the fundamental assumption upon which graduated pressure depended: that, "like the commitment to get the missiles out of Cuba in 1962," the enemy would be convinced that the U.S. was "prepared to meet any level of escalation they might mount"; that it had "established a consensus to see through this course of action both at home and on the world scene"; and that it would not "not buckle politically" if North Vietnam failed to "comply." The wargame's results suggested that graduated pressure could lead to disaster in Vietnam. The President, it seemed, would have to confront a difficult decision between a large-scale protracted war or disengagement under the auspices of a negotiated agreement. [42]

Incredibly, the conclusions of SIGMA II were never seriously studied and had no discernible impact upon the Administration's Vietnam policy. The effect of the wargame on William Bundy and other civilian advisors responsible for Vietnam planning "was not great." [43]

Military Theology

The growing consensus behind the strategic concept of graduated pressure overpowered SIGMA II's unpromising conclusions because the President and his civilian advisors were unwilling to risk either escalation or disengagement. In their minds, a rash application of force would be disastrous and lead, in the worst-case scenario, to nuclear war with the Soviet Union. Doing nothing would lead to defeat in South Vietnam and an associated loss of credibility that could undermine the West's alliance structure and result in defeat in the Cold War. [44]

The fear of escalation reinforced the Administration's perception that the Chiefs' doctrinal focus on employing overwhelming force to destroy the enemy's will and capability to fight was not only irrelevant but dangerous. Soviet Premier Nikita Khrushchev had warned President Johnson that aggressive U.S. policies, such as those recommended by Greene and LeMay, could lead, in the worst-case scenario, to nuclear war. McGeorge Bundy remarked that LeMay assumed away the possibility of an escalation of the war. McNamara agreed that the Chiefs "downplayed" risks of escalation and that he had to keep the Chiefs in check to "avoid the risk of nuclear war." [45]

Considering military action an extension of diplomacy discouraged analysis based on military considerations, such as the SIGMA II findings. McNaughton shared McNamara's and Bundy's views that the use of force should aim to communicate with the enemy rather than to inflict destruction. Even Taylor had come to believe that military force should "signal intention." Citing the Cuban Missile Crisis to support his view, Taylor warned that "too much in this matter of coercing Hanoi may be as bad as too little." He hoped that severely limited force would induce the leadership in Hanoi to become "cooperative" and "wind up the VC insurgency on terms satisfactory to us and our South Vietnamese allies." To satisfy the conflicting objectives of avoiding escalation and demonstrating resolve to the enemy, the President's civilian advisors felt not only justified but compelled to discount the Chiefs' doctrinal advice. [46]

The blurred distinction between diplomatic communication and military action helped draw military planning for Vietnam further away from the Chiefs and toward the State Department and interdepartmental committees. William Bundy and McNaughton became the principal planners for Vietnam. Both men believed that coordinating the use of force with diplomacy called for a high degree of precision and control, a lesson they had drawn from the Cuban Missile Crisis. The triumvirate of McNamara, Bundy, and McNaughton would determine the right "mix" of military and diplomatic measures necessary to attain a settlement in Vietnam. They would then supervise military operations to "tighten the screw" on the North Vietnamese leadership. [47]

The triumvirate was intent upon breaking with past interventionist formulas in favor of applying the least amount of force to achieve the desired end. The incremental nature of their novel approach allowed for hope and optimism in the face of adversity. If some bombing of North Vietnam was insufficient, then more bombing might work, or if this failed, the introduction of troops, or more troops, would end the war. Because this was a new approach to warfighting, the triumvirate felt prudent in being equivocal and tentative in their management of violence. Experimentation with the level and type of military force was acceptable because the policy being formulated was new and unprecedented. [48]

Wheeler, the Chiefs, and senior military commanders strongly voiced their doctrinal objections. "I do not regard combat as a baseball game — nine men on each side, with neither side allowed to increase its strength regardless of need or capability," Wheeler argued. "War may quite properly be limited by national policy as to area, weapons, targets, and objectives. Within these parameters, however, force should be employed in the kind, degree, and timing necessary to achieve national objectives." [49]

To his military colleagues, Wheeler privately derided the triumvirate's novel warfighting approach as "military theology," since its prospects for success were long on hope but short on empirical merit. [50]

The military understood and articulated to the unreceptive civilians what Welsh Major General Henry H. E. Lloyd wrote in the 18th Century. "This art [of war], like all others, is founded on certain and fixed principles, which are by their nature invariable; the application of them can only be varied: but they are themselves constant." [51]

The February 1962 edition of Field Manual 100-5, Field Service Regulations, Operations, describes the "Principles of War" as *fundamental truths governing the prosecution of war. Their proper application is essential to the exercise of command and to successful conduct of military operations. These principles are interrelated and, dependent on the circumstances, may tend to reinforce one another or to be in conflict. Consequently, the degree of application of any specific principle will vary with the situation.* [52]

The first principle is "Objective." *Every military operation must be directed toward a clearly defined, decisive and attainable objective. The ultimate military objective of war is the destruction of the enemy's armed forces and his will to fight. The objective of each operation must contribute to this ultimate objective. Each intermediate objective must be such that its attainment will most directly, quickly, and economically contribute to the purpose of the operation. The selection of an objective is based upon consideration of the means available, the enemy, and the area of operations. Every commander must understand and clearly define his objective and consider each contemplated action in light thereof.* [53]

As Wheeler defined it, "War is a political act; it is the employment of military force to achieve a political objective. Put another way, war is violence organized and utilized to destroy the capability and will of a hostile state to pursue a course of action inimical to national interests." [54]

To the military, victory over North Vietnamese aggression was the only acceptable objective. Wars, when entered, are fought to be won. The inconclusive armistice that ended the fighting in Korea but failed to resolve the underlying political causes of that war, was unsatisfactory. "There can be no substitute for victory", MacArthur famously asserted to Congress in 1951. MacArthur also remarked to the United States Corps of Cadets in 1962, "Your mission remains fixed, inviolable … it is to *win* our wars". [55]

While "Objective" focuses attention on *what* is to be accomplished, the principle of "Offensive" states in general terms *how* the objective is to be attained. *Offensive action is necessary to achieve decisive results and to maintain freedom of action. It permits the commander to exercise initiative and impose his will upon the enemy; to set the pace and determine the course of battle; to exploit enemy weaknesses and rapidly changing situations, and to meet unexpected developments. The defensive may be forced on the commander, but it should be deliberately adopted only as a temporary expedient while awaiting an opportunity for offensive action or for the purpose of economizing forces on a front where a decision is not sought. Even on the defensive the commander seeks every opportunity to seize the initiative and achieve results by offensive action.* [56]

The military had no use for the triumvirate's carrots and sticks. They wanted offensive sledgehammers to attack North Vietnam rapidly, unrelentingly, and with overwhelming force to destroy its airbases, planes, and antiaircraft defenses, to cripple its few industries, to tear up its bridges and railroads, and to cut off its fuel and power supplies – as rapidly as possible.

Instead, the military had to settle for a finely adjusted mix of restraints, and fits and starts emanating from Washington. They saw this approach as absurd, unsound, dangerous, and futile. Yet, respectful of civilian control over them, the military would attempt to play the weak hand they had been dealt to the utmost of their abilities. [57]

The President rejected recommendations for reprisal airstrikes from Rusk and the Chiefs because he and his other advisors were afraid of losing control. The ability to control events precisely — rather than what effect those operations might have upon the enemy — became a principal criterion for approving operations. The belief that the Administration could maintain close control from Washington over the actions of U.S. forces engaged in combat in Vietnam carried over to an assumption that it could anticipate, even script, the enemy's response to military operations. [58]

Despite SIGMA II's findings, the triumvirate clung to its "military theological" assumptions about how Hanoi's leadership would respond to coercive military pressures. These unrealistic assumptions continued to guide the evolving strategy for the war. The principal elements of the policy of graduated pressure — maximum results with minimum investment, and the belief that the enemy would respond rationally to precisely controlled military stimuli

— were consistent with the educational backgrounds and professional experiences of the economists, managers, attorneys, and systems analysts who became the architects of American intervention in Vietnam. The warfighting doctrinal principle of employing overwhelming force seemed unnecessary, wasteful, and inefficient. [59]

The triumvirate failed to consider that Hanoi's commitment to revolutionary war made losses that seemed unconscionable to American white-collar professionals of little consequence to the Hanoi government. They instinctively discounted military advice that questioned their assumption that Ho Chi Minh, when confronted with military action designed to affect his calculation of interest, would respond as they anticipated.

Unsuccessfully, the military attempted to educate the triumvirate on warfighting. The Assistant to the Chairman of the Joint Chiefs of Staff, Army General Andrew J. "Andy" Goodpaster, warned McNamara in the fall of 1964, "Sir, you're trying to program the enemy and that is one thing that we must never try to do. We can't do his thinking for him." [60]

Goodpaster's admonition fell on deaf ears. Besides hostility, the triumvirate confronted their senior military counterparts with an admixture of arrogance and ignorance. "Military judgment was a term you just never even mentioned," recalled Army Lieutenant General James K. Woolnough, "because military judgment didn't mean anything to any of those people. They were new, and they just discovered the wheel." [61]

When Woolnough assumed duties as the Army's Deputy Chief of Staff for Personnel, "Johnny" Johnson cautioned him. "Your military judgment doesn't count for a thing," Johnson said. "You have got to prove it statistically if you're going to sell it to these directors of today." [62]

"Throughout the war, the Joint Chiefs of Staff and Westmoreland lived in a different world and fought a very different war than McNamara and his civilian colleagues," political scientist Dale R. Herspring observes. "It is not surprising that the two camps often spoke *past* one another." [63]

Other Options

On 3 October, President Johnson asked Under Secretary of State George W. Ball to play devil's advocate against the Administration's Vietnam policy and its strategic concept of the war. Two days later, Ball responded with a lengthy memorandum that challenged "assumptions of our current Vietnam policy." Ball urged the President to assess the potential cost of the war "before we commit military forces to a line of action that could put events in the saddle and destroy our freedom to choose the policies that are at once the most effective and the most prudent." Ball's recommendations also fell on deaf ears. [64]

The following week, the Chiefs discussed the deteriorating situation in Vietnam. Lamenting that their previous recommendations for action against North Vietnam had gone unheeded, LeMay urged Wheeler to be more argumentative with the President and press for a full air campaign against the North Vietnamese during White House meetings on the war. "Johnny" Johnson maintained his contrary belief that the principal problem in Vietnam involved "a struggle for the loyalty and support of the population" rather than North Vietnamese support for the insurgency. Unrelenting, LeMay argued that the solution to the problem in Vietnam would not be found through "political, economic, psychological, and military actions proposed by the Army," but by the unconstrained application of firepower against North Vietnam. [65]

Wheeler forged a consensus among the Chiefs. On 23 October, they issued a memorandum again recommending action against the North to destroy its "will and capability" to support the insurgencies in South Vietnam and Laos. The memo advanced versions of both LeMay's and Johnson's recommendations. "Accelerated and forceful actions both inside and outside of the Republic of Vietnam" would support a four-fold strategy to cut off Viet Cong insurgents from assistance from the North; separate the Viet Cong from the population in the South; continue to seek a viable and legitimate South Vietnamese government; and maintain a threatening military presence in Southeast Asia for the purposes of coercion and deterrence. Because of the Saigon government's political instability, the memo described the struggle in Vietnam as requiring "a combination of political and military action" and argued that "there is an interaction between the two that permits a political success to be exploited militarily and vice versa." [66]

Recommending fourteen military actions in ascending order of severity, the Chiefs predicted "the entire program of courses of action may be required." Six immediate actions would influence the situation within South Vietnam while eight actions would isolate the Viet Cong in the South from their base in the North. The Chiefs deferred proposing additional actions until they could convince the triumvirate and the President that such actions had become necessary, as they knew would be the case. [67]

Incorporating the vernacular of "military theology," the Chiefs' program of actions was "arranged so that any of the actions may be selected, implemented, and controlled, as required to produce the desired effect on analyzing and estimating the Communist reaction." At the extreme end of the scale, the Chiefs' program included mining and blockading North Vietnamese ports, an all-out air campaign against North Vietnam, amphibious and airborne ground offensives into the coastal areas of North Vietnam, as well as the commitment of increasingly large numbers of ground forces into Southeast Asia. [68]

The Chiefs assessed that there was "not a high risk" of Chinese intervention on the ground unless the U.S. and South Vietnam occupied areas of North Vietnam or northern Laos, or the U.S. attacked Chinese air bases. If the Chinese did intervene, the Chiefs believed it was "within the capability of U.S. force to deal with large-scale aggression." They did not cite SIGMA II's findings that air action against the North would provoke an intensified ground war in the South, which in turn would require the introduction of large numbers of U.S. ground troops. [69]

Bien Hoa

On 1 November - two days before American voters went to the polls - the Viet Cong launched a nighttime raid on Bien Hoa airfield that killed four Americans, wounded 72, and damaged or destroyed 17 of 36 U.S. Air Force aircraft.

Taylor furiously described the attack as "a deliberate escalation and a change of the ground rules" and recommended that it "be met promptly by an appropriate act of reprisal." Westmoreland and Sharp agreed with Taylor that Bien Hoa was precisely the kind of attack for which the President, just over a month earlier, had approved "tit-for-tat" reprisals. [70]

With increasing unanimity, the Chiefs argued that Taylor's recommendation didn't go far enough. They saw Bien Hoa as an opportunity to begin "systematic bombing" of North Vietnam and recommended progressive attacks against all targets on their 94-target list. In conjunction with initial airstrikes, the Chiefs planned to dispatch Marine and Army units to secure the Danang and Saigon areas. After flying U.S. troops and supplies into Saigon, the aircraft would evacuate U.S. military dependents. Although the bombings might initially appear to be reprisals, they would mark the beginning of a sustained air campaign to "punish" North Vietnam and interdict infiltration routes to the South. [71]

Immediate retaliation was out of the question, however. With the election looming and wary of the internal situation in South Vietnam, the President did not seriously entertain Taylor's and the Chiefs' recommendations. [72]

Wheeler warned McNamara that the Chiefs were so frustrated about the situation in South Vietnam that "if the United States did not take action against North Vietnam immediately it should withdraw all forces from South Vietnam." They requested McNamara send a memo to the President to that effect. [73]

McNamara responded by promising that the President would soon decide to use military force in Vietnam. He reassured the Chiefs that their recommendations were vital to the decision-making process. He appeared sympathetic to their view that disaster would ensue if the U.S. continued to follow the current policy in Vietnam. He directed the Chiefs to "re-examine the forces which should be required to support a major effort in South Vietnam and the logistics to back up these forces." LeMay took solace in McNamara's tough talk about a systematic bombing program. McNamara spoke extensively about airstrikes against China, suggesting that once the U.S. completed the destruction of the 94 targets on the Chiefs' list, airstrikes might be launched against nascent Chinese nuclear facilities. McNamara reassured "Johnny" Johnson that ground troops should deploy at the outset of an air campaign because bombing alone "would not bring any major changes in the attitude of the dissident Viet Cong in the South." McNamara even spoke unreservedly about a land war in Southeast Asia that would pit the U.S. armed forces against the combined armies of China and North Vietnam. [74]

The response to Bien Hoa typified what would become a pattern in the relationship between the Chiefs and the Administration. Although McNamara shared the President's constant dread of escalation, he made empty promises of future action and requests to re-examine plans for a large-scale war in Asia that assuaged the Chiefs' discontent in the short term but would strain their civilian-military relationship over time. [75]

Another Committee

The day after Bien Hoa, the President authorized intensive planning for future action in Vietnam. Despite intelligence that bombing North Vietnam would not decisively affect the war in the South, a firm consensus would emerge within the Administration by the end of November that the U.S. must soon employ airpower against the North in some form. Presidential advisors disagreed among themselves on reasons for the bombing, some viewing it as a way to boost morale in South Vietnam, others as a means to reduce infiltration from the North, while still others saw it as a weapon to force Hanoi to stop supporting the insurgency. They also disagreed on the type of bombing. Wheeler and the military continued to advocate a "fast and full squeeze" — massive attacks against major industries and military targets. Civilian advisors advocated a "slow squeeze," a graduated series of attacks beginning with infiltration routes in Laos and slowly extending to North Vietnam. [76]

After Johnson's crushing defeat of Goldwater in the election, his top priority became to pass his Great Society social legislation, which he believed would secure his place in history.

Because the Great Society constrained exploration of policy options in Vietnam, the probable consequences of the most desirable course of action — the gradual application of military pressure against North Vietnam — received scant attention. Indeed, the triumvirate of McNamara, McNaughton, and William Bundy recognized that their strategy was unlikely to achieve the

Administration's stated foreign policy objective of guaranteeing the freedom and independence of South Vietnam. However, rather than explore alternative courses of action, the triumvirate rationalized that committing the U.S. military to war in Vietnam and losing would be preferable to withdrawing from what they considered an impossible situation. They believed that if the U.S. demonstrated that it would use military force to support its foreign policy, its international stature would be enhanced, regardless of the outcome. Because the triumvirate conceived of the gradual application of force as a political, rather than a military, operation, they did not seriously evaluate its practical military consequences. [77]

The President approved the formation of another interdepartmental committee to examine U.S. interests and objectives in Vietnam; to assess the situation there and its global and regional implications; to define the major courses of action; and to argue the pros and cons of each. The triumvirate constrained the Chiefs' inputs and steered the committee's deliberations so that its final recommendation accorded with their own "military theology." [78]

The triumvirate believed that it would be preferable to fail in Vietnam after attempting some level of military action than to withdraw without first committing the U.S. military to direct action against North Vietnam. They thought the principal objective of military activities was to protect U.S. credibility. Because they assumed that graduated military pressure could be stopped at any time and would not commit the U.S. to any further military measures, they saw less risk in using force than not doing so. Failure to uphold the Administration's commitment to preserve the independence of South Vietnam would be acceptable so long as the world recognized that the U.S. had done all it could under the circumstances. McNaughton believed that the U.S. would be in "no worse position" in Southeast Asia if graduated pressure failed to secure U.S. policy objectives there than it was already. Indeed, the loss of South Vietnam after the direct intervention of U.S. armed forces "would leave behind a better odor" then an immediate withdrawal and would demonstrate that the U.S. was a "good doctor willing to keep promises, be tough, take risks, get bloodied, and hurt the enemy badly." [79]

Bundy earnestly believed his "undramatic 'water drip' technique" would have a more disquieting psychological effect on North Vietnam than the "more dramatic attacks" advocated by the Chiefs. [80]

Although the committee did solicit the Joint Staff for "specific military facts," the Chiefs were unable to influence the committee's vital early deliberations that established the limits of its examination. By the time Wheeler first received a coordinating draft of the committee's analysis for the Chiefs to assess, Rusk, McNamara, and McGeorge Bundy had already briefed the President on the scope of the study. Once again, the Chiefs were forced to dissent from a consensus position devised through civilian interdepartmental coordination. The Chiefs were frustrated by the triumvirate's elimination of the only two options that made any military sense: get in fully to win, or stay out. [81]

On the collective assumption that progress in the South was nearly hopeless, the triumvirate focused the committee's attention on putting pressure on Hanoi. All options considered called for the gradual application of limited military force against North Vietnam and fell within a narrow range of all feasible actions open to the United States. [82]

Wheeler disdained the weakness of the committee's recommendations. Vital military targets, such as the North Vietnamese MIG fighter base at Phuc Yen, would be off-limits under any of the options for fear of antagonizing either the Chinese or the Soviets. [83]

The Chiefs rejected the triumvirate's notion that gradual military pressure would secure U.S. objectives in Southeast Asia and enable the U.S. to withdraw from Vietnam whenever it wished. They urged McNamara to develop a "clear set of military objectives before further military involvement in Southeast Asia is undertaken." The Chiefs were convinced that the U.S. should either fully commit itself and all its resources to the defense of South Vietnam, or nothing at all. They argued that once the U.S. began using force in Vietnam, it could not terminate military activities until it had attained freedom and independence for South Vietnam. Reflecting MacArthur's "no substitute for victory" maxim, the Chiefs denounced the idea that the U.S. should commit military force and expend American lives without fully committing to the policy objective that the intervention was supposed to achieve. They could not fathom the notion of employing military force to "leave behind a better odor" should the U.S. lose. [84]

The Chiefs' "hard knock" recommendation was an intensive air campaign against North Vietnam to destroy the 94 targets on their list. The Chiefs requested that McNamara forward their recommendation to the President for his consideration. He refused on the grounds that Johnson would receive the Chiefs' position when the working group completed its study. [85]

In a meeting with the President, Rusk, the Bundy brothers, Vance, and McCone, McNamara did not mention the Chiefs' request for a clarification of objectives nor their advocacy of a "hard knock" military option that went beyond those being considered by the committee. When the President expressed his desire that no "firm decisions" be made without military advice, McNamara failed to disclose how closely he had curtailed the scope of Joint Staff planning to conform with his own preconceptions of how the war should be fought. [86]

The President's desire for consensus and McNamara's sensitivity to that desire helped preclude a full examination of the differences of opinions between the Chiefs and the triumvirate's committee. These fundamental differences included the appropriate objective for military action and the "degree of firmness" with which the U.S. should pursue those objectives. The Chiefs remained committed to the application of the "full limits" of U.S. combat power to secure the freedom and independence of South Vietnam, whereas the triumvirate sought only a "limited objective" in South Vietnam itself and was interested primarily in preserving America's "credibility" worldwide. [87]

The committee's final report ostensibly reaffirmed the U.S. commitment to a free and independent South Vietnam and Laos, but it contained "fall-back objectives" consistent with McNaughton's "good doctor" metaphor. [88]

Although not immediately apparent in Washington, the growing momentum behind the Administration's evolving strategy of graduated pressure would have profound consequences. Because the President and his civilian advisors continued to regard graduated pressure as a sensible way to prevent a wider war, they never considered alternatives to that ostensibly expansive policy, such as neutralization or diplomacy. Despite predictions that graduated pressure would fail and isolated calls for a negotiated settlement to extricate the U.S. from a commitment with little prospect for success, U.S. involvement in Vietnam continued in the face of increasing governmental instability in Saigon. [89]

Meanwhile, a working group of representatives from the CIA, Defense Intelligence Agency, and the State Department's Bureau of Intelligence and Research concluded that the chances of political stability in South Vietnam were less than even, and that it would be "extremely difficult" to reverse the deteriorating security situation. Sanctions against the North would change the situation in the South only if they affected the will of North Vietnam to contribute to the war effort there. The analysts suggested that the threat of destruction of the North Vietnamese industrial sector and its transport and communications system would probably not bring the country to its knees and that Hanoi would be prepared to endure it. [90]

The analysts also assessed that strong U.S. pressure on North Vietnam would pose painful questions for the North Vietnamese leadership and doubt-less occasion sharp debates within the upper echelons of the Hanoi government. They believed, however, that Hanoi would refrain as long as possible from requesting Chinese assistance, such as large-scale ground force "volunteer" intervention, which might endanger North Vietnamese independence. This hesitancy would, of course, be overcome if North Vietnamese leaders considered the existence of their regime to be at stake. [91]

Taylor Visits Washington

In an Executive Committee session of the National Security Council on 26 November, Taylor proposed a two-phase "Scenario for Controlled Escalation" to begin the application of military pressure on North Vietnam through gradually intensifying airstrikes. Phase I, lasting nearly one month, would aim to "bolster the local morale and restrain the Viet Cong" by conducting covert operations, limited airstrikes against infiltration targets in Laos, and reprisal bombing against North Vietnamese targets in response to any provocations. Meanwhile, Taylor would leverage the promise of airstrikes to induce the South Vietnamese to put their government in order. If, as hoped, the Saigon government survived and an acceptable level of stability was achieved, the U.S. would initiate Phase II, which Taylor described as a "methodical program of mounting air attacks" of two to six months duration against North Vietnam, followed if necessary, by a naval blockade. [92]

Perhaps in deference to Taylor, his old boss and mentor, Wheeler did not press the Chiefs' view during the Executive Committee session. He may also have recognized the futility of doing so since only the Chiefs advocated the "hard knock" course of action. [93]

In late November, McNamara approved a National Security Action Memo (NSAM) that closely followed Taylor's two-phase proposal. This document authorized time-phased military actions, such as air deployments, bombing targets, and the numbers of sorties required per target. William Bundy lauded McNaughton's "impressive array of facts on available forces" as "the best thinking available." [94]

While the Chiefs did not contribute to the triumvirate's document, they did not take substantive issue with it. The document indicated that the President would escalate the level of military activities. It affirmed the U.S. policy objective in Vietnam was to secure an independent, non-Communist South Vietnam and did not list lesser "fall-back" objectives. It permitted airstrikes on all 94 targets recommended by the Chiefs, as well as aerial mining of North Vietnamese ports and a naval blockade of North Vietnam. [95]

The Chiefs were also satisfied that the document included a paragraph describing their "hard knock" course of action. They were unaware that McNamara removed that paragraph from the final version submitted to the President. William Bundy later justified this excision because the triumvirate had reached a "crucial consensus," and the Chiefs' position was "without institutional support." [96]

Setting the Stage for Escalation

On 1 December, Wheeler seized an opportunity to propose the Chiefs' "hard knock" recommendation when the National Security Council Principals

Group briefed the President on the options put forward by the triumvirate's committee. Wheeler informed Johnson that the Chiefs recommended "sharp military actions," including the destruction of the Phuc Yen MIG fighter base, other airfields, and major petroleum facilities within three days. These initial attacks would "establish the fact that the U.S. intends to use military force, if necessary, to the full limits of what military force can contribute to achieving U.S. objectives in Southeast Asia." Airstrikes would then continue against infiltration targets in North Vietnam and eventually expand to areas throughout the country. Wheeler said the program "could be suspended short of full destruction of [North Vietnam] if our objectives were earlier achieved." [97]

More significantly, Wheeler put the President and his civilian advisors on notice that the Chiefs' collective judgment was that solving the conflict in Vietnam would ultimately require a much greater level of force than the triumvirate's committee recommended. "Johnny" Johnson believed it would take five years and 500,000 troops to win in Vietnam. To emphasize the Chiefs' recommendation, Wheeler read the following statement:

> The JCS recognize that any course of action we adopt, except early withdrawal from SVN, could develop eventually into the course they advocate. This fact reinforces our belief that we should profit by the several advantages of forthright military action initiated upon our decision. In other words, if we must fight a war in Southeast Asia, let us do so under conditions favorable to us from the outset and with maximum volition resting with the United States. [98]

The President expressed agreement with several points in the Chiefs' position and was amenable to tougher military action. He left open the degree to which he was willing to commit military force, and he concurred with Wheeler's statement that military action should aim to preserve "maximum volition." The President was reluctant to take immediate military action due to the instability of the South Vietnamese government and the precarious position of American civilian dependents living in South Vietnam, but he pledged a willingness to reconsider Wheeler's proposal later. [99]

The President approved the immediate initiation of Phase I l operations in the Laotian panhandle to hinder infiltration of North Viet troops and supplies down the Ho Chi Minh Trail. At least 12,000 regular North Vietnamese Army (NVA) troops had already moved south and were poised to cross the Laotian frontier into South Vietnam's Central Highlands. [100]

In approving what amounted to decisions for war, Johnson demanded absolute secrecy. Recognizing that even with his huge electoral mandate, he would have only a brief honeymoon period to achieve his ambitious legislative goals, he was unwilling to permit the war to thwart his Great Society. If he had to go to war, he would do everything possible to obscure and conceal it. Johnson made it a matter of "highest importance" that the December decisions be kept from the public. [101]

For the same reasons, Johnson continued to move cautiously for more than a month. He was disinclined to escalate rapidly in view of his campaign promises of no wider war. He refused to send U.S. troops while the political situation South Vietnam remained in disorder. He and his advisors also feared that U.S. reprisals might provoke further Viet Cong attacks at a time when South Vietnam was still in turmoil. [102]

Consistent with Johnson's effort to keep Vietnam out of the press, the triumvirate were determined to keep the Phase I pressures sharply limited. They continued to block the Chiefs' calls for further action and a relaxation of restrictions on authorized military actions. Still, the Chiefs persisted. [103]

On Christmas Eve, a powerful explosion destroyed the Brinks Hotel, an American officers' quarters in Saigon. The blast killed two Americans and wounded 63 others. Four days later, Taylor recommended a retaliatory air-strike against North Vietnam.

The Chiefs' quickly endorsed Taylor's suggestion. Wheeler requested authorization from McNamara for a reprisal raid against Taylor's preferred target, a military barracks in the southern portion of North Vietnam. McGeorge Bundy and Rusk opposed a retaliatory strike, and their opinion prevailed. [104]

Military preparations for Phase II operations were completed in mid-December. Three target packages for airstrikes against North Vietnam were available; U.S. Navy and Air Force aircraft were standing by; and destroyer patrols off the North Vietnamese coast were set to resume on 3 February. The stage was set for U.S. intervention. [105]

The President's political position in late 1964 was as strong as it ever would be. He had just won an overwhelming electoral victory and had firm control of Congress. Public opinion was apathetic and permissive to Johnson's increasing involvement in the Vietnam conflict. [106]

CHAPTER 2

ENOUGH, BUT NOT TOO MUCH
(JANUARY – JUNE 1965)

War is not a human activity that can be precisely — and conveniently —
divided between military and political components. ... Military action should
never be seen as an end unto itself. One might even argue that attempting to
separate the military from the political is dangerous business. ... [Conflict
should be viewed] as a constant dialogue between civilian policy makers and
their wartime subordinates. This dialogue should focus on what military force
can achieve politically, how strategies are best employed, and what state of
peace follows in the aftermath of man's most destructive act. None of these
aspects of war are the special preserve of either political or military leaders.
War has long been about political-military interaction.
Vietnam was no exception.
— Colonel Gregory A. Daddis, 2014 [1]

Plunging Ahead

Following the President's approval of the triumvirate's committee
report, the deteriorating political and military situation in South Vietnam and
pressure from Johnson's advisors would move the President toward deepening
U.S. military intervention. [2]

Between late 1964 and early 1965, the President would fundamentally
alter the U.S.commitment by initiating the regular bombing of North Vietnam
and by sending the first U.S. ground combat troops to South Vietnam. [3]

"I don't think anything is going to be as bad as losing," Johnson told
McNamara in January 1965, "and I don't see any way of winning." Nevertheless,
Johnson plunged ahead as he, the triumvirate, and McGeorge Bundy hoped
that by gradually increasing the bombing and introducing U.S. combat forces

into the ground war, they could coerce North Vietnam into abandoning its support for the insurgency in the South. This strategy of gradual escalation was based on the dubious assumption that North Vietnam would give up its goals rather than risk complete destruction. The result for the U.S. would become an irreversible commitment to a major war and Americanization of the conflict in South Vietnam. [4]

Johnson was determined to maintain control in his own hands. He also feared that a potentially divisive debate on Vietnam would distract attention from the domestic issues he wished to focus on. Thus, while taking major steps toward war, Johnson would carefully and skillfully silence public discussion and obscure the significance of his decisions. By stressing the continuity of his policies and emphasizing that he was giving equal attention to military measures and negotiations, he would persuade both "hawks" and "doves" that he was moving in their direction. By deceit and obfuscation, he would brilliantly mobilize a consensus behind his policies while blurring what these policies actually entailed. [5]

Despite divergent policy opinions between the President's military and civilian advisors on the direction and magnitude the war should take, Wheeler loyally struck a conciliatory note to the press on 14 January:

> The first point I want to make — and I want to make it with emphasis — is that no matter what rumors or assertions you may have heard to the contrary, there is no boiling dissension between the military and civilian leaders within the Department of Defense. It appears to me that the current relationship between the soldier and the state is possibly the best we have had in many years. [6]

Rather than expose differences of opinion among the Chiefs to McNamara and the President, Wheeler would convince his colleagues to submit consensus recommendations. Seeking to protect the Chiefs' limited influence, Wheeler knew "the highest authorities" would leverage the Chiefs' differences to further diminish their influence on Vietnam policymaking. [7]

McConnell

On 1 February, General John P. McConnell was sworn in as Chief of Staff of the Air Force. [8]

Back in early 1964, when the President was considering McConnell to replace LeMay, he asked McConnell whether he would support policies inconsistent with his professional military opinion. McConnell assured him that, even if he did not have faith in the Administration's policies, he "would still go ahead and carry out [the President's] decisions to the best of my ability, and I would see, also, to it that the entire Air Force did the same." McConnell saw his role as providing McNamara and Johnson "suitable alternatives for the application of military power" so they might "choose the one which best solved the problem *as they saw it*." This was the correct answer the President wanted to hear. [9]

Time magazine announced that McConnell's appointment "marked the end of an era in military leadership." By appointing McConnell, the President completed the shift of the Joint Chiefs of Staff away from World War II "heroes" to military men who were McNamara-style "planners and thinkers." [10]

ROLLING THUNDER

Meanwhile, by the end of January, the President could not delay any longer making vital decisions about Vietnam. Signs of intensifying conflict had appeared in South Vietnam in late 1964 and into 1965, as the Viet Cong strengthened its forces at all echelons, from village guerrillas to main-force regiments. One of the major arguments against escalation — the weakness of South Vietnam — had become the most compelling argument for it. Most of Johnson's advisors agreed that the threat to the South and the ominous military danger required the U.S. to bomb the North. Throughout the month, Taylor strenuously warned Washington that failure to take drastic action could only lead to "disastrous defeat." [11]

Speaking in "apocalyptic" language, McGeorge Bundy warned that continuation of existing policy would lead to "disastrous defeat." The choice, he advised, was between using U.S. military power to change Communist policy or trying to negotiate a way out. Favoring the more aggressive option, he pushed for implementation of retaliatory airstrikes at the first opportunity, followed by Phase II bombing operations. [12]

On 7 February, Viet Cong forces attacked an American barracks in Pleiku in the Central Highlands and a nearby helicopter base, killing nine Americans and destroying five aircraft. Pleiku provided a convenient pretext for escalation, and the President soon ordered retaliatory airstrikes against North Vietnam. [13]

The military scrambled. "Bus worked all day Saturday [the day of the Pleiku attack] and slept in the Pentagon," Betty Wheeler recorded. [14]

When another Viet Cong attack occurred at Qui Nhon three days later, the President not only ordered another series of airstrikes against North Vietnam but also "continuing action against North Vietnam … with modifications up and down in tempo and scale in the light of our recommendations … and our own continuing review of the situation." The air war against North Vietnam had commenced. [15]

The objectives for the bombing campaign were to raise South Vietnamese morale, compel Hanoi to abandon the Viet Cong, and to interdict the flow of men and supplies moving into South Vietnam. While the rationale was clear, the President's civilian and military advisors held opposing views on *how* to conduct the bombing. [16]

Johnson's military advisors strongly recommended hitting North Vietnam immediately and hard through an intensive strategic air campaign that would apply maximum practicable pressure within a short period of time to achieve a quick and decisive solution to the war. Former President Dwight D. Eisenhower advised Johnson that "centralization is the refuge of fear" and urged him to "trust" the military to conduct operations against North Vietnam. Airpower doctrine emphasized the destruction of an enemy's warmaking capabilities to force him to come to terms. Hearkening back to the bombing campaign against Germany, the Chiefs reiterated their 94-target plan to destroy North Vietnamese economic centers in just sixteen days. [17]

The President disliked the Chiefs' options of extensive bombing and mining harbors for their potential to trigger a Chinese intervention. A Korean War-type situation would again require a large U.S. ground force commitment and a belated admission that the U.S. was at war. Thus, to avoid a moral dilemma and other complications, Johnson was inclined to severely limit the bombing. The "slow squeeze" bombing strategy was attractive to him because it promised quick results without troop deployments. [18]

Most of the President's civilian advisors continued to advocate this gradual approach, which would intensify if North Vietnam persisted in supporting the war. They acknowledged the military's warning that limited, gradual bombing would exert less pressure upon North Vietnam and that it was less likely to compel Hanoi to scale down or cancel the insurgency or enter negotiations.

McNaughton conceded these risks but argued that "measured against the cost of defeat" the program would be "cheap," and even if it failed to turn the tide, "the value of the effort" would "exceed the costs." The triumvirate echoed Johnson's concern that an all-out bombing campaign would pose a greater risk of widening the war. Plus, it would transmit a signal out of all proportion to the limited objectives and interests of the U.S. in Southeast Asia; incur unacceptable political penalties; and perhaps foreclose the promise of achieving U.S. objectives at a relatively low level of violence. [19]

Ultimately, the President decided to sustain the triumvirate's graduated pressure program. Dubbed Operation ROLLING THUNDER, the bombing would continue in a slow, steady, deliberate manner, beginning with a few infiltration-related targets in southern North Vietnam and gradually ascend in tempo while moving northward with progressively more severe attacks on a wider variety of military and industrial targets. This pattern was intended to preserve the Administration's options of whether to proceed or not, escalate or not, or quicken the pace or not, dependent upon Hanoi's reactions. The triumvirate considered the carrot of halting the bombing as important as the stick of continuing it, and bombing pauses were provided for. They hoped this track of major military escalation would be accompanied by a parallel diplomatic track to bring the war to an end and that both tracks could be coordinated. Thus,

ROLLING THUNDER was designed to force favorable negotiation and not achieve victory on its own. [20]

Almost as soon as the bombing program commenced, pressures mounted to expand it. The initial attacks achieved meager results. Complaining that ROLLING THUNDER had merely amounted to a "few isolated thunderclaps," Taylor called for a "mounting crescendo" of airstrikes against North Vietnam. Meanwhile, intelligence reports ominously warned that the military situation in South Vietnam was steadily deteriorating. [21]

Three weeks after ROLLING THUNDER commenced, Westmoreland complained to Wheeler about the absurdity of the civilians' tight control of the operation from Washington, considering that the weather changed faster than people in Vietnam could inform Washington of those changes. Westmoreland asked for greater authority to orchestrate the airstrikes with other operations against North Vietnam over which he enjoyed more control. Westmoreland prophetically warned Wheeler that "experience indicated that the more remote the authority which directs how a mission is to be accomplished, the more we are vulnerable to mishaps resulting from such things as incomplete briefings and preparation, loss of tactical flexibility and lack of tactical coordination." [22]

"The problems in dealing with Washington were myriad," Sharp recalled. "One of the most aggravating was the frequently inordinate delay we experienced in receiving a reply from the [Joint Chiefs of Staff] to proposals that required their approval. The reason was regrettably simple: the Chiefs could not get a decision from McNamara." [23]

Although Wheeler and the Chiefs shared Westmoreland's and Sharp's dissatisfaction with the bombing plan, Wheeler urged them to be patient and let him handle the political problem of control over ROLLING THUNDER. He asked them to be sensitive to the "sizable and vexing" domestic and international political considerations that impinged on operations against North Vietnam. Once ROLLING THUNDER was underway, Wheeler believed he would have greater success in removing restrictions on the operation. [24]

Ground Troops

Johnson's decision to wage a bombing campaign against North Vietnam provided the pretext for the introduction of U.S. ground combat forces into South Vietnam. Anticipating Communist retaliatory attacks for ROLLING THUNDER, Westmoreland urgently requested in late February two Marine landing teams to protect the airbase at Da Nang. [25]

On 1 March, the President indicated that he was willing to look with favor upon a recommendation for the deployment of more U.S. ground combat forces to boost the counterinsurgency effort, but without drawing public attention to the escalation of the war. [26]

"Seven o'clock, no Bus," Betty Wheeler informed her mother that evening. "He has put [in] long hours the last little bit, or is it always? Our trip to [Fort] Benning was cancelled on Saturday. Bus worked all day [instead]. He hadn't gotten home until ten-thirty the night before." [27]

Painting a bleak picture of the South Vietnamese Army (ARVN), Westmoreland asked for reinforcements to provide "a substantial and hard-hitting offensive capability on the ground to convince the [Viet Cong] that they cannot win." [28]

The Chiefs quickly endorsed Westmoreland's troop request. Over the next several months, they would also endorse the deployment of additional U.S. troops to buttress South Vietnam. [29]

The President asked his military advisors whether the enemy could match an U.S. buildup. The "weight of judgment" was that the enemy could not, Wheeler responded. The President also consulted the "wise men," a bipartisan group of elder statesmen who seconded the military in recommending an expanded war. McNamara believed the only options were to withdraw and be humiliated; continue the same failed strategy; or expand the effort, with the latter option presenting "the best odds of the best outcome with the most acceptable cost to the United States." [30]

Dissenting voices were few. Among them, Ball predicted that approval of Westmoreland's request would result in "a protracted war involving an open-ended commitment of U.S. forces, mounting U.S. casualties, and no assurance of a satisfactory solution, and a serious danger of escalation [involving the Chinese or Soviets] at the end of the road." [31]

Taylor also questioned the wisdom of introducing U.S. troops and transcending the barrier that had kept the U.S. from assuming a larger responsibility for the ground war in South Vietnam. Although he conceded the importance of protecting U.S. airbases, Taylor expressed grave concern about the long-range implications of Westmoreland's request. Once the first step was taken, it would be "very difficult to hold [the] line." [32]

Ball's and Taylor's objections were ignored. Johnson's decision to send troops to secure an U.S. airbase was not perceived as a major policy decision, but as a minor supporting contingency. The need for them appeared so pressing and immediate, the commitment so small, that the decision was made routinely, with little discussion of its long-range consequences. After less than a week of perfunctory debate, the President approved Westmoreland's troop request. [33]

Once ashore, the Marines soon discovered that they had neither the capability nor freedom of action to adequately secure the airbase. However, once the barrier had been broken, military considerations would increasingly justify the introduction of more troops and greater operational authorities.

Civilian policymakers in Washington could resist this pressure for more troops so long as their present Vietnam policy was successful. Initially, ROLLING THUNDER seemed to produce a positive effect, as ground combat in South Vietnam declined in March. A feeling of cautious optimism existed in Washington throughout the spring despite Westmoreland's gloomy reports. [34]

Alarmed by the slow pace of the South Vietnamese Army's buildup and fearful of a major enemy offensive in the Central Highlands, Westmoreland concluded by mid-March that if the U.S. was to avert disaster in Vietnam, there was "no solution... other than to put our own finger in the dike." He advocated, therefore, the immediate commitment of two U.S. Army divisions, one to the Highlands and the other to the Saigon area. [35]

Long impatient with the Administration's caution, Wheeler and the Chiefs were eager for the U.S. to assume full responsibility for the war. Not only did they strongly endorse Westmoreland's request, but they would also argue for the deployment of as many as three Allied divisions for use in offensive operations. [36]

The Administration found itself on what McNaughton called "the horns of a trilemma." The options of withdrawal and a massive air war against North Vietnam had been firmly rejected. It was apparent by mid-March, however, that the limited bombing campaign undertaken in February would not produce immediate results, and Westmoreland's urgent warnings raised fears that further inaction might result in a South Vietnamese collapse. Many Administration officials reluctantly concluded, therefore, that U.S. ground forces must be introduced into Vietnam. They fully appreciated, on the other hand, the possible domestic political consequences of the sort of commitment Westmoreland proposed. [37]

"Johnny" Johnson openly wondered whether the U.S. military even belonged in Indochina. For more than six months, he had tried to persuade his fellow Chiefs to adopt an either-or position, saying that the Chiefs should tell the President to "either get into this thing and win, or not go in at all." [38]

After visiting Saigon, Johnson reported that U.S. ground troops would have to intervene directly in the counterinsurgency. He recommended a substantial increase in U.S. military assistance, including several combat divisions to either to interdict the Laotian panhandle to stop infiltration or to counter the growing threat in the central and northern provinces. Convinced that committing U.S. troops should be the nation's last resort and undertaken only if civilian leaders were willing to make "an irrevocable commitment," Johnson also pushed his fellow Chiefs to convince the President to authorize full mobilization of the reserves. [39]

Sensitive to the myriad diplomatic, political, and military reasons leading the President to approach with great caution any large commitment of ground combat forces to South Vietnam, Wheeler urged an incremental approach toward troop deployments. Westmoreland agreed so long as the President remained committed to "do whatever is necessary militarily to prevent defeat." "Johnny" Johnson warned that "temporizing or expedient measures will not suffice," but also agreed that the Administration should "take whatever actions are necessary" to "buy time." Once the impending disaster in Vietnam was averted, the Chiefs could press for further deployments. Instead of recommending the deployment of five divisions, the level of force that he and Army planners felt was necessary to achieve a free and independent South Vietnam, "Johnny" Johnson agreed with the "politically feasible" recommendation for one U.S. division, so long as the others deployed later. [40]

On 15 March, "Johnny" Johnson provided the President his estimation that up to 500,000 troops and five years would be required to win the war. The President and McNamara were shocked. "None of us had been thinking in anything approaching such terms," McNamara recalled. [41]

The President merely authorized the deployment of additional Marines to secure the air base at Da Nang and other coastal enclaves. He also authorized the Army to commence deploying nearly 20,000 logistics troops to Southeast Asia. At the same time, the President modified the Marines' mission to allow them to conduct offensive operations close to their bases. Despite the added numbers and expanded missions, U.S. ground forces had yet to engage the enemy in large-scale combat.

Although the President had again deferred authorizing the deployment of additional ground forces, he made concessions to the Chiefs in other areas. He convinced them that he was committed to taking any action necessary to preserve South Vietnam and held out the promise of more decisive military action in the future. He loosened controls on ROLLING THUNDER, approved most of "Johnny" Johnson's recommendations, and directed the Chiefs to identify ways to improve the military situation in the South. The President's tough talk galvanized the Chiefs and convinced Wheeler that the President was committed to "do everything possible to better our situation" in Vietnam. [42]

Indeed, the question of how best to employ large numbers of U.S. ground forces was still unresolved on the eve of their deployment. Focusing on population security and pacification, some planners saw U.S. combat forces concentrating their efforts in coastal enclaves and around key urban centers and bases. Under this plan, such forces would provide a security shield behind which the Vietnamese could expand the pacification zone. When required, U.S. combat units would venture beyond their enclaves as mobile reaction forces.

This concept, largely defensive in nature, reflected the pattern that the first Army combat units to enter Vietnam had established. But the mobility and offensive firepower of U.S. ground units suggested their use in remote, sparsely populated regions to seek out and engage main force enemy units as they infiltrated into South Vietnam or emerged from their secret bases. While secure coastal logistical enclaves and base camps still would be required, the weight of the military effort would be focused on the destruction of enemy military units. Yet, even in this alternative, U.S. forces would serve indirectly as a shield for pacification activities in the more heavily populated lowlands and Mekong Delta.

A third proposal particularly appealing to "Johnny" Johnson was to employ U.S. and Allied ground forces across the Laotian panhandle to interdict enemy infiltration into South Vietnam. This was a more direct and effective way to stop infiltration than the use of airpower. Encumbered by military and political problems, the idea would be revived periodically, but always rejected. The pattern of deployment that would develop in South Vietnam was a compromise between the first two concepts. [43]

Vietnam planning over the past several months had meant extra-long hours for Wheeler and Chiefs. "I'm working on Bus in the hopes that he will take a long weekend," Betty Wheeler wrote. "God knows he needs it more than I do." [44]

In a meeting with McNamara, Wheeler, and the Chiefs on 29 March, Taylor disagreed with the Chiefs on the number of U.S. forces that should be deployed to Vietnam and how they should be employed. Westmoreland cabled his support for Wheeler's proposals to change the mission of U.S. forces from maintaining security in the South to conducting active counterinsurgency operations and to introduce a three-division force to secure coastal areas and fight Communist forces in the Central Highlands region. Taylor, however, remained opposed to additional ground forces.

Although McNamara believed that some U.S. troops were needed, he agreed with Taylor that three divisions "seemed high." McNamara, who still wished to carefully control each incremental increase in the use of force in Vietnam, recommended that only two additional Marine battalions be deployed. McNamara considered the primary contribution of ground forces would be to signal resolve to Hanoi and gave his tentative endorsement to Taylor's "enclave" concept. [45]

Taylor and McNamara also overruled the Chiefs' calls to intensify ROLLING THUNDER. To forestall their opposition, McNamara held out the promise of future action. He suggested that in four to twelve weeks the mining of Haiphong Harbor and other actions that the Chiefs had previously recommended might become "politically feasible." McNamara assured the Chiefs that if they supported restrictions on the air campaign in the short term, they would eventually be permitted to place "very strong pressure" on North Vietnam. [46]

Hanoi Escalates

Meanwhile, Ho Chi Minh and his advisors also debated how to proceed. They understood that a protracted war might be necessary. Nurturing political support would take time, and a powerful adversary would not be quickly defeated. They reasoned, however, that time was on their side since the U.S. had no compelling national interest to fight in Vietnam. Hanoi's goal would be to deflate America's "aggressive will;" to win a political and psychological victory to make the U.S. unwilling to continue fighting; to avoid losing long enough; and to inflict a constant drip of casualties. Over time, the U.S. would accept defeat. [47]

As a result of this strategic debate, Hanoi decided to match the U.S. escalation, with the objective of bogging down U.S. forces in a protracted struggle and creating a stalemate that would sap American and South Vietnamese morale. Hanoi directed much of its effort to convince the U.S. that its "limited war" had failed. For the U.S. to win, it would have to escalate dramatically, possibly igniting a "general war" involving the Chinese or Soviets. When confronted with the choice between "general war" or de-escalation, most Hanoi strategists presumed the U.S. would choose the latter. [48]

Naval Operations

Although the ground war would be of paramount importance, surface ships of the U.S. Navy's 7th Fleet would also play a major role. Approved in March, Operation MARKET TIME would interdict the steadily growing North Vietnamese seaborne supply effort in South Vietnamese waters. American naval forces would augment South Vietnamese coastal surveillance and anti-infiltration operations with radar surveillance and anti-infiltration operations with radar surveillance ships, small craft, and aerial patrols. The operation would prove so successful in disrupting the North's maritime resupply lines that Hanoi would hasten improvements to the Ho Chi Minh Trail and develop Sihanoukville in ostensibly neutral Cambodia as a transshipment point. [49]

A complementary operation, GAME WARDEN, would seek to deny enemy access to the Mekong Delta's rivers and the mouth of the Saigon River. Bombers, fighters, and electronic warfare planes flying from aircraft carriers in the South China Sea would also fly ROLLING THUNDER missions, interdict the Ho Chi Minh Trail, and support ground operations inside South Vietnam. [50]

Closer offshore, Task Force 77 would provide air and naval gunfire support along South Vietnam's 1,200-mile coastline, although after mid-1966 it would concentrate on the northernmost portion, the narrow coastal lowlands in the I Corps Tactical Zone (I CTZ). Comprised of aircraft carriers, cruisers, and destroyers, and briefly including the battleship *New Jersey* in 1968, the task force would provide accurate naval gunfire day or night, with 8-inch guns striking targets as deep as 16 miles inland. [51]

Pacification

The fifth Allied war front would be a pacification campaign to confront several challenges: Communist military strength in the countryside; jurisdictional disputes among competing U.S. bureaucracies; weak South Vietnamese local leadership; and an overemphasis on the bestowal of material benefits and equating them with progress in winning the peasants' loyalty. Pacification measures would preserve the status quo, but at a higher standard of living.

Westmoreland would gladly leave this "other war" to the South Vietnamese Army (ARVN), supplemented by South Vietnamese Territorial Forces. The division of labor between the Americans and South Vietnamese seemed logical because U.S. forces could best take on large Viet Cong and North Vietnamese Army units and minimize the involvement of foreign troops in politically sensitive activities, while indigenous forces understood local conditions and spoke the language. However, beset by poor leadership, low morale, and corruption, the ARVN would often victimize rather than aid the peasants. Even when support for the Viet Cong later dropped as the violence escalated, and the Communists' demands for taxes, labor, and recruits increased, the ebbing enthusiasm would not translate into appreciable gains for Saigon.[52]

Political stabilization of South Vietnam would form the bedrock of Westmoreland's three-phase sustained campaign plan. In Phase I, U.S. and Allied forces would be committed as necessary to halt the losing trend by 1965. Tasks included securing major military bases, defending major political and population centers, and preserving and strengthening the South Vietnamese Armed Forces (RVNAF). In Phase II, U.S. and Allied forces would assume the offensive to destroy enemy forces and reinstitute rural construction activities. In this phase, intended to begin in 1966, U.S. forces would participate in clearing, securing, reserve reaction, and offensive operations as required to support and sustain the resumption of pacification. Finally, in Phase III, U.S. and Allied forces would ensure the defeat and destruction of the remaining enemy forces and base areas.[53]

Decision

In a meeting with the triumvirate, McCone, Rusk, Taylor, McGeorge Bundy, and Wheeler on 1 April, the frustrated President wanted to place greater pressure on Hanoi.

Wheeler seized upon the President's exhortation by urging an expansion of ROLLING THUNDER and the deployment of ground combat units to Vietnam. Wheeler complained that the twelve-week bombing program developed under McNamara's guidance was inadequate. It did not make sense militarily to avoid hitting the MIG airfields in North Vietnam. Because the U.S. was "losing the war," the President should approve the Chiefs' recommendation to deploy the remainder of a Marine division, a U.S. Army division, and a South Korean division. The ground forces, Wheeler argued, would have a major effect on the war, signal U.S. determination and purpose to North Vietnam, serve as a deterrent to escalation, position U.S. military power forward if deterrence failed, and provide bargaining leverage for negotiations. Wheeler pressed the President for a decision, telling him that with three divisions and logistical improvements, "your problem [is] solved." Wheeler minimized the cost of his proposal, noting that reserve forces would not have to deploy and could be used to replenish the strategic reserve. [54]

Instead of spurring a debate about the nature of the problem in Vietnam and examining possible U.S. responses, Wheeler's proposal ran into the President's preoccupation with consensus and his desire to keep U.S. involvement in the war as quiet as possible. Johnson decided upon a middle course designed to satisfy all parties. He deferred deciding on Wheeler's three-division recommendation. Instead, he approved the deployment of two additional Marine battalions and expanded the Marine mission from defensive security to offensive counterinsurgency operations. In the long run, the change of mission that committed U.S. troops to offensive combat was more significant than the deployment of additional troops, but the former decision was easy easier to conceal from the American public in the short term. The President reassured Wheeler that he would consider sending additional forces to Vietnam soon and told him to prepare two U.S. divisions for deployment. [55]

McCone realized the President had made his decision without an informed, comprehensive estimate of the situation and without fully considering the consequences of expanding the mission of U.S. ground forces in Vietnam. He argued that the decisions to change the mission of U.S. ground forces in Vietnam to one of "active combat" was justified only if the U.S. "hit" North Vietnam "harder, more frequently, and [to] inflict greater damage." [56]

> McCone argued:
>
> Instead of avoiding the MIGs, we must go in and take them out. A bridge here and there will not do the job. We must strike their airfields, their petroleum resources, power stations, and military compounds. This, in my opinion, must be done promptly and with minimal restraint. If we are unwilling to take this kind of decision now, we must not take the actions concerning the mission of our ground forces. [57]

McCone warned that unless the President made a clear choice between a negotiated settlement and a decisive expansion of the war, the United States would incur an "ever-increasing commitment of U.S. personnel without materially improving the chance of victory." [58]

The President listened to McCone's views but remained resolved to take only the minimal actions necessary to prevent defeat in South Vietnam.

Agreeing with McCone about what the situation in Vietnam demanded, Wheeler responded to the President's reluctance to commit fully to either negotiation or the use of military force by pressing him for a gradual intensification of the war effort, as the President's domestic political concerns permitted. [59]

When Wheeler informed his wife on 5 April that "he has got to go to Hawaii the end of this month", Betty was hopeful they "can have a weekend on the beach". It would not materialize. [60]

By this time, the President recognized that achievement of U.S. objectives in Vietnam would require a sustained and costly commitment, but he continued to refuse to submit his policies to public or congressional debate. Although the Administration effectively concealed the direction of its policy, the obvious expansion of the war, particularly the bombing, attracted growing criticism. The Administration sought to disarm its critics by several dramatic peace initiatives.

In a speech at Johns Hopkins University on 7 April, Johnson affirmed that the U.S. was prepared to enter "unconditional discussions" and even offered Hanoi a billion-dollar economic development program for the Mekong River Valley region. The President was unquestionably sincere in his desire for peace, but his initiatives were designed primarily to silence domestic and international critics rather than set in motion determined efforts to find a peace settlement. Johnson made clear in his Johns Hopkins speech that the U.S. would not compromise its fundamental objective of "an independent South Vietnam — securely guaranteed and able to shape its own relationships to all others — free from outside interference", which, by implication, meant a non-Communist South Vietnam. [61]

An independent South Vietnam was nonnegotiable to North Vietnamese leaders, who remained determined to unite Vietnam under Hanoi's domination. The day after the Johns Hopkins speech, Hanoi responded with "four points" as preconditions for any negotiations. The U.S. had to withdraw unconditionally from Vietnam. A coalition government in the South (which Hanoi planned to dominate) would be formed to negotiate the unification of Vietnam. Until that government was formed, the Viet Cong's political arm, the National Liberation Front (NLF), would be the only legitimate representative of the Vietnamese people.

Although it had taken less than twenty-four hours for Ho Chi Minh to reject Johnson's export version of the Great Society, the response in the United States was generally positive. [62]

The introduction of ground troops to South Vietnam and their employment in offensive operations was the first natural breakpoint in Johnson's Vietnam policy since the President approved graduated pressure thirteen months earlier. The Chiefs seized this opportunity to voice their opposition and urge more resolute action in Southeast Asia. They agreed among themselves to insist to the President that the immediate deployment of three divisions was necessary to win the war in Vietnam. Wheeler asked his colleagues to stand firmly behind this recommendation. [63]

Meanwhile, due to international and domestic political pressure to stop ROLLING THUNDER, the President assured the American people that he would continue to exercise "restraint." Concerned that he would, the Chiefs recommended in a meeting with Johnson, McNamara, and Vance on 8 April lifting the restrictions on the air campaign. Intelligence assessed that ROLL-ING THUNDER had not reduced the overall military capability of Vietnamese Communist forces in "any major way." [64]

The President appeared committed to invest whatever level force the Chiefs determined was necessary to "win" the war in the South. He observed that "at present we are limited as to what we can do in North Vietnam, we have almost free rein in South Vietnam, and I want to kill more Viet Cong." [65]

Greene, who had grown frustrated with the disparity between the President's tough talk and his limitations on the use of force, argued for a much larger Marine Corps effort in South Vietnam. The President, however, was not yet prepared to consider specific proposals and deferred any consideration of Greene's recommendation until their next meeting. Unwilling to intensify the air campaign or deploy large numbers of U.S. troops to the South, the President still pressured the Chiefs to "kill more Viet Cong" with the troops and matériel currently available to Westmoreland. [66]

Recognizing that temporizing measures would not produce tangible results, Greene believed the U.S. faced the difficult decision of either withdrawing from Vietnam or staying to fight a "major campaign." He agreed with his fellow Chiefs' calls for the immediate deployment of a Marine expeditionary force, one Army division, and one South Korean division to South Vietnam. The U.S. should soon "commence a rapid, significant, sustained increase" in pressures against North Vietnam, including unrestricted airstrikes on enemy military and industrial targets, the mining of Haiphong Harbor, shore bombardment of coastal and island targets, and seizure of the latter with South Vietnamese troops. Simultaneously, the U.S. should prepare for a "total blockade" of North Vietnamese ports and put the U.S. economy "on a wartime footing." [67]

A week later, the President continued to play for sympathy from the Chiefs while criticizing their performance. Determined to preempt discussion of intensification of military actions against the North, Johnson once more made clear his intention of retaining tight control over military operations.

He promised more determined action in the future and vowed to increase the tempo of bombing targets below the 20th Parallel. Johnson professed enthusiasm for any proposal from the Chiefs to intensify the war in the South and told them he would invest whatever amount of money, matériel, or effort necessary "to win the game in South Vietnam." This sounded to the Chiefs like classical victory was their military objective.[68]

The President asked for Wheeler's recommendations. Wheeler restated the Chiefs' recommendation of 20 March that three divisions deploy to South Vietnam. Despite his pledge to commit to South Vietnam the forces the Chiefs deemed necessary, the President said he could never get Congress to go along with that many troops. Besides, Johnson noted, a large troop deployment might incite a reaction from North Vietnam and China.

Unhappy with Wheeler's advice, the President indicated that he would be willing to approve the deployment of 5,000 troops, instead of the 90,000 that would attend the deployment of three divisions. Intent upon the Chiefs giving him a quick and inexpensive way to reverse the deteriorating situation in South Vietnam, the President then asked "Johnny" Johnson for his assessment. Johnson backed Wheeler and reiterated that three divisions were the minimum force necessary.

The President had leveraged differences among the Chiefs to his advantage before. Now, Greene's desire to increase the Marine Corps' role in Vietnam led him to urge a "cheap" deployment of 5,000 more Marines, one-hundred-fold fewer than he thought would ultimately be required to fight a "major campaign." Instead, the President approved Westmoreland's request for the 173rd Airborne Brigade.[69]

Angry that the President had led them "into a trap," Wheeler later chastised Greene for not having "stuck by their original agreement to hold fast on the Chiefs' previous recommendation to introduce three divisions into South Vietnam."[70]

The Chiefs were becoming increasingly outspoken about their frustration with the President, who seemed more concerned with avoiding defeat than developing an overall strategy. They understood he wasn't really interested in their opinions — his primary goal was to keep them on board. When senior generals began complaining to the Senate Armed Services Committee about how Johnson was conducting the war, Mississippi Senator John C. Stennis went to the President. Thereafter, Johnson began including Wheeler in many key sessions, but the result was the same: "More visible consultation calmed the critics, but Johnson went right on taking the crucial measure of events with his four or five most trusted civilians." [71]

Wheeler, who had already reconciled himself to working for a gradual intensification of the war, got on with the business of deploying more troops to South Vietnam. Having succeeded in reconciling the Chiefs' previously divergent views, he determined to ensure consistent messaging among the Chiefs to prevent the President and McNamara from continuing to leverage any differences between them to discount the Chiefs' recommendations. [72]

"Now despite what you may have heard to the contrary, my colleagues and I get along very well indeed," Wheeler would recall in 1969. "We see eye to eye much more than we disagree. In fact, we have been accused of being too cozy on occasion. Insofar as [what is required to win] the war in Southeast Asia, there hasn't been a divergency of view among the Joint Chiefs of Staff since the fall of 1964." [73]

The two April meetings between the President and the Chiefs added greater confusion to an already muddled strategic picture of what the U.S. military was supposed to accomplish in Vietnam. The President's curtailment of their discussion to only those initiatives that would "kill more Viet Cong" prevented the development of a comprehensive plan for the war. Instead of defining policy goals precisely and then determining how military force might contribute to those goals, the President's discussion with the Chiefs began with how much force he was willing to invest in the near term and assumed, with no thought for the nature of the war, that any action would constitute progress in the war effort. The Chiefs were to make their recommendations not according to agreed-upon objectives but according to the means the President made available, based on domestic political priorities. [74]

McNamara later admitted, "The Joint Chiefs, CINCPAC, Westy, and I all continued to react on a day-to-day basis to the gathering force of events when we – and especially I, as Secretary – should have been far more forceful in developing a military strategy and a long-term plan for the force structure required to carry it out." [75]

In the absence of clearly defined strategic objectives, "killing more Viet Cong," a tactical mission, became the basis for the Chiefs' plans and recommendations. They concluded that, with the current force levels, they might "kill more Viet Cong" through the massive application of airpower in the South. It was unclear, however, how the tactic of using massive airstrikes against an enemy who was intertwined with the noncombatant population would help to establish strategic conditions conducive to ending the war. [76]

Having thwarted opposition from the Chiefs, the President now faced a potential threat from Taylor in Saigon. Johnson's decision to deploy the 173rd Airborne Brigade had come as a "complete surprise" to Taylor. He responded by renewing his argument that the presence of U.S. ground combat units was not only unnecessary but counterproductive. He restated his judgment that these U.S. forces would "sap the [South Vietnamese government's] initiative and turn a defense of the [South Vietnamese] homeland into what appears a foreign war." [77]

Taylor sensed the Administration's policy had devolved into a collection of disparate initiatives lacking any unifying strategic concept or clear objective. He was "greatly troubled" by its proclivity to equate any new program or initiative with an improvement in the situation in Vietnam. [78]

While Taylor pressured the President to halt the increase in U.S. forces, the Chiefs urged McNamara to dismiss the Ambassador's objections. Rather than assess the validity of Taylor's reservations about the consequences of introducing progressively larger numbers of troops, the Chiefs remained focused on gaining approval for additional deployments.

Honolulu

The President, unwilling to risk open dissent with either Taylor or the Chiefs, depended on McNamara to affect a compromise between them. Johnson suspended the deployment of the 173rd Airborne Brigade while the triumvirate and Wheeler met with Taylor, Westmoreland, and Sharp in

Hawaii. McNamara would have to persuade Taylor to accept the deployment of additional troops while parrying calls from the military for an intensification of the air campaign against North Vietnam. [79]

The Administration resolved its "trilemma" in Vietnam with a compromise, rejecting the military's proposals, but still recommending that the President approve a significant commitment of ground forces and an enlargement of their mission. The conference attendees agreed upon a hastily improvised strategy to "break the will of the [North and the Viet Cong] by depriving them of victory." The bombing would be maintained at its "present tempo" for six months to a year, although the conferees agreed that bombing "would not do the job alone." Therefore, they decided that a large increment of additional U.S. ground combat forces should be sent to Vietnam. Troop strength would more than double from 33,000 to 82,000. [80]

These additional forces were not to be used in the Central Highlands or given an unrestricted mission, as Westmoreland, Wheeler, and the Chiefs advocated, but would be used in the more cautious, low-risk "enclave strategy" devised by Taylor. This experimental strategy required U.S. troops to occupy coastal strongpoints or enclaves around the major U.S. bases, provide security for these areas, and be prepared to reinforce South Vietnamese Army (ARVN) forces within a fifty-mile radius. The Administration hoped this limited commitment would deny the enemy a knockout blow and control of certain crucial areas, thus allowing time for the South Vietnamese buildup and for ROLLING THUNDER to take effect on the North. Additionally, it would release ARVN forces from the security mission so they could actively pursue the enemy's main force units. Although the Honolulu decisions stopped short of the commitment urged by the military, they advanced well beyond the original objective of base security and marked a major step toward large-scale involvement in the ground war. The new strategy shifted emphasis from the air war against North Vietnam to the war in the South, and by adopting it, the Administration at least tacitly committed itself to expand U.S. forces as the military situation required. [81]

The President authorized the establishment of five enclaves with seventeen battalions of U.S. troops. This "low profile" strategy assumed that the

ARVN could defeat the Viet Cong, an assumption that was not universally accepted. Westmoreland considered the ARVN too ineffective for the task. He also found the static defense role for U.S. forces too restrictive. Events would seem to prove him right as the Viet Cong offensive gained momentum.

Ball recognized that the President was failing to consider the likely consequences of his decisions to gradually increase the number of U.S. troops in Vietnam. Yet, he stopped short of forcefully objecting to the vector of U.S. policy. Like the Chiefs, Ball did not press the President to choose between large-scale intervention and withdrawal. Because the President's advisors did not directly confront the confusion and contradictions apparent in Johnson's "middle course," the U.S. continued to deepen its involvement in the war without a clear objective or strategy for the employment of U.S. military force. McNamara's effort to satisfy the President's desire for consensus had obscured the long-term implications of the Administration's decisions.

Wheeler and Ball both questioned the wisdom of the President's chosen course, yet they both supported Johnson's decisions. Ball resolved to impede greater military involvement. Wheeler sought to accelerate it.

Only McCone sounded an objection. He again urged the President to consider possible enemy reactions to the introduction of U.S. ground forces. McCone again predicted that the North Vietnamese would respond in kind to the U.S. effort in South Vietnam meaning that troop deployments would produce "no definite result." Aware that his recommendations had again fallen on deaf ears, McCone soon resigned in frustration. [82]

Meanwhile, the Communist build-up that McCone predicted was well underway. Encouraged by popular unrest in the South, persistent instability in the Saigon government, and growing antiwar sentiment in the U.S., Hanoi sensed an opportunity to gain a decisive victory. With U.S. ground combat units arriving in the South, a combined Viet Cong/North Vietnamese Army offensive might achieve victory before the U.S. could intervene in force. By mid-April, it was apparent to U.S. intelligence officials that Hanoi was dispatching not only individual soldiers, but trained and ready NVA units to South Vietnam. The offensive would begin in May with the onset of the monsoon season. [83]

After Honolulu, Sharp sent a message to his subordinate commanders that he was loath to send, considering his misgivings about ROLLING THUNDER. He reminded them that "in the day-to-day pressure of an operational environment it was not easy to remember that the air campaign was not just another war with the objective of inflicting maximum damage to the enemy." Sharp, like Westmoreland, Wheeler, and the Chiefs, knew this was a lousy and ineffective way to fight a war. Still, he was duty-bound to remind his forces that ROLLING THUNDER was "a precise application of military pressure for the specific purpose of halting aggression in South Vietnam," and that there was no doubt as to the damage the strikes had accomplished. Sharp advised his commanders to "continue to expect various restrictions on their operations, some explicitly stated, others implied, and that the fundamental importance of the air campaign, executed as ordered, required careful compliance with the spirit and intent of each instruction." [84]

The Chiefs and the Joint Staff were exceptionally busy implementing recent presidential decisions on Vietnam by identifying and preparing units for movement overseas and refining mobilization plans for Selected Reserve forces, as well as monitoring the deteriorating situation in the Dominican Republic. The frenetic pace led "Johnny" Johnson to exclaim, "There just isn't enough thinking time in this job!" [85]

On 28 April, an exasperated Betty Wheeler wrote, "It's now seven-thirty. Bus just called and said that he didn't know when he'd get home. If it's not one thing it's another." [86]

The following Sunday, Betty wrote, "Bus ate and went to the office at the usual time. You can imagine what these days have been." [87]

Dominican Republic

Although Europe and Asia remained critical to the Administration's containment policy, U.S. interests in the Caribbean increased sharply after Cuba embraced Communism. In the Dominican Republic, a military counterrevolution followed a military revolt to oust a civilian junta.

In May, when the country's capital city, Santo Domingo, became a bloody battleground and diplomacy failed to restore peace, the President decided to deploy a U.S. contingent that soon reached 23,000 troops. [88]

Although the deployment of U.S. forces to the Dominican Republic necessitated only minor adjustments to the buildup plans for Vietnam, the Chiefs would repeatedly point out to the Administration that the operation demonstrated how unexpected demands elsewhere in the world could deplete the strategic reserve, and that it underscored the importance of mobilization if the Services were to continue to meet worldwide contingencies while supplying trained combat units to Westmoreland. [89]

Funding Request

In early May, the President approved a five-day bombing pause, accompanied by private messages to Hanoi indicating that a decrease in North Vietnamese and Viet Cong military activity could lead to a scaling down of U.S. air attacks. Johnson's peace moves helped to quiet domestic and foreign criticism, at least temporarily. The Administration used the respite to solidify congressional support. On 4 May, Johnson requested $700 million for military operations in Vietnam and made clear that he would regard a vote for the appropriation as an endorsement of his policies. The basic decisions had already been made, of course, and the President did nothing to clarify the policy he was pursuing. It was very difficult for the legislators to vote against funds for troops in the field, and Congress approved the request quickly and without dissent. [90]

A week later, the Communists commenced their summer offensive. To make matters worse, the South Vietnamese government was again in turmoil. As it faltered and the Viet Cong offensive gathered momentum, the President and his civilian advisors remained ambivalent about how U.S. military force should be used in Vietnam and, indeed, for what purpose. On 18 May, Johnson resumed the bombing. He was one of the first to admit that the pause had been "a total failure. It produced nothing." [91]

Wheeler and the Chiefs continued to press McNamara for a full U.S. commitment. They argued their "quick war" scenario would not only mean that the U.S. had a chance of winning the war, it would send a clear message to North Vietnam's leadership, something the bombing campaign had not accomplished. The Chiefs asked to speak directly with the President. [92]

Wheeler and the Chiefs also continued to argue for mobilization in the Administration's upper foreign-policy echelons. The primary critic of mobilization was McGeorge Bundy, who was convinced that the American people would not tolerate an expanded conflict. McNamara, however, was willing to be pushed. The Chiefs' plan – declare a national emergency, mobilize the reserves, get in, win, and get out –seemed an elegantly simple (and cost-effective) plan. Finally, tentatively, McNamara agreed. [93]

On 18 May, Wheeler informed his wife that he had arranged to take four days of much-need leave, which they would spend by continuing to scout around the region for a weekend retreat. [94]

ROLLING THUNDER

Meanwhile, the Chiefs forwarded to McNamara a proposal from Sharp to shift the air effort against the North to a combination of around-the-clock small strikes and deliberately planned large strikes aimed at inflicting maximum damage in a single day. McNamara, however, endeavored to keep the bombing restricted, retained tight control of the air campaign, and coordinated all targets with Rusk. McNamara formally disapproved the Chiefs' recommendation a full month later.

The development of a weekly ROLLING THUNDER program remained cumbersome and fragmented. The Chiefs focused on the "positive" objectives of interdicting the flow of men and supplies into the South and of destroying the will and capability of North Vietnam to continue its support for Communist forces in South Vietnam, whereas civilian officials in the Departments of State and Defense emphasized the "negative" objectives of preventing further international and domestic opposition to the war, minimizing civilian collateral damage, and preventing the conflict from escalating.

The process focused Pentagon civilian and military officials on selecting specific targets to hit in each ROLLING THUNDER program, rather than on developing a comprehensive strategic assessment of the air campaign. It was not surprising, therefore, that intelligence indicated that ROLLING THUN-DER had neither significantly impeded the flow of supplies to Communist forces nor discouraged North Vietnam from continuing its support for the war in the South. It had not facilitated negotiations nor relieved external pressure on the South Vietnamese political system.

"This strategy has [employed] air power inefficiently and expensively and has achieved results far short of potential," Westmoreland warned presciently. "The enemy now has a comprehensive air defense system under centralized control, [which] will result in mounting casualties as the war goes on – perhaps more than we will be willing or even able to sustain, given the present limitations on targets." [95]

Wheeler and the Chiefs intensely resented the President's elimination of any professional military input to the decision-making process while personally regulating the pace of escalation, minimizing autonomy in the field, discouraging the development of comprehensive campaign plans, and refusing to accept bombing proposals in more than weekly target packages. [96]

More than any President before him, Johnson sought personal supervision and close, centralized control over the military. Because of his lingering distrust of senior military officers, he had ignored the advice of his military advisors and discounted their judgments on what it would take to be successful. Influenced by the triumvirate's "military theology", Johnson would continually misread the enemy's intentions and make wrong decisions that the military opposed. [97]

> Wheeler recalled:
> We, in my judgment, misused our naval and air power with the result that the North Vietnamese were able to accommodate over time to what little destruction, to the destruction that was caused, with the help of the Russians and the Eastern European satellites, to a lesser degree the Chinese, were able to maintain themselves and continue the war. [98]

Under pressure from the Chiefs between May and July, McNamara would authorize several extra armed reconnaissance missions under certain conditions. Geographic limitations on interdiction missions and strikes against fixed military targets would gradually recede, as well. [99]

An Appropriate Juncture

During the three months that followed the May bombing pause, the Administration would take the final steps toward an open-ended commitment to war. Despite the bombing, continued increases in aid, and the infusion of U.S. ground forces, the military situation had deteriorated drastically, and the political situation in Saigon showed no signs of improvement. Johnson requested new initiatives that would reverse, or at least retard, the adverse flow of events. His advisors began pressing for vigorous action to stave off certain defeat. [100]

"In the summer of 1965 it became amply clear that it wasn't a matter of whether the North Vietnamese were going to win the war," Wheeler recalled, "it was just a question of when they were going to win it." [101]

By early June, the Administration had reached an appropriate juncture for a thorough policy review and new initiatives. Although time was available for a thorough, in-depth formulation process, major decisions would be made in a crisis management atmosphere that severely limited meaningful deliberations or a reassessment of options. Therefore, the Administration would consider only short-range options or remedies. [102]

"One reason the Kennedy and Johnson Administrations failed to take an orderly, rational approach to the basic questions underlying Vietnam was the staggering variety and complexity of other issues we faced," McNamara recalled. "Simply put, we faced a blizzard of problems, there were only 24 hours in a day, and we often did not have time to think straight." [103]

McNamara elaborated:

> We had no senior group working exclusively on Vietnam, so the crisis there became just one of many items on each person's plate. When combined with the inflexibility of our objectives, and the fact that we had not truly investigated what was essentially at stake and important to us, we were

left harried, overburdened, and holding a map with only one road on it. Eager to get moving, we never stopped to explore fully whether there were other routes to our destination. [104]

Taylor returned to Washington for consultations. Neither the bombing program, nor the ground war in South Vietnam, nor the political war was going well. The original hope that with U.S. forces securing the major bases, the South Vietnamese Army could carry the fight to the enemy was fading fast. There was talk of an eventual deployment of between 300,000 to 500,000 U.S. troops to South Vietnam. [105]

The Administration was forced to confront the decision it had avoided until now: Would the U.S. seek a negotiated settlement and unilaterally withdraw under unfavorable circumstances, or would it commit ground forces in an expanded combat role to achieve its policy objectives? "I can't get out," Johnson agonized. "I can't finish with what I've got. So, what the hell can I do?" [106]

Some of the President's civilian advisors, notably Ball and Chairman of the President's Intelligence Advisory Board Clark M. Clifford argued for a negotiated settlement, but they were a small minority. Long frustrated by restrictions on the bombing, Director of Policy Planning Walt W. Rostow and the President's military advisors urged intensification of the air war. The present level of bombing, they contended, was merely inconveniencing Hanoi. American restraint had allowed Hanoi to strengthen its offensive and defensive capabilities. Rostow argued that victory could be attained if the U.S. struck North Vietnam's industrial base. Sharp and Westmoreland recommended, and Wheeler and the Chiefs seconded, a more intensive bombing effort that included "lucrative targets" near Hanoi and Haiphong. [107]

"If you're going to fight a war, you shouldn't fight in South Vietnam," Wheeler advised. "You'd better fight it in North Vietnam because that's where the problems arose. In other words, it was the source." [108]

Sharp recalled:

From the very beginning I recommended to the Joint Chiefs of Staff that we take military action to resolve this conflict as quickly as possible. I wanted to hit the enemy where it hurt — in the heartland of North Vietnam. We should have done this before the enemy was given a chance to deploy an effective air defense system. The JCS strongly supported my recommendations and did everything in their power to get on with the war, but the roadblocks were unbelievable. [109]

Only What Necessary

In the face of the deteriorating military situation within South Vietnam, Westmoreland had concluded by the end of May that a drastic expansion of U.S. ground forces would also be required to avert defeat. On 7 June, he requested more troops and authorization for them to locate and destroy Vietnamese Communist forces in the South. The number of troops he requested was more than two and a half times larger than the limit the President had approved on 22 April. [110]

According to Westmoreland, the U.S. could no longer avoid committing its ground troops to combat because the South Vietnamese "can no longer cope alone" with Communist forces. It was time, he said, to "take the war to the enemy." [111]

Although Taylor suggested that the situation in South Vietnam was not as dire as Westmoreland had reported, the Chiefs backed Westmoreland's assessment that the South Vietnamese Army lacked sufficient military strength to hold the line on its own. Wheeler told the President that the Chiefs supported Westmoreland's request in full. They also requested authorization for U.S. and Allied reinforcements to undertake offensive operations. [112]

"The Joint Chiefs of Staff are good at some things and not good at others," Wheeler recalled. "They are good at developing and issuing strategic guidance. But they are not good at developing force levels or guiding the use of forces. These activities must be left to the field commander." Thus, the Chiefs had no desire to second-guess Westmoreland concerning the need for or the employment of U.S. forces in Vietnam. It was Westmoreland, therefore, who developed the strategy, and it was he who calculated the force levels necessary to implement that strategy. [113]

Ball pointed out that the number of troops was not as important as how they would affect the nature of U.S. involvement in Vietnam. Would U.S. forces remain in enclaves to provide security and serve as "ready reaction" forces, or would they conduct large-scale offensive operations aimed at finding and destroying enemy troop concentrations. [114]

"Although a commander must observe caution," Westmoreland observed, "he wins no battles by sitting back waiting for the enemy to come to him." [115]

"You *must* take the fight to the enemy," Wheeler urged the President. "No one ever won a battle sitting on his ass." [116]

Even Taylor now conceded that "the strength of the enemy offensive had completely overcome a former reluctance to use American ground troops in general combat." As the chief advocate of the enclave strategy, Taylor had clung to his conviction that no additional substantive improvements would be gained for the additional costs of switching to a more aggressive military strategy. He thought only the South Vietnamese could save their country. The introduction of many foreign troops would transfer the relationship between the U.S. and South Vietnam from one of partnership to one of American dominance, thus adding further cause for poor morale on the part of the South Vietnamese. [117]

Pressure for direct involvement came not only from the military, but from within the Administration and from others who wished to see more positive results, as well as from the public, which perceived that the U.S. was losing. [118]

Ball argued to the contrary that it was unreasonable to expect U.S. military action to defeat the Communists or force them to negotiate. For him, Westmoreland's proposed offensive strategy represented a greater cost without a corresponding benefit. Others in the State Department feared that North Vietnam would respond in kind by matching or surpassing the U.S. force levels and receive additional aid from the Soviet Union and China. The threat of direct Chinese intervention was also a possibility. [119]

"We – certainly I – badly misread China's objectives and mistook its bellicose rhetoric to imply a drive for regional hegemony," McNamara recalled. "We also totally underestimated the nationalist aspect of Ho Chi Minh's movement." [120]

McNamara recommended only that the President delay in making a comprehensive assessment and deploy only enough troops to hold the situation together throughout the summer. [121]

The President, however, was convinced that U.S. national interests were better served by further military intervention, and he would ultimately authorize the deployment of substantial U.S. ground forces to South Vietnam. Johnson would also allow the enclave strategy to lapse in favor of Westmoreland's proposed offensive strategy. With superior mobility and firepower, these forces would locate, destroy, and displace the Viet Cong's main force units, enabling South Vietnamese Army forces to assume the missions of security and internal development. [122]

Westmoreland was not "a dolt who single-handedly lost the war by leading an equally unimaginative U.S. Army to employ a 'strategy of attrition' based solely on killing." Rather, he developed an intelligent and comprehensive military strategy consistent with U.S. national policy and the President's larger political agenda. Destroying the enemy, while an important part of the strategy, was but one means to the ultimate end of building a viable nation in Vietnam. [123]

Westmoreland explained:

> It was the only strategy that I could come up with that was viable if there were no change in policy, if we were not going to widen the war, and if we were not going to call up the reserves. One of the things that worried me was my conclusion that this strategy bought a long war and that casualties on the battlefield were going to be heavy. It was my strategy, and I portrayed it as such. [124]

When asked by the Washington press to clarify the U.S. military role in Vietnam, the State Department issued a statement on 8 June that was widely interpreted to mean that in recent weeks the President had authorized Westmoreland to conduct offensive operations. The following day, the White House issued a qualified (and grossly misleading) denial. In fact, however, Johnson had authorized implementation of Westmoreland's proposed three-phase military strategy. [125]

"The first large continent [of U.S. combat troops] … would be enough to halt the swift disintegration of the South Vietnamese forces, blunt the main thrust of the Viet Cong offensive, and permit the construction of an American logistical base," Westmoreland explained. "Those objectives achieved, additional American troops, supplemented by contributions from other countries, would enable me to seize the initiative. In a third phase, the enemy would be worn down to the point where the South Vietnamese – with their manpower mobilized and their forces retrained and re-equipped – could gradually take over." [126]

Thus, the main effort of U.S. military strategy had shifted from inflicting pain on North Vietnam through bombing to denying the Communists a military victory in the South. Short of defeating the enemy, the U.S. could negotiate from a position of strength, if the North Vietnamese and Viet Cong came to the realization that further military action was futile. [127]

The fulfillment of Westmoreland's strategy rested not only upon the success of American efforts to locate and defeat enemy forces, but also upon the success of the South Vietnamese government's pacification program. In mid-June, in what would be the last in a series of coups that followed Diem's overthrow, Lieutenant General Nguyen Van Thieu became Chief of State, and Air Vice Marshal Nguyen Cao Ky became Prime Minister. Their new government would provide the political stability requisite for successful pacification. Success also hinged upon the effectiveness of the bombing campaign against the North to reduce infiltration of men and matériel, dampen the intensity of combat in the South, and induce Communist leaders in Hanoi to alter their long-term strategic goals. Should any strand of Westmoreland's threefold strategy falter, prospects for overall success would diminish. [128]

Mushy Middle Ground

The focus on justifying the President's middle course preserved confusion in strategic planning. Without a clear idea of the objective, the military strategy under which U.S. forces would operate remained unclear, as well. [129]

McNamara was challenged to explain to the Chiefs the President's decision to authorize only a portion of Westmoreland's request. He recognized the incompatibility between Johnson's desire to take the middle approach and pursue a "stalemate" in the near term and the Chiefs' belief that, once committed, the U.S. should apply whatever level of force necessary to defeat the Communists. However, McNamara had neither communicated to the Chiefs the limitations on commitment, nor did he ask them what might be achieved with the additional troops or what strategy was appropriate to that level of force. Wheeler first gained knowledge of the President's decision to commit only those troops necessary to hold on throughout the summer during a meeting on 11 June. [130]

Johnson limited the scope of the meeting to "ways of holding the situation" in South Vietnam. Taylor, who had agreed to McNamara's force ceiling of 100,000 troops, minimized the difficulty of the situation. McNamara misrepresented the scale of Westmoreland's troop request. He also highlighted divisions among the Chiefs to suggest that they did not fully support Westmoreland's request or his advocacy of an aggressive war against the Viet Cong. [131]

Wheeler challenged both Taylor's depiction of the situation and McNamara's misrepresentation of the Chiefs' position. "The Chiefs are impressed by General Westmoreland's presentation of the need for more U.S. forces," Wheeler affirmed. "The Chiefs favor taking a decision now on sending the number of troops recommended by General Westmoreland." [132]

Wheeler's effort was futile because the President had already made his decision. "We must delay and deter the North Vietnamese and Viet Cong as much as we can, and as simply as we can, without going all out," Johnson stated. "When we grant General Westmoreland's request, it means that we get in deeper, and it is harder to get out. They think they are winning, and we think they are. We must determine which course gives us the maximum protection at the least cost." [133]

"In any kind of endeavor, avoiding the difficult decision, treading the mushy ground of the middle road, is guaranteed to produce something less than notable success," Sharp recalled. "In war it is guaranteed to produce a true strategy for defeat." [134]

The President would continue to pursue a policy that would allow him to maintain a consensus, although, as William Bundy recalled, "just what this meant in terms of U.S. forces was not spelled out or decided." [135]

"Buzz, what do you think it'll take to do the job?" Johnson asked Wheeler. Wheeler responded first by seeking clarification of the military objective. The President answered ostensibly that victory meant driving the Communists from South Vietnam and pacifying the country. In that case, Wheeler estimated, it would require between 700,000 to 1,000,000 men and take seven years. [136]

Johnson countered angrily, "No one's using a figure like that."

Clifford then asked Wheeler, "If we win, do we still have to stay there?"

Wheeler replied, "Yes, we would have to keep a major force there for twenty or thirty years." [137]

Thus, the President knew the cost of winning the war, but he never wanted to commit the resources to win it. He remained resolved to do only what was necessary to avoid defeat in Vietnam. Fixated on short-term expedients and lacking a comprehensive estimate of what the war might cost the U.S. in the long term, the President focused on the more easily discernible price of withdrawal. [138]

As Johnson approved additional troop deployments, he continued to defer a decision on the fundamental nature of his policy. After September, he hoped to forge a "united front" in Congress behind his policy. Ball suggested that Johnson keep new troop deployments to a minimum, so he could "keep the power of decision" and "keep control." With each troop deployment, however, Johnson was sinking the U.S. deeper into a quagmire. [139]

On 16 June, Eisenhower advised Johnson that since the U.S. had "appealed to force" in Vietnam, "we have got to win." Therefore, Westmoreland's troop request should be approved. [140]

Two days later, Johnson formally approved a portion of Westmoreland's request. Nine battalions of the 1st Cavalry Division, amounting to 23,000 troops, would be sent to South Vietnam. [141]

Westmoreland complained to Sharp and Wheeler, "It is difficult, if not impossible for me to imagine how we can commit and sustain U.S. forces, air, surface and naval, without backing them up for the long pull by mobilization of manpower, industrial and training resources at least to a limited degree." Westmoreland reminded them of his firm belief that "extraordinary measures were necessary just to stabilize the situation; and that more combat strength would probably be required to carry the war to the enemy." [142]

McNamara had kept the military onboard while concealing from them his determination to keep the U.S. commitment sharply limited. To help Johnson maintain the middle ground, McNamara began to develop a program aimed at achieving a "stalemate in Vietnam." McNamara's objective did not entail compelling the enemy to accept terms favorable to U.S. interests. Thus, U.S. involvement in the war would continue to escalate without a clear plan of action aimed to achieve decisive results. [143]

The President recognized the consequences of the decisions he had made over the previous five months. He discovered that once U.S. forces were committed to direct combat in the air against the North and on the ground in the South, he had no option but to continue to deepen U.S. intervention and assume even greater responsibility for the war effort. The rationale of graduated pressure, that incremental intensifications of the war were reversible and therefore could be pursued at low cost, had committed the U.S. to war before Johnson had given himself and the country an opportunity to determine whether that commitment would be in the nation's interest.

Sensing the President's desire for an easy answer to what seemed an intractable problem, the triumvirate gave him what he wanted. By the end of June, however, the mushy middle ground had led the President to a dead end.

He had used rhetoric equating opposition to his policy with the abandonment of U.S. soldiers on the front lines. If he rejected military requests for additional forces, the same charges could be leveled against him. [144]

Presciently, the President confided to McNamara on 21 June:

> I think that in time ... It's going to be difficult for us to very long prosecute effectively a war that far away from home with the divisions that we have here and particularly the potential divisions. And it's really had me concerned for a month, and I'm very depressed about it because I see no program from either Defense or State to give me much hope of doing anything except just praying and grasping to hold on during [the] monsoon [season] and hope they'll quit. And I don't believe they're ever going to quit. [145]

ARC LIGHT

Meanwhile, Operation ARC LIGHT had commenced. In this operation, U.S. Air Force B-52s conducted huge strikes against Communist base camps, troop concentrations, and supply lines in South Vietnam. [146]

The air war over South Vietnam was an essential adjunct to ground combat operations, and just as fragmented as ROLLING THUNDER. Unlike ROLLING THUNDER, the President imposed few restrictions on these air operations since neither the Soviets nor the Chinese cared whether the U.S. bombed its Ally's homeland. Before the war ended, approximately 4,000,000 tons of bombs would fall on South Vietnam — four times the tonnage the U.S. would drop on North Vietnam. [147]

CHAPTER 3

FATEFUL DECISIONS
(JULY – DECEMBER 1965)

Once our leaders, our authorized leaders, the President and the Congress,
decide that fight we must … we should fight to win; and we should not go in
for a limited war where we put our limited manpower against the unlimited
hordes of Communist manpower which they are willing to expend lavishly,
and do. They have no value for human life or respect for it at all.
— General Mark W. Clark, 1953 [1]

Defiance in Hanoi

In early July 1965, North Vietnamese General Secretary of the Central
Committee Le Duan assessed various contingencies, including an invasion of
North Vietnam by U.S. forces. While recognizing that the U.S. might commit
up to 400,000 troops to South Vietnam, he emphasized factors which would
make it disadvantageous for the U.S. to do so. He predicted that the U.S. would
not invade the North with its own forces because it would bring China into
the war. The use of nuclear weapons by the U.S. was also virtually ruled out. [2]

The possibility of broadening the direct war to the North is a possibility which we must pay utmost attention, because U.S. imperialism could
be adventurous. We must be vigilant and prepared to cope with each worst
possibility. The best way to cope … is to … make the puppet military units —
the primary mainstay of U.S. — rapidly fall apart, push military and political
struggle for it, and quickly create the opportunism and to advance [the] complete defeat of U.S. imperialism and its lackeys in the South. [3]

Decision Point

The next decision point for the Administration came in July and focused on the number of troops that would be necessary to accommodate the first phase of Westmoreland's offensive strategy for the ground war. It had become clear by the end of June that the enemy was much stronger than earlier intelligence estimates had indicated. Consequently, if Westmoreland's ground strategy was to be the heart of U.S. policy in Vietnam, the Administration would have to provide more troops. It was no longer a question of *whether* the U.S. would further deepen its involvement in Vietnam, but *how* the President would reconcile the demands of war with those of his Great Society legislative agenda. In the coming weeks, Johnson's series of "small decisions" on ground troops would push the number of troops approved for deployment to South Vietnam over 120,000. [4]

Goodpaster's Study Group

On 2 July, McNamara asked Wheeler to form a small study group within the Joint Staff to address the ostensible question, "If we do everything we can, can we have assurance of winning in Vietnam?" Although McNamara merely intended for the study to solidify consensus behind the President's pursuit of the "middle ground," Wheeler sensed the opportunity to reassert the Chiefs' recommendations to take the gloves off. He appointed Goodpaster to lead the study group. [5]

McNamara undermined Goodpaster's study group by restricting the number of participants in accordance with the President's instructions to reduce the chance of leaks.

"I would hope that the study could produce a clear articulation of what our strategy is for winning the war in South Vietnam," McNaughton instructed Goodpaster. The triumvirate continued to define the policy goal for South Vietnam as maintaining U.S. credibility and prestige. They envisioned achieving that goal by pursuing the military objective of stalemate. To "win" in Vietnam, the U.S. would merely have to "succeed in demonstrating to the [Viet Cong] that they cannot win." A stalemate, McNaughton suggested, would be tantamount to "victory" if it served as a "way station along toward a favorable settlement." [6]

Wheeler instructed Goodpaster to downplay McNaughton's guidance and instead base the study group's assessment on the Administration's *stated* policy goal of maintaining a stable and independent non-Communist government in South Vietnam. Although McNamara had told the President that he had "very different definite limitations on commitment in mind," he had not informed Wheeler and the Chiefs that such a constraint existed, lest they balk at explicit limitations. [7]

Goodpaster's study group established objectives that would require larger forces and fewer restrictions on military planning and operations than the triumvirate envisioned. The group answered the question of whether the U.S. could win in Vietnam with a qualified yes. Victory was possible with the establishment of a military force capable of seizing and retaining the initiative. At Wheeler's direction, Goodpaster inserted a significant caveat: "Within the boundaries of reasonable assumptions ... there appears to be no reason we cannot win if such is our will ... and if that will is manifested in strategy and tactical operations." [8]

The study group urged the destruction of the "war-supporting power of North Vietnam" and the defeat of Viet Cong and North Vietnamese main force units in the South. Consistent with the Principles of War, military action would force the Communists to end the war or render them incapable of continuing it, rather than merely imposing a stalemate as a "way station" to negotiations. [9]

To accomplish this military objective, the Administration must lift restrictions and controls on the use of military force, except for prohibitions on a land invasion of North Vietnam, the use of nuclear and chemical weapons, and mass bombings of population centers. Short of these few restrictions, the military would require complete freedom of action, including ground operations in Laos to cut the Ho Chi Minh Trail, a full-scale air campaign against the North, and offensive operations in the South aimed at the destruction of enemy units. Once the President approved this strategy, military actions could "not be subject to restriction, delay, or planning uncertainties." Through Goodpaster, Wheeler explicitly informed McNamara that the U.S. would have to remove virtually all restrictions on the application of conventional military power to win in Vietnam.[10]

Moving Forward

On 8 July, the President formally nominated Henry Cabot Lodge to resume his post as U.S. Ambassador to South Vietnam in place of Taylor, who had submitted his resignation.[11]

Two days later, McNamara informed the Chiefs that the President had decided to "move forward" in South Vietnam but had not yet decided on a specific course of action. The President had approved the deployment of the full thirty-four battalions that Westmoreland had requested. This would raise the total number of U.S. troops in South Vietnam beyond 200,000 by 1 November.[12]

McNamara then reviewed the details of the impending mobilization and deployment. The Marine Corps would mobilize a fourth Marine division and air wing and add three new brigades to its force structure. The reserve and newly formed units would be combat ready within four to six months. The Army would call-up 27 reserve battalions and, to eventually replace the reserve units, would organize another 27 Regular Army battalions from scratch. If the need existed, the reserves might remain on active duty. McNamara told the Chiefs that the first priority would be to get troops "into South Vietnam as fast as they can be absorbed." All that remained, he said, was the formal announcement of the decision. The Congress and the American public would have to be "softened up" first.[13]

Greene was astonished by McNamara's announcement and thought the "requirement for additional forces and the deployment of both regulars and reserves had not been carefully thought through." Greene felt that the Chiefs had been reduced to technicians whose principal responsibility was to carry out decisions already made rather than fully participating in the planning and advisory process.[14]

Despite having excluded the Chiefs from policy discussions, McNamara still needed to keep them "on the team." He ostensibly retained the full list of military actions developed by Goodpaster's study group, even though it included military measures that went far beyond the limitations he envisioned. In the first draft of his paper on the expansion of U.S. military pressure, McNamara recommended the deployment of 40 battalions to raise the number of U.S. troops to 200,000. Consistent with the Chiefs' plans for mobilization, the paper suggested a reserve call up of 100,000 and the extension of tours of duty for those already in the service. The paper also proposed expanding the air campaign against North Vietnam, including bombing port facilities, mining harbors, destroying transportation and industrial targets closer to Hanoi, and intensifying aerial interdiction. Aircraft would attack North Vietnamese airfields and surface-to-air missile sites as necessary. [15]

In truth, McNamara never genuinely considered advocating these measures the Chiefs had recommended. McGeorge Bundy, who believed the principal purpose of ground troops would be to preserve U.S. credibility by covering "an eventual retreat," criticized the military actions in the paper as "rash to the point of folly." McNamara appeased the Chiefs by keeping his memo unchanged, but privately indicated his willingness to drop military recommendations to preserve the support of McGeorge Bundy and Rusk, who favored limited military actions. [16]

McNamara did not forward the Goodpaster study to the White House. In consequence, the U.S. military commitment in Vietnam would continue to grow without a reconciliation of the military's and McNamara's fundamentally different conceptions of how to prosecute the war. [17]

Saigon Trip

Neglecting strategic thought and unreceptive to "alternative courses of action and their consequences," McNamara was focused entirely on tactical issues during a fact-finding trip to South Vietnam. He hoped to obtain from Westmoreland an estimate of the number of troops needed to impose a stalemate, whereas Westmoreland sought an open-ended commitment to the objective of "overwhelming" the enemy. McNamara asked him whether, based on the assumption that enemy efforts did not increase, 34 additional U.S. battalions would suffice "to prove to the [Viet Cong and North Vietnamese] that they cannot win in South Vietnam." Doctrinally rejecting stalemate as a military objective, Westmoreland argued that the enemy was "too deeply committed to be influenced by anything but [the] application of overpowering force." Even the full level of force that he had requested would "not per se cause the enemy to back off." Westmoreland said, "Instinctively, we believe that there may be substantial additional U.S. forces requirements." After the forces included in his request had stabilized the military situation, Westmoreland intended to use unspecified numbers of additional troops "to gain and maintain a military initiative" in 1966. [18]

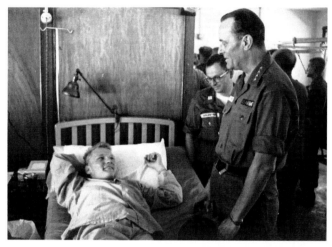

Wheeler visits wounded servicemembers in a field hospital in South Vietnam, July 1965. (Office of the Chairman of the Joint Chiefs of Staff)

The Chiefs Testify

While Wheeler was in Vietnam with McNamara, the Chiefs testified before the House Armed Services Committee on 15 July. Asked by legislators to provide a comprehensive estimate of the amount of force the war would ultimately require, the Chiefs gave varied estimates. Greene estimated 500,000 troops. He believed the legislators must have inferred the need for mobilization, but neither he nor his colleagues made that requirement explicit.

Questioning moved from troop requirements and mobilization to military action against North Vietnam. Again, the Chiefs did not want to get ahead of the Administration. One legislator admonished them that they were "creatures of the Congress and therefore have a duty to tell them as well as to the Executive Branch." [19]

Later that day and in private, Greene provided to a congressional staffer the true assessment that the Chiefs declined to provide publicly to the committee. The U.S., he asserted, was on the verge of a "major war" that ultimately would involve a minimum of 500,000 troops. The war would take at least five years, and the U.S. would suffer many casualties. To set conditions for winning the war, the U.S. would have to undertake an "immediate intensification" of operations against North Vietnam and within South Vietnam. [20]

Fateful Decisions

After McNamara's party returned to Washington on 21 July, the President and his chief advisors began a week-long series of discussions to hammer out major decisions about U.S. military, political, and economic involvement in South Vietnam. Defusing potential opposition to his fateful Vietnam decisions by the week's end, the President would set the U.S. on a course from which it would not deviate for nearly three years. [21]

In his Saigon trip report to the President, McNamara described the objective of military force as demonstrating to the enemy "that the odds are against their winning." He predicted that his proposal — if "properly integrated and executed with continuing vigor and visible determination — [stood] a good chance of achieving an acceptable outcome within a reasonable time." His recommendation reiterated those actions the President had already decided to support. American ground force deployments would increase to 34 battalions or, if South Korea failed to provide 9 battalions promptly, 43. Limitations on the air campaign would continue. McNamara omitted actions that he had included in earlier papers, such as the mining of Haiphong Harbor. [22]

If the Chiefs found limitations on the level of force under McNamara's plan unsatisfactory, the other options the President presented, "bugging out" and "maintaining present force and losing slowly," were even more unacceptable to them. [23]

In a meeting with the Chiefs and the Service Secretaries on 22 July, the President expressed his fear that if he "gave Westmoreland all he asked for" and expanded the air campaign in accordance with the Chiefs' advice, China might "come in." [24]

A new CIA estimate concluded, however, that China would not intervene unless the U.S. invaded North Vietnam or attacked air bases in China. The CIA also predicted that the Chinese would conclude that deployments consistent with Westmoreland's full request would only postpone and worsen the eventual U.S. defeat.

Greene expressed with great candor his frustration over limitations on military force. He urged intensifying ROLLING THUNDER, blockading North Vietnam, and mining Haiphong Harbor. He warned the President that winning the war in South Vietnam would take five years and 500,000 troops.

After Greene recommended the deployment of 80,000 more Marines than Westmoreland had requested, the President asked, "Won't this cause them [China and the Soviet Union] to come in?"

"Johnny" Johnson responded, "No, I don't think they will."

The President replied, "MacArthur didn't think they would come in either." [25]

McDonald observed that while the U.S. "can't win an all-out war," he thought a loss of international credibility that would attend a U.S. withdrawal left the Administration no choice but to send more troops. [26]

There was little discussion of how the additional troops would be employed or how their actions might contribute to achieving policy goals. Wheeler made several references to the stated policy goal of maintaining "South Vietnam as free and independent," but there was no discussion of how to reconcile that goal with McNamara's proposal that military force should aim to achieve a stalemate in the South. [27]

McNamara had previously recommended that the President ask Congress for authority to call to active duty 235,000 men from the reserves. In addition to increased draft calls and involuntary extensions of tours of duty, the Armed Forces would be increased by 600,000.

No shrinking violet, Wheeler staunchly urges the President to mobilize the reserves if Johnson will involve the U.S. in a major ground war in Vietnam, the White House Cabinet Room, Washington, DC, 22 July 1965. (LBJ Library)

The Chiefs "made their most convincing case" for mobilization of the reserves and calling up the National Guard. Wheeler recalled, "All of our contingency plans were based upon the assumption that if we made a sizable commitment of our forces anyplace in the world, we would immediately reconstitute the strategic reserves of the U.S. by the call-up of the reserve units." Obviously, such a large mobilization of manpower and the necessary supplemental appropriations to support it would have spurred a national debate. [28]

Wheeler implores the President to heed sound warfighting principles as Johnson considers involving U.S. ground combat forces in Vietnam, the White House Cabinet Room, Washington, DC, 22 July 1965. (LBJ Library)

"We didn't think it was going to prove to be a two-penny military adventure by any manner or means," Wheeler recalled. "It was for the same reason that we advocated and continue to advocate such things as closing the port of Haiphong and really undertaking an air and naval campaign against North Vietnam that would teach them what war was all about, [so] they wouldn't be so damned eager to indulge in one." [29]

Now, McNamara informed the President that he was "not pressing" him to order national mobilization since it was tantamount to a declaration of war. [30]

The question of how many troops were required could never be answered. McNamara left the absolute number dependent on "developments." The President accepted such imprecision in assessing the cost of ground intervention because it avoided having to make a clear funding choice between intervention and domestic priorities. The question of how many soldiers was linked to the miltary's bottom line question of what ground forces were supposed to accomplish. Johnson had never clearly articulated a policy goal to the Chiefs beyond generalities because then they would have had adequate justification for demanding the means to accomplish their specific objective — an intolerable situation for Johnson because it would mean a full mobilization of the economy for war, consuming resources from his beloved welfare programs. [31]

The President ignored Wheeler's estimate that success would require between 700,000 to 1,000,000 men and take seven years because it was associated with a mission that Johnson had no intention of clearly assigning to the military. Any stipulation of a goal beyond denial of a Communist victory would again bring the conflict between economic priorities into sharp focus and cause a national debate. [32]

Thus, the President's military advisors did not understand what the intervention was to accomplish. Without a clear military objective, the total cost of reaching the goal could not be estimated. Only incremental expenses had to be explained and financed. Johnson treated the Vietnam intervention much like an open-ended domestic program that was to achieve whatever possible within the fiscal restraints placed on it by funding. This economic bent in his decision-making style attempted to keep both the Great Society and the Vietnam War affordable and beyond the necessity of choosing one or the other. [33]

McNamara's determination to give the President what he wanted had overcome his earlier recommendation. Although he had allowed the Chiefs to continue planning under the assumption that the reserves would be mobilized, McNamara told the President the following day that mobilization was unnecessary and assured him that he could fight a war without it. [34]

Johnson continued to fear that anything resembling a declaration of war might provoke the Soviet Union and China. While concern over escalation of the war was genuine, he exaggerated the danger of Chinese intervention to justify his unwillingness to ask for congressional approval of measures that might jeopardize his civil rights and Medicare bills, which were then at crucial stages in the legislative process. Congressional approval was pending on numerous other proposals, as well. Johnson was determined to establish his place in history through the achievement of sweeping domestic reforms, and he feared that seeking congressional authority to wage war in Vietnam would destroy his dreams of a Great Society at home. With McNamara's assistance, Johnson contrived rationalizations that mobilization alone might provoke escalation of the war and that a sharp congressional debate over appropriations risked sending the wrong "signal" to Hanoi about American resolve. Thus, he informed his advisors that he wanted his decisions to be implemented in a "low-key manner in order to avoid an abrupt challenge to the Communists, and to avoid undue concern and excitement in the Congress and in domestic public opinion." [35]

On 23 July, it finally became clear to the Chiefs that the President's domestic political priorities had overwhelmed the assumptions upon which they had based their Vietnam planning. Orders from the President were to hold down the "political noise level" of escalation. Instead of the $12.7 billion that the Chiefs estimated the new deployments would cost, the Administration would limit additional funding to the $1 billion already included in the 1966 Defense Appropriations Bill. The reserves would not be called up. [36]

Wheeler and the Chiefs were incredulous. They had left the meeting with the President the day before with the clear understanding that he had decided to mobilize the nation for war. Greene lamented that the U.S. was on the "verge of escalating the South Vietnam emergency into a full-scale war and that the failure to treat it as such was a grave error. The reserves should be called up and the full supplemental budget required should be asked of Congress." [37]

"It came as a total and complete surprise," "Johnny" Johnson recalled. "And I might say a shock. Every single contingency plan that the Army had that called for any kind of expansion of force had the assumption in it that the reserves would be called." [38]

"Confining yourself to the active forces alone to supply the manpower and not being able to call upon the very sizable reserve in manpower and units in the reserve components meant that you had to stretch your talent in the regular forces very, very thin," Wheeler recalled. "It meant that you had to increase the call-up or the draft by a substantial percentage. And if started, it would, over time, spread your leadership thin. I'm speaking of both officers and noncommissioned officers." [39]

Meeting with the Chiefs and the Service Secretaries the following day, McNamara outlined his plan to meet Westmoreland's troop request without mobilization and without asking Congress for sufficient funding to carry it out. Mobilization, extension of tours of duty for those already in the Services, and supplemental funding would all require legislative action and were, therefore, rejected. To "reduce the political noise level in Communist China and the Soviet Union," the President would delay all funding requests until January 1966 and then understate the need by half. [40]

McDonald immediately called out McNamara, exclaiming that the decision was based more on the "domestic political noise level" than on international considerations. McNamara admitted that mobilization of the reserves would cause a serious domestic debate. During the Korean War and the 1961 Berlin Crisis, mobilization elicited public outcries and sapped morale. Backtracking on his exaggerated concern over an escalation of the war, McNamara insisted that such a congressional debate would give the Communists the "wrong impression of U.S. resolve." [41]

The Chiefs were stunned. Every war plan conceived since World War II required mobilization of the reserves to augment the standing armed forces after the initial round of hostilities had commenced. "No prudent nation can allow commitments and power to get out of balance," Wheeler argued. [42]

To prevent potential opposition, McNamara promised the Chiefs that the Administration would take more resolute action in the future, and he appealed to their parochial Service interests. As with other denials of the Chiefs' recommendations, McNamara promised that the President would reconsider the decision against mobilization later.

"Johnny" Johnson realized that the President's decision not to mobilize was a prescription for disaster both for his Service and for the war, but the decision left him "tongue tied." All he could do was tell McNamara that "the quality of the Army is going to erode to some degree that we can't assess now." Although he thought that fighting a war while adhering to "peacetime practices" was "unconscionable" and recognized that "our self-imposed restraints exceeded by far the objectives that we sought," Johnson determined to "try and fight to get the best posture that we can." [43]

At a cabinet meeting four days later, Wheeler again strenuously urged the President to choose the quick war alternative and argued that mobilization was the best way to assure victory in Vietnam. Quickly dismissing Wheeler's argument, Johnson announced he would not call up the reserves. In agreement with McNamara's assessment of the situation in South Vietnam, the President said he favored the strategy of graduated response. Wheeler was stunned into silence. [44]

The President had helped preserve the confusion and lack of clear direction that attended deepening U.S. military involvement in the war. The ambiguous nature of his Vietnam policy offered certain advantages in the domestic political realm, permitting disparate constituencies to read into Johnson's policy whatever they wanted to. For those opposed to deepening the U.S. commitment in Vietnam, Johnson seemed devoted to the pursuit of "peace," emphasizing careful controls and tight restrictions on the use of military force. For the Chiefs and others pressing for more resolute military action, Johnson appeared tough and privately characterized the initial military actions as first steps toward a much larger war effort. To both doves and hawks, he stressed continuity with the policies of previous Administrations. For the doves, he described the intensified American military role as essentially no different from the policies of Kennedy, Eisenhower, or Truman. For the hawks, he affirmed his commitment to "save South Vietnam and to help the South Vietnamese to preserve their freedom." [45]

The President excluded Congress from any real decision making on Vietnam intervention. He avoided any formal restraints on his policy and a divisive national debate that may have affected his domestic programs. Yet, without active Congressional involvement and consent for the swift application of overwhelming military force, Johnson had no popular mandate to initiate more than a highly restricted intervention. Without congressional support for a war, the President would be forced into a self-restrained policy of overly controlled, incremental escalation of force that would ultimately prove ineffective for defeating the determined Communists. [46]

The President overestimated the willingness of the nation to support the costs of the war. Montana Senator Michael J. Mansfield prophetically cautioned his friend in late July that Congress and the American people supported him, not because they understood or were deeply committed to his Vietnam policies, but because he was the President. Lingering beneath the surface, he warned, was confusion and uncertainty that could develop over time into outright opposition. If U.S. objectives could be attained at minimal cost, Americans were willing to remain committed to Vietnam. Should the war last much longer and cost much more than had been anticipated, Johnson's support would wither away, and the advocates of escalation and withdrawal whom he had so skillfully parried would turn on him. Johnson disregarded Mansfield's warnings. [47]

During the last week of July, Johnson molded an apparent consensus for his Vietnam policy, which sought "the maximum protection at the least cost." He did not wait for a consensus to emerge over troop deployments to Vietnam but forced one upon his advisors. Johnson did, however, listen carefully to arguments presented by Ball and the Chiefs and asked numerous probing questions before ultimately rejecting their respective proposals for withdrawal and large-scale escalation. [48]

The President would authorize the immediate deployment of 50,000 ground troops to South Vietnam and a new strategy for their deployment. Johnson acknowledged that this would not be enough and tacitly agreed to commit another 50,000 before the end of the year. Implicitly at least, Johnson also committed himself to furnish whatever additional forces might be required later. By ratcheting up the war's scale and intensity, both in the skies over North Vietnam and especially inside South Vietnam, Johnson hoped to find Hanoi's breaking point. When the destruction reached the right intensity, he believed the enemy would negotiate on U.S. terms to avoid greater suffering. In making an open-ended commitment to deploy U.S. military forces as the situation demanded and in giving Westmoreland a free hand for employing them, Johnson cleared the way for the U.S. to assume the burden of fighting in South Vietnam. [49]

The President would not approve the all-out bombing campaign urged by Westmoreland and the Chiefs. Besides fearing that a direct, full-scale attack on North Vietnam might provoke Chinese intervention, Johnson and his civilian advisors also felt that the industrial base around Hanoi was a major trump card for the United States. The threat of its destruction might be more useful than destruction itself. The President would, however, permit a gradual intensification of the bombing of North Vietnam. [50]

Johnson had also decided to commit massive U.S. ground forces to war without mobilization. The draft, which would be doubled from 17,000 to 35,000 each month, rather than a call up of the Army Reserves, was a non-mobilization that could provide the manpower without declaring a national emergency. Voluntary enlistment programs would also be intensified. [51]

Although Johnson's fateful decisions conformed to the majority judgment that massive ground force intervention was required, they fell well-short of authorizing the measures necessary to ensure favorable termination of the war and placed strong emphasis on moderation and negotiation. [52]

The President's desire for consensus within the Administration had stifled any meaningful debate over goals or the efficacy of intervention as a policy end. Such an irreversible and perilous course of action was worthy of longer, more deliberate consideration. Instead, Johnson had made his decisions and quickly sought reassurance and consensus among his advisors, as if they were parliamentarians being caucused to promote a congressional bill. [53]

Johnson wanted to avoid potential congressional opposition to his Vietnam decisions. Meeting with the Senate and House leadership on 27 July, McNamara sensed what the legislators wanted to hear and attempted to fulfill their expectations. He lied that U.S. troops were not engaged in combat operations and tried to allay fears that the U.S. was intervening on behalf of a weak client. McNamara misrepresented the scale of Westmoreland's troop request, understating by half the 100,000 troops that Westmoreland had requested to arrive in South Vietnam by the end of the year. He also understated the funding required by approximately $10 billion and argued that mobilization was not only unnecessary but undesirable from a military perspective. Although he had once favored mobilization, McNamara now contended that calling-up the reserves would be an inefficient use of a "perishable asset." The President could only mobilize the reserves by requesting a congressional resolution declaring a national emergency. Such an emergency permitted only a one-year mobilization. Since Westmoreland expected the war to last longer than that, a call-up was of limited utility. [54]

Wheeler remained silent before the legislators, although inside he was burning. He realized the President's decisions and the triumvirate's "military theology" that underpinned them constituted a disaster in the making, yet he would not publicly challenge McNamara and Johnson. Like the Chiefs, Wheeler acknowledged his subordination to "the highest authority." [55]

As "Johnny" Johnson later explained, "You argue your case up to the point of decision. Having been given a decision, you carry it out with all the force that you can, put all your effort behind caring it out." Loyally, Wheeler would continue to execute McNamara's and Johnson's decisions. He would also continue to incrementally shape them toward greater adherence to the Principles of War. [56]

Palmer recalled:

> Many American leaders, myself included, realized the serious disadvantages of the limiting ourselves to the defensive and confining our ground operations to the territorial boundaries of South Vietnam, but still believed that we would somehow find a way to overcome these handicaps — the 'can do' syndrome. But for most of us the realization that time would run out on us very quickly came too late. [57]

The President attempted to flatter and thereby placate the frustrated and disappointed Wheeler during a Pentagon awards ceremony the following day.

> I want to publicly thank General Wheeler, the Chairman of the Joint Chiefs of Staff, for his wise counsel during the period that I have been President. There are many honored and hallowed names on the honor roll of the Chiefs of Staff and Chairmen of the Chiefs of Staff, but there is none that is greater or has contributed finer service or more wisdom and understanding than the man who now occupies that high office. ... I would say that I sleep better at night when I sleep, because of General Wheeler. [58]

In a press conference later that day, the President announced plans to deploy additional combat units and increase U.S. troop strength in South Vietnam to 170,000 by the end of the year. Together with hundreds of support and logistical units, these combat units would constitute the first phase of the buildup during the summer and fall of 1965. Johnson described his decision to commit the U.S. to war in Southeast Asia as "the most agonizing and the most painful duty of your President." Commenting that the war might go on seven or eight years, Johnson had committed the U.S. to an open-ended, limited war of attrition. [59]

The President's decisions between December 1964 through July 1965 were based on two fatal miscalculations. In seeking to do what would be "enough but not too much," the Administration never analyzed with any real precision how much would be enough. Military estimates of the forces and time required would eventually prove quite accurate. But Johnson had devoted his energy to neutralizing his military advisors politically rather than seeking their views.

The President's decisions had also taken place in a strategic vacuum. Scant consideration was given to a precise formulation of goals and how the elements of national power might be best used to achieve them.

Everyone engaged in the U.S. effort in Vietnam, from the White House to the Vietnamese hinterlands, went to war with the certainty of success. On the twentieth anniversary of the victorious end to World War II, Johnson had staked everything on the unexamined assumption that the enemy could be quickly brought to bay by the application of U.S. combat power. [60]

As U.S. involvement in Vietnam deepened, the gap between the true nature of that commitment and the President's depiction of it to the American people, the Congress, and members of his own Administration would widen. Johnson and the triumvirate had set the stage for America's disaster in Vietnam. [61]

Hanoi Reevaluates

To the North Vietnamese leadership, Johnson's decisions marked the failure of America's "special war." But rather than negotiate, as Hanoi had hoped, the U.S. was escalating to what North Vietnamese strategists labeled a "limited war," sending its own forces to rescue the disintegrating South Vietnamese Army. [62]

Hanoi decided to match the U.S. escalation, with the objective of bogging down U.S. forces in a protracted struggle and creating a stalemate to sap American and South Vietnamese morale. The North would direct much of its effort to convincing the U.S. that its "limited war" had failed. For the U.S. to win, it would have to escalate dramatically, possibly igniting a "general war" involving the Chinese or Soviets. Most North Vietnamese strategists presumed the U.S. would choose de-escalation over "general war". [63]

Washington

Wheeler replaced the President's photo on the wall behind his desk with a giant relief map of Southeast Asia. Clearly, Vietnam was now front and center on his mind. [64]

Wheeler carried the Administration's optimistic message on the ABC News "Issues & Answers" program:

> Due to the sizeable increase in the Viet Cong forces in the past year, the situation has changed. … I believe, then, that our U.S. forces in conjunction with the Vietnamese forces should be able to defeat the Viet Cong and to re-establish this favorable balance that we had a couple years ago. … No, we are not turning it into an American war. Our forces are not there to replace the Vietnamese forces; they are there to supplement the Vietnamese forces. General Westmoreland understands this clearly. [65]

Wheeler's workload was wearing on him. "Hopefully, Bus is going on a week's leave starting the sixteenth," Betty informed her mother on 9 August. "I don't know yet where we'll go or what we'll do. Bus needs rest and quiet. I wish that we could stay right here but he seems to feel that he wouldn't be let alone."

Ten months into Bus's term as Chairman, Betty was already looking forward to it being over. "Hopefully, [we'll] be through in a year. Don't know what makes me think so."

"I may talk to you later tonight if Bus ever gets home," Betty added. "He's been at the White House almost all day briefing Senators on Vietnam." [66]

Combat Operations

Over the summer, Communist forces spearheaded by at least three North Vietnamese Army (NVA) regiments had mounted a strong offensive in South Vietnam's Central Highlands. Overrunning South Vietnamese Army (ARVN) border camps and besieging some district towns, the Communists seemed poised to cut the nation in half. To counter the threat, Westmoreland proposed to introduce the Army's newly organized airmobile division, the 1st Cavalry Division, with its large contingent of helicopters, directly into the highlands.

In September, the 1st Cavalry Division established its main base at An Khe, halfway between the coastal port of Qui Nhon and the highland city of Pleiku. From this strategic location, the division could help keep open the vital east-west road from the coast to the highlands and could pivot between the highlands and the coastal districts, where the Viet Cong had made deep inroads. [67]

Westmoreland shared Wheeler's conviction that "it was the basic objective of military operations to seek and destroy the enemy and his military resources." Like the Korean War, the conflict in South Vietnam was complicated by enemy sanctuaries and by geographical and political restrictions on Allied operations. American ground forces were barred from operating across South Vietnam's borders in Cambodia, Laos, or North Vietnam. The CIA correctly predicted that the Communists would avoid major confrontations and withdraw into their sanctuaries whenever they began incurring unbearable losses. The President's prohibition on pursuing enemy forces into their sanctuaries — although these border areas were vital to the enemy's war effort — would narrow Westmoreland's freedom of action and detract from his efforts to make effective use of U.S. military power, thus enabling the Communists to dictate the frequency and intensity of combat and precluded the high attrition rate Westmoreland sought. [68]

Military historian and Army Lieutenant Colonel Dave R. Palmer observed:

> The Johnson Administration's avowed purpose of limiting the ground war to South Vietnam alone was patently irrelevant. The North Vietnamese themselves had already involved all of Indochina. They had established base camps, artillery positions, supply depots, major headquarters, training complexes, and hospitals just behind the borders. Enemy forces staged in safe areas, struck swiftly into South Vietnam, and retreated as quickly back to secure havens. In full view of the Allies, they contemptuously stockpiled supplies to support guerrilla and regular forces operating within South Vietnam. [69]

In October, the 1st Cavalry Division received its baptism of fire in the Battle of the Ia Drang. Despite terrific U.S. casualties, the battle was lauded as the first major U.S. triumph of the Vietnam War. The airmobile division had relentlessly pursued the enemy over difficult terrain and defeated crack North Vietnamese Army units. [70]

Meanwhile, Wheeler sought more direct ways of taking the fight to the enemy. A large amphibious operation against North Vietnam had been an element of U.S. strategy for defeating major Communist aggression in mainland Southeast Asia since 1959. Wheeler now tasked Sharp to prepare a feasibility study for the seizure of a lodgment in the littoral of North Vietnam to sever the principal lines of communication by which forces and supplies were introduced into South Vietnam. [71]

"The idea [of a U.S. invasion] reminds me of a fox with one foot caught in a trap," North Vietnamese President Ho Chi Minh stated that fall. "He starts leaping about trying to get out, and – pouf — he gets a second one in another trap." North Vietnamese Army General Vo Nguyen Giap boasted, "Let them try! We would welcome them wherever we can get at them with modern weapons. … But they will also find themselves caught up in a People's War. The whole people are united as they were under our ancestors, and invaders will find every village a hornets' nest." [72]

Build-up

Meanwhile, Westmoreland's troop buildup was proceeding slowly, although by year's end, the U.S. would have almost 184,000 troops in Vietnam. One hindrance was logistical support. Problems began in the U.S., where the production base operated at a low level. As the war geared up, production would lag behind demand, partly because most strategists assumed the war would be over no later than 1967. Due to the lead times involved, many manufacturers feared production would peak just as the war was winding down. In Vietnam, the U.S. Military Assistance Command, Vietnam (MACV) had to build a logistics infrastructure that eventually would include six deep water ports, 75 tactical airfields, 26 hospitals, a road network, and several dozen permanent base facilities, all from scratch. Despite activation of the 1st Logistical Command in April 1965 to oversee the effort, requirements would often overwhelm the military's ability to transport, unload, and distribute supplies. [73]

A second factor constraining the buildup was the President's refusal to authorize mobilization of the reserves, whose units included logistics and engineering skills that would have mitigated, although not eliminated, the logistics problem. [74]

"In mid-October, Westy sent us revised estimates of his 1966 requirements," McNamara recalled. Instead of the 275,000 Westmoreland had previously stated he would need by July 1966, he now wanted 325,000, with the possibility of even more later, "and with no guarantee that the United States would achieve its objectives." [75]

"Westy's troop request troubled us all," McNamara continued. "We worried that this was the beginning of an open-ended commitment. The momentum of war and the unpredictability of events were overwhelming the Joint Chiefs' calculations of late July and Westy's predictions of early September. I sensed things were slipping out of our control." [76]

Lambasted

Wheeler and the Chiefs were discontent with the President's considerable restrictions on the application of U.S. combat power in Southeast Asia. They continued to express their professional convictions and planned for offensive contingencies on the possibility that Johnson would eventually relax such restrictions.

In late October, the Chiefs resumed their push for a "sharp blow," a series of airstrikes against Hanoi, Haiphong, airfields, surface-to-air missile sites, roads, and railroads in a period of just a few days, with at least some targets hit by B-52s. [77]

The uncertain direction of the Vietnam War also troubled Wheeler and the Chiefs. After several disagreements with McNamara about strategy, they requested another private meeting with the President. The Chiefs hoped the meeting would determine whether the U.S. military would continue its seemingly directionless buildup to fight a protracted ground war or take bold measures that would bring the war to an early and victorious end.

Despite the lack of a clear-cut intelligence estimate, Wheeler and the Chiefs were unanimous that the risk of the Chinese or Soviets reacting to massive U.S. measures against North Vietnam was acceptably low, but only if the U.S. acted without delay. In the Chiefs' view, the triumvirate had been piling on forces in Vietnam without understanding the consequences. The Chiefs requested, and McNamara granted, a private meeting to express their views directly to the President.

The President greeted the Chiefs warmly. "He personally ushered them into his office", recalled McDonald's aide, Marine Major Charles G. Cooper, "all the while delivering gracious and solicitous comments with a Texas accent far more pronounced that the one that came through when he spoke on television." With no easel provided for the map board that Cooper intended to drop off, Johnson invited him in as well, saying, "You can stand right over there." [78]

Johnson positioned Cooper in front of the windows and the Chiefs in a semi-circle in front of it. He did not offer them seats. Wheeler, McDonald, and McConnell stood closest to the President, who stood nearest the door. [79]

The President peered at the map as Wheeler began speaking. In about five minutes, Wheeler summarized the U.S. entry into Vietnam, the current status of forces, and the purpose of the meeting. He then thanked Johnson for having given his senior military advisors the opportunity to present to him their opinions and recommendations. Finally, Wheeler noted that although the Secretary of Defense did not subscribe to their views, he did agree that a presidential-level decision was required. His arms crossed, the President seemed to listen intently.

The essence of Wheeler's remarks was that the U.S. had come to an early decision point or "moment of truth" in its ever-increasing involvement in Vietnam. The U.S. must begin to employ its principal strengths – air and naval power – to punish the North Vietnamese, or we would risk becoming involved in another protracted Asian ground war with no prospects of a satisfactory conclusion. Speaking for his colleagues, Wheeler proposed a bold course of action that would avoid protracted land warfare. He suggested the U.S. isolate the major ports through naval mining, blockade the rest of the North Vietnamese coastline, and simultaneously commence bombing Hanoi with B-52s. [80]

Wheeler then asked McDonald to describe how the Navy and Air Force would combine forces to mine the waters off Haiphong and establish a naval blockade. When McDonald finished, McConnell added that speed of execution would be essential, and that the U.S. would have to make the North Vietnamese leadership believe that the U.S. would increase the level of punishment if they did not sue for peace.

As Wheeler, McDonald, and McConnell spoke, the President seemed to be listening closely, nodding occasionally. When McConnell finished, Wheeler asked the President if he had any questions. After a moment, Johnson turned to Greene and "Johnny" Johnson, who had remained silent during the presentation, and asked, "Do you fully support these ideas?" He followed with the thought that it was they who were providing the ground forces, essentially acknowledging that the Army and Marine Corps had the most to gain or lose because of this discussion. Seemingly deep in thought, the President turned his back on the group for a minute or so. [81]

Suddenly discarding the calm, patient demeanor he had maintained throughout the meeting, Johnson whirled to face the Chiefs and exploded. Startled, Cooper nearly dropped his map board. He later recalled:

He screamed obscenities, he cursed them personally, he ridiculed them for coming to his office with their 'military advice'. Noting that it was he who was carrying the weight of the free world on his shoulders, he called them filthy names – shitheads, dumb shits, pompous assholes, — and used 'the F-word' as an adjective more freely than a Marine in boot camp would use it. He then accused them of trying to pass the buck for World War III to him. It was unnerving, degrading. [82]

After the President's tantrum, he resumed the calm, relaxed manner he had displayed earlier and again folded his arms. "It was as though he had punished them, cowed them, and would now control them," Cooper recalled. "Using soft-spoken profanities, he said something to the effect that they all knew now that he did not care about their military advice." After disparaging the Chiefs' abilities, Johnson added that he did expect their help. [83]

The President suggested that each one of them change places with him and assume that five incompetents had just made these military recommendations. "He told them that he was going to let them go through what he had to go through when idiots gave him stupid advice, adding that he had the whole damn world to worry about, and it was time to see 'what kind of guts you have.'" Johnson paused, as if to let it sink in. "The silence was like a palpable solid, the tension like that in a drumhead," Cooper recalled. "After thirty or forty seconds of this, he turned to General Wheeler and demanded that Wheeler say what he would do if he were the President of the United States." [84]

Wheeler took a deep breath before responding. He was not an easy man to shake. His calm response set the tone for the Chiefs. They had known coming in that Johnson was an exceptionally strong personality, and a venal and vindictive man, as well. They had known that the stakes were high, and now realized that McNamara had prepared Johnson carefully for this meeting, which had been a charade.

Looking the President squarely in the eye, Wheeler told him that he understood the tremendous pressure and sense of responsibility Johnson felt. He added that probably no other President in history had had to make a decision of this importance, and further cushioned his remarks by saying that no matter how much about the presidency he did understand, there were many things about it that only one human being could ever understand.[85]

"You, Mr. President, are that one human being," Wheeler said. "I cannot take your place, think your thoughts, know all you know, and tell you what I would do if I were you. I can't do it, Mr. President. No man can honestly do it. Respectfully, sir, it is your decision and yours alone."[86]

Apparently unmoved, Johnson asked the Chiefs the same question. In turn, each supported Wheeler and his rationale.

"The President ... looked sad for a moment, then suddenly erupted again, yelling and cursing, again using language that even a Marine seldom hears," Cooper recalled. "He told them he was disgusted with their naïve approach, and that he was not going to let some military idiots talk him into World War III." Johnson ended the conference by shouting, "Get the hell out of my office!"[87]

Cooper credited the Chiefs for having done their duty. "They knew that the nation was making a strategic military error, and despite the rebuffs of their civilian masters in the Pentagon, they had insisted on presenting the problem as they saw it to the highest authority and recommending solutions." The Chiefs had done so and had been rebuffed. "That authority had not only rejected their solutions but had also insulted and demeaned them." As McDonald and Cooper drove back to the Pentagon, McDonald said he had known tough days in his life, and sad ones as well, but "this has got to have been the worst experience I could ever imagine."[88]

"One can only wonder at the Chiefs' willingness to continue to serve after such an experience," Herspring observes. "Maybe we military men were all weak," McDonald later pondered. "Maybe we should have stood up and pounded the table. ... I was part of it and I'm sort of ashamed of myself too. At times I wonder, 'Why did I go along with this kind of stuff?'"[89]

Wheeler later explained, "Our recommendations may not always be accepted to the degree which we consider *militarily* desirable, but once the decision has been made, it has been our job to implement the decision to the best of our ability. This is as it should be." [90]

Consistent Advice

Paradoxically, the President placed heavy emphasis on military force as a foreign policy instrument but sought to exclude his uniformed military advisors from the Vietnam policy formulation process. Nevertheless, Wheeler and the Chiefs would persist in advocating stronger measures against North Vietnam. Wheeler would advocate ever more forcefully the Chiefs' recommendations for expanded military actions against North Vietnam and the removal of politically self-imposed restrictions on the application of military power, mobilization of the reserves, and, through March 1968, increased ground force deployments to South Vietnam. [91]

Now was the time for the U.S. to take the offensive. Although in theory the best route to victory would have been a strategic offensive against North Vietnam, such action was not in line with U.S. strategic policy which called for the *containment* rather than the destruction of Communist power. [92]

"The Johnson Administration had already barricaded the one sure route to victory — to take the strategic offensive against the source of the war," Dave Palmer noted. "America's fear of war with Red China protected North Vietnam from invasion more surely than any instrument of war Hanoi could have fielded." [93]

"While a strategic offensive against North Vietnam may not have been politically feasible, we could have taken the tactical offensive to isolate the battlefield," military historian and Army Colonel Harry Summers observes. "But instead of orienting on North Vietnam — the source of the war — we turned our attention to the symptom — the guerrilla war in the South. Our new 'strategy' of counterinsurgency blinded us to the fact that the guerrilla war was tactical and not strategic. It was a kind of economy of force operation on the part of North Vietnam to buy time and to wear down superior U.S. military forces." [94]

"We took the *political* task (nationbuilding/counterinsurgency) as our primary mission and relegated the *military* task (defeating external aggression) to secondary consideration," Summers continues. "The effect was a failure to isolate the battlefield, but because of the confusion over objectives this fact was not readily apparent. Not only was it not apparent to the American field commander in Saigon, it was also not apparent to the decision makers in Washington." [95]

Prussian military theorist General Carl von Clausewitz defined the enemy's *center of gravity* as "the hub of all power and movement on which everything depends. ... The point against which all energy should be directed." Summers argues that the U.S. "adopted a strategy that focused on none of the possible North Vietnamese centers of gravity — their Army, their capital, the Army of their protector, the community of interest with their allies, or public opinion. ... Instead, by seeing the Viet Cong as a separate entity rather than as an instrument of North Vietnam, we chose a center of gravity which in fact did not exist." [96]

The President would listen to Wheeler's recommendations and gradually approve expanded bombing and larger deployments, but always at slower and smaller rates than those advocated by the Chiefs. Such gradualism, they repeatedly warned, would fail to punish the Communists sufficiently to compel them to end the war. [97]

No shrinking violet, Wheeler asserted, "I have, in the past, and will, in the future, furnish the President with the most realistic advice the [Joint Chiefs of Staff] can develop." [98]

Secretary of State under President Ronald Reagan and White House Chief of Staff under Presidents Richard Nixon and Gerald Ford, Army General Alexander M. Haig, Jr. stated:

> Conceding to the politically expedient path is not the role of a military advisor. Generals have a sacred obligation to speak the truth to their political leaders. But we have produced on occasion, since World War II, a breed of military leader unwilling to stand up if doing so would risk his career.

If one is not willing to jeopardize his or her career by telling the truth to his political superiors – who are generally not trained or steeped in the art of warfare – then you invite the worst outcome. There is nothing in a military career more important than integrity and a sense of political obligation. Nothing. This is what the American people expect from their professionals. [99]

Wheeler and the Chiefs spoke truth to power to McNamara and Johnson, but they moderated their arguments based on their shared conviction that it was the President's ultimate prerogative to wage the war as he saw fit. "It has always been my view that the role of the military under civilian authority and the need for discipline and obedience of orders of civilian leaders is absolute, paramount, in a democracy," Wheeler later testified. "Otherwise, you would have nothing but chaos in your Armed Forces; in fact, you wouldn't have Armed Forces, you would have a mob. I don't think any of us want that." [100]

"We were following a classic role of military subordination to political authority, to civilian authority," said Johnson. "The viewpoint all along was that we [the Joint Chiefs of Staff] were adhering to the President's statement, basically enunciated in the Johns Hopkins University speech in April of 1965 that 'We seek no wider war and that we do not seek the overthrow of the North Vietnamese regime.'" [101]

Those who questioned the direction of the President's Vietnam policy, including Vice President Hubert H. Humphrey, Jr., were excluded from future deliberations. Johnson's other advisors considered Humphrey's treatment an object lesson. Those with doubts arrived at the paradoxical conclusion that to protect their influence with the President, they had to spare him their most deeply held doubts. If they voiced their reservations, they would join Humphrey in exile. [102]

ROLLING THUNDER

By the end of 1965, ROLLING THUNDER airstrikes had destroyed or damaged approximately 1,500 waterborne logistics craft, 800 trucks, and 650 pieces of railroad rolling stock. Yet, the operation's objectives had not been achieved because, as Sharp pointed out, the operation had failed to abide by its basic concept and principle of applying a continual and steadily increasing level of pressure. Expressing a view that would be repeated by military leaders many times throughout the war, Sharp exclaimed, "The Armed Forces of the United States should not be required to fight this war with one arm tied behind their backs." Thus far, execution had been intermittent and variable, bolstering Hanoi's morale, tenacity, and conviction that the patience of the American public would expire before a just peace could be obtained. Communist leaders stated publicly that enormous costs and casualties would persuade the United States to negotiate on North Vietnamese terms. [103]

At Christmas, the President discounted the Chiefs' advice and halted the bombing of North Vietnam in the hope that the Communists would respond in kind by stopping their aggressive activities and reducing the scope and level of conflict. Several such unilateral truce efforts would occur between May 1965 and late 1966. In every instance, the Communists used the bombing pause to rush troops and supplies to reinforce their forces in South Vietnam. [104]

Throughout the pause, the Chiefs urged the immediate resumption of bombing, asserting that its cessation placed U.S. forces "under serious and progressively increasing military disadvantage." [105]

Wheeler explained the Chiefs' point of view:

> If you are sensible, you don't give the enemy an even break. War is not a game. So we advocated, militarily, that we should undertake the most sizable effort that we could against remunerative targets, excluding populations for targets. None of us believed in that at all. [We advocated that we] close the port of Haiphong as the first major target, as a matter of fact, by mines and by destroying the docks of the other facilities there by bombing [and that we] utilize our naval forces out there to help out with targets that were closest to the shore. [106]

Wheeler's persistence would lead the President to gradually authorize an expansion of the bombing of North Vietnam and relaxation of the restrictions under which it was carried out. The air war would quickly grow from a sporadic, halting effort into a regular, determined program of eventually massive proportions. Sorties would increase from 25,000 in 1965 to 79,000 in 1966 and to 108,000 in 1967. Bomb tonnage would increase from 63,000 to 136,000 to 226,000. [107]

> Wheeler recalled:
>
> Another viewpoint which was advocated... wanted to give signals to the enemy. So this meant that we used a sort of eye-dropper approach to applying our part. This had no effect at all, none. As a matter of fact, all it did was permit the North Vietnamese to improve their defenses, get more assistance from the Soviets and from the Eastern European satellites. I think it probably strengthened the will of Hanoi, rather than the contrary. Now this was one of these political-military theories people come up with who are not professionals.
>
> The third point of view ... recognized the undesirability of embroiling the Soviet Union and/or the Chicoms [Chinese Communist] in this mess.
>
> So here you have the President presented with viewpoints, and he chose the slow approach. It was just a question of which line of advice he was going to take. For his own reasons, he chose the slow approach rather than the one we advocated. [108]

CHAPTER 4

Escalating Stalemate
(1966)

[The] JCS believe ... greater weight should be given to ... the constancy of will
of the Hanoi leaders to continue a war which they realize they cannot win in
the face of progressively greater destruction of their country.
— Joint Chiefs of Staff Memorandum, 24 January 1966 [1]

Economy of Force

Westmoreland had received fairly explicit directives from Washington
on what he was not to do, imprecise instructions on what he was expected to
accomplish, and very vague information on what he would have on hand to
do it with. His limitations and strictures were carefully delineated but his missions and resources were left open for interpretation. [2]

Westmoreland assessed several military tasks confronting the U.S.
Military Assistance Command, Vietnam (MACV) at the beginning of the
year: 1) the protection of the [South Vietnamese Government] and the South
Vietnamese people; 2) the protection and development of U.S. installations
and logistics bases to keep pace with the continuing deployment of major U.S.
combat forces; and 3) the qualitative and quantitative improvement of the
South Vietnamese Armed Forces.

Westmoreland could not accomplish all these tasks with equal emphasis everywhere simultaneously. Therefore, he would concentrate efforts in the
most vital areas. Elsewhere, he would apply *Economy of Force*, the Principle of
War of employing all available combat power in the most effective way possible, in an attempt to allocate a minimum of essential combat power to any
secondary efforts. Next to the populated area around Saigon in the III Corps

Tactical Zone (III CTZ), he judged the coastal lowlands of the I and II CTZs farther north as the critical regions requiring immediate attention.

With these priorities and considerations in mind, Westmoreland would deploy the bulk of reinforcements into these areas. Accordingly, the 1st Marine Division was allocated to the heavily populated southern provinces of I CTZ.

The Communists viewed the critical areas much the same as Westmoreland did. Consequently, the major battles of the year would develop in these critical areas. [3]

I CTZ

Westmoreland was concerned that the demilitarized zone (DMZ) between North and South Vietnam offered the Communists an avenue into one of the South's most critical areas. The mountainous borderlands were porous, allowing the North Vietnamese to infiltrate with ease.

Westmoreland's fears intensified with the Buddhist Crisis, which had virtually stalled South Vietnamese Army (ARVN) activity in I CTZ for months. Marine Major General Lewis W. Walt's III Marine Amphibious Force (MAF), the corresponding U.S. headquarters, had also become embroiled in these political troubles. As a result, MACV diverted some newly arrived U.S. Army units to the III MAF area of operations, which until then had been a purely Marine Corps area. Meanwhile, Hanoi continued with its own build-up above the DMZ. [4]

North Vietnamese Army (NVA) units deployed just north of the DMZ posed a serious and continuing threat to the security of Quang Tri and Thua Thien Provinces. This region was isolated from the remainder of South Vietnam by a mountain spur running to the sea just north of Da Nang. The highway over this obstacle was narrow, winding, and vulnerable. No all-weather ports existed north of the Hai Van Pass. The ancient, imperial city of Hue in Thua Thien Province was politically and psychologically important to all Vietnamese. The populated coastal strip in this region was very narrow and difficult to defend. Enemy lines of communication, however, were shorter than those required to support operations in any other area of South Vietnam.

Additionally, the Communists were able to use to their great advantage their sanctuary across the DMZ. [5]

In early 1966, MACV observed indicators of a major Communist attack across the DMZ. On 4 January, NVA forces attacked the American Special Forces camp at Khe Sanh with 120-mm mortars, the heaviest weapons yet employed. [6]

ROLLING THUNDER

On New Years Day, no U.S. combat air operations over North Vietnam were underway due to the bombing halt that had gone into effect on Christmas 1965.

On 12 January, Sharp submitted to the Chiefs a detailed discussion of the interrelationship between military operations in North Vietnam and the overall strategy of the war in South Vietnam. Sharp discussed this relationship in terms of three objectives: 1) to deny effective North Vietnamese direction and assistance to the war-making capability of the Communists in South Vietnam; 2) to assist the GVN in protecting the South Vietnamese people from Communist subversion and oppression, to liberate areas dominated by the Viet Cong, and to assist in the establishment of a stable economy and the continuation of an independent, non-Communist government; and 3) to defeat the Viet Cong and NVA forces and destroy their base areas in South Vietnam. It was essential, Sharp asserted, that to achieve success in each of these three components of strategy through simultaneous applications of appropriate military force.

Sharp cited the first objective of denying the Communists in South Vietnam effective North Vietnamese direction and assistance as the basis for the renewed air campaign. It should be conducted to accomplish this objective most effectively. Access to external assistance that enabled Hanoi to sustain military operations must be denied, and the resources already in North Vietnam would be destroyed. All known military material and facilities would be destroyed, and military activities and movements would be continuously harassed and disrupted. This approach would require intensive air operations very unlike those conducted before the bombing halt.

Sharp argued that the nature of the war had changed since the air campaign began. ROLLING THUNDER had not forced Hanoi to the decision sought in Washington. In fact, intelligence indicated that Ho Chi Minh would continue to support the Viet Cong until he was denied the capability to do so.

Sharp argued that effective accomplishment of the three objectives of U.S. strategy would either bring Hanoi to the conference table or cause the insurgency to wither from lack of support. The alternative, he warned, appeared to be a long war, costly in lives and material resources. [7]

The Chiefs echoed Sharp's arguments and called for an all-out effort to destroy the North's ability to support the South Vietnamese insurgency. They argued that a renewed and greatly intensified program of bombing, which should begin with petroleum products (POL), should also destroy large North Vietnamese military facilities and electric power facilities, interdict land routes from China, and close all North Vietnamese ports. [8]

Sharp was convinced that such an aggressively executed air campaign could win the war by the end of 1966 and would certainly do so before mid-1967. Heavier bombing, not pauses, he asserted, would produce negotiations. Sharp was incensed at how long it had taken to obtain presidential approvals for expanding the air war.

In late January, McNamara submitted recommendations to the President on the resumption of ROLLING THUNDER that included the issue of POL. During 1965, North Vietnam had imported roughly 170,000 tons of POL. Despite skepticism from other agencies, the Chiefs, Sharp, and Westmoreland considered POL essential to the North's infiltration capability. They pushed hard for attacks against North Vietnam's fuel storage and transport system. McNamara's recommendations focused on countering infiltration, mainly by blocking routes that led to the Ho Chi Minh Trail, but viewed attacks on POL as contributory to that effort. [9]

McNamara recalled:

[President] Johnson clearly believed that the pause had been a mistake and that the bombing had to be resumed. Although I remained convinced the Joint Chiefs had overestimated interdiction's effectiveness, I now recognized resumption was necessary. We had to start bombing again to blunt criticism that the pause was leading to even higher levels of infiltration, and to avoid sending the wrong signal to Hanoi, Beijing, and our own people. [10]

On 30 January, the President decided to end the pause. A Harris poll released the same day reported that the vast majority of Americans would support an immediate escalation of the war – including all-out bombings of North Vietnam and increasing U.S. troop commitments to 500,000 men. [11]

In a press conference on 2 February about the resumption of bombing, McNamara attempted to convince Hanoi not to overreact. "Our objectives in South Vietnam are limited," assured McNamara. "Our objectives are not to destroy the Communist government of North Vietnam." Wheeler remained stone-faced as McNamara spoke, but inwardly he cringed. *Surprise* is one of the Principles of War, and one of its precepts is to keep the enemy ignorant of your intentions. Yet, this is precisely what McNamara did, informing Hanoi, the Soviet Union, and China that would they incur little or no risk to themselves, thus freeing them to continue their involvement in the war to the same extent that each felt served its own interest. [12]

"The United States should have kept its intentions ambiguous and never taken Hanoi off the hook with respect to an invasion," Bruce Palmer argued. "By maintaining a clear amphibious threat off the coast of North Vietnam we could have kept the North Vietnamese off-balance and forced them to keep strong troop reserves at home." [13]

Westmoreland recalled:
In efforts to allay public outcry, authorities in Washington frequently made known to the world, including the enemy, through off-the-record press sessions or leaks to favorites in the media, what we were, or were not, going to do militarily; and some newsmen deemed any secret fair game for revelation. Both practices tended to deny us the advantages of flexibility, surprise, and strategic deception. They also provided

COLONEL MARK A. VINEY

the enemy critical response time and must on many an occasion have afforded him hope when otherwise his morale might have flagged. [14]

Armchair Generals

It seemed that everyone had ideas on how to fight the Vietnam War better. However, owing to the President's intentional deception of Congress, the military, the media, and the American public, considerable confusion existed over just what combat operations were supposed to accomplish. Was it classical victory as in World War II, or was it something less?

On *Meet the Press*, Taylor remarked, "It is very curious, as I read the comments on the situation in South Vietnam, that in some quarters the word 'victory' has acquired an evil connotation. It is something that one shouldn't strive for. Well, I hope we are striving for victory … victory is just accomplishing what we set out to do. … That's victory." [15]

Wheeler and his fellow senior military leaders understood the Administration was intent upon the doctrinal definition of victory. Wheeler defended the feasibility of that objective in secret testimony before a subcommittee of the Senate Armed Services Committee. "I myself have no doubt that, in the long term, we can achieve military victory." [16]

Sharp was equally sanguine in an interview with *U.S. News & World Report*. "We can take the initiative and win in Vietnam. … Go out and get them. That's the way you win." [17]

At a White House meeting with Johnson and his cabinet, Eisenhower remarked, "If force is going to do the bidding, you must commit the amount of force necessary to bring the conflict to a successful conclusion." [18]

Westmoreland saw it the same way. Complaining about Washington's micromanagement and lamenting the constant "help" offered him by well-intentioned armchair generals back in the States, he observed that "a major problem in those early days, as through the entire war, was that Washington policy decisions forced us to fight with one hand." Westmoreland had been given considerable leeway in implementing ground operations, but he resented what he later described as "naïve, gratuitous advice" from the "self-appointed field marshals" in the State and Defense Departments, and he was frustrated by restrictions that forbade him from going into enemy sanctuaries. [19]

On 8 February, Wheeler's long-time friend and former fellow West Point instructor, Lieutenant General (Retired) James M. Gavin, gave testimony to the Senate Foreign Relations Committee critical of the way the war was being fought. Gavin's testimony stirred up a controversy in the press. He was sensitive to the fact that his comments were critical of Wheeler's advice and support to the President.

"[Bus] had a letter from Jim Gavin," Betty Wheeler wrote. "Jim said he hoped that he hadn't caused him any discomfort and that he never dreamed that he would stir up so much. Bus said he wrote and told him the only discomfort caused was to have disagreement with a good friend and a fine soldier, publicly." [20]

Speaking out on a "sure way for [the] U.S. to end the war in Vietnam in a hurry," General John K. Waters, who had recently retired as the Commanding General, U.S. Army Pacific, wrote in U.S. News & World Report:

> The time has been long overdue for the United States to take the necessary aggressive and offensive action on the ground to win the war in South Vietnam. This can be accomplished by employing the U.S. Army, ably supported by the other services of our armed forces, to isolate the South Vietnam battlefields and interdict the enemy on the ground.

More specifically, Waters advocated establishing a blockade by U.S. ground forces across the midsection of Vietnam and Laos to cut the Ho Chi Minh Trail. Later, they would clear out Communist forces in Laos, down to the Cambodian border. He proposed to assign to the South Vietnamese the job of aggressively going after Communist forces in South Vietnam, with the U.S. providing supplies and air support. Waters suggested warning China to stay out of North Vietnam, and if Chinese or North Vietnamese armies massed against the U.S. blockade to attack the South, then "smash them with U.S. air and ground weapons." [21]

Hanson W. Baldwin, military editor of the *New York Times*, echoed similar hawkish sentiment:

> We faced the 'hordes of Asia' in Korea and defeated them. If we cannot win the kind of war now being fought in Vietnam, then God help us, for we are undone throughout the world! … Our military leaders believe we can win. … Escalation in Vietnam accompanied by mobilization actually will help to *strengthen* our global posture. … The Korean War tremendously increased the U.S. military potential. … Indeed, there is a very strong belief among our strategists that if, once again, we must fight Chinese manpower on the ground, South Vietnam and Southeast Asia is, from our point of view, a good place to do it. … We scare ourselves with shadows. [22]

A Constant Threat

In March, Westmoreland urgently requested authority to bring U.S. combat power to bear along enemy avenues of approach into South Vietnam. On 1 April, he was given primary responsibility for armed reconnaissance and intelligence analysis in the southernmost portion of North Vietnam. Removing any doubt about where the emphasis now lay, McNamara would state on 16 April that operations north of this southernmost portion of North Vietnam would only be conducted when they incurred no penalty to operations required in "the extended battlefield." [23]

Meanwhile, Hanoi had several reasons for optimism. In the United States, opposition to the war grew daily more vocal and violent; in Saigon, war weariness was evident and the political situation potentially explosive; on the battlefield, Allied forces forfeited much of their strength by assuming the strategic defensive and by surprisingly permitting snug sanctuaries to exist right under their noses. [24]

Despite the aggressive U.S. air effort in Laos, the North Vietnamese continued to extend the Ho Chi Minh Trail toward the Cambodian border.

Accomplishing this in 1966, Hanoi gained bases backing the mountains all the way to the Central Highlands.[25]

Political limitations obliged Westmoreland to fight only inside South Vietnam, while the Communists could move in and out of the country at will. The location, timing, size, and duration of each battle was left to the Communists' initiative. Westmoreland had to wait for his foe to move. So long as the sanctuaries existed, Allied forces remained on the strategic defensive. In blunt military terminology, the United States had forfeited the initiative to the enemy.[26]

Hanoi's strategists sought to maintain a constant threat in the highlands to diverge Allied forces from pacification efforts and to preserve their own influence among the population near the coast, from which the Communists obtained considerable support. This strategy for dealing with U.S. forces was like that employed by the Viet Minh against the French and by Communist forces in 1964-65 against the South Vietnamese Army (ARVN).[27]

Since February, the North Vietnamese 324B and 341st Divisions had threatened an invasion across the demilitarized zone (DMZ), and infiltration of enemy forces was under way. At this point, only the 1st ARVN Division and a single U.S. Marine battalion were deployed north of the Hai Van Pass in the two northern provinces of I Corps Tactical Zone (CTZ).

In response to this imminent threat, Westmoreland progressively shifted the bulk of the 3rd Marine Division north of the pass and also introduced the first U.S. Army units into the northern provinces, including a infantry battalion from the 173rd Airborne Brigade and 175-mm artillery batteries capable of providing long range fire support from their positions near the coast all the way to Khe Sanh near the Laotian border. They could also range into and across the DMZ.[28]

Relative calm had followed the Ia Drang battle in October 1965. However, in March 1966, the North Vietnamese Army (NVA) demonstrated its intent to continue infiltration and to challenge U.S. forces in II CTZ when its 95B and 101C Regiments overran the Special Forces camp at A Shau in Thua Thien Province on the remote western border of I CTZ.

Short of troops and helicopters and threatened by a major invasion along the DMZ, Westmoreland decided against reinforcing or reoccupying the A Shau base. This decision denied MACV one of its best jumping off points for special operations against the Ho Chi Minh Trail and would allow Communist forces free rein to establish the A Shau Valley as a major logistic base. Over the next two years, the NVA would construct roads into Laos to tie-in with the extensive network of trafficable routes leading from North Vietnam, and the valley would become a staging area for forces infiltrating into the piedmont and coastal areas around Hue. During 1966, more than 58,000 men, equivalent to five divisions, would infiltrate into South Vietnam. By the end of the year, Communist strength in South Vietnam would rise to more than 280,000 and was augmented with an estimated 80,000 additional political cadre. [29]

MACV interpreted the infiltration of new enemy divisions and the stockpiling of equipment as evidence that the Communists intended to open a new front in northern I CTZ to divert Allied forces from the heavily populated region around Saigon, which was the enemy's preferred objective. Westmoreland also believed that the enemy hoped to seize and hold the northern areas as a base for a so-called liberation regime that could be parlayed into a winning "compromise" in future peace talks. The Communists' ultimate objective appeared to be the seizure of complete control of the two northernmost provinces. [30]

From the Communists' perspective, the northern provinces of I CTZ had advantageous features. Between March until mid-summer, Thua Thien Province would be rocked by political unrest marked by riots and civil disorders by militant Buddhists and students. The situation was particularly acute in Hue and Da Nang. The loyalty of many ARVN troops in the northern region remained in question since some had actively supported the rebel movement.

Another factor that drew the Communists' attention to northern I CTZ was its proximity to North Vietnam and the subsequent need for shorter land routes for resupplies and reinforcements. [31]

Differences Among Us

In April, divergent perceptions of progress became apparent between the triumvirate of McNamara, McNaughton, and William Bundy, and the President's other senior foreign policy advisors. "There comes a time in every battle – in every war – when both sides become discouraged by the seemingly endless requirement for more effort, more resources, and more faith," Westmoreland advised. "At this point, the side which presses on with renewed vigor is the one to win." [32]

McGeorge Bundy had departed the Administration and was replaced as National Security Advisor by Walt Rostow. Having participated in strategic bombing against Germany during World War II, Rostow was an enthusiastic advocate of bombing POL. Rostow would never waver in his conviction that the war could be materially shortened only by putting substantial U.S. forces on the ground astride the Ho Chi Minh Trail in Laos or into the southern part of North Vietnam to cut off North Vietnamese supplies to the South. Without such decisive action, the U.S. would be committed to a long, uncertain struggle. "I regarded as ridiculous the view that you couldn't make the cost too high to the enemy," Rostow stated. [33]

Rostow was a natural ally for the Chiefs, nudging the President as hard as the military and much more effectively since he had daily access to Johnson. "Walt ... was an extraordinarily bright man with a warm personality and an open approach with his colleagues," McNamara recalled. "But Walt viewed our Vietnam involvement, the conduct of our operations, and the prospects for achieving our political military objectives there very uncritically. Optimistic by nature, he tended to be skeptical of any report that failed to indicate we were making progress." [34]

A CIA intelligence estimate released in March strengthened the hand of POL advocates by concluding that bombing tactics so far had been flawed. In April, the Joint Staff and DIA concluded that a program of POL attacks would limit the infiltration of Communist main force units in the South, but that the North Vietnamese could still exert greater effort than they had in 1965.

McNamara and Rusk were more reluctant, fearing that effective POL attacks could draw China or the Soviet Union into the war. [35]

In early April, the triumvirate prepared what they called a "possible 'fall-back' plan" based on their belief that "while the military situation is not going badly, the political situation is in terminal sickness and even the military prognosis is of an escalating stalemate." They concluded that the U.S. should consider seizing on the troubles as the vehicle for disengagement. [36]

"Most of my colleagues viewed the situation quite differently," McNamara recalled. "They saw (or wish to see) steady political and military progress." That summer, Rusk would comment that "the situation has reached the point where North Vietnam cannot succeed." Rostow wrote, "Mr. President, you can smell it all over: Hanoi's operation, backed by the [Chinese Communists], is no longer being regarded as the wave of the future. ... We are not in, but we're moving." Lodge cabled that "the military side of this war is going well. ... This means that the real danger – and the only danger – would be if the American people were to lose heart and choose 'to bring the boys home'. This would indeed be the first domino to fall." White House Vietnam Assistant Robert W. Komer reported after a trip to South Vietnam that he was "both an optimist and a realist." [37]

Little support existed among the President's senior advisors for McNamara's view that "an acceptable military solution was not possible and therefore we should 'get in direct touch' with the North Vietnamese and Viet Cong to work out the best settlement obtainable." He later wrote, "My disagreement with the President's other senior advisors deepened as the year progressed. The divergence grew increasingly sharp and obvious." [38]

McNamara reflected in his memoirs:

> The differences between me and the Chiefs were not hidden, yet they were also not addressed. Why? Most people wish to avoid confrontation. They prefer to finesse disagreement rather than to address it head-on. Also, I speculate that LBJ – like all Presidents – wanted to avoid an open split among his key subordinates, especially during wartime. So he swept our

divergence of opinion under the rug. It was a very human reaction. But I regret that he, Dean [Rusk], and I failed to confront these differences among us and with the Chiefs directly and debate them candidly and thoroughly.[39]

Reappointment

In late April, the President reappointed Wheeler for a second, two-year term as Chairman. "You don't get extended as Chairman unless you're doing something right, and they like what you're doing," observes General (Retired) George W. Casey, Jr., former Chief of Staff of the Army (2007-2011).[40]

At the blistering pace Bus had maintained, it is understandable that Betty wrote, "The reappointment is viewed with mixed emotions. Certainly, to live in the manner in which we do for another two years, can't be hard to take. I just wish that there was some way for Bus to have more rest and also a real vacation."[41]

Wheeler leveraged Rostow's influence to insist upon a regular seat for himself at the President's Tuesday lunches. Sharp later complained, "That no professional military man, not even the Chairman of the JCS, [had been] present at these luncheons … whether by deliberate intent or with the indifferent acquiescence of Secretary McNamara, was in my view a grave and flagrant example of his persistent refusal to accept the civilian-military partnership in the conduct of our military operations."[42]

Wheeler had long resented how these private forums among Johnson's closest civilian advisors had contributed to the Chiefs' isolation from the planning and decision-making process. Because the advice that Johnson received during these lunches had been pre-coordinated between McNamara and Rusk, it was unlikely that the President or other civilian advisors present would question it. This arrangement had kept Johnson ignorant of the Chiefs' opinions, and the Chiefs had remained ill-informed of the true direction of the Administration's Vietnam policy. Not anymore.[43]

The President had come to value and trust Wheeler's judgment. "I would put forward the military point of view when it was necessary or comment on anything else as far as that goes," Wheeler recalled. "Mr. Johnson didn't confine me to commenting on military affairs at all." [44]

Wheeler explained:

> When I talked to the President or to the Secretary of Defense, I knew what the other Chiefs' views were. Not only that, if a particular problem was coming up, I always consulted with them if I had time. ... I always reported to them practically verbatim what went on at the meetings, what I had said. And if we were talking about a problem where there was a divergency of view among the Chiefs, I would always express the divergent view. I made this a practice. So that [the President] was not receiving merely my advice, but he was receiving the corporate advice of the other Chiefs. [45]

Ground Combat

Meanwhile throughout the spring and early summer in I Corps Tactical Zone (CTZ), U.S. Marines had concentrated their operations along the coastal plain in Quang Nam, Quang Tin, and Quang Ngai Provinces. In conjunction with South Vietnamese Army (ARVN) forces, U.S. Marines radiated out from secure enclave areas to bring large portions of the coastal region back under Saigon's control. [46]

Like Wheeler, Westmoreland wanted to take the ground war to the enemy in North Vietnamese territory inasmuch as existing authorities would allow. In early May, Westmoreland sought approval from Sharp to execute Operation SHOTGUN, a series of amphibious and psychological operations against North Vietnam. This operation would create the impression that a larger scale amphibious operation was imminent; divert North Vietnamese troops from employment in South Vietnam; and develop lucrative targets of troop concentrations for airstrikes. [47]

Sharp acknowledged that while the concept appeared feasible and had certain tactical advantages, "its many ramifications and implications, both political and military, give rise to certain reservations." He observed that the concept of deliberately creating the impression of an imminent U.S. invasion of North Vietnam was inconsistent with current national policy. The enemy, he also noted, was aware of U.S. military potential for amphibious operations against North Vietnam. Besides potentially triggering an undesirable Chinese reaction, Sharp was also concerned that the close association of covert operations and overt U.S. ships and aircraft would hinder the U.S. from denying association with the covert program. [48]

Sharp also acknowledged that the operation could help develop lucrative targets of troop concentrations for airstrikes but questioned "whether this effect would be worth the risks involved." He directed Westmoreland to develop more detailed outline plans that addressed Sharp's concerns before he would make a recommendation on it to the Chiefs. [49]

ROLLING THUNDER

"Americans often grow impatient when they cannot see light at the end of the tunnel," the President stated in a speech on 17 June. Johnson had recently authorized the military's proposed shift in bombing from interdiction to POL targets, beginning with attacks on small storage facilities. [50]

In late June, U.S. aircraft struck large POL facilities in Hanoi and Haiphong, which had previously been off-limits. The POL campaign was an apparent success, as 80% of North Vietnam's bulk fuel capacity was destroyed. Yet, it would make little difference. Never requiring much fuel to begin with, North Vietnam would now receive more POL supplies from China and the Soviet Union, and it would disperse 55-gallon fuel drums along transportation routes and in small underground storage sites. [51]

In a think tank study that summer, a group of leading scientists examined data provided by the Administration and concluded that "North Vietnam has basically a subsistence agricultural economy to present a difficult and rewarding target system for air attack." [52]

An intelligence estimate compiled by the CIA and DIA in July determined, "The U.S. bombing of North Vietnam has had no measurable effect on Hanoi's ability to mount and support military operations in the South at the current level." [53]

Through October 1968, ROLLING THUNDER would increasingly grow in geographic scope, additional sorties (the number would increase four-fold), bomb tonnages, and expanded target lists. But political, military, and operational constraints would prevent it from ever becoming the unrestricted effort that senior military leaders had consistently recommended.

"In the final analysis," Bruce Palmer argued, "airpower against the North without a credible and integral ground threat to Hanoi was indecisive." Political constraints flowed from the President's "negative objectives," the things he did not wish to occur. While pursuing his stated positive objective of an independent, non-Communist South Vietnam, Johnson wished to avoid alienating NATO Allies, undermining his Great Society agenda by diverting attention and money from it, or, most importantly, provoking large-scale Chinese or Soviet participation in the war. Paradoxically, to save South Vietnam, the United States had to apply force, but to avoid a wider war, it had to limit the force applied. For the Vietnamese, of course, it was always a war without limits. [54]

No American knew for sure what the Chinese or Soviet threshold was for entering the war. Along with economic aid and military equipment, China would send 320,000 troops to North Vietnam between 1965 and 1969, primarily engineer and anti-aircraft units. China assured North Vietnam that if the U.S. invaded, China would intervene. The Communists made sure the U.S. knew of these assurances. The Soviets provided North Vietnam with everything from medical supplies to fighter jets, and by 1969 would eclipse China as Hanoi's primary benefactor. The Soviet Union would also supply 3,000 "advisors," some of whom manned antiaircraft defenses. It also threatened to send "volunteers" to North Vietnam.

Because North Vietnam had two "big brothers that have more weight and people than I have," Johnson hedged the bombing with restraints, which would loosen as the war continued but never disappeared entirely. He specified strike days, selected targets, limited the number of sorties, and for most of ROLLING THUNDER forbade attacks within thirty nautical miles of Hanoi and ten miles of Haiphong, and in a 25-mile-wide buffer zone along the Chinese border. McNamara said deciding whether to hit a target required balancing the target's value, the risk of pilot loss, and the possibility of widening the war. [55]

On 28 June, Johnson told a White House party that he had said to his daughter Lucy, "Your daddy may go down in history as having started World War III. You may not wake up tomorrow." [56]

According to Bruce Palmer:

Ironically, the United States misjudged the cohesion of the Communist alliance opposing it — the Soviet Union, China, and North Vietnam. We were slow to recognize the depth of the Sino-Soviet split, overestimated the threat of Chinese Communist expansion, and misunderstood Chinese equities in the Vietnam War. China and the Soviet Union did deter a U.S. invasion of North Vietnam, and the United States did avoid war with those two superpowers. ... This failure to understand the nature of Sino-Soviet relations cannot be charged to any particular person or group. Rather, it is a reflection of unsophisticated and uninformed American views at the time. [57]

Another political constraint would consist of bombing halts — eight in all — most of them lasting only a few days, but one would extend more than a month. Because North Vietnam insisted it would not negotiate while being bombed, the Administration confronted pressure to stop the bombing as a diplomatic signal that the U.S. was willing, even eager, to negotiate. Wheeler and his fellow senior military leaders correctly predicted and warned the Administration each time that the enemy would use these halts, not to negotiate, but to rebuild defenses, repair damage, and hasten troops and material southward.

Three military constraints would limit the success of ROLLING THUNDER. Initially, airfield construction was so slow it delayed the build-up. Even as aircraft arrived, they would confront a shortage of 500- and 750-pound bombs until the spring of 1967. A tangled command system continued to hinder ROLLING THUNDER since, in violation of the Principle of War of *Unity of Command*, no single commander controlled all air operations in theater. The most significant military restraint was a bombing doctrine that emphasized destroying an enemy's capability to fight by ruining its vital centers. The military leadership developed plans to wreck the North's economy by attacking its transportation system, POL, its few factories, and electric power. But with a rudimentary transportation system and tiny industrial base, North Vietnam would not prove a vulnerable target for a sustained air campaign against urban-industrial targets.

Operational controls, such as the weather and enemy air defenses, would also impose limitations. From May through August, the skies over North Vietnam were relatively cloud-free. For the remainder of the year, weather conditions made daylight bombing difficult. Most U.S. aircraft lacked all-weather capability, so pilots had to drop flares to see their targets. They located them less than one-third of the time. Over time, North Vietnam would respond to the bombing by mobilizing repair crews and evacuating its cities. It would also adjust work schedules to reduce vulnerability, which was fairly easy, since bombing raids followed predictable routines, and strike packages were big, obvious, and often compromised in advance by enemy spies and signals intelligence. With Soviet and Chinese assistance, North Vietnam would develop a formidable, layered, active air defense system integrating radar, antiaircraft artillery, surface-to-air missiles (SAMs), and MiG fighters. [58]

"We repeatedly killed dedicated professional air officers and lost expensive and irreplaceable aircraft," wrote Air Force fighter pilot Jack Broughton, "because of the maze of restrictions imposed on those of us assigned the task of fighting in a nearly impossible situation." [59]

Ground Combat

By this point, Westmoreland had halted the losing trend of 1965 and could begin the second phase of his general campaign strategy. On 30 July, the Joint Staff informed Sharp that U.S. and Allied forces were authorized to maneuver in the DMZ south of the demarcation line when in contact with Viet Cong/North Vietnamese Army forces, or when such an engagement was imminent, as necessary for preservation of friendly forces. They were not authorized, however, to advance north of the demarcation line and would withdraw south of the DMZ when contact with the enemy was broken. Westmoreland would have to inform the Chiefs immediately of any actions taken under this authority. This entailed aggressive operations to search out and destroy Communist main-force units in addition to continued efforts to improve security in the populated areas of III Corps Tactical Zone (III CTZ). [60]

Westmoreland's search and destroy operations highlighted a basic problem. These large, multi-division operations into the enemy's war zones had produced some benefits for the pacification campaign. By keeping Communist main-force units at bay, Westmoreland had impeded their access to heavily populated areas and prevented them from reinforcing Viet Cong provincial and district forces. Yet, when U.S. units were shifted to the interior, local Viet Cong units gained a measure of relief. Westmoreland faced a strategic dilemma. American forces in Southeast Asia now numbered more than 350,000 troops, but he could not afford to keep substantial forces away from their bases for more than a few months at a time without jeopardizing local security. Unless he received additional forces, Westmoreland would always be torn between two operational imperatives. [61]

Doubts

Meanwhile, "Johnny" Johnson felt the Chiefs should be more forceful in arguing their disagreements with civilian leaders. What bothered him the most about the growing civilian-military discord over war strategy was the Administration's shameless public relations campaign to sell the war to the American people, a spin tactic that embittered Johnson against the President and McNamara.

While Johnson was beginning to believe the U.S. should turnover responsibility for the war to the ARVN and push for a change in strategy, Wheeler advocated an increase in U.S. troop deployments. Wheeler argued that the U.S. might require more than 500,000 soldiers to meet the growing North Vietnamese Army threat, a figure that made Administration officials uncomfortable. Although Westmoreland continued to provide Washington with reports that he was making progress – evidenced by the big unit battles of late 1965 and early 1966 — Wheeler realized that the war could not be won without the nation's irrevocably committing itself to South Vietnam's defense.

Wheeler continued to push tirelessly for full mobilization, crafting a policy that made troop increases look incremental but brought the Administration inevitably closer to full mobilization. By agreeing to an ever-larger commitment of U.S. forces, Wheeler realized he was slowly moving closer to the upper limit of U.S. troop availability; when he reached that upper limit, he believed, the President would have little choice but to mobilize the nation. Using increased troop deployments in early 1966 as a gauge, Wheeler knew the Army would start scraping the bottom of the manpower barrel in late 1967 or early 1968 (and the war still would not be won). Throughout most of 1966, Wheeler was confident his plan would work. Not only were U.S. troop levels in Vietnam being consistently increased, but McNamara remained an invaluable pro-mobilization ally. [62]

Ground Combat

Meanwhile, North Vietnamese Army (NVA) troops had entered Quang Tri Province from the north and west in divisional strength from March through June, while U.S. Marine Corps, U.S. Army, and South Vietnamese forces had progressively pushed north and west from the coast. A major clash resulted. Intelligence indicated that no less than 5,000 regular troops of the NVA 324B Division were in South Vietnam preparing to overrun Quang Tri Province.

To counter this threat, Walt had only the reinforced 3rd Marine Division, an ARVN division, and some smaller Vietnamese Marine units. His other division, the 1st Marine Division was fully engaged in southern I CTZ.

Operation HASTINGS commenced on 15 July to counter the NVA threat immediately south of the DMZ. The largest ground combat operation of the war to date, it involved more than 8,000 Marines and 3,000 South Vietnamese troops against an estimated 12,500 NVA troops. The operation preempted a major enemy attack, succeeded in overrunning several enemy positions and capturing large quantities of supplies, and killed 882 enemy soldiers. [63]

The NVA's 324B Division withdrew across the DMZ by the end of July after suffering severely during Operation HASTINGS. In late August, the division returned to Quang Tri Province and positioned itself deep in the jungles of the western mountains. The Marines countered with Operation PRAIRIE to check the threat of another Communist foray into the populated eastern region.[64]

Meanwhile in the Pentagon, the Chiefs approved an outline plan for an operation to seize a lodgment near Vinh, North Vietnam. The genesis of this plan was a feasibility study that Wheeler had tasked Sharp to prepare in October 1965 for the seizure of a lodgment in the littoral of North Vietnam to sever the principal lines of communication by which forces and supplies were introduced into South Vietnam. Wheeler had always intended to convince the President to take the ground war into North Vietnamese territory. Thus far, however, the Chiefs had not included the establishment of such a lodgment among the measures they recommended for the prosecution of the war. This reflected the Administration's policy, reiterated by Rusk in a news conference on 5 August that, "We have no desire to destroy the regime in North Vietnam."[65]

Rostow echoed this policy in a later television interview. "Our objectives have been remarkably clear and stable in Vietnam. It is to defeat this aggression being imposed on the South. We have no interest whatsoever in overthrowing the government of the North. … The President's objective is to get this aggression defeated and get this to an honorable peace as soon as possible."[66]

As frustrated as Wheeler was over the Administration's self-imposed restrictions on waging the war and its public pronouncements about such restrictions, he and his fellow senior officers were confident that the U.S. would ultimately muddle its way through to a successful conclusion. On 31 August, Wheeler stated publicly that the process of establishing a "free, stable" South Vietnam "may take years and it will take great patience … but there is every reason to have hope that it will be done."[67]

"The thing that impressed me most was the tremendous progress that's been made in the seven months since my last inspection – progress that augurs a definite victory," Greene told the press during a visit to South Vietnam a few days later. "I know I sound optimistic to you, and I'm enthusiastic about what I see, because I'm convinced, if we keep on with what we're doing, that we can bring a satisfactory close to this conflict in South Vietnam." [68]

ROLLING THUNDER

In August, a CIA assessment determined that the North Vietnamese had built "the most formidable air defense system in the history of modern warfare" and argued that the U.S. bombing campaign against North Vietnam was failing. More ominously, the CIA believed North Vietnamese willpower to persist was greater than the United States' own. [69]

Wheeler initially believed the CIA report would reinvigorate McNamara's call for mobilization and convince the President that the triumvirate's strategy of graduated response was bankrupt, that not only was it not working, that it could never work. To Wheeler's amazement, however, the report had just the opposite effect. It destroyed McNamara's morale and, with it, his support for the Chiefs' argument for mobilization. [70]

McNamara had begun losing faith in the air war against North Vietnam months earlier. "To bomb the North sufficiently to make a radical impact upon Hanoi's political, economic, and social structure," McNamara told the President in October, "would require an effort which we could make but which would not be stomached either by her own people or by world opinion, and it would involve a serious risk of drawing us into war with China." McNamara recommended that the bombing be stabilized at its present level and "at the proper time ... I believe we should consider terminating bombing in all of North Vietnam or at least in the Northeast zones for an indefinite period in conjunction with concurrent moves toward peace." [71]

Senior military leaders, on the other hand, merely believed that the bombing had not been allowed to achieve its full potential. Interdiction and attacking POL had only marginally influenced the war, so now the military focused its targeting recommendations against North Vietnam's industry and electric power. Although some advisors warned the President that North Vietnam was devoid of any worthy industrial target system, Johnson sanctioned raids on the North's only steel factory, its sole cement plant, and all its thermal power plants, although the largest of these only produced the kilowatts required by an American town of 25,000.

Soon, 87% of North Vietnam's electric generating capacity and its few industries were in ruins, but the North compensated with thousands of generators and additional Chinese and Soviet aid. Another think tank study determined that the bombing "had no measurable effect on Hanoi's ability to mount and support military operations in the South." [72]

Sharp, on the other hand, would categorize the year-end results of ROLLING THUNDER more optimistically. Approximately 9,500 waterborne logistic craft, nearly 4,100 trucks, and over 2,000 pieces of railroad rolling stock had been either destroyed or damaged by airstrikes.

Even though North Vietnam had been able to compensate for much of the damage to its transportation system and industrial capability, the air campaign had at least accomplished several tasks, Sharp pointed out, which if left undone, would have resulted in an increased ground threat to South Vietnam. The combination of attacks against North Vietnamese petroleum facilities and the transportation system increased pressure to maintain adequate stocks, required increased imports, and added to port congestion in Haiphong. Constant harassment of lines of communication prevented the uninhibited movement of military forces to the South and caused them to move primarily at night, appreciably extending their transit time. Added to the disruption of Hanoi's timeline for operations in South Vietnam, ROLLING THUNDER had brought about economic deterioration, disrupted normal transportation and logistics networks, and aggravated management problems and manpower shortages.

After a comprehensive review of the objectives, results, and future courses of action for ROLLING THUNDER operations, Sharp would conclude that the basic objectives and tasks set forth for the program were still valid. He asserted that an effective air campaign, together with continued successful operations in South Vietnam, offered the greatest prospects for bringing the war to a successful conclusion on terms advantageous to the U.S. and its Allies. [73]

Sharp urged:

If the enemy avoids major engagements in South Vietnam and gets back to Phase II of their plan, the guerrilla phase, then it becomes urgently important to step up the pressure in the North by hitting targets that hurt them. And if some civilians get killed in the course of these stepped-up air attacks, then we should recognize it as part of the increased pressure. This war is a dirty business, like all wars. We need to get hardheaded about it. That is the only kind of action that these tough Communists will respect. That is the way to get this war over soonest. Let's roll up our sleeves and get on with the war. We have the power; I would like to have the authority to use it. [74]

Anti-Infiltration System

Against this backdrop, a special study group of scientists conceived an anti-infiltration system that would popularly become known as the McNamara Line or Electric Fence. The system featured a 40-kilometer-long physical barrier supported by early warning devices and carefully selected fortified positions constructed on key terrain, manned with adequate forces, and supported by artillery, airstrikes, and naval gunfire. It was intended to thwart the massive infiltration of North Vietnamese troops and equipment across the DMZ. The early warning device sensors were designed to be employed in a linear obstacle field. The balance pressure system would indicate any increase in weight, such as that produced by a person walking over it. The infrared intrusion detector operated similarly to home security detectors. Unattended seismic detectors were used to note and report earth vibrations, such as those caused by a group of persons walking down a trail. Acoustic sensors transmitted the sound when persons stepped on small explosive devices.

The system was designed to reduce the need for costly operations in an area constantly subjected to enemy-directed artillery and mortar fire from adjacent sanctuaries within and across the DMZ. The anti-infiltration system would also detect enemy incursions and movements at greater distances. The system was an overall effort to counter both enemy infiltration and direct invasion by making enemy movement across the DMZ simultaneously costlier to the attacker and less expensive for the defender. [75]

"We anticipate that the North Vietnamese would learn to cope with a barrier built this way after some period of time which we cannot estimate, but which we fear may be short", wrote Director of the Joint Staff Army Lieutenant General Berton E. Spivy, Jr. to Sharp on 8 September. "Weapons and sensors which can make it much more effective barrier, only some of which are now under development, are likely not to be available in less than 18 months to 2 years. Even these, it must be expected, will eventually be overcome by the North Vietnamese, so that further improvements in weaponry will be necessary." Thus, the Joint Staff envisioned a dynamic "battle of the barrier", in which the barrier would be continually improved and strengthened by the introduction of new components, and which, it was hoped, would keep the North Vietnamese off-balance by continually posing new problems for them. [76]

Wheeler promotes Berton E. Spivy, Jr. to Lieutenant General, The Pentagon, Washington, DC, 1 April 1965. (Office of the Chairman of the Joint Chiefs of Staff)

Spivy continued:

Apart from North Vietnamese countermeasures against the barrier itself, the U.S. had to consider other strategic alternatives available to the enemy in case the barrier was successful, including a move into the Mekong plain; infiltration from the sea either directly to [South Vietnam] or through Cambodia; and movement down the Mekong from Thakhek (held by the Pathet Lao and North Vietnamese) into Cambodia. [77]

Spivy also noted that "it will be difficult for us to find out how effective the barrier is in the absence of clearly visible North Vietnamese responses, such as end runs through the Mekong plain. Because of supplies already stored in the pipeline, and because of the general shakiness of our quantitative estimates of either supply or troop infiltration, it is unlikely to be some time before the effect of even a wholly successful barrier becomes noticeable." This would necessitate a vastly increased intelligence effort, "including continued road-watch activity in the areas of the multiple roads, and patrol and reconnaissance activity south of the anti-personnel barrier." [78]

SEA DRAGON

Meanwhile, ROLLING THUNDER was not the only means by which the Allies were taking the war to the enemy in North Vietnam. Naval surface forces were also conducting a vigorous and unremitting campaign against logistics craft in North Vietnamese waters and against land targets within the range of their guns.

Since May 1965, naval gunfire had been employed in support of U.S. and Allied forces in South Vietnam. To augment ROLLING THUNDER, particularly during periods of adverse weather and reduced visibility, Sharp believed that naval gunfire should also be employed against North Vietnam. Naval forces within the Gulf of Tonkin were already engaged in early warning, search and rescue, and aircraft carrier support missions.

Sharp argued that naval gunfire could divert and dilute some North Vietnamese defensive efforts, which were concentrated on air defense. On 13 May 1966, the Chiefs recommended to McNamara that naval gunfire be authorized against targets ashore and in the coastal waters of North Vietnam in the area 17-20 degrees North.

Typifying how the Johnson Administration belatedly granted the military only a portion of the authorities it had requested and deemed necessary for prosecuting the war toward a successful outcome, authority was finally granted on 15 October to conduct surface ship operations against waterborne traffic in North Vietnamese coastal waters, but only south of 17 degrees 30' North. Shore bombardment was only authorized in self-defense. Attacks against watercraft engaged in fishing or in nonmilitary pursuits were prohibited. On 11 November, the northern boundary of SEA DRAGON operations would be extended northward to 18 degrees North.

The DMZ had been a secure sanctuary for the Communists during the first half of 1966, not because of a lack of friendly firepower capability, noted Sharp, but because of self-imposed U.S. restraint. On 20 July, however, the Chiefs convinced McNamara to authorize limited U.S. actions to counter the serious threat from North Vietnamese infiltration through the DMZ. Thereafter, airstrikes, artillery, and naval gunfire targeted clearly defined military activity in the area south of the demarcation line, the actual boundary between North and South Vietnam.

As late as 24 November, the would prohibit the use of artillery and naval gunfire against even clearly defined military activity in the DMZ north of the demarcation line. This restriction, Sharp lamented, had enabled the Communists to construct extensive fortifications with particular emphasis on air defense positions.

By the end of 1966, SEA DRAGON forces would destroy 382 waterborne logistics craft and damage another 325, destroy 5 shore batteries and damage 2 others, and destroy 2 radar sites and damage 2 more. Equally significant, SEA DRAGON forced the bulk of logistic movement that had been seaborne back into the crowded land routes or into the inland waterways, where it was subject to aerial attack. [79]

Manila Conference

On 24-25 October, President Johnson met with South Vietnamese Chairman Thieu and Premier Ky and other Allied leaders in Manila. While enroute to the conference, Johnson proclaimed in Australia, "I believe there is a light at the end of what has been a long and lonely tunnel." His outlook may have been buoyed by a growing list of recent military successes and by greater political stability in South Vietnam. [80]

On the final day of the conference, the seven participants from Australia, New Zealand, South Korea, South Vietnam, the Philippines, Thailand, and the United States signed a communiqué pledging to withdraw troops from Vietnam within six months if North Vietnam "withdraws its forces to the North and ceases infiltration of South Vietnam." A four-point "Declaration of Peace" stressed the need for a "peaceful settlement of the war in Vietnam and for future peace and progress" in the rest of Asia and the Pacific. [81]

Mitigating Shortfalls

By this point, the III Marine Amphibious Force (MAF) had been obligated to shift more of its forces north to the DMZ area. The 3rd Marine Division headquarters moved to Phu Bai near Hue with a forward command post at Dong Ha. The 1st Marine Division covered down on the rest of I Corps Tactical Zone (I CTZ) south of Thua Thien.

Several more batteries of U.S. Army 175-mm guns and 105-mm howitzers were introduced into the northern I CTZ to provide long-range fire support, bombardment into and across the DMZ, and direct fire support for ground troops. More substantial reinforcements were required if the northern provinces were to be held. Enemy forces in I CTZ had grown from 23 battalions in the summer of 1966 to 52 by the end of the year. The III MAF was stretched to the limit with inadequate helicopter and logistical assets and could do no more than hold its own. [82]

Even before the 1965 buildup was completed, Westmoreland requested additional U.S. troops to bring the total to 450,000 by the end of 1966. While the Administration had retained tight control over the air war, it had given

Westmoreland broad discretion in developing and executing the ground strategy, and it saw no choice but to give him most of the troops he asked for. In June 1966, the President approved a force level of 431,000 to be reached by mid-1967. Even while these deployments were being approved, Westmoreland developed yet another request to increase the number of troops to 542,000 by the end of 1967. [83]

With insufficient forces available to adequately cover all South Vietnamese territory, the Allies could not concentrate their efforts everywhere. American operations proceeded, therefore, with economy of force. Throughout 1966 and into 1967, U.S. forces would continually search for tactical concepts and techniques to maximize their advantages of firepower and mobility and to compensate for the constraints of time, distance, difficult terrain, and an inviolable border. Along the border regions, the Allies fought primarily to prevent the incursion of North Vietnamese units into South Vietnam and to erode their combat strength. There, each side pursued a strategy of military confrontation, seeking to weaken the fighting forces of its opponent through attrition. Each sought military victories to convince opposing leaders of the futility of continuing the contest. [84]

Sharp Recaps

By the end of 1966, U.S. military strength in South Vietnam had grown to 385,000. It had been a productive year, Sharp reported. Since mid-March 1965, U.S. forces had exerted increasing pressure on Communist forces in South Vietnam as the U.S. logistics capability expanded. During 1966, the U.S. had deployed a balanced and effective combat force. Successful spoiling operations had prevented a Communist military takeover and had forced them to employ their main force units defensively. Nevertheless, the capable and resourceful Communists had continued their overt warfare and developed a strong logistics base, much of which in Laos and Cambodia. They had also retained their capability to deploy substantial, additional NVA regular forces. [85]

While Allied air operations over North Vietnam had attrited but not prevented the introduction of external assistance into North Vietnam, substantial progress had been made in destroying war supporting industries and resources. Emphasis on harassing, disrupting, and impeding the movement of men and material to South Vietnam had proven costly to Hanoi, which was forced to exert a prodigious effort to continue it. The Communists had adjusted to aerial attacks by ingeniously hiding and dispersing their logistics activities and had demonstrated remarkable recuperative capability along their main supply routes. [86]

Allied forces had seized the initiative against NVA main force units in South Vietnam. However, the Communists had been able to disengage many units and had found refuge in sanctuaries in Laos, Cambodia, and North Vietnam, where allied ground forces were not authorized to strike them. This restriction had allowed the Communists to set the pace of ground combat to their advantage. Although they had not reverted to guerilla actions as their primary mode of operations, the Communists had found that they could not defeat and eject Allied forces by large unit operations. They had proven themselves sufficiently flexible to strike at places and times of their choosing under circumstances that offered them reasonable chances of success. Communist unit integrity had remained intact, and their logistics capability was sufficient for continuing the war. [87]

Nation building, the ultimate goal of U.S. involvement in Vietnam, had continued in concert with military operations. Progress was often interrupted by enemy attacks or harassment, but the demonstration of South Vietnamese Government concern and aid in every village and hamlet in South Vietnam had remained the focus. Growth of this effort had been slow and painstaking. Although the South Vietnamese Armed Forces had the primary mission of supporting pacification, U.S. forces had provided direct support in various capacities. South Vietnamese Army units had been redeployed and retrained to support pacification programs, but instilling motivation had proven difficult, and progress in orienting these forces had been slow.

Thus, 1966 came to a frustrating conclusion, capped off by 48-hour stand downs observed on both Christmas and New Year's. "[The Chiefs and I] had made many attempts throughout the year to initiate a hard-hitting air campaign, [yet] the restrictions continue to dominate the ROLLING THUN-DER program," Sharp reported. "I have no *doubt* in my mind that Secretary

McNamara understood the military recommendations, but he was determined, in accordance with his own political view of the situation, to hold the air war against North Vietnam to what was in essence an ineffectual level." [88]

CHAPTER 5

A FOOT IN THE DOOR
(JANUARY – JUNE 1967)

Planning is the art and science of understanding a situation, envisioning a
desired future, and laying out effective ways of bringing that future about.
–United States Army, *Field Manual 6-0 (Commander and Staff Organizations
and Operations)*, 5 May 2014 [1]

Failed Expectations

"Militarily, we are succeeding," was Wheeler's public message about
Vietnam in early 1967. [2]

This, though, is a hard task — do not underrate this enemy; the difficulty of the environment; or the political, economic, and social complexities involved. … In less than two years, the United States has worked logistic
miracles, deployed a major expeditionary force some 10,000 miles, seized the
initiative, and inflicted major damage on the enemy. In the months ahead we
can expect even greater military success. [3]

"The need, now and in the future, is for persistence and determination,"
Wheeler asserted. "What we have done in Vietnam, especially in the past year
and a half, is to make it possible for freedom to triumph. If we *determine to
persist*, the recent past can be prologue to victory. [4]

Taylor stated after a tour of Vietnam in late January, "I have a feeling
that the enemy situation may change drastically for the better by the end of
1967." [5]

Despite Wheeler's and Taylor's optimism, over two years of fighting along
five fronts had produced two unhappy results in Vietnam. One was a stale-
mated war at ever higher levels of violence, notwithstanding Westmoreland's

assertion that he had breached the crossover point. The U.S. had won almost every battle, yet the war was no closer to an end. The Communists simply refused to give in. The second unsatisfactory result was growing dissent on the American home front. [6]

Within the Department of Defense, divergent opinions over what to do about Vietnam became ever starker. On one side, the military urged doing more. McNamara, on the other, had begun thinking the U.S. should cut its losses and get out. [7]

Wheeler and the Chiefs were not surprised by the sorry progress of the war. They found no "substantial trend" toward attaining the U.S. objective of ending Communist efforts to conquer South Vietnam. All along, they had warned Johnson and McNamara that failure to apply overwhelming force from the get-go would ultimately lead to a protracted struggle and greater casualties. [8]

Regarding "the campaign of slowly increasing pressure which was adopted," Wheeler pointedly reminded McNamara, "we deprived ourselves of the military effects of early weight of effort and shock and gave the enemy time to adjust to our slow quantitative and qualitative increase of pressure." [9]

The military still believed that progress was being made and that the war could be won if the U.S. used its military power more effectively. [10]

Admiral U. S. Grant Sharp, Jr. greets Wheeler upon his arrival in Hawaii, 12 January 1967. (Office of the Chairman of the Joint Chiefs of Staff)

In mid-January, Sharp reiterated his concerns regarding the restrictive nature of the 1966 ROLLING THUNDER campaign. He pointed out, for example, that of the 104 lucrative targets in the Northeast sector North Vietnam, only 20 had been hit. "I outlined emphatically what I considered must be our future concentration relative to the enemy's known strengths," Sharp recalled. [11]

Sharp cited a recent CIA analysis postulating that restricting the bombing to the southern panhandle of North Vietnam and Laos "would tend to strengthen Hanoi's will." North Vietnam regarded such a restricted bombing pattern "a clear victory — evidence that international and domestic pressures on the U.S. are having an effect." Their leaders were encouraged to believe that the U.S. was tiring of the war and was being forced to retreat. [12]

"Closing the port of Haiphong and other minor ports in North Vietnam … would be the single most effective and economical method of drastically reducing the enemy's capability to carry on the war in South Vietnam," Sharp asserted. "The military advantages of this action would be manifold." [13]

Although the Chiefs had succeeded in lifting many restrictions on the bombing, they remained deeply dissatisfied with the conduct of the air war and were angered by the President's continuing refusal to mobilize the reserves. The Chiefs would continue to develop plans for beginning to achieve an elusive victory, and Wheeler would seize every opportunity to recommend them.[14]

"As I see them," Wheeler continued, "our objectives in Vietnam are to honor a commitment, halt external aggression, defeat externally directed subversion, and give the South Vietnamese the chance freely and peacefully to determine their own destiny. These objectives are related to our strategic position in the Pacific and are interrelated with our larger objectives throughout the world. It is important that we succeed — and we will — but it is also important that we do so by employing our power with care so that it does not unbalance the world situation."[15]

Across much of the nation, the military's hawkish stance found considerable support. The inane policies founded upon the triumvirate's "military theology" had utterly failed. It was high time to wage the war in accordance with proven warfighting doctrine. As British Admiral John A. Fisher noted in 1905, "Moderation in war is imbecility!"[16]

From the opposite perspective, some of Johnson's civilian advisors openly advocated the abandonment of the policies they had come to regard as bankrupt. Opposition to the war had increased within the Administration over the previous year. Ironically, the major advocate for change was McNamara, the person so closely associated with escalation that the war had once been dubbed "McNamara's War."[17]

McNamara was forced to admit that escalation of the war had not produced "broken enemy morale and political effectiveness." The South Vietnamese government seemed no more stable than before, while the air war had produced limited results at heavy costs, including in terms of domestic and world opinion. The triumvirate of McNamara, McNaughton, and William Bundy were also disillusioned with the ground war in South Vietnam. Increased U.S. troop levels had not yielded correspondingly larger Communist losses, and there were no indications that further expansion of the war would induce any substantive strains on North Vietnam. [18]

The President, however, was still thinking in terms of winning in Vietnam. Under increasing pressure from critics of his Administration's conduct of the war, Johnson communicated to his senior national security advisors an openness to consider alternative strategies and a desire to accelerate military operations toward an acceptable conclusion. [19]

"We can *win* the war," Wheeler urged the President, "if we apply pressure upon the enemy relentlessly *in the North* and in the South [author's emphasis]." [20]

President Johnson with the Joint Chiefs of Staff outside the White House, Washington, DC, early Spring 1967. (LBJ Library)

Westmoreland's Objectives

By the end of 1966, the Allies had achieved considerable momentum in ground combat operations in South Vietnam. Westmoreland intended to retain it throughout 1967. Additional U.S. forces and other available resources would enable the scope and pace to steadily increase. With these larger forces, additional firepower, and improved mobility, the Allies would carry the battle to the Communists on a sustained basis. Concurrently, the pacification effort would be intensified and expanded.

Westmoreland's strategy envisioned establishing unrelenting but discriminating military, political, and psychological pressure upon the Communists at all levels. Military efforts in the III Corps Tactical Zone (III CTZ) would be intensified. Allies would begin to expand combat operations into the IV CTZ area. Expansion would continue in the populous southern portion of I CTZ while continuing to guard the demilitarized zone (DMZ) with minimum forces, while forces would be economized in the II CTZ area.

In the northern part of I CTZ, Westmoreland intended to meet and defeat an anticipated North Vietnamese invasion through the DMZ and Laos, interdict enemy infiltration routes in South Vietnam, and neutralize Communist base areas near the coastal plain that had provided the Viet Cong much of its support. Equally important in the southern portion of I CTZ would be the protection of Allied base areas and the lines of communication that enabled the South Vietnamese government to extend its control. Having largely denied the rice-producing coastal regions of II CTZ and much of the Quang Nam Province of I CTZ to the Communists in 1966, Westmoreland intended to link those areas and expand Allied control into Quang Ngai and Quang Tin Provinces. [21]

ROLLING THUNDER

"There is no question in my mind that our air interdiction program has imposed serious problems on the enemy," Westmoreland informed Sharp and Wheeler on 6 February. "I do not consider it likely that air interdiction is capable of stopping movement by foot though it can complicate the enemy's efforts in this regard," he wrote. "In contrast, there can be no doubt that bombing and interdiction in North Vietnam and Laos have inflicted appreciable damage on the enemy's logistical system. This, in my judgment, is the salient factor to be weighed in assessing the effectiveness of our air operations in these areas." [22]

"Although we cannot expect to cut off the enemy's sources of supply through the use of airpower, we can do a much better job than we are doing now if some of the restrictions were removed," Westmoreland wrote Sharp and Wheeler eleven days later. "I agree with Oley [Sharp's] comments on the air campaign to the North and again emphasize the importance of relaxing the political controls imposed on our air campaign in Laos. ... I view this matter with deep concern. The enemy is being allowed an advantage which will ultimately be measured in American lives. ... Time marches on with the enemy devoting his full resources to moving supplies energetically to his troops in the South with our counter efforts falling short of our capability." [23]

"Once again Washington," Sharp recalled, "that is, of course, Secretary McNamara — was on the tack that the object of the air war was to stop infiltration, and since it had not done so we need to look at more productive alternatives." Sharp had made the point many times that airstrikes on lines of communication had never been able to stop infiltration, only hinder it. The primary objective of airpower should not be to try to stop infiltration, but rather to destroy the sources of the material being infiltrated. [24]

Losses in North Vietnamese military equipment, raw materials, and vehicles had more than been offset by significantly increased aid from the Soviet Union and China. American escalation had not forced the two Communist rivals back into a close alliance, as the triumvirate had feared. Nevertheless, along with their increasingly heated rivalry, it had permitted Hanoi to play one against the other to obtain greater aid and prevent either from securing predominant influence. Between 1965 and 1968, North Vietnam would skillfully exploit divisions between its Communist allies to receive more than $2 billion in aid.

"I consider the bombing and use of naval gunfire in North Vietnam essential and vital to our military strategy," Westmoreland stated publicly on 3 March. The air campaign, he noted, had forced the enemy to divert significant manpower to the maintenance of lines of communication and to the manning of a sophisticated air defense system. It had also destroyed a significant portion of the enemy's war economy. "However, from my point of view, the most important reason for this bombing campaign is that it saves American and Vietnamese lives on the battlefield as well as those of our [Allies]," Westmoreland asserted. "If not for the bombing, we would have taken many more casualties because the enemy would have been better armed and supported by larger quantities of war supplies. Also, he could have put more armed troops into South Vietnam." [25]

Another bombing pause would cost many additional lives and probably prolong the conflict, Westmoreland noted. "I can understand why some of the American people would like to see the bombing stop. I can understand the things they worry about. But what they don't understand is the terrible cost in lives that our troops, the gallant South Vietnamese and our [Allies] would have to pay for a nebulous result. I don't want to pay one drop of blood for a 'pig in a poke'." Westmoreland knew the enemy was attempting to win the battle in the propaganda arena and had been encouraged by "a number of unwitting, if well-meaning, groups. I am confident that the American people will back their troops on the battlefield as they have done in the past and that they will close ranks and give us unstinting support." [26]

On the other hand, the bombing campaign still had not achieved its goals. It had also absorbed a great deal of personnel and resources that could have been diverted to other military uses. Official U.S. estimates would concede that infiltration had increased from about 35,000 troops in 1965 to as many as 90,000 in 1967, even as the bombing had grown heavier and more destructive. The U.S. was now paying a heavy price for marginal gains in the air war.

Ground Combat

Infiltration into South Vietnam was a crucial element of Hanoi's strategy, and the Ho Chi Minh Trail was its key. From the beginning of the U.S. war, the North Vietnamese had committed vast human and material resources to expanding and improving this vital lifeline. During peak periods in the late 1960s, North Vietnam would move an estimated 400 tons of supplies per week and as many as 5,000 soldiers a month into South Vietnamese battle zones.

Throughout 1965 and 1966, the Communists attempted to keep the U.S. forces off-balance, thereby disrupting Westmoreland's search and destroy operations. In 1967, they would engage U.S. forces in major actions around the DMZ, giving themselves short supply lines and convenient sanctuary and helping to draw U.S. forces away from the populated areas while leaving the countryside vulnerable to the Viet Cong. [27]

Westmoreland's ground strategy of attrition had serious flaws. It assumed that the U.S. could inflict intolerable losses on the Communists while keeping its own within acceptable bounds, an assumption that flew in the face of experience with land wars on the Asian continent and the realities in Vietnam. An estimated 200,000 North Vietnamese reached draft age each year. Thus, Hanoi was able to replace its losses and match each U.S. escalation. Moreover, the Administration's self-imposed restrictions under which the war was being fought had permitted the Communists to control their casualties. The North Vietnamese and Viet Cong remained extraordinarily elusive and were generally able to avoid contact when it suited them. They fought at times and places of their own choosing and on ground favorable to them. If losses reached unacceptable levels, they simply disappeared into the jungle or retreated into sanctuaries in North Vietnam, Laos, and Cambodia.

Thus, the U.S. had achieved no more than a stalemate. The Communists had been hurt, in some cases badly, but their main forces had not been destroyed. They retained the strategic initiative and could strike sharply and quickly whenever and wherever they chose. [28]

The Administration clearly perceived the deployment of North Vietnamese divisions near the DMZ as the invasion threat it represented. It was also disappointed that the Communists still controlled the same areas they had in 1965. Pacification data had tilted barely five percentage points in Saigon's favor. Meanwhile, infiltration and order of battle estimates indicated the Communists had only grown in power. Despite known losses, the enemy had been able to maintain a proportional counter-buildup to the growth of U.S. forces. Westmoreland would later cite this fact in demanding the deployment of thousands more troops. Still, all things considered, the atmosphere in Washington remained one of "hedged public optimism." [29]

Engaging Congress

The President had been forced to ask for a tax surcharge on all Americans to help pay for the war. "The burden of Vietnam had become inescapable,"

Prados writes. "Gone were the days when Johnson could engage on the sly, failing to disclose the full extent of troop deployments and disguising their budget implications." The Administration would request $12 billion in supplemental funds, plus $21.9 billion for Vietnam in the new fiscal year. [30]

On 23 January, Wheeler helped McNamara and Johnson loosen the congressional purse strings. "Bus worked all weekend for his session on the hill this week," Betty Wheeler reported. His intensive preparation paid off. Wheeler was highly esteemed for his intelligence, integrity, and charm by members on both sides of the Senate Armed Services Committee. "Victory can be achieved in the Vietnam war," said Texas Senator John G. Tower during the hearing. "We've got the highest caliber of professional military men in our history." [31]

Growing Unpopularity

With U.S. troop strength in Vietnam still growing and the President's recent calls for alternative strategies to "win" in Vietnam, the military was optimistic that the authorities and capabilities for taking the war to the Communists more effectively were finally coming together. "The enemy's chance for a military victory is gone," said Wheeler. "The North Vietnamese have learned that there is an increasing toll to pay for aggression." [32]

"We are enjoying a greatly improved military situation in Vietnam as compared with a year ago," Wheeler stated publicly on 26 February. "I am confident that a year from now our military progress will have been at least as great and probably greater than in the calendar year 1966. ... I think it should be rather apparent by now, both to the North Vietnamese and the Viet Cong, that they are not going to win a military victory." [33]

The military's optimism was contrasted by the growing unpopularity of the war at home. Draft calls had risen dramatically and were increasing. Selective Service began to eliminate deferments that had shielded graduate students, as well as families with members already serving in the military. Public opinion polls remained stable but fragile, with slight gains for the antiwar side and fewer respondents who expressed no opinion. Protesters were marching in greater numbers. At Stanford University on 20 February, the Secret Service had to physically extricate Vice President Humphrey from his limousine when protesters swarmed and pummeled it.[34]

Congressional backing for the war had also weakened. While attempting to evaluate the potential for replacing the Tonkin Gulf Resolution with a more explicit grant of authority, Johnson was informed by congressional leaders that there was no chance of that at all. Instead, opponents of the war attached amendments to the budget supplement, supporting negotiations and prohibiting the use of funds for operations in North Vietnam or for augmentation of U.S. forces. Although another amendment approved of the U.S. effort, it too backed negotiations. Johnson prevailed on Mansfield to table both in favor of a rider that — Mansfield assured him —- consisted entirely of things Johnson himself had said, but this too noted hope for a settlement and deplored expansion of the war. Johnson signed it into law on 4 April, and he would never again raise the matter of new authority.[35]

The McNamara Line

The bombing campaign's failure and the discrepancy between the military's optimistic pre-strike predictions and the disappointing post-strike reality had compelled McNamara to search for a better option to impair Hanoi's ability to continue supporting the war in the South. He settled on a special study group's proposal for a high-tech barrier, or "strongpoint barrier system," just below the DMZ that would stretch across Vietnam and into the Laotian Panhandle to inhibit the growing rate of infiltration of North Vietnamese men and materials into South Vietnam, a problem that had bedeviled the Allies since 1961. McNamara had advocated this strongpoint barrier system since October 1966, and it had become known as "the McNamara Line".[36]

The President signed a directive on 13 January, giving the strongpoint barrier system the highest national priority. Doctrinally oriented toward the *Offensive*, the military was generally opposed to the strongpoint barrier system, but they were not unanimous that it would necessarily detract from offensive operations by siphoning off manpower. "The Joint Chiefs reacted coolly to this idea but did not actively oppose it," McNamara recalled.[37]

"I think it is going to have minimum effectiveness for the cost that has been associated with it," stated "Johnny" Johnson in later testimony. "My own description of it is that it is like closing the window and leaving the door open," Greene would testify. "From the very beginning, I have been opposed to this project."[38]

The strongpoint barrier system would not stop all infiltration, Westmoreland stressed on 26 January, but it would make it more difficult and more costly to the enemy. To man an effective obstacle system, MACV determined that a minimum additional force of one division and one armored cavalry regiment would be required. "I do not consider the end result to be the final solution to stop infiltration," Westmoreland stated. "An obstacle or barrier system must be regarded as only one of many anti-infiltration programs. The proper balance of all these programs must be preserved to prevent undue reliance on any single system."[39]

Over the next month, the Joint Staff would flesh out an outline plan for the strongpoint obstacle system under the name Operation PRACTICE NINE.[40]

On 22 February, the Chiefs forwarded Westmoreland's requirements for manning the anti-infiltration system to McNamara. They noted two fundamental disadvantages: the increased anti-infiltration capability would be established would be in northeastern South Vietnam where North Vietnamese infiltration had been minimal, and the diversion of resources required to execute the plan would reduce the emphasis and impetus of essential ongoing programs.

Accordingly, the Chiefs, did not recommend execution of the plan. They considered that "military actions now in progress in Southeast Asia … are demonstrating substantial successes toward national objectives and that, if expanded and pressed with continued vigor, the successes will accelerate." They concluded that "any additional resources that might be provided can be used to a greater advantage in executing Sharp's concept of operations for Southeast Asia."[41]

Wheeler, however, disagreed with the Chiefs. In a rare instance of publicizing a split opinion among his colleagues, he wrote:

> ... although I support much of the [PRACTICE NINE Requirements Plan], I disagree with the [Chiefs'] recommendation that the plan not be approved for execution. ... Again, while I recognize that the obstacle system ... may require an undesirable diversion of in-country resources, it is not clear to me that this will of necessity be so; it is also possible that the level of activity in the vicinity of the DMZ will require the commitment of comparable forces to that area whether or not construction of the obstacle system envisaged by [Westmoreland] is undertaken. *Furthermore, proceeding now with the actions required to provide additive assets for support of the ... plan does not, in my view, rule out subsequent decision to utilize these assets in other ways should the turn of events so require. Thus, it is my view that proceeding now with preparatory actions to implement the [PRACTICE NINE] plan may enhance rather than inhibit the flexibility available to* [Westmoreland]. (author's emphasis) [42]

The rationale underlying Wheeler's curious dissent was not understood until 2010, when this author discovered in the National Archives a plan that Wheeler was then contemplating for taking the ground war to the enemy in North Vietnam. Wheeler viewed manning the strongpoint barrier system as a conveniently plausible cover story for shifting the 1st Cavalry Division to northern Quang Tri Province, where the division would occupy an attack position preparatory to a multi-division invasion of North Vietnam. [43]

Wheeler's Invasion Plan

Amid growing domestic frustration with the war and the President's stated willingness to consider more decisive action against North Vietnam, Wheeler conceived a strategic offensive that would make it as difficult and costly as possible for the North Vietnamese Army (NVA) to continue effective support for the Viet Cong (VC) and to cause North Vietnam to cease direction of the VC insurgency. Wheeler considered North Vietnam's army its "center of gravity" - *the hub of all power and movement on which everything depends. ... The point against which all energies should be directed.* [44]

Wheeler wanted to assess the feasibility of an offensive operation that would directly attack North Vietnam's ability to infiltrate men and supplies into South Vietnam. If such an operation was feasible considering other requirements in Southeast Asia and worldwide, he could suggest it to the President, who just might authorize it under the appropriate circumstances. [45]

In late February, Wheeler met several times with the President and his civilian advisors in the White House to discuss options for intensifying operations against North Vietnam.

Wheeler also met with Army Colonel George C. Viney, a Joint Staff action officer. Wheeler confided to Viney his belief that the President was losing faith in McNamara and that Johnson would eventually seek Wheeler's opinion on "how to get the war off the dime". Wheeler needed a plan for solving the President's dilemma, or at least to begin solving it. [46]

Admired by Viney as "the consummate Beltway staff officer with an uncanny talent for anticipating future requirements," Wheeler envisioned a short-duration raid by substantial U.S. forces into the southern portion of North Vietnam to attack enemy sanctuary areas there. He tasked Viney to develop an operational concept for this operation. [47]

Assisted by Marine Colonel Evans C. "Bones" Carlson, Viney developed a concept of operations that featured an amphibious assault in conjunction with a ground attack through the demilitarized zone; an airmobile operation to block and screen to the west and northwest of the principal enemy forces; and an airborne assault in sufficient strength to establish blocking positions astride the avenues of approach for enemy reinforcements moving from the north. Ground forces would include two U.S. Marine Corps divisions, an airmobile division, an airborne division, and supporting units. [48]

Reinforcements

Meanwhile, Wheeler invited Westmoreland's views on troop deployments as part of the Chiefs' deliberations on how to exert more pressure on the Communists. On 18 March, Westmoreland requested an "optimum force" increase of four and two-thirds divisions, plus ten tactical fighter squadrons. This 201,250-man increment would raise the total number of U.S. troops in South Vietnam to 671,616 troops. Of his total request, Westmoreland identified two and one-third divisions as a "minimum essential force" to be in place before 1 July 1968.[49]

Intent upon sending one and a half divisions to the I Corps Tactical Zone (I CTZ) and two to the Central Highlands, Westmoreland urged expanding ground operations into Laos and Cambodia; advocated heavier bombing and mining of North Vietnam; and contemplated an amphibious invasion north of the demilitarized zone. McNamara measured the cost of Westmoreland's proposals. "This meant mobilizing the reserves, boosting active-duty forces by 500,000 men, and spending another $10 billion annually on the war – in addition to the roughly $25 billion already directed toward Southeast Asia out of a total Pentagon budget of approximately $71 billion."[50]

Meanwhile, McNamara had requested the Chiefs provide recommendations on how to deploy as soon as possible additional forces required to man the strongpoint barrier system. After considering all possible assets in the continental United States (CONUS), Hawaii, and Okinawa, the Chiefs responded on 23 March that to minimize unfavorable personnel impacts on existing forces and without mobilization of any reserve units, the Army would have to withdraw some units designated to reinforce western Europe in the event of a Soviet invasion. These repurposed units could arrive in South Vietnam in October.

To mitigate the negative impact of this deployment, the Chiefs recommended:

> If the units deployed from CONUS to meet this requirement are not restored, the CONUS sustaining base would be reduced. Additional resources, both personnel and

equipment, must be provided in order to maintain the CONUS sustaining base and to rectify the loss in capability to respond to contingencies or other worldwide commitments. Even with reconstitution of the CONUS sustaining base there will be an increase in the number of Army personnel required to return to Southeast Asia with less than 25 months between tours. [51]

Escalation Speculation

In a speech in Nashville on 15 March, the President seemed combative and spoke of the need "to exact a penalty against North Vietnam for her flagrant violation of the Geneva Accords." Some observers likened Johnson's calm determination to that of a poker player who had decided to raise the stakes. A journalist noted that Johnson's "references to ending the war by negotiation have increasingly a perfunctory and repetitious sound as though they were made solely for the record." [52]

Columnist Walter Lippmann referred to Johnson's carrot-and-stick technique, "which has become routine since 1965," and worried that "gestures about peace have been the preludes to an escalation of the war." [53]

The question of new strategies was paramount. There were really only two alternatives: to invade North Vietnam and engage Hanoi on its own ground or to invade Laos and shut off the tap for infiltration by cutting the Ho Chi Minh Trail. Both options were on the table.

Mansfield was sufficiently concerned that he warned against an invasion of North Vietnam in a meeting with journalists on 17 March. Assuming that the President was sincere about keeping the Chinese and Soviets out of the war, Mansfield would not consent to any invasion plan. He was concerned about "high-level American military officers in Vietnam" wanting "a coastal landing like that at Inchon in the Korean War." Such an operation was impermissible under the Tonkin Gulf Resolution, Mansfield said. It would bring China into the war, as well as end the Sino-Soviet dispute, both inimical to U.S. policy interests. [54]

A few months earlier, noted Vietnam expert Bernard B. Fall had predicted that if there were an amphibious invasion of North Vietnam, it would occur around Vinh. Skeptically, he noted legal problems that would preclude the use of Allies such as the Koreans, insufficient South Vietnamese troops, and the fact that U.S. forces were already stretched thin. Marcus G. Raskin, Fall's collaborator on a Vietnam reader and former National Security Council staffer, noted several indicators that an invasion might be under consideration. There were leaks about mass troop movements and amphibious exercises. Congressional aide Gar Alperovitz had been told by a friend in the White House that invasion planning was underway. Another source quoted Rostow as saying, "We'll soon have to go North." [55]

Guam

Wheeler departed for the Far East on the evening of 15 March after working a full day in the office. After a stopover and coordinations with Sharp in Hawaii, Wheeler and Sharp travelled together to Vietnam enroute to Guam. [56]

While Bus was away in Vietnam, Betty Wheeler woke up from an afternoon nap to discover an antiwar protest being staged in front of their quarters on Fort Myer:

I could hardly believe my eyes. There were at least thirty pickets going round and round on the sidewalk taking in the area of the house. The signs were mostly 'Peace', 'Get out of Vietnam', nothing personal, but I must say not a very pretty sight. ... Believe the purpose was for Bus to mend his ways and at Guam recommend getting out of Vietnam. They should have arrived a few days sooner. [57]

Although the Guam conference between senior U.S. and South Vietnamese officials was primarily devoted to political development in Saigon, South Vietnamese Chief of Staff General Cao Van Vien presented a plan for an attack into Laos to cut the Ho Chi Minh Trail. Westmoreland made a few comments about it and presented his request for additional troops. [58]

On 1 April, Wheeler reviewed Viney's and Carlson's preliminary analysis on the lodgment operation in North Vietnam, which they had dubbed

Operation MULE SHOE. Wheeler gave them additional guidance to examine how to provide the forces that Westmoreland had requested simultaneously with forces for the lodgment operation. A selective call up of reserve forces and certain changes in personnel retention and assignment criteria were to be considered. Wheeler directed they brief their findings to the Chiefs on 10 April. [59]

I CTZ

"We have been watching closely the growing enemy buildup in and south of the demilitarized zone (DMZ) and in Laos," Westmoreland informed Sharp and Wheeler on 5 April. A serious threat to northern I Corps Tactical Zone (I CTZ) had developed, and the North Vietnamese were likely planning a major campaign there soon. Enemy-initiated actions in northern I CTZ had steadily increased, and enemy pressure in Quang Nam, Quang Tin, and Quang Ngai Provinces persisted. Artillery, rocket, and mortar attacks had increased in frequency and intensity. The North Vietnamese could attack with up to two divisions south of the DMZ. A major enemy build-up was underway on the border of Laos and Thua Thien Province. Westmoreland expected the North Vietnamese to infiltrate additional forces and supplies to augment their capability to launch a major offensive to secure the northern provinces of I CTZ while maintaining pressure on Quang Nam, Quang Tin, and Quang Ngai Provinces. [60]

Installation of the strongpoint barrier system commenced, although McNamara would not formally announce the decision to construct it until five months later. The line of fortified strongpoints would eventually extend from the coast to the mountains west of Khe Sanh and served as observation posts, patrol bases, and fire support bases.

The strongpoint barrier system had been designed as an *Economy of Force* measure. After III Marine Amphibious Force (III MAF) developed the system, Westmoreland intended to turn the strongpoints over to the South Vietnamese Army (ARVN), thereby freeing U.S. forces for mobile operations. Westmoreland also hoped to cut down on costly search operations near the DMZ. The proximity of enemy artillery and mortar fire had made operations there particularly bloody. Westmoreland also hoped to enhance Allied reaction by fire to Communist incursions by canalizing enemy movement, detecting the enemy at greater distances, and inflicting greater losses.[61]

As the year progressed, the evolving military situation and the intensity of enemy indirect fires would slow development of the strongpoints and cause Westmoreland to defer construction of obstacles and to restudy their practicability and useful location. Ultimately, the project would be shelved when the build-up of U.S. forces in I CTZ pre-empted the logistical support required to transport the construction materials.

Although the strongpoint barrier system would never be completed, certain portions of it were sufficiently developed to permit their use. As Westmoreland intended, ARVN units would take over manning the defensive positions, freeing more U.S. forces for mobile operations. Some of the early warning devices would later be used in the siege of Khe Sanh and effectively provided targeting data for bombing and artillery strikes.[62]

MULE SHOE

On the afternoon of 10 April, the Chiefs received a briefing on Viney's revised concept for Operation MULE SHOE, which incorporated Wheeler's latest guidance. Running nearly three and a half hours, this meeting was substantially longer than most of the Chiefs' other "tank sessions" that year. After much discussion, the Chiefs agreed that much staff work was still required to determine the feasibility of Wheeler's proposed operation.[63]

Three days later, Wheeler directed Spivy to continue development of the concept. "In furtherance of discussions of the Joint Chiefs of Staff at their meeting on 10 April 1967, I would like the Joint Staff, in conjunction with the Services to prepare a detailed analysis of the feasibility of a limited lodgment operation into southern North Vietnam (Operation MULE SHOE)."[64]

The analysis would inform a feasibility assessment by the Chiefs. Specific areas to be examined included, but were not limited to: an operational concept; forces required to execute the operation; augmentation or replacement of forces currently deployed in South Vietnam that would be employed in this operation; forces required to restore and/or enlarge the CONUS (continental

United States) reserve and sustaining base; as well as sources and equipage of forces, logistical support, and any major problems anticipated for all these requirements; plus transportation requirements and sources thereof. An assessment of the best time period to conduct such an operation in southern North Vietnam, considering weather, planning time, force availability, and other limiting factors was also required. The time necessary to maximize damage to VC/NVA forces and logistics facilities within the proposed area of operation would be estimated, as was the impact on worldwide military posture during preparation, execution, and reconstitution periods.

Wheeler directed numerous assumptions to be made: The U.S. would maintain its commitment to reinforce NATO within 30 days. Drawdown of European pre-stocks would not be authorized. Operation PRACTICE NINE commitments would be met. Planners were also to examine the alternative that PRACTICE NINE requirements would *not* be met. Westmoreland's troop request for 1968 and Operation MULE SHOE requirements were to be met simultaneously. Selective mobilization of industrial resources would be undertaken. (A very big assumption.) Mobilization of the reserves would be authorized. (Another very big assumption.) A freeze on rotation of personnel currently serving in Vietnam would be authorized for a necessary period. Plus, repetitive tours for Southeast Asia would also be authorized. (These last three assumptions were a significant departure from existing personnel policy and reflected the deleterious effect of the President's decision not to mobilize the reserves in 1965.)[65]

Wheeler granted Spivy six weeks to present the analysis to the Chiefs. Considering the magnitude of this tasking, he encouraged Spivy to form an ad hoc study group with representatives from each of the Services. Brigadier General V.W. Banning, USMC, served as Chairman. Viney and Carlson remained the primary action officers.[66]

"I would prefer that [Pacific Command] not be brought into this problem at this time," Wheeler instructed Spivy. "However, if in your judgment, an analysis in the depth required for a decision on the feasibility of the plan cannot be accomplished without the assistance of [Pacific Command], please inform me at your earliest opportunity and I will re-examine this issue."

Although Wheeler, Westmoreland, and Sharp maintained very close coordination and situational awareness through almost daily back channel traffic, Wheeler wanted to maintain the politically explosive MULE SHOE plan in "close-hold" status to avoid potential leaks.[67]

On 21 April, Viney, Carlson, and eleven other members of the Joint Staff, were joined by twelve consultants from the Services and two from the Defense Intelligence Agency (DIA). These consultants would advise on specialized matters, such as climatology, airlift capabilities, combat air operations, force generation capabilities, alterations to personnel policies, and logistics support capabilities.[68]

U.S. Military Posture

In late April, the Chiefs merged Westmoreland's troop request and his manning requirements for the strongpoint barrier system into a broader analysis of U.S. military commitments worldwide. This analysis would become the Chiefs' justification for insisting upon mobilization.[69]

The Chiefs saw a need for no fewer than 29 Army and five-plus Marine divisions. This growth would have created the largest U.S. military establishment since World War II. Later compromises by the Chiefs would bring the number down to a peak Korean War size, which still amounted to about a one-third increase in endstrength. No such force could be created without a partial mobilization.[70]

On 19 April, the Chiefs discussed the force requirements that Westmoreland and Sharp had submitted for Fiscal Year (FY) 1968. According to Wheeler, "All of the Chiefs expressed the view that, since political costs of a call-up of reserves will have to be paid in order to supply the forces requested by [Sharp] and [Westmoreland] in FY' 68, we should go ahead with the generation of additional forces sufficient to give us flexibility in Southeast Asia operations and provide ample forces to deal with other contingencies."[71]

"I believe that the [Chiefs] should point out possible contingencies we might have to face," Wheeler specified to Spivy the following day regarding formulation of a Joint Chiefs of Staff memorandum on the U.S. military posture. "The paper would close with forces which the Joint Chiefs of Staff believe we should undertake to generate over the next couple of years." Wheeler felt the Chiefs should point out that North Vietnam remained intransigent to any suggestion of negotiations or reduction of hostilities. Moreover, very substantial aid, without which North Vietnam could not continue in the war, was being imported. "In effect, while North Vietnam is the cutting edge of the Communist effort in Southeast Asia, the power behind the blade is supplied by China, the Soviet Union, and the Eastern European satellites." Wheeler also wanted to emphasize that the Communists were using both Laos and Cambodia as sanctuaries and base areas from which to conduct and support military operations in South Vietnam. [72]

The Chiefs agreed with Wheeler that U.S. military forces might be required to cope with several worldwide contingencies, including: overt engagement of Soviet or other foreign 'volunteer' military units in both North and South Vietnam; an increase of tensions or even low-level military actions from North Korea against South Korea; an increase of tensions in central Europe, perhaps centered on Berlin, to a degree that would require U.S. reinforcement of NATO; as well as overt military intervention by Chinese Communist forces in South Vietnam.

Reflecting Wheeler's actual conception of MULE SHOE as a "foot in the door" for sustained combat operations, he also specified, "The requirement [is] for us to invade North Vietnam in order to destroy enemy forces threatening the northern provinces or, alternatively, *to seize territory* in North Vietnam which would block access to infiltration routes through Laos into South Vietnam and to become *a blue-chip* in peace negotiations." (Author's emphasis). [73]

"I do not believe it necessary for us to advocate a total mobilization of World War II dimensions," Wheeler also wrote. "The real need, it seems to me, is to establish a training and production base which will give us the capability of generating expeditiously the military forces required to deal with an expansion of operations in Southeast Asia while, at the same time, being able to honor our full NATO commitments." He believed that the U.S. had lost this capability because of drawdowns on military stocks for the Vietnam War and "the freezing of men into non-Vietnam available status due to our tour lengths policy. Apropos of the latter, I do not advocate changing tour lengths nor the criteria for a second tour in Vietnam." [74]

Along the DMZ

Meanwhile, as the North Vietnamese continued to turn their half of the DMZ into a vast armed camp, Allied offensive operations in northern I Corps Tactical Zone (I CTZ) were exacting a heavy toll on Communist forces and meeting what looked like a conventional invasion. U.S. Army heavy artillery engaged in almost daily duels with North Vietnamese guns across the border, and III Marine Amphibious Force (MAF) conducted a battalion-size amphibious landing below the DMZ as a spoiling operation. In early April, a week after the Marines reembarked, the NVA struck Quang Tri City in a coordinated attack with four separate assault forces. [75]

"In my opinion, the forthcoming summer campaign in I Corps could be a decisive period of the war," Westmoreland informed Sharp and Wheeler on 12 April. "It is essential that we provide every reinforcement available to ensure that the campaign is a success and the enemy suffers a decisive defeat. This would not only improve the general security of the area but could have a profound effect on the strategic thinking of the leadership in Hanoi." [76]

The Communists would strike across the length of Quang Tri Province throughout the year. In the eastern area of the DMZ, two miles south of it and ten miles northwest of Dong Ha, was a small defensive position near Con Thien. Situated on a commanding hilltop, Marine observers there had a commanding view of any activity in the area. [77]

Con Thien anchored the western end of the barrier system that extended eight miles eastward to Gio Linh. This strip was bulldozed flat to aid with visual observation. Obstacles were emplaced to canalize enemy movement and provide protection for the various electronic sensor devices. Strong points such as Con Thien served as patrol bases, fire support bases, and stations for monitoring the sensors.

Communist forces had made several attempts to capture or destroy the Marine base at Con Thien. In late May, the Marines would counter with

Operation HICKORY, a multi-battalion sweep that produced several fierce small-unit engagements. [78]

Farther west, the Khe Sanh plateau was ideal terrain for the Communists. The rugged, mountainous countryside provided natural infiltration routes. Most mountain trails were obscured by triple canopy jungle, dense elephant grass, and bamboo thickets. Concealment from aerial reconnaissance was good, and the heavy jungle undergrowth limited ground observation to five meters in most places.

Fighting around Khe Sanh commenced in late April when Marine reconnaissance prematurely triggered a major enemy attempt to overrun the combat base. At least one regiment of the NVA's 325C Division was mauled in subsequent fighting by Marine units supported by massive airstrikes and artillery. The NVA threat to the area was reduced for a time. [79]

Thus, while the U.S. Military Assistance Command, Vietnam (MACV) continued to gain momentum in both clearing operations and strikes against enemy main force units, Westmoreland was compelled to either build up his forces near the DMZ or lose the northernmost provinces to increasingly large NVA forces. [80]

Westmoreland transferred U.S. Army units from II and III Corps Tactical Zones into the area the Marines had vacated and formed Task Force Oregon, which was activated at Chu Lai on 12 April and placed under the operational control of III MAF. As the departed Marines had done, Army forces in Chu Lai supported the extensive South Vietnamese pacification effort in Quang Tin and Quang Ngai Provinces in addition to conducting their own mobile combat operations. [81]

Meanwhile, U.S. battlefield successes had not been matched by political progress in Saigon. Lodge, the outgoing U.S. Ambassador, warned President Johnson that if the South Vietnamese "dribble along and do not take advantage of the success which MACV has achieved against the main force and the Army of North Vietnam, we must expect that the enemy will lick his wounds, pull himself together and make another attack in '68." Westmoreland's achievements, Lodge added, would be "judged not so much on the brilliant performance of U.S. troops as on the success in getting [the South Vietnamese Army, Regional Forces, and Popular Forces] quickly to function as a first-class... counter-guerrilla force." [82]

Westmoreland Returns to Washington

Meanwhile, Westmoreland had cabled a request for another 200,000 troops to offset the Communists' increased posture near the DMZ; to improve the environment for Revolutionary Development in I and IV Corps Tactical Zones; to destroy enemy main force units; to locate and destroy district and provincial guerilla forces; and to provide security for the population. [83]

"We were always worried about whether we had enough stuff and the authority to do anything with it," Spivy recalled. "We always felt like we were just a dollar short and a day late on almost everything we were doing. We were just terribly unhappy and dissatisfied with the way we had been able to put things together as we were building up. We were upset with the situation at home, too. All of us were worried about that." [84]

The Chiefs were fully supportive of Westmoreland's request, and on 20 April they recommended yet again to McNamara an expanded air campaign to further reduce the flow of men and supplies to the South. They also urged the President to mobilize the reserves and allow the military to pursue the Viet Cong and North Vietnamese Army into Laos, Cambodia, and even North Vietnam. The Chiefs further recommended that North Vietnamese ports be mined and that Washington "make a solid commitment in manpower and resources to a military victory." Once again, the Chiefs were telling the President that it was time to get serious about fighting the war because the graduated response program was not working. [85]

"Both Westy and the Joint Chiefs stated their belief that this program would require mobilizing the reserves and utilizing the nation's full military capability, including the possible use of nuclear weapons," McNamara recalled. "They recognized these actions could lead to confrontation with China and/ or the Soviet Union in Southeast Asia or elsewhere, but they considered such steps necessary to shorten what they predicted would otherwise be five more years of war." [86]

Westmoreland was summoned back to Washington for consultations. Enroute, he gave briefings at Da Nang and Honolulu on his plans to invade Laos, one of them a division-sized operation to sever the Ho Chi Minh Trail, but neither as ambitious as Vien had advocated at Guam. [87]

On 25 April, Westmoreland addressed the annual Associated Press editors' luncheon to build public support for the war. Convinced that the crossover point had been surpassed — meaning that Allied forces were now killing more of the enemy than Hanoi and the Viet Cong could replace them — Westmoreland asserted that Communist hopes were bankrupt and that a U.S. victory was imminent.

"I only hope that he has not dug a hole for himself with regard to his prognostications," a less sanguine "Johnny" Johnson wrote. "The platform of false prophets is crowded!" [88]

Strategy Sessions

The following day, President Johnson held two off-the-record to discuss Vietnam strategy with his senior national security advisors.

In preparing the President, Rostow cautioned him against making any immediate decisions, provided talking points, and reminded him to have McNamara and Rusk comment on Westmoreland's presentation. [89]

At the map board, General William C. Westmoreland outlines his recommendations for alternative Vietnam War strategy, the White House Cabinet Room, Washington, DC, 26 April 1967. (LBJ Library)

In the morning session, Westmoreland described the situation in Vietnam, sector by sector. He was concerned about ammunition stocks and expressed his frank dismay "at even the thought of stopping the bombing program." Mentioning contingency plans, Westmoreland said, "I believe we should confront [North Vietnam] with South Vietnamese forces in Laos," and he advised the same for Cambodia. [90]

When Westmoreland asserted that "last month, we reached the crossover point," the President asked, if that were the case, then why did he require reinforcements.

"When we add divisions, can't the enemy add divisions?" Johnson asked. "If so, where does it all end?"

"The [Viet Cong and North Vietnamese] strength in South Vietnam now totals 285,000 men," Westmoreland explained. "If we add two and a half [sic] divisions, it is likely the enemy will react by sending troops," probably only four more divisions, and it might not be able to supply all those troops.

The President asked, "At what point does the enemy ask for volunteers [from China and the Soviet Union]?"

Westmoreland replied, "That's a good question."

The President asked, "What if we do not add the two and one-third divisions?"

Wheeler responded, "The momentum will die; in some areas the enemy will recapture the initiative. We won't lose the war, but it will be a longer one."[91]

Without the "minimum essential force" augmentation, Westmoreland explained, we "we will not be in danger of being defeated, but it will be nip and tuck to oppose the reinforcements the enemy is capable of providing." In the final analysis, we are fighting a war of attrition in Southeast Asia, Westmoreland said. "The next step if we are to pursue our present strategy to fruition, would probably be the second addition of two and one-third divisions, or approximately another 100,000 men." Westmoreland reiterated his assessment that the war would not be lost, but that progress would certainly be slowed down. To him, this was "not an encouraging outlook, but a realistic one."[92]

At McNamara's prompting, Westmoreland estimated that under the current program of 470,000 troops, the war would continue for five more years, only two more years if MACV received the "optimum" force package of four and one-third divisions leading to a total deployed force of 665,000 troops, or three more years with the "minimum essential" augmentation.

Rusk asked about alternatives for the bombing program. Rostow mentioned the options of going into Laos or southern North Vietnam. Westmoreland described his plans for an invasion of Laos.

Wheeler interjected that the Chiefs were concerned about military threats in other parts of the world simultaneous with an increase of end-strength in Vietnam. They were currently reviewing possible responses to threats in South Korea, Soviet pressure on Berlin, the appearance of Soviet, North Korean, and Chinese "volunteers" in Vietnam, and even overt intervention by China. As the President well-knew, these threats underlay the Chiefs' repeated calls for mobilization to reconstitute the strategic reserve.

Despite other threats worldwide, Wheeler emphasized the potential necessities for employing U.S. troops outside of South Vietnam's borders. On North Vietnamese activity in Cambodia and Laos, he said, "U.S. troops may be forced to move against these units." To keep the pressure on Hanoi, he suggested, "We may wish to take offensive action against [North Vietnam] with ground troops". He added, "The bombing campaign is reaching the point where we will have struck all worthwhile fixed targets, except the ports." [93]

After the meeting adjourned, Rostow wrote a memo for the President, urging him to consider offensive ground operations against North Vietnam with an eye toward domestic opinion:

> As I see it, it is difficult to ask for the calling up of reserves if we are to do just a bit more of the same. We would be creating a major political crisis in the U.S. without being able to promise an early or decisive result. ... We should consider whether there are ways of using our military power to turn off the tap at higher — but acceptable — risk. For example, we can mine Haiphong and other harbors, which partially closes off, at least, the tap some distance from the bathtub. We can come nearer the bathtub and partially turn it off by: landing forces north of the DMZ and cleaning out the three divisions which are [Hanoi's] principal instrument for diverting and harassing U.S. forces; putting in additional forces to cut the infiltration routes on the ground in Laos just south of the DMZ; we could mount the landings and clean out the three divisions and have them come south to assume these blocking positions south of the DMZ, including Laos. [94]

Rostow and Wheeler had long seen eye-to-eye on Vietnam. The details of Rostow's recommendations suggest that Wheeler had shared the operational concept for Operation MULE SHOE with Rostow, despite having kept Westmoreland and Sharp in the dark about it – for the time being.

"The American people — if they are going to be asked for major additional sacrifices of men and money — and additional risk — would rather do something big and hopefully decisive," Rostow argued. He did not ignore Communist counter intervention or other challenges that Wheeler had equitably cited. Rostow mentioned the diplomatic and technical difficulties entailed, but he clearly favored a large solution, suggesting that Johnson put aside "the political problems objectively involved" and ask Westmoreland what his plan would be to win the war in the shortest time possible. (This was precisely the question that Wheeler anticipated back in February the President would eventually ask *him*.) [95]

In the second strategy meeting with the President that afternoon, Rostow opined that if additional troops were authorized, "they should be committed in such a way as to gain a spectacular advantage." The solution, he argued, was an amphibious invasion north of the DMZ. Rostow moved to the map and vigorously laid out his rationale. He considered the invasion "a more effective way to proceed than going into the difficult terrain of Laos during the dry season, which, in any case, lay a half-year more in the future." Rostow believed – as did the Chiefs — that the Chinese would not intervene if the U.S. stayed below Vinh, and he claimed that the intelligence estimate supported him. [96]

Westmoreland responded that his staff had studied such an amphibious operation and agreed that it could achieve significant results. However, an invasion would have to be conducted during the southwest monsoon season, already in progress, which would end in a few months. Since no troops were currently available, it would mean waiting until the spring or summer of 1968.

According to Westmoreland, "No one around the table, to include the President, expressed any great enthusiasm for the operation, and the discussion died with only Rostow and me participating." [97]

Wheeler was a firm believer in the Principles of War, yet he did not bolster Rostow's argument because his special study group had yet to determine MULE SHOE's feasibility. "As the Joint Chiefs of Staff are the *responsible* officials on matters of military advice, we are also directly *accountable* for the advice we provide," Wheeler would later state publicly. "In short, if our advice is accepted, and some action is called for, it falls upon the uniformed heads of the Services — my JCS colleagues — to give effect to their earlier advice with resources at hand. The ancient jibe 'to put up or shut up' is built into the system. We have learned long ago not to press for action where we cannot 'put up.'" [98]

Far better at this juncture, Wheeler thought, to keep his cards close and gauge the responses of the President's other advisors to Rostow's pitch. Wheeler merely summarized the Chiefs' position that they firmly believed the President must review the contingencies which they faced, the troops required to meet them, as well as additional punitive action against North Vietnam. [99]

In another memorandum for the President after the meeting, Rostow undercut Westmoreland's argument for reinforcements with data showing that enemy loss rates had varied little, regardless of the numerical strength of U.S. forces. "Johnson took it all in and bided his time," Rostow recalled, "chewing over the problem for many weeks." Influenced by Rostow's statistics, a newly reluctant Johnson would eventually approve only 45,000-50,000 more troops, plus additional bombing. [100]

Westmoreland departed the White House determined to preserve the invasion options. "I will proceed to work out alternative courses of action in the event the Administration decides to pursue a different strategy," he recorded. Wheeler would do the same. [101]

"While we had studied the possibility of invading North Vietnam, I had never recommended it," Sharp recalled. "In my view it was not necessary, since with proper use of airpower we could bring the North Vietnamese to heel." [102]

A few days later, the triumvirate's William Bundy commented upon the "contingency thought" of ground action in North Vietnam. "I would be totally against it," Bundy stated, "for the simple reason that I believe the chances are 75-25 that it would bring the Chinese truly into the war." [103]

Worried over flagging domestic support for a prolonged and indecisive war, Westmoreland believed, as did the Chiefs, that only through disruption of the enemy's sanctuaries could the Allies force Hanoi to accept a negotiated peace. Such an alternate military strategy, however, came with an unacceptable political cost at the grand strategic level. Johnson, already uneasy about the war's ascendancy over his prized Great Society programs, could not sanction the additional 200,000 troops that Westmoreland requested. Nor could the President answer satisfactorily why Americans continued to bear a heavy load while Saigon's leaders seemed unwilling to make the necessary political and social reforms. Nearing an election year, Johnson would refute any widening of an increasingly unpopular war. [104]

HICKORY

Meanwhile, things were heating up again in I Corps Tactical Zone (I CTZ). The III Marine Amphibious Force (III MAF) responded to increased North Vietnamese Army (NVA) infiltration from Laos into the northwestern corner of South Vietnam by shifting two Marine battalions to Khe Sanh. On 3 May, in some of the heaviest fighting of the war to date, the NVA attacked the Special Forces camp at Lang Vei while the Marines seized Hill 881N from the North Vietnamese. This key terrain northwest of Khe Sanh dominated the airfield and Special Forces camp at Khe Sanh and overlooked Communist infiltration routes. [105]

"I found things in I Corps better than I had expected," Westmoreland informed Wheeler and Sharp on 8 May. "Although combat has been intense and our casualties have been high, morale seemed to be good and there is an obvious feeling that the situation is in hand. I was particularly impressed with the spirit of the Vietnamese 1st Division. They have enjoyed considerable success during the last two weeks and are proud of their accomplishments." [106]

In response to NVA artillery bombardments and ground attacks emanating from the DMZ, the Administration authorized for the first time on 18 May a U.S. Marine-South Vietnamese Army (ARVN) clearing operation in the southern half of the DMZ. Over an eleven-day period, these forces, supported by artillery, naval gunfire, tactical air, and B-52 strikes killed over 780 enemy and temporarily neutralized the Communists' offensive capability in the area. [107]

On 16 May, Sharp advised Wheeler that he was planning to conduct an intensive firepower campaign against enemy concentrations and gun positions in the northern portion of the DMZ and the area to the immediate north. The continued buildup of North Vietnamese Army (NVA) offensive forces, as recently evidenced by the obvious attempt to position surface-to-air missiles (SAM) in the area was a matter of increasing concern.

"Artillery and mortar fire from within and North of the DMZ falling on Marine positions in northern I CTZ at a stepped-up pace calls for increased effort to prevent the enemy from attaining a position where constant harassment across the DMZ is carried on with impunity," Sharp explained. "Tactical air, naval gunfire, and artillery have kept the enemy off balance in the past and slowed his rate of infiltration into [South Vietnam], but I believe it is time to increase the tempo of activity in and North of the DMZ." [108]

Sharp intended to silence the SAM threat before employing ARC LIGHT bombers on selected areas previously approved. Concentrated tactical airstrikes would be conducted throughout the entire area. Artillery and naval gunfire would be employed on suitable targets. However, Sharp pointed out, to provide the amount of tactical airpower considered necessary and at the same time continue adequate support of ground forces in South Vietnam, an additional 125 tactical air sorties per day for three days from Task Force 77 would be required. D-Day for Operation HICKORY was tentatively scheduled for 18 May.

Sharp also requested authorization to conduct an amphibious demonstration off the beaches of North Vietnam in support of HICKORY. This would occur approximately 30 kilometers north of the demarcation line separating North and South Vietnam. [109]

Initially skeptical "of the wisdom of going ahead" with the amphibious demonstration, the Joint Staff J-3 provided a fact sheet on Sharp's proposed operation to Wheeler. Advantages to be gained from the amphibious operation included delaying and/or precluding enemy deployment of reinforcements to the DMZ; generating enemy concern for future amphibious attacks that might cause a withdrawal of forces from South Vietnam or restrict further deployment south; and creating confusion in the enemy's ability to exercise decisive command-and-control of defensive operations in the HICKORY area of the DMZ. [110]

On the other hand, the J-3 noted, a demonstration would provide North Vietnam with credible evidence of success in repulsing a U.S. amphibious operation against North Vietnamese shores. Coordination with the Secretary of Defense and the President would be necessary, which would require time beyond the scope of current planning for the operation. Political concern for other military operations in the timeframe of British Foreign Minister George A. Brown's visit to Moscow would apply. Furthermore, the area chosen for the demonstration coincided closely with the proposed landing area of MULE SHOE. A demonstration in the proposed area might attract additional North Vietnamese forces into the anticipated MULE SHOE landing area, which would impose greater liabilities to the success of that operation. Political repercussions resulting from a demonstration could be expected to outweigh possible military advantages, and it would impose increased difficulty in gaining authority for execution of a possible lodgment in North Vietnam.

For these reasons, the J-3's initial review indicated that "execution of the amphibious demonstration off [North Vietnam] in concert with Operation HICKORY would not be worth the candle." [111]

That evening, Wheeler cabled Sharp that "no repeat no demonstration or feint employing [US/South Vietnamese forces] off beaches of [North Vietnam] is authorized." [112]

Meanwhile in Saigon, widespread recognition of the fact that pacification and the main force war were essentially inseparable had led to the establishment within the MACV headquarters of the Office of the Assistant Chief of Staff for Civil Operations and Revolutionary Development Support (CORDS). On 4 May, Army General Creighton W. Abrams, Jr. and Ambassador Robert W. Komer arrived to assume their respective duties as Deputy Commander, U.S. Military Assistance Command, Vietnam (DCOMUSMACV) and Deputy to COMUSMACV for CORDS. Going forward, the pacification program would receive additional resources, increased military support, and unified civil-military manning, thus creating a single, more forcefully directed U.S. pacification support effort. [113]

Wheeler promotes Creighton W. Abrams, Jr., to General, The Pentagon, Washington, DC, 4 September 1964. (Office of the Chairman of the Joint Chiefs of Staff)

Opposition Mounts

"In a long letter to the President, [McGeorge Bundy] analyzed the pros and cons of strategic bombing and generally advised against major escalation (specifically noting that he was opposed to closing the port of Haiphong)," Sharp recalled. "In [Bundy's] view, escalation would not bring a visible victory over Hanoi before our 1968 election. ... In effect, he was counseling that we concentrate on continuing to simply prevent defeat rather than taking decisive strategic action to achieve a clear and early military victory." [114]

Predictably, Wheeler and the Chiefs completely disagreed with the thrust of Bundy's analysis and assertions. "In providing the President with their views, the Chairman took particular issue with the recommendation against interdicting Haiphong harbor," Sharp recalled. [115]

"As a matter of cold fact," Wheeler wrote on 5 May, "the Haiphong port is the single most vulnerable and important point in the lines of communication system of North Vietnam." [116]

Two days later, word of the top secret White House deliberations leaked to the press. The *St. Louis Post-Dispatch* reported that the Administration had been debating an invasion of the North, explicitly mentioning an "Inchon Landing." Politicians soon took positions on the issue. Missouri Senator William Stuart Symington, Jr. observed that an invasion would involve the Chinese and have incalculable results. Michigan Governor George W. Romney, a prominent Republican and early candidate for the presidential nomination in 1968, told audiences he feared intervention by both the Chinese and the Soviets. [117]

On 19 May, McNamara recorded his opposition to a U.S. invasion of North Vietnam in a draft presidential memorandum (DPM). In such an event, "we would expect China to respond by entering the war with both ground and air forces," while the Soviets would increase their support to Hanoi. He also advised against an invasion of Laos. [118]

"It is important to note that a DPM is more than a statement of the views of the signator (in this case the Secretary of Defense)," Sharp explained. "Its intent is to put on record the pertinent views of all the cognizant officials, hopefully by consensus." [119]

Rostow wrote to the President three days later that McNamara's memorandum "appears [to be] a reaction against the [Chiefs'] position as he understands it and projects it – a reaction that goes a bit too far." Rostow's proposed alternative strategy involved mobilizing the reserves to "seriously impress Hanoi that the jig was up." He had long favored "the shallow invasion of North Vietnam" and again endorsed such an action as necessary and advisable. "I do not believe the best use of our forces is to invade Cambodia or Laos. Nor should we decide *now* to invade the southern part of North Vietnam to cut infiltration routes. I would, however, like us to have that option next year, if necessary; for example, if they bring several more divisions down to the DMZ area." Rostow added, "I myself do not believe that the Soviet Union would go to war with us over Vietnam unless we sought to occupy North Vietnam, and even then a military response from Moscow would not be certain." Wheeler considered Rostow's stance a green light to continue developing MULE SHOE. [120]

McNamara Wavers

"After much thinking, struggling, and searching, I had concluded – and I bluntly told President Johnson – that 'the war in Vietnam is acquiring a momentum of its own that must be stopped 'and that Westy's approach 'could lead to a major national disaster," McNamara recalled. [121]

In his DPM, McNamara warned the President that there might be "a limit beyond which many Americans and much of the world will not permit the United States to go. The picture of the world's greatest superpower killing or seriously injuring 1,000 noncombatants a week, while trying to pound a tiny, backward nation into submission on an issue whose merits are hotly disputed, is not a pretty one." [122]

McNamara recommended assuming a less aggressive course in Vietnam. He called for either an unconditional bombing halt or restriction of the bombing to the area south of the 20th Parallel. Such a move, he cited, would appease critics of the war and might lead to negotiations. McNamara also called for a ceiling on deployed endstrength with additional forces capped at 30,000 over an 18-month period — a formula for "slow progress," as well as a shift from Westmoreland's aggressive ground war strategy to a more limited one focused on securing the South Vietnamese population. [123]

McNamara's recommendations reflected his loss of faith that the U.S. could achieve its objectives in Vietnam at an acceptable cost. "The memo crystallized my growing doubts about the trend of events and set the stage for the increasingly sharp debate that followed," McNamara recalled. For some time, his repeated public assertions of confidence had cloaked growing private doubt. McNamara's pessimism was now emerging, first within the Administration and later in the year in public. [124]

McNamara's confidence had begun to waver in the fall of 1965. He confided to a select group of reporters at the Honolulu conference in February 1966 that "the sustained United States air offensive against North Vietnam launched exactly a year before by President Johnson had not succeeded — and would not. An agrarian society could not be blasted into submission, he said with unusual passion: 'no amount of bombing can end the war." [125]

During the summer of 1967, McNamara began to fear that the vast expansion of the war was endangering the global security position that he had labored so diligently to construct since becoming Secretary of Defense in 1961. He was troubled by the destructiveness of the war, particularly casualties among Vietnamese civilians, and by growing domestic opposition. McNamara and his civilian deputies were also disillusioned by the lack of progress in the ground war. [126]

McNamara warned the President that actions might not yield the results anticipated. In response to Westmoreland's request for 200,000 more troops, McNamara had come out against the large solution and warned against what he saw as false strategic options, such as invading North Vietnam or Laos. This was ironic because in 1964-1965 McNamara had conspired with Rusk and McGeorge Bundy to keep Ball's objections to Americanizing the war from the President.

Henceforth, McNamara would diverge even more from Rusk, who would remain steadfast in backing force until early 1968. Many years later, McNamara would note the irony of the Secretary of Defense spearheading negotiation efforts while the Secretary of State demanded military action. [127]

That the President did not promptly endorse McNamara's recommendations as he had on previous occasions was not surprising. Now, he faced a situation where the Chiefs were in ardent opposition to anything other than a significant escalation of the war with a call-up of the reserves. This put them in direct opposition to McNamara and his civilian advisors and created a genuine policy dilemma for the President who had to consider the necessity of keeping the military "onboard" in any changes to the U.S. policy for Southeast Asia. [128]

The Chiefs Counter

"In the two weeks after McNamara's DPM," the Pentagon Papers revealed, "the Washington paper mill must have broken all previous production records. The [Chiefs] literally bombarded the Secretary with memoranda, many of which had voluminous annexes." Their direct comments on the DPM did not come until ten days after McNamara transmitted it to the President.

Before then, however, aware of McNamara's proposals, the Chiefs forwarded several studies, each of which advanced their own arguments for escalation. [129]

On 20 May, "[the Chiefs] sent me another memo repeating their view that invasions of North Vietnam, Laos, and Cambodia might become necessary, involving the deployment of U.S. forces to Thailand and, quite possibly, the use of nuclear weapons in southern China," McNamara recalled. "All of this, they emphasized, highlighted the need to mobilize U.S. reserves." [130]

While the Chiefs may have been annoyed at what they felt was a misrepresentation of their views on the best course of action for the United States, they were outraged by an "alarming pattern" in McNamara's DPM that suggested an effort to change U.S. objectives in Southeast Asia to a compromise with the Communists. Furthermore, McNamara's recommended strategy was completely anathema to their view of how the war should be conducted. "The current [Office of the Secretary of Defense] thrust is at considerable variance with our own thinking and proposals," Wheeler informed Sharp. [131]

In a strongly worded rebuttal on 20 May, Wheeler and the Chiefs wrote, "The Joint Chiefs of Staff view with increasing concern the loss of the strategic initiative in Southeast Asia and the current restrictive worldwide U.S. military posture." They recommended expanded naval and air operations in North Vietnam; significant and progressive increase in U.S. and [Allied] military pressures in South Vietnam; a build-up of forces to achieve the capabilities they had recommended; an immediate decision regarding selective call-up of reserves and extension of terms of service for 12 months; increased authority for accelerated procurement to include delegation of authority to the Services to negotiate noncompetitive, cost-reimbursable contracts, and to provide necessary facilities; as well as immediate authority to initiate procurement of long lead-time materiel items required to accomplish their recommended force build-up. [132]

Regarding McNamara's proposed military strategy for the air and naval war in the north, the Chiefs countered, "While limiting the bombing to South at 20° might result in increased negotiation opportunities with Hanoi, such a new, self-imposed restraint resulting from this major change in strategy would most likely have the opposite effect." Any possible political advantage gained by confining the interdiction campaign to the panhandle, they noted, would be offset decisively by allowing North Vietnam to continue unobstructed importation of war matériel. The Chiefs were also convinced that "such a drastic reduction in the scale of air operations against North Vietnam could only result in the strengthening of the enemy's resolve to continue the war. No doubt, the reduction in scope of air operations would also be considered by many as a weakening of U.S. determination and a North Vietnamese victory in the air war over North Vietnam. ... It would most likely strengthen the enemy's alternate hope of victory and lead to a redoubling of his efforts." [133]

As for McNamara's assertions about domestic attitudes and predicted reactions to several occurrences, the Chiefs were "unable to find due cause for the degree of pessimism expressed in the DPM." They firmly believed that "the American people, when well-informed about the issues at stake, expect the government to uphold its commitments. History illustrates that they will, in turn, support their government and its necessary actions." The Chiefs believed that there was no significant sentiment for peace at any price. They also believed that despite some predictable debate, a reserve call-up would be willingly accepted and that there would be "no 'irresistible' drive from any quarter for unnecessary escalation of the conflict." [134]

To McNamara's claim that "there is strong likelihood of a confrontation between the United States and the Chinese Communists or the USSR, as a result of intensification of air and naval operations against North Vietnam and/or a major increase in U.S. forces in South Vietnam," the Chiefs simply countered, "Intelligence estimates do not support this contention." [135]

"Most of the foregoing divergencies between the DPM and the stated policies, objectives, and concepts are individually important and are reason for concern," the Chiefs wrote. "However, when viewed collectively, an alarming pattern emerges which suggests a major realignment of U.S. objectives and intentions in Southeast Asia without regard for the long-term consequences." The Chiefs stated their unawareness of any decision to retract the policies and objectives that had been affirmed by senior Administration officials many times in recent years. "Thus, the DPM lacks adequate foundation for further consideration." [136]

The DPM did not support current U.S. national policy and objectives in Vietnam and should not be considered further, the Chiefs continued. There was no basis for change in the Chiefs' views on the major issues in the DPM, which had been stated clearly in their recent memorandums and in this rebuttal. The U.S. national policy objectives should be reaffirmed, the Chiefs insisted. "The U.S. military objectives for Vietnam as restated in JCSM-218-67 support current U.S. policy objectives. Implementation of [McNamara's recommendations] would serve to prolong the conflict, reinforce Hanoi's belief in ultimate victory, and probably add greatly to the ultimate cost in U.S. lives and treasures." Unaware that the President had seen the DPM ten days before, the Chiefs concluded by recommending that the DPM not be forwarded to Johnson. [137]

"This was typical of the way Secretary McNamara operated," Sharp recalled, "often taking a controversial issue directly to the President before obtaining comments from the [Chiefs]." [138]

On 20 May, the Chiefs also recommended authorization for a selective call-up of the reserves so that the U.S. could more effectively fulfill its worldwide commitments. The nation must be able to send large U.S. forces to any of several trouble spots, such as Korea and Berlin, yet the U.S. could not respond fast enough with sufficient forces to meet most of these contingencies. [139]

The Chiefs insisted that mobilization was necessary because during the past several months, there had been a marked increase in deliberately flagrant North Korean activities. "Korea provides an attractive place for the Communist Chinese (CHICOM) to stage a diversionary effort. In the event of a major CHICOM/North Korean attack on South Korea, the U.S. strategic reserve might not be capable of adequate, timely reinforcement. Under these circumstances, the prompt use of nuclear weapons, coupled with air and naval operations against bases and LOCs [lines of communication] in Manchuria, would probably become necessary to preserve the integrity of South Korea." Moreover, a Chinese attack on Thailand could trigger the use of nuclear weapons against lines of communication and supply bases in southern China. Similarly, should the Chinese intervene overtly with major combat forces in Vietnam, "it might be necessary to establish a strategic defense in South

Vietnam and use tactical nuclear weapons against bases and LOCs in South China." [140]

The Chiefs also believed that the U.S. had to "regain the Southeast Asia initiative and exploit our military advantage." They argued that present air restrictions crippled our war effort and that limitations should be reduced on targets, as well as the rules of engagement, and that more forces, primarily air, should be deployed. Moreover, they believed the U.S. should reinforce as fast as possible, to prevent the enemy from adjusting to the increases in pressure, as they had been able to do thus far. [141]

The Chiefs were particularly exercised at the prospect of a very slow U.S. build-up over time that would continue to permit the Communists to react. They emphasized, "It is fundamental to the successful conduct of warfare that every reasonable measure be taken to widen the differential between the capabilities of the opposing forces. Target system limitations, rules of engagement, and force curtailments have combined to militate against widening the gap between the total Free World force capability, including South Vietnam, and the capability of the enemy to generate, deploy, and sustain his forces while improving the defense of his homeland." [142]

In a memorandum to Vance and William Bundy on 22 May, Rostow wrote, "Only the President can assess the political difficulty of the reserve call-up. But it should be noted: nothing we could do would more seriously impress Hanoi than we had the capacity to see it through." [143]

"Those thoroughly professional men in Hanoi would, I believe, be profoundly impressed by a call-up," Rostow continued. "They would know that even if we did not use much of that call-up immediately, we would be in a position to deal with whatever manpower requirements emerged. ... I have a feeling that it would be wise to have some sort of reserve call-up this summer if the President `judges it politically possible." [144]

Rostow also quoted North Vietnamese General Tran Do to explain the Communists' view on negotiations:

> Our basic intention is to win militarily. We use military victories as decisive factors to end the present conflict. We want to

end the war through military victories and not peace negotiations. … And what is our concept of peace? To have peace, for us, is to have the Americans withdraw and the National Liberation Front accepted as the only organization which truly represents the [South] Vietnam people. Someone asked Chairman Ho Chi Minh: 'What do you think of the Saigon government?' The Chairman's answer is definitive: 'There is no government in Saigon. There is only a clique of U.S. lackeys in Saigon.' Then, you understand easily that negotiations are not possible. [145]

Agonizing Dilemma

After two years of major combat operations, the President's optimism of 1965 had eroded into deep frustration. The U.S. had deployed almost 500,000 troops, sustained almost 13,000 killed, dropped more bombs than in all theaters in World War II, and it was spending more than $2 billion per month on the war. [146]

Johnson was physically and emotionally exhausted, frustrated by his lack of success, torn between his advisors, and uncertain which way to turn. He was caught in an agonizing dilemma. Unable to conclude the war by military means and unwilling to make the concessions necessary to secure a negotiated settlement, Johnson discovered belatedly what Ball had warned him about in 1964, that "once on the tiger's back, we cannot be sure of picking the place to dismount." [147]

Westmoreland continued to report steady progress, yet Johnson was worried about the implications of Westmoreland's ground strategy and his request for more troops. Still, Johnson would not consider a return to the enclave strategy or place a ceiling on the troop level. He remained firmly opposed to mobilizing the reserves and expanding the war, as he continued to fear a direct confrontation with the Soviet Union or China. [148]

McNamara recalled that by June, "It was clear to me that our policies and programs in Indochina had evolved in ways we had neither anticipated nor intended, and that the costs – human, political, social, and economic – had grown far greater than anyone had imagined. We had failed." [149]

"The onslaught of memos from the Chiefs did not persuade me," McNamara recalled. On 12 June, he and Vance again counseled the President to reject the Chiefs' plan, citing a CIA analysis and asserting their conviction that a large-scale escalation could lead to disaster. "Nothing short of toppling the Hanoi regime will pressure North Vietnam to settle so long as they believe they have a chance to win the 'war of attrition' in the South. … actions sufficient to topple the Hanoi regime will put us into war with the Soviet Union and China." McNamara and Vance also argued that the Chiefs' plan would be costly in American lives, as many of their recommended targets were heavily defended and hitting them would involve losses per sortie several times higher than the program McNamara had proposed. [150]

While Johnson shared some of McNamara's reservations about the war, he was gradually losing confidence in his dovish Secretary of Defense, just as Wheeler had foreseen. Johnson did not accept McNamara's recommendations to scale back U.S. political objectives in Vietnam; yet, Johnson had flatly rejected military proposals to expand the war. "Bomb, bomb, bomb, that's all you know," he complained to the Chiefs on several occasions. [151]

Although Johnson agreed with McNamara that the bombing had not accomplished much, he was not prepared to stop or even limit it. Mississippi Senator John C. Stennis was planning an investigation into the conduct of the air war. The President was not prepared to risk a confrontation with the hawks or a potentially explosive public debate on the bombing. Moreover, many of the President's other advisors argued strongly against McNamara's recommendations. Rusk, Rostow, Taylor, Clifford, and McGeorge Bundy all agreed that domestic critics would not be appeased by a bombing halt. Bundy added that to stop the bombing would "give the Communists something for nothing," and would be seen by Hanoi as a sign of weakness. [152]

Differences over bombing strategy were coming to a head between McNamara and the Chiefs and Sharp. The Chiefs denounced McNamara's proposals as an "aerial Dien Bien Phu," a term Wheeler calculated would resonate with the President. Appearing before the Senate Armed Services Committee early in the year, McNamara had expressed doubt that ROLLING THUNDER had significantly reduced infiltration and certainty that no alternative bombing strategy could do so. Wheeler testified that in the military's opinion, some reduction in infiltration had resulted. [153]

The Chiefs now renewed their demands for authorization to strike targets within the Hanoi-Haiphong exclusion zones. The issue had come up during the Guam conference and again during the strategic review of Westmoreland's troop request. With reservations, the President approved specific airstrikes, such as on the thermal power plant in Haiphong. Post-strike assessments claimed the airstrikes were effective. Ninety percent of attack sorties flown continued to target North Vietnamese transportation systems or were for armed reconnaissance. Thus, the debate focused on only a small fraction of U.S. air capability.

McNamara had resisted the expansion of target authorizations, citing doubts about its effectiveness, the cost in domestic and world opinion, and the possibility that Soviet or Chinese ships would be hit, potentially triggering an international incident leading to their intervention. Fortunately, when such incidents did occur at Haiphong and another port, the Soviets confined themselves to diplomatic protests. [154]

The President continued to hold the shrinking middle ground between his advisors' recommendations. Johnson's decisions were improvisations that defied military logic and did not confront, let alone resolve, the contradictions in U.S. strategy. He continued the bombing because he deemed it necessary to pacify certain domestic factions and because terminating it might be considered a sign of weakness. He refused to provide Westmoreland all the troops he considered necessary to implement his strategy, but he did not confront the inconsistencies in Westmoreland's strategy itself. The Administration also informed the Soviets that the President had completely ruled out an invasion of North Vietnam and the use of tactical nuclear weapons. [155]

"If Washington was unwilling to allow professional warriors to make war professionally," Dave Palmer observed, "there was no option other than continuing the unpopular war of attrition." To Westmoreland, results obtained would be a function of resources committed. It merely remained a matter of how soon Washington expected victory; the more men available, the sooner it would come. [156]

MULE SHOE

While McNamara recommended easing off and taking a different tack in Vietnam, Wheeler was quietly planning for full speed ahead on a more aggressive course. His special study group spent the month of May assessing the feasibility of Operation MULE SHOE.

Wheeler had specified on 6 March that the feasibility of retaining a lodgment area in North Vietnam as a "Blue Chip" negotiating asset was to be studied as an alternative to withdrawal upon completion of MULE SHOE. However, because he did not restate this requirement in his 13 April directive or verbally to Viney, MULE SHOE was developed strictly as an "in-and-out" operation. Tacitly though, Wheeler anticipated the success of a limited invasion might entice the President to approve a longer campaign in North Vietnam. Wheeler had already employed similar incremental approaches toward troop deployments and the bombing program. He did not specify retention of the lodgment area in writing because "to have done so would have killed the plan politically from the get-go." Viney clearly understood, however, that Wheeler intended MULE SHOE as a "foot in the door, although you could not have sold it to anyone that way." [157]

Against this background, the study group determined the force and logistics requirements and capabilities, related these values to the other programs of concern, measured their overall impact on the U.S. political-military posture worldwide, considered the political implications of the operation, and estimated possible reactions by Hanoi, Peking, and Moscow. [158]

For MULE SHOE, the Commander-in-Chief, Pacific (CINCPAC) would be assigned the mission of "establishing a limited lodgment in southern North Vietnam to fix and destroy Viet Cong and North Vietnamese Army (NVA) forces and their installations in and near the DMZ; thereafter, to abandon the lodgment and withdraw from North Vietnam as directed." [159]

Forces would be rapidly introduced through a four-pronged, simultaneous assault by airmobile and airborne forces, an amphibious landing force, and other ground forces. [160]

The lodgment area was bounded in the north by the Kien Giang and Dai Giang Rivers, by the DMZ demarcation line in the south, and by the foothills west of Highway 101. Thus, the lodgment area was approximately 40 miles long and 20 miles deep from the coast. Landing beaches were located just south of Dong Hoi. [161]

The 1st Cavalry Division (Airmobile) would conduct an airmobile assault across the DMZ to seize critical terrain in the foothills west of Highway 101 (Objectives MULE, CAT, and DOG), thereby blocking the enemy's escape to the west and northwest and preventing his reinforcement from Laos.

Assault elements of the 82nd Airborne Division would parachute onto the northern portion of the lodgment area to seize critical terrain objectives at the Kien Giang and Dai Giang Rivers (Objectives YOKE and ZEBRA), thereby blocking the advance along the coastal plain of enemy reinforcements from the northwest, sealing off that portion of the lodgment perimeter, and securing the right flank of the landing beaches.

An additional airborne brigade would constitute a force reserve during the initial assault and link-up operations. Once enemy intentions for reinforcement became clear, this reserve could support the 5th Marine Division landing force in its assault toward the DMZ.

The embarked 5th Marine Division would conduct an initial feint northward toward Vinh, (110 miles north), then, by amphibious assault, establish a beachhead south of Dong Hoi about 30 statute miles north of the demarcation line (Objective ECHO). It would then attack southeastward along two avenues (Routes RED and BLUE) to crush enemy forces against another Marine division attacking northwest. [162]

The last division-sized amphibious assault conducted by the U.S. had occurred at Inchon sixteen years earlier. Among the complexities and associated logistical challenges involved, more than 20% of all the Navy's amphibious shipping was already in use. Two-thirds of the large landing craft (LSTs) in the Pacific, along with 36 more operated by the Military Sea Transport Service, were already committed to providing supply services to MACV. [163]

The study group tasked an unspecified Marine division from the III Marine Amphibious Force (most likely the 3rd Marine Division) to conduct a ground attack across the DMZ to attain a limited objective (Phase Line BRAVO), destroy enemy forces in the DMZ, continue the attack northward to complete the encirclement, and to provide the anvil upon which the enemy forces would be destroyed by friendly forces attacking from the northwest.

For operational security reasons, no role was assigned to the South Vietnamese Army (ARVN) either in execution of or support to MULE SHOE. American units deploying to South Vietnam in Fiscal Year 1968 would replace those in-country that had been diverted for the operation. [164]

For three years, the President had restricted the application of U.S. combat power against targets in North Vietnam, in part, for fear of provoking overt Chinese intervention. In a Special Intelligence Estimate attached to the MULE SHOE study, the Defense Intelligence Agency (DIA) assessed that Communist leaders would not believe U.S. assurances that the assault was limited and did not have as its objective the overthrow of the Hanoi government. The Chinese might consider the U.S. invasion to have created political and psychological opportunities to increase their presence in and influence over North Vietnam. Under such circumstances, there would be a high risk that China would introduce ground combat forces into North Vietnam during MULE SHOE. Such forces would most likely deploy into northern North Vietnam and remain there after U.S. forces withdrew south of the DMZ. The DIA considered it probable that such intervention would be conducted in a manner so as not to precipitate an overreaction from the U.S. leading to a nuclear attack on mainland China. It was possible, however, that China would not intervene at all if the U.S. withdrew promptly. [165]

Thus, only fourteen days were allocated for ground combat operations and the withdrawal of forces. The operation would conclude with the destruction of enemy logistics facilities and installations and the evacuation of all friendly forces.

The study group determined that weather and surf conditions during the months of June through August were the most favorable period to execute MULE SHOE, meaning that it would have to be executed the following summer. Forces to execute the operation would not become available until March 1968.

North Vietnamese Army (NVA) forces within the lodgment area or which quickly could be brought to bear against it totaled about 31,400 troops. The study estimated the NVA could reinforce at the DMZ with an additional 56,000 men within nine days of the U.S. assault. With U.S. air superiority, the ability of the North Vietnamese Air Force to disrupt the operation was minimal. Likewise, the threat posed by the tiny North Vietnamese Navy was insignificant.

Massive use of combat airpower would prepare the objective areas, destroy or neutralize anti-aircraft artillery (AAA) and surface-to-air missile (SAM) sites, isolate the lodgment area, support the ground force in destruction of the enemy, and prevent the arrival of major NVA reinforcements. ARC LIGHT bombing operations would support MULE SHOE, as required. ROLLING THUNDER operations would continue, but coordination and/or curtailment would be required in southern North Vietnam during MULE SHOE.

The total U.S. Air Force commitment to MULE SHOE was 8 tactical fighter squadrons (TFS), 1 tactical reconnaissance squadron (TRS), 162 C-130 aircraft, and 174 C-141 aircraft. During the 11-day commitment, 100% of the C-130 and C-141 inventories would be obligated, which would degrade the ability of Strike Command to deploy forces elsewhere for any worldwide contingency operations.

Naval surface forces would conduct diversionary and preparatory operations, and then provide naval gunfire support throughout the assault. Increased air and naval surface operations and special operations outside the lodgment area would assist in isolating the objective area and limit North Vietnamese capability to influence the outcome. Combatant ships and aircraft of the Pacific Fleet would conduct pre-assault operations, feints and demonstrations, and operations in continuing support of the lodgment. The total U.S.

Navy commitment to MULE SHOE was 39 combatant ships and 76 amphibious ships.

An integrated cover and deception plan would be implemented to cause the North Vietnamese leadership to conclude that an impending U.S. offensive would target Laos, instead of being launched across the DMZ into southern North Vietnam.

MULE SHOE would include coordinated diplomatic and psychological programs to make clear to the enemy and to domestic and international public opinion the limited nature of U.S. and South Vietnamese objectives in North Vietnam and to demonstrate U.S. and Allied resolve to attain these objectives.

Civil affairs actions were considered to control, protect, and if necessary, evacuate elements of the local North Vietnamese population. While most of the 290,000 civilian non-combatants in the lodgment area would be hostile or neutral at best, it was possible that a significant number might appeal to U.S. forces for assistance and evacuation. In such event, U.S. forces would grant assistance and arrange for asylum in South Vietnam.

Okinawa, Taiwan, and the Philippines would be the final staging areas for airborne and other forces committed to MULE SHOE. Japan, Guam, Okinawa, and the Philippines would provide external base support, as appropriate. Bases in Thailand and South Vietnam would be utilized as recovery and/or diversion bases, as required.

The State Department informed the study group that the Japanese government would not consent to an offensive operation being launched from its territory. The solution devised was for U.S. aircraft transiting Japanese airfields to keeps their cargo ramps closed. The U.S. could get away with that one time, the State Department advised, and the Japanese would be furious. [166]

The study group addressed in considerable detail the logistics, transportation, and combat engineer requirements for MULE SHOE. It also estimated that U.S. forces would sustain 144 killed in action and 900 wounded in action per day. This casualty rate, which was substantially above the current experience in South Vietnam, would equate to 10,440 total casualties, or 8.7%

of the 82,977-man Army and Marine Corps ground force, during ten days of projected combat operations.

Within the parameters of the study, the study group determined that the Services could provide the forces, transportation, and supplies for MULE SHOE while concurrently meeting other program commitments. However, this would require the significant changes to personnel policy assumed by Wheeler, changes he would be hard pressed to convince the President to approve.

The study concluded that, subject to certain enabling decisions and preparations, the operation was feasible, could be one of the most significant military actions in the conflict thus far, and would accelerate the attainment of U.S. objectives in Vietnam. The study recommended that the operation be endorsed by the Chiefs and included in the program of actions for prosecution of the war in Southeast Asia; and that the study be transmitted to CINCPAC for use in operational planning. "The conclusions and recommendations notwithstanding, there are serious problems that require solution and risks that would have to be assumed," the study concluded. [167]

Other Matters

In his memoirs, McNamara posed the rhetorical question of "how presumably intelligent, hard-working, and experienced officials – both military and civilian – failed to address systematically and thoroughly questions whose answers so deeply affected the lives of our citizens and the welfare of our nation." He asserted, "Simply put, such an orderly, rational approach was precluded by the 'crowding out' which resulted from the fact that Vietnam was but one of a multitude of problems we confronted." [168]

"The crush of events that summer and fall made it increasingly hard for the President and the senior officials in State, Defense, and the National Security Council to focus sharply on Vietnam," McNamara recalled. "We were confronted with a deluge of other crises and problems: a Middle East war that led to the first use of the hotline between Moscow and Washington; a Soviet anti-ballistic missile program that threatened to upset the nuclear balance between East and West; a looming conflict between Greece and Turkey over Cyprus that endangered NATO's eastern flank; race riots in our major cities; and, of course, rising protests against the war, which included a massive attempt to shut down the Pentagon." [169]

With NATO, Vietnam, and now another Arab-Israeli war competing for his time, Wheeler was keeping long hours. "It's now eight-thirty (P.M.) and still no Bus," Betty Wheeler wrote on 7 June. "Bus cancelled out on the West Point trip. We did have a beautiful weekend in the country. … Bus needless to say, is up to his ears. What a muddle." [170]

Eisenhower delivered the commencement address to the West Point Class of 1967. His comments reflected the military's continuing optimism that the war was certainly winnable. "Whatever happens in Vietnam, I can see nothing but military victory." [171]

ROLLING THUNDER

"On 23 May, we received word from the [Chiefs] that no further targets would be authorized within the Hanoi prohibited area," Sharp recalled. "When I promptly fired back 'why?', I was advised by General Wheeler that it was indirectly related to the present strategy of cutting back our air campaign North of 20° latitude, although there were other factors involved. These included the feeling in high circles that our recent strikes in the Hanoi area had raised the temperature of the war to a degree that might elicit additional Soviet assistance to the North Vietnamese, as well as a perception that the losses sustained by our forces were not commensurate with the results obtained. Also, there was that old recurrent desire to let the dust settle while we watched for Soviet and Chinese communist reaction." Wheeler also informed Sharp that the Chiefs had made a strong recommendation on the continuing need to obstruct and reduce the flow of war-supporting material into South Vietnam through various actions against ports, airfields, and rail lines.

"And so once more," Sharp complained, "the political decision-makers evidenced the same stultifying combination of attitudes — a complete lack of understanding the results of the air campaign, and a tendency to be more influenced by possible Soviet reaction than by what we could do to end the war." [172]

"We are at an important point in this conflict," Sharp observed on 21 June. "We have achieved a position, albeit late in the game, from which a precisely executed and incisive air campaign against all the target systems will aggregate significant interrelated effects against the combined military, political, economic, and psychological posture of North Vietnam. In our judgment, the enemy is now hurting and the operations to which we attribute this impact should be continued with widest latitude in planning and execution in the months of remaining good weather." [173]

CHAPTER 6

Expert Opinions
(June – December 1967)

I am mindful of Patrick Henry's succinct warning: 'The battle, sir, is not to the strong alone; it is to the vigilant, the active, the brave.' Thus, we can assure our strength by being *vigilant* — thinking through present problems and planning for the future; by being *active* in support of our ideals and commitments, and, finally, by being *brave* enough to stand up for what we believe wherever and whenever we are challenged.

– General Earle G. Wheeler, 26 October 1967 [1]

Special Tank Session

The number of hours that Wheeler devoted to Operation MULE SHOE during this incredibly busy period reflected the great importance he placed upon it. It was, after all, the best way he saw for "getting the war off the dime" and on toward victory.

"This has been a seemingly endless week," Betty Wheeler reported on 16 June. "If I feel so – how must poor Bus feel? … Bus has gone to the White House every evening at six thirty. It's been nine or nine-fifteen before he gets home." [2]

The previous day, Viney briefed Wheeler on the study group's report. Wheeler was very pleased with the 158-page document and directed Viney to brief the Chiefs as soon as possible. [3]

This "close hold" briefing occurred on 23 June and was remarkable in that the Chiefs' operations deputies were not present, as was typical for their routine tank sessions. Besides Wheeler and the Chiefs, the only other persons present were Viney and Air Force Colonel Ralph J. Hallenbeck, whose job it was to record the Chiefs' discussion by shorthand notation. [4]

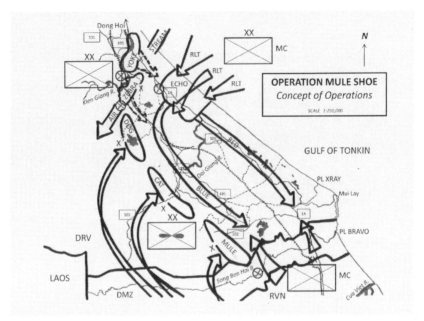

On 23 June 1967, Colonel George C. Viney briefed the Joint Chiefs of Staff on Wheeler's concept for Operation MULE SHOE using a map like this one. (Author)

The Chiefs were well-informed of the current situation in northern I Corps Tactical Zone (I CTZ) and Westmoreland's concern that the buildup of Viet Cong and North Vietnamese Army (NVA) forces in and above the demilitarized zone (DMZ) presaged a second North Vietnamese invasion of South Vietnam across the DMZ. Viney got right to the point of describing the proposed lodgment to destroy enemy forces and logistics facilities above the DMZ. The operation would be necessarily brief in order to reduce the high probability of Chinese intervention. [5]

After Viney concluded, the Chiefs deliberated. "Wally" Greene was all for it. There was some discussion about the Navy's initial concern over the availability of 8-inch shells for naval gunfire requirements. That had already been addressed to the Navy's satisfaction, so "Mac" McDonald was onboard for MULE SHOE, too.

The Chiefs also discussed the enemy's considerable antiaircraft defenses in the southernmost portion of North Vietnam. Near the lodgment area, the NVA had approximately 452 light anti-aircraft artillery guns, about 100 of which were in the lodgment area itself or presented a threat to air operations over the lodgment area. Three identified SA-2 antiaircraft missile sites were in the general vicinity, two in the lodgment area and one to the north. The study group had already wargamed this threat to the Air Force's satisfaction, so McConnell also concurred with the operation. [6]

During the Chiefs' deliberations throughout the year, McConnell had remained a consistent advocate of the use of more airpower against North Vietnam, convinced this would minimize the need for more troops, decrease Allied casualties, and shorten the war. In the absence of more authority for stronger air programs, he agreed with the other Chiefs on virtually all measures they mutually thought might shorten the conflict. [7]

Only "Johnny" Johnson opposed MULE SHOE — firmly. This surprised Viney, who recalled, "The Army kept their cards close to them on that one." [8]

An aide to Wheeler later praised Johnson for his "reputation of being the best prepared Chief when he went to the tank". Historian Martin Blumenson calls him "a moderating and stabilizing influence in the Joint Chiefs of Staff … because his intellectual and moral leadership consistently advocated the balanced view." [9]

"Johnny feels very deeply," Spivy recalled. "His views on the way things ought to go and were going were always quite sharp, quite precise. … He was very precise about his feelings. He took very strong feelings, either pro or con. There is nothing very gray. It's either good or bad." [10]

Wheeler knew the triumvirate of McNamara, McNaughton, and William Bundy would strenuously oppose another recommendation for escalation from the Chiefs, particularly one so likely to provoke Chinese intervention and fan domestic antiwar demonstrations. To have any hope of overcoming the triumvirate's growing calls for de-escalation, Wheeler had to achieve unanimity among the Chiefs. [11]

Johnson did not oppose MULE SHOE on philosophical grounds. Although he had been deeply critical of Westmoreland's search and destroy strategy and had advocated a population-centric strategy in 1966, Johnson's reasons for dissension were purely practical. [12]

Johnson and Wheeler had both served in the Army Staff's Operations Directorate and as Chief of Staff of the Army. "They each knew the Army inside and out," said Viney. For over two hours, a point-by-point debate ensued between the two Army generals on every issue raised by Johnson. "Now Johnny, what's your next objection?" Wheeler baited him. "What's your next concern?" In modern parlance, "the elephants danced." [13]

The enemy air defense threat to the 82nd Airborne Division and the 1st Cavalry Division was one issue. Another was that the 82nd was woefully short of airborne qualified personnel. Viney, whose brigade spearheaded the division's assault landing into the Dominican Republic two years earlier, bolstered Wheeler's assertions that the associated hurdles could be overcome. Johnson was not so sanguine and didn't buy Viney's claim of how rapidly he would bring the 82nd back into a state of combat readiness if Johnson would give him command of the division. This audacious remark elicited a chuckle from all the Chiefs. [14]

Viney would not have argued with Johnson so insistently had he known of the Army's many debilitating personnel issues that were Johnson's paramount concern. The President's decision in July 1965 not to mobilize the reserves had profoundly affected the way the Army had supported and sustained the war. To meet Westmoreland's calls for additional combat forces, to obtain manpower to enlarge its training base, and to maintain a pool for rotation and replacement soldiers in South Vietnam, the Army was in the process of increasing its active strength by nearly 1.5 million men. Necessarily, it had relied on larger draft calls and voluntary enlistments, supplementing them with heavy drawdowns of experienced soldiers from units in Europe and South Korea and by extending some tours of duty to retain specialists, technicians, and cadres to train recruits and round-out deploying units. Combat units assigned to the strategic reserve had been used to meet a large portion of Westmoreland's force requirements, and reservists were not available to replace them. Mobilization would have eased the additional burden of providing officers and noncommissioned officers (NCOs) to man the Army's growing training bases. As matters stood, requirements for experienced cadres competed with the demands for seasoned leaders in units deploying to South Vietnam. The personnel turbulence caused by competing demands for the Army's limited manpower had been exacerbated by a one-year tour of duty in South Vietnam. [15]

After more than three hours, the Chiefs' special tank session adjourned with the Army "splitting out". Wheeler and Johnson continued their debate in Wheeler's office. Wheeler summoned Lieutenant General Jim Woolnough, the Army's Deputy Chief of Staff for Personnel, to join them. Woolnough had been Wheeler's best man and West Point roommate, and his stance in the matter is speculative. Ultimately, Johnson still refused to endorse MULE SHOE. [16]

One of the plan's key assumptions was that the President would authorize mobilization. Johnson argued that it was a bad assumption since the President had disapproved all the Chiefs' previous calls for mobilization.

Johnson probably also argued that the plan's fourteen-day timeline was wildly unrealistic. To have any lasting impact, the operation would require more time to destroy enemy logistics facilities. Yet, if U.S. forces remained in North Vietnam any longer, they might find themselves battling Chinese reinforcements in an open-ended campaign.

At the current rate of operations, the Army was already over-extended and scraping the bottom of the manpower barrel. Without mobilization, the Army could not shoulder the additional burden MULE SHOE would impose, nor could it meet competing worldwide force requirements, despite the study group's optimistic conclusion that it could do both.

· "In those days," Spivy recalled, "if necessity if for no other reason, the Chiefs were objective and very cooperative with each other. They stood up for their own Services, of course. They were far more statesmanlike than perhaps they had the opportunity to be in earlier years. ... The circumstances of the McNamara era did a lot to make them a lot more cooperative. They couldn't afford to split or disagree." [17]

Without the unanimous endorsement of the Chiefs, Wheeler could not recommend MULE SHOE to the President. He would not, however, forgo the centerpiece of his strategy for starting to win the war. For the remainder of his tenure as Chairman, he would continue to advocate ground combat operations against North Vietnamese sanctuary areas. He would continue to refine MULE SHOE in anticipation that a suitable spark might prompt the President to authorize more radical action against North Vietnam and the mobilization to support it. [18]

MULE SHOE contained several spectacular and incredibly risky components: the first air assault of an entire airmobile division over enemy territory through an advanced, integrated air defense; the first division-size amphibious assault landing since Inchon; the first strategic deployment of an entire airborne division from its home station in the continental United States directly into combat through parachute assault, as well as the commitment of every C-130 and C-141 aircraft in the inventory for the duration of the operation.

Wheeler's very big assumptions that the President would authorize selective mobilization of industrial resources, and that he would finally authorize mobilization of the reserves were remarkable. Most incredible of all was that three of the four Chiefs agreed with Wheeler's assumptions and that they accepted MULE SHOE's very high risks, including Chinese intervention. They were willing to put their stars on the line behind an operation that was a 180-degree divergence from Administration policy, was incompatible with the triumvirate's "military theology," and would certainly inflame the antiwar movement. However, Wheeler and the Chiefs (minus Johnson) were convinced that MULE SHOE would accelerate attainment of U.S. objectives in Southeast Asia.

Wheeler Pushes Mobilization

Since late July 1965, Wheeler had pressed the Administration to mobilize the reserves and commit the nation to an all-out war in South Vietnam. Indeed, his arguments had been so persistent that the Chiefs' views were greeted with dismissive resignation by most members of the Administration.

Wheeler now decided to let the war itself act as a catalyst for changing the Administration's policy.

Not only was Wheeler certain that Westmoreland would need more troops, he realized the nation had reached what Administration officials were beginning to call the Plimsol Line – the point at which further call-ups would automatically trigger a full-scale American mobilization. In August 1967, the U.S. had 490,000 troops in South Vietnam, and another 35,000 were preparing for deployment. The total number of deployed U.S. troops would soon reach the 525,000 level. Beyond that number, the Joint Staff had determined that the U.S. would be in an untenable military readiness situation, meaning it would be forced to activate the reserves or fight the war with the troops it had.

I CTZ

"[The Communists] have shifted into an attritional offensive," Rostow confirmed in an interview on 9 July, "based on a different principle; namely, the pinning down of our forces by using the area north of the DMZ and areas of Laos as safe haven. … They have shifted from a posture of trying to win the war to keeping the war going." [19]

Hanoi's new strategy was consistent with an Asian warfighting maxim recently espoused by Mao Tse-tung: "Cause the enemy to waste his resources." This strategy manifested itself in heavy fighting in I and II Corps Tactical Zones (CTZs). [20]

Throughout the summer, U.S. Marine forces endured some of the most intense enemy artillery barrages of the war and fought several battles with North Vietnamese Army (NVA) units that infiltrated across the 17th Parallel. The Marines' stubborn defense, supported by massive counterbattery fire, naval gunfire, and air attacks, thwarted the Communist offensive in northern I CTZ, but not before Westmoreland had to divert additional Army units as reinforcements.

Even as Westmoreland shifted Allied forces from II CTZ to I CTZ, fighting intensified in the highlands. After U.S. Army units made several contacts with NVA forces during May and June, Westmoreland moved the 173rd Airborne Brigade from III CTZ to II CTZ to serve as an operational reserve. [21]

"As we weigh and balance the situation in the North and the situation in the South, as I see it, the North is paying a tremendous price and is deteriorating whereas the South is being successful in resisting this invasion and is progressively improving," Westmoreland stated in a press briefing on 29 June. "It would appear to me that history weighs rather decidedly in favor of the South."[22]

Meanwhile, to bolster his arguments for MULE SHOE, Wheeler had requested the Joint Staff study the impact of the build-up of Communist forces at the DMZ. Submitted on 11 July, the study determined that NVA forces had tripled in number near the DMZ since April 1966. Current intelligence slightly raised the Mule shoe study's estimate of the number of NVA forces in and immediately north of the DMZ to 41,800 in three divisions. North Vietnamese artillery, rocket, and heavy mortars concentrated at the DMZ exposed U.S. and Allied forces to a volume and weight of fire not encountered elsewhere in South Vietnam. NVA antiaircraft capabilities near the DMZ had increased fivefold and had doubled since November 1966. Six surface-to-air missile sites provided the NVA a quantum increase in its air defense capabilities. Increased capacity of logistics installations and road networks in the DMZ and in southern North Vietnam gave the NVA the capability to support its forces in sustained combat in and near the DMZ.

"The outlook is for continued high friendly casualties as long as the NVA is afforded the advantage of a secure base in and free transit through the DMZ," the study determined. Current U.S. forces within South Vietnam and those out-of-country were adequate to conduct an offensive operation to decisively defeat and destroy all major enemy forces in and adjacent to the DMZ. The study also recommended that "existing constraints at the DMZ must be removed and a decision made to proceed with an operation similar to that proposed in Mule shoe."[23]

Saigon Trip

Meeting with Averell Harriman on 1 July, McNamara pessimistically complained that Rusk was "too optimistic over what could be achieved." McNamara told Harriman that it was impossible to win the war militarily;

that he hoped the pressure on the President from the hawks would not be so great that the war would expand into a confrontation with the Soviet Union or China; and that he felt the most helpful way of ending the war through negotiations would be for Saigon to negotiate with the National Liberation Front. [24]

Abrams and Wheeler in Saigon, Republic of Vietnam, July 1967.
(Office of the Chairman of the Joint Chiefs of Staff)

McNamara, Wheeler, and Under Secretary of State Nicholas D. Katzenbach visited Vietnam on 5-12 July for an update on recent developments. Upon arrival, McNamara's party immediately began ten hours of meetings and briefings in Westmoreland's headquarters. [25]

According to Army Major General Philip Davidson, Westmoreland's Intelligence Officer, McNamara made clear his utter lack of interest in the briefings presented to him by Bunker, Sharp, and Westmoreland. Davidson recalled that "during most of the briefings [McNamara] read or worked on paper spread out before him; and he asked almost no questions of the briefers. His indifference to the presentations left no doubt that McNamara believed that none of the presenters could tell him anything he wanted or needed to hear." McNamara's demeanor did nothing to improve his relations with the military. [26]

Two days of intensive briefings were followed by visits to combat zones, a tour of pacification programs in the Mekong Delta, and private meetings with Thieu and Ky. While climbing a steep hill near Pleiku, Wheeler became acutely short of breath and nauseated. He sensed there was something not right with his heart but attributed it to the heat, humidity, and being out of shape. He felt better the next day but experienced more fatigue during and immediately after the trip than usual. [27]

Westmoreland's staff had optimistically informed McNamara that U.S. operations were keeping the Communists off balance and inflicting tremendous losses. The Viet Cong was encountering increasingly difficult problems in recruiting. The South Vietnamese Army's (ARVN's) desertion rate had declined noticeably, and the combat performance of some ARVN units had improved. After months of floundering, the pacification program seemed to be gaining traction. Prior to departing Vietnam, McNamara concealed his own reservations and dutifully informed the press, "There is no military stalemate." [28]

"The slow pace of the war, the mounting casualties, and the increasing polarization it was generating at home frustrated and troubled the President," McNamara recalled. "When Nick, Bus, and I reported our findings on July 12, following our return, he at one point asked, 'Are we going to be able to win this goddamned war?'" Again concealing his personal reservations, McNamara informed the President that, "operations are proceeding well" and "reports on the scene are better than press reports at home." McNamara also denounced pessimistic stories in the press, reiterating the talking point, "There is no military stalemate in Vietnam!" [29]

In a joint news conference the next day with McNamara and Wheeler, the President put the best spin on the situation. "We are generally pleased with the progress that we have made militarily. We are very sure that we are on the right track. We realize that some additional troops are going to be needed and are going to be supplied." [30]

Behind the scenes, the President finally authorized the aerial assault to isolate Haiphong that Sharp, General William W. Momyer, the new 7th Air Force commander, and Admiral John J. Hyland, the 7th Fleet commander, had vigorously advocated to McNamara in Saigon. They had already completed preparations for it. In approving the assault, Johnson remarked ominously, "The U.S. people do think, perhaps, that the war cannot be won." [31]

On 1 August, Admiral Thomas H. Moorer replaced McDonald as the Chief of Naval Operations. "[Tom] impressed me as a very down-to-earth, practical, very stable guy," Spivy recalled. "He took his place very quickly and became an outstanding member [of the Joint Chiefs of Staff]. He was a good deal smarter than some of them. … A first rate guy, I thought. I thought a great deal of Tom Moorer." [32]

Hanoi Senses Opportunity

The battles along South Vietnam's borders led Hanoi to reassess its strategy. Unwavering in their ultimate objective of unification, North Vietnamese leaders acknowledged that their strategy of military confrontation had failed to halt the U.S. buildup in the South or to reduce U.S. military pressure on the North. Regular and main force units had failed to inflict a significant military defeat on U.S. forces. Although the North Vietnamese Army (NVA) maintained the tactical initiative, Westmoreland had kept NVA units at bay, and in some areas, like the Binh Dinh Province, diminished Communist influence in the contest for control of the rural population. Many military leaders in Hanoi viewed the war as a stalemate and believed that maintaining the present course would yield diminishing returns, especially if their local forces were drastically weakened. [33]

Giap observed that the United States had been trying to confine the conflict within a limited war framework. He suggested a go-for-broke offensive to counter the Americans' intent. Giap rationalized immediate or near-term action, noting the possibility that President Johnson might send another 100,000 or 200,000 troops to Vietnam. Giap was aware that Johnson had already approved an additional 55,000 troops, which would mean the U.S.

would have more than a half-million troops in Vietnam by mid-1968 — thus indicating a need for Hanoi to strike before those reinforcements arrived.

Giap also foresaw an opportunity. Those reinforcements, he noted, represented a mobilization level far beyond initial U.S. forecasts and at variance with U.S. global strategy. Pressing the U.S. to the wall might force it to yield. [34]

Hanoi decided to launch a two-phased campaign consisting of a deception phase followed by a "General Offensive-General Uprising." Designed to lure U.S. troops out of South Vietnam's populated areas, the deception phase began in the fall with a series of assaults in isolated border areas. It would culminate with the siege of the Khe Sanh combat base near the Laotian border. [35]

Stennis Hearings

Despite extensive damage inflicted upon the North, the bombing campaign had not achieved its goals. The U.S. was paying a heavy price for marginal gains. The cost of the air war, in terms of flying costs, munitions, and replacement aircraft, was estimated more than $1.7 billion during 1965-66, a period in which the U.S. lost more than 500 aircraft. Between 1965 and 1968, the U.S. would lose more than 950 aircraft at a cost of $6 billion. By mid-1967, the limited success of the air war prompted McConnell to lament, "I can't tell you how I feel. … I have never been so goddamn frustrated by it all. … I'm so sick of it." [36]

"[Hawks in] both parties – fully supported by the Joint Chiefs – pressed for a widening of the war," McNamara recalled. "The latter group worried Johnson, [Rusk], and me most." Polls showed public sentiment moving in their direction. A Harris survey in mid-May reported slightly stronger support for increased military pressure than for withdrawal. This rising hawkishness was manifest in the Senate Armed Services Committee's Preparedness Investigating Subcommittee, which had taken a hard line on airpower and would harshly criticize the Administration's bombing program for months. "When [the legislators] learned through the Chiefs in June that the President had accepted my recommendation to keep the bombing limited, they went on the warpath." [37]

In August, Stennis convened the Preparedness Investigating Subcommittee to investigate "whether we are doing what we can and should do *in the opinion of our military experts* to hit the enemy when and where and in a manner that will end the war soonest and thus save American lives." [38]

Stennis greatly respected the nation's top military leaders, especially the Chiefs. During the two years since U.S. troops landed in Vietnam, the hawkish Senator had applauded their testimony, praised their sacrifices, valued their opinions, and greeted their programs with approval. [39]

"The question is growing in the Congress," Stennis said his opening remarks, "as to whether it is wise to send more men if we're going to just leave them at the mercy of the guerrilla war without trying to cut off the enemy's supplies more effectively. … My own personal opinion is that it would be a tragic and perhaps fatal mistake for us to suspend or restrict the bombing." [40]

Praising the Chiefs for their opposition to what he called "the doctrine of gradualism," Stennis listened closely as they publicly castigated the Administration for failing to listen to their advice. Sharp and Momyer also provided pointedly critical testimony. McNamara was sandwiched among them. "The hearings, which went on in executive session for seven long days between August 9 and August 29, proved to be one of the most stressful episodes in my life," McNamara recalled. [41]

Testifying on 9 August, Sharp stressed the imperative to cut the flow of military aid to North Vietnam from the Soviet Union. The ratio of war supplies entering North Vietnam, he said, was "four to one, the Soviets to China." [42]

"Although initiated with modest efforts and slowly expanded under carefully controlled conditions, the growing weight of our efforts has brought extensive destruction or disruption of North Vietnam's war supporting resources," Sharp testified. "Approximately half of the country's war supporting industry has been destroyed or disrupted." [43]

Much remained to be done, Sharp testified, particularly in the important northeast sector, which was the North Vietnamese main base area for the war the South. It contained numerous fixed and transitory targets that had not been struck. Here, key elements of the transportation system, industrial facilities, and important military complexes continued to function. Large quantities of supplies and war material from external sources moved through this area. This material was stored in and immediately adjacent to Hanoi and Haiphong, where it was moved out under cover of darkness and bad flight weather. An extensive and continuous effort was required to locate and destroy this material as it moved southward.

"No war has ever been brought to a successful conclusion by defensive action alone," Sharp testified. "During the last three months, we have begun to hurt the enemy in his home territory. He is suffering painful military, economic, and psychological strains. The best way to persuade the ruling element in North Vietnam to stop the aggression is to make the consequences of not stopping readily and painfully apparent." [44]

On 15 August, Stennis released to the press Sharp's statement before the subcommittee during the previous week. Stennis made clear his own views on the air war, which largely reflected testimony from Sharp and other senior military leaders. The air war against North Vietnam, Stennis was convinced, remained a vital and indispensable military measure. The support and protection that it provided U.S. forces in the South, by slowing and limiting the infiltration of men and material, was absolutely essential to the ground war.

"I support the bombing campaign because I am convinced that it significantly lessens the pressure on our ground forces in the South and thus reduces our casualties," Stennis said. "I support it also because I believe that without it, the ground war would last indefinitely, at least for many years." [45]

"I sincerely and earnestly share the desire for a speedy end to the war and the fighting and killing," Stennis continued. "However, the suspension or substantial curtailment of the air war would be a step backward which would lengthen and protract the war rather than shorten it." [46]

The air war against North Vietnam had clearly hurt the enemy, particularly in the last two or three months, Stennis noted. "It is no time to reduce the military pressure when the enemy is thus hurt. Instead, the pressure should be increased and sustained so that the military and economic consequences of continuing with the war will become painfully apparent to Hanoi." [47]

"To my mind, it would make absolutely no military, political, or moral sense whatsoever – indeed, it would be tragic – for us to dispatch 45,000 or so additional ground troops to South Vietnam and, at the same time, to halt or substantially curtail the air war and thus give Hanoi unrestricted freedom to introduce the men and goods to counter them," Stennis remarked.[48]

Highly esteemed by members on both sides of the committee, Wheeler testified on 16 August. Virginia Senator Harry F. Bird, Jr. called him "one of the ablest military officers I have ever known."[49]

Corroborating Sharp's testimony, Wheeler testified that the war was not being won and could not be won until North Vietnamese support for the southern insurgency was broken. He repeated his own judgment that the bombing had reduced movement to the South, "particularly supplies over the last several months." While Wheeler refused to say that the war was being lost, he made it clear that the Administration's failure to increase pressure on North Vietnam might mean that it could not be won. He testified that there was unanimous agreement among commanders that the Administration's policy of aerial interdiction of supplies to the Viet Cong was doomed to failure unless U.S. forces could "go to the source" to effectively close the port of Haiphong and the rail lines in North Vietnam through and over which Soviet war supplies were transported.[50]

"There is no question but that lacking support in the Soviet Union – that is, getting the means of war – that any sizeable conflict would be impossible for the North Vietnamese and the Viet Cong," Wheeler stated. The war could be ended "in a relatively short period of time" if Haiphong were closed, he asserted. If the Administration was serious about winning the war, Wheeler testified, then it must take steps against North Vietnam that included approval of the Chiefs' full target list to stop the flow of supplies to North Vietnam. But he also implied that even this action would not be enough, a clear indication to the Administration that he still advocated full mobilization.[51]

Between 1954 and the end of 1967, Hanoi would receive some $2.9 billion in foreign military aid, mostly from the Soviets. It also maintained annual aid agreements with Communist China, North Korea, Mongolia, Romania, Bulgaria, and Cuba.

The Soviets had provided North Vietnam with about 35 surface-to-air missile (SAM) battalions, a sophisticated communications and radar network, numerous light bomber and fighter plane aircraft, and large quantities of anti-aircraft weapons. Together, these weapons constituted one of the most sophisticated air defense systems ever faced by any force in combat. Additionally, the Soviet Union provided the NVA with modern ground force equipment, such as 122-mm and 140-mm rockets, 120-mm mortars, and 130-mm field guns.

The Soviet Union had also provided priority support to the North Vietnamese transportation system. It had not only supplied a large percentage of the vehicles needed to move supplies south, but also the road construction equipment required to keep existing roads serviceable and to build new military roads in North Vietnam, Laos, and Viet Cong-controlled areas of South Vietnam. The Soviets had also provided railroad equipment, barges, bridging equipment, and petroleum.

Although the percentage of foreign aid that North Vietnam received from Communist China had declined steadily since 1965, such aid was significant and included the rehabilitation and development of North Vietnam's railways, highways, and communications facilities, reconstruction and improvement of irrigation systems, and construction of heavy and light industrial facilities. In 1966, some 40,000 Chinese performed road and rail maintenance and other repair work in North Vietnam. By early 1968, that number would grow to 50,000. American intelligence believed some antiaircraft units there were manned by Chinese soldiers. Military equipment from China mostly included small arms, ammunition, and light antiaircraft artillery, as well as some fighter aircraft.

In the early stages of the conflict with the United States, Vietnamese Communist forces were handicapped by weapons and ammunition shortages, and they often relied upon captured and homemade items. By this point, however, they possessed an abundance of the latest models of conventional Communist weapons. [52]

"The generals and admirals hammered at what they considered the central problem in the way we were fighting the war – meddling by the civilians in Washington," McNamara recalled. "In their minds, it stood in the way of victory and got men killed. I strongly believed we were saving American lives without penalizing progress in the war. ... I was left with quite a case to rebut." [53]

McNamara's testimony was widely anticipated. For subcommittee insiders, it was the culmination of months of work, a fragile strategy designed to expose the unacknowledged breakdown of the military-civilian consensus on Vietnam policy. [54]

McNamara testified that it would be impossible to cut off supplies from the North solely using an air campaign. He then contradicted the Chiefs' testimony. "A selective, carefully targeted bombing campaign, such as we are presently conducting," McNamara insisted, "can be directed toward reasonable and realizable goals. This discriminating use of air power can and does render the infiltration of men and supplies more difficult and more costly." While Johnson's policy might be debatable, its impact wasn't. It was working. The North Vietnamese were buckling. America was winning the war in Vietnam. [55]

McNamara stuck to his guns before the committee, but the senators faulted him for micromanaging the air campaign. "The case against expanding the air war was clear," McNamara recalled. "All you had to do was look at the numbers. My testimony generated considerable controversy." [56]

South Carolina Senator Strom Thurmond called it "a statement of appeasing the Communists and of no-win. ... If we follow what you have recommended, we ought to get out of Vietnam at once, because we have no chance to win." [57]

Symington told reporters, "If the position as presented by the Secretary this morning is right, I believe the United States should get out of Vietnam at the earliest possible time, and on the best possible basis; because with his premises, there would appear to be no chance for any true 'success' in this long war." [58]

The Chiefs were stunned and furious with McNamara's testimony. He had dismissed their most crucial contention that a successful conclusion to the war could only be gained by shutting off supplies to the North, not to the South. Moreover, as Wheeler had testified, the effectiveness of the U.S.

bombing campaign was not a matter of opinion but the most important sta-tistical measure of progress in the war. If the air campaign was working, as McNamara asserted, why were shipments of men and arms to South Vietnam increasing? In other words, McNamara had lied. What Wheeler and his fel-low senior officers testified might be discomfiting, but it was also transpar-ently provable: the U.S. strategy was not working; the North Vietnamese were not buckling; the U.S. probably could not win by continuing the triumvirate's graduated escalation policies.

Civilian-military relations had not been so seriously undermined since World War II. McNamara's testimony broke the unofficial contract between civilian leaders and senior military officers that, by necessity, exists in every democratic society: members of the military pledge they will obey civilian authorities without question; in return, civilian leaders pledge that those orders will not lead to useless sacrifice of military life. [59]

In Wheeler's office that afternoon, the Chiefs decided to resign en masse. They would sleep on their decision and announce it the next day. Wheeler spent an almost sleepless night grappling with his sense of loyalty and his mil-itary oath. Although he had pushed his colleagues to resign, his instinct now told him that it was the wrong thing to do, and he changed his mind. [60]

Reconvening in Wheeler's office the following morning, Wheeler told the Chiefs, "We can't do it. It's mutiny." Their resignation would not make a damn bit of difference because the President would merely replace them with other officers more amenable to his policies. The Chiefs agreed and swore an oath never to reveal the matter. Moorer and Johnson would later officially deny it. [61]

"A downside of *hari-kari* is that one only gets to commit it once," Military historian Army Brigadier General John S. Brown observes. "Until and unless the right moment comes, officers obey the lawful orders of those appointed over them. In Earle G. Wheeler we find a soldier who had been dealt a bad hand, but nevertheless believed results would be better if he stayed at his post than if he left it. His example remains relevant today." [62]

Given McNamara's bad-faith defense of a clearly discredited strategy, there was little reason to hope for an eventual U.S. victory. On one level, the Chiefs believed that to continue the war under current conditions would be immoral in that it would lead to a useless sacrifice. On another level, they believed that the crisis had more practical consequences. It convinced many three- and four-star general officers and flag officers that the military itself must have a greater voice in determining U.S. policy. The change in attitude was fundamental and marked an unprecedented break in U.S. military tradition. Wheeler believed that the Chiefs now had a unique opportunity to convince the American people to pressure the President to make an unambiguous stand in Vietnam or to get out. [63]

"That the air campaign has not achieved its objective to a greater extent cannot be attributed to inability or impotence of air power," the Stennis subcommittee's damning report stated. "It attests, rather, to the fragmentation of our air might by overly restrictive controls, limitations, and a doctrine of 'gradualism' placed on our aviation forces which prevented them from waging [the] air campaign in the manner and according to the timetable which was best calculated to achieve maximum results." [64]

The subcommittee's report argued, "It is high time, we believe, to allow the military voice to be heard in connection with the tactical details of military operations." [65]

The President considered the hearings a political disaster. "Your generals almost destroyed us with their testimony before the Stennis Committee," Johnson scolded Wheeler. "We were murdered in the hearings!" [66]

Shortly after the subcommittee released its report and the President learned of the Chiefs' anger over McNamara's testimony, Johnson approved 52 of the 57 bombing targets that McNamara had previously prohibited the Chiefs from attacking. McNamara had lost the President's confidence. His resignation was now only a matter of time. [67]

The fallout from the Stennis hearings also prompted some members of the Administration to reconsider its ground strategy. Wheeler asked Westmoreland to comment upon Rusk's suggestion that Westmoreland might make better use of his on-hand forces by concentrating them in critical areas to achieve decisive results in a timelier manner.

"Secretary Rusk is thinking in terms of the more conventional type warfare where our forces could launch such an all-out offensive from a reasonably secure area of departure, leaving behind a pacified rear area, and against identified enemy formations disposed along a recognizable front," Westmoreland replied on 26 August. "Such is not the case in [South Vietnam]. … We are pursuing a strategy which applies relentless pressure against the entire spectrum of enemy forces. As additional assets become available, our operations will be stepped up. If more dramatic evidence of our determination to win this war at the earliest date is required, I suggest that consideration be given to carrying the ground attack to the known areas of enemy concentration north of the DMZ and along the border sanctuaries. These moves would not be without their pitfalls, but I am confident that they could be undertaken successfully." [68]

Wheeler briefs the President and his closest national security team, the White House Cabinet Room, Washington, DC, 29 August 1967. (LBJ Library)

Heart Attack

"Strong differences of judgment did divide us," McNamara recalled, "and the frictions they caused created stress, which took its toll." [69]

More than a month after his Pleiku incident, Wheeler still wasn't feeling completely well. A cardiologist at Walter Reed determined that Wheeler had suffered a heart attack and admitted him immediately for testing and several weeks of rest. "Johnny" Johnson would serve as Acting Chairman in the interim.

Remarkably, despite the substantial professional differences between Johnson, McNamara, Wheeler, and the Chiefs, and the tremendous pressure upon all of them, they and their wives were on very friendly personal terms. They would grow increasingly closer as the Vietnam predicament wore on. [70]

"I appreciate greatly your thoughtfulness in sending me the two autographed books which I shall treasure," Wheeler wrote to the President on 5 September. "Even more, I appreciate the letter which you wrote to me. Knowing as I do the tremendous domestic and international burdens which you must shoulder, I also note the extra exertion needed to add even one more letter to the stack of work which you must do."

Wheeler continued:

Also, your reminder that you too have gone through this experience is a heartening and sustaining thought as to my own future. No doubt Bob McNamara has told you that the doctors believe that I am doing quite well. Apparently, this attack occurred in early July with Bob and I were visiting Vietnam and, therefore, much of the recuperation period is behind me. This is not to say that I don't have an additional convalescent period ahead because I do. The doctors told me this morning that they are engaged in reviewing all of the tests and will give me within the next couple of days a schedule for me to follow. As soon as I know where I stand, Mr. President, I shall report the facts to you. [71]

"I am distressed to learn that you have suffered a heart attack," Sharp cabled Wheeler two days later. "Glad it was only a minor one and that your progress is good and you'll return to duty soon. Having been with you each day during the July Vietnam visit I must say you were a healthy looking and vigorous patient."[72]

Discharged from Walter Reed after resting for two weeks, Wheeler still required additional rest time. Concerned that he physically might not be able to continue the job, Wheeler offered to resign. "When I got out on convalescent leave, I went to see President Johnson," Wheeler recalled. "I told him what my physical condition was and the what the prognosis was and so on, and the fact that I was going to be out of action for at least another six weeks, and it could be considerably more than that. I suggested to him that I should retire and that he should appoint somebody else as Chairman of the Joint Chiefs of Staff."[73]

"Well, he talked to me about 45 minutes," Wheeler recalled. "Finally, he said to me, 'Now, Buzz,' he said – Buzz was what he always called me – 'You just go along and do what the doctors tell you to do to improve your health. I don't want anybody else as Chairman of the Joint Chiefs of Staff,' he said, 'but, on the other hand, I don't want you to kill yourself in that job. After you've had another checkup in about six weeks or so, if the doctors say you can do the job,' he said, 'then I want you to stay on.' Then – we were in his office, this was about 7:30 or so at night – he got up, and walked to the door with me, and put his arm around my shoulder, and said, 'I can't afford to lose you. You have never given me a bad piece of advice.'"[74]

The cardiologist prescribed exercise, which Wheeler endeavored to fit into his schedule, at least on weekends in the country. "Bus never stopped smoking," his son Bim says, "although after his heart attack he did switch to a pipe and milder cigarettes."[75]

"He had really worn himself out," Spivy recalled. "Doc Upton, who was in the Pentagon or JCS dispensary, was a heart specialist. [Henceforth,] he traveled with Wheeler all the time." The Wheelers' household staff took lessons in cardiopulmonary resuscitation and practiced it semiannually as a precautionary measure.[76]

Home Front

The President recognized that he could not ignore domestic opposition to the war. From the beginning, he perceived that "the weakest chink in our armor is public opinion." Initially, Johnson feared the hawks more than the doves, but by the fall of 1967 he reassessed. "The major threat we have is from the doves," he told his advisors on 5 September. [77]

"There are signs that the Administration is getting fed up with the deceit, wrong decisions and dictatorial arrogance of Robert Strange McNamara, the man who never yet has been right about Vietnam or any other military matter," Goldwater wrote in a scathing syndicated newspaper column two days later. "The major visible sign of McNamara's slippage in the court of LBJ is the fact that, for the first time, military men seem free to voice the opposition to McNamara which always has been present. ... The fact that the Chiefs are now fighting him openly can only mean, it seems to me, that there is certain knowledge now that the White House is withdrawing some of that support." [78]

Increasingly fearful that the war might be lost at home, Johnson launched a two-pronged offensive to silence his most outspoken enemies and win public support for his policies. Johnson was convinced that the peace movement was turning the public against the war, so he set about to destroy it. The President instructed the CIA to implement a surveillance program of antiwar leaders to confirm his suspicions that they were Communists operating on orders from foreign governments. [79]

This campaign against the peace movement soon shifted from surveillance to harassment and disruption, often by illegal means. In violation of its charter prohibiting domestic surveillance, the CIA's Operation CHAOS — and the FBI's Operation COINTELPRO — employed illicit wiretaps and forged documents, framed protesters on drug charges, and incited violence through agents provocateur to subvert antiwar protesters. [80]

The President also launched a "Success Offensive" to shore up popular support by disseminating positive information as "sound evidence of progress in Vietnam." The embassy in Saigon and military leaders responded with a barrage of optimistic data. [81]

"We're really doing the job now," said Brigadier General J.M. Philpott, Director of Intelligence for the 7th Air Force, in the 8 September edition of *Time* magazine. [82]

Buoyed by the President's concessions to their demands for increased bombing authorities, the Chiefs contributed their own messages of optimism. "In my opinion, our new air effort against North Vietnam is making a major contribution to the achievement of our objectives," Moorer was quoted in *Time* magazine. [83]

Even "Johnny" Johnson enthused in *U.S. News & World Report* the following week:

> We are very definitely winning in Vietnam. ... There has been a marked turnabout. ... Now there is forward movement everywhere. ... I think we have a momentum going now that we have not had before, and in order to increase this momentum and to bring the active hostilities to a conclusion faster, we want to reinforce success. ... I think we have come a very long way in the past two years – and I see no reason why we can't keep this momentum going. [84]

"Categorically, I reject the all-too-frequent use of the word 'stalemate,'" Wheeler stated in a speech on 26 October. "Anyone who knows the dictionary definition of this word and knows the true nature of our campaign in Vietnam must reject the term." [85]

During his weekly luncheon on 12 September attended by Rusk, McNamara, Rostow, and "Johnny" Johnson, the President asked Johnson to have the Chiefs "search for imaginative ideas to put pressure to bring this war to a conclusion." He did not want them to "just recommend more men or that we drop the atom bomb." The President said he could think of those ideas himself. He wanted the Chiefs to come up with some new programs. He also predicted that when Congress reconvened in January it would try to bring the war to a close either by getting out or by escalating significantly. [86]

Con Thien

The North Vietnamese Army (NVA) had begun firing 152-mm artillery from within or above the demilitarized zone (DMZ) back in July and was now concentrating indirect fires of all types against the U.S. Marine outpost at Con Thien. These fires peaked on 19-27 September when 3,077 mortar, artillery, and rocket rounds hit the base. The Marines responded with increased counterbattery fire, airstrikes, and naval gunfire, which forced the enemy fire to slacken. [87]

Despite U.S. spoiling operations, enemy activity in the DMZ had intensified. MACV estimated that the North Vietnamese wanted to draw U.S. forces into the region in order to check Allied success in other areas, and in the process of creating a major diversion, to achieve a significant military victory. [88]

"I am concerned over the situation near the DMZ," Westmoreland informed Sharp and "Johnny" Johnson – who was serving as Acting Chairman in Wheeler's absence — on 27 September. "The casualties which our forces have been taking are high and our ability to suppress enemy fires into our positions has not been effective." During the first 24 days of September, the U.S. had incurred 52 killed in action (KIA) and 994 wounded in action (WIA) in Quang Tri Province from artillery, rocket, and mortar fire. "This is a high price to pay for holding the enemy along the DMZ front," Westmoreland wrote. "Our serious losses are not significantly greater this month, but the fact that they are being suffered while in a defensive posture has an unfortunate psychological impact." [89]

Although all the North Vietnamese artillery fire was being delivered from positions north of the Ben Hai River, some of their rockets and all their mortars were located south of the river. Westmoreland was also aware that the enemy had significant maneuver forces south of the river. On two occasions since Westmoreland had been granted authority to move into the southern portion of the DMZ, sweeps to the river were made to clear the area. Both operations were successful but incurred heavy casualties due to U.S. troops' exposure to enemy fire from north of the river, that Westmoreland was not authorized to suppress or take by ground attack.

"Our fundamental problem," Westmoreland explained, "is that our posture south of the DMZ is defensive, and, around Con Thien, relatively static. To shift to the offensive without going all of the way to eliminate positions north of the Ben Hai would invite heavy casualties on a repetitive basis. To launch a major combined attack from the sea and across the DMZ to eliminate the enemy position was "undoubtedly out of the question until May or June, because of weather even if political obstacles could be overcome." [90]

Westmoreland tasked the III Marine Amphibious Force and 7th Air Force to prepare plans for limited offensive operations across the DMZ against artillery positions in the event that the situation required it and presidential authorization was granted. He pointed out that any offensive operations north of Con Thien would be extremely difficult to conduct and support because of the poor weather and prospect of heavy mud during the next four months. "Confronted with the current situation, it is my judgment that we should not increase the forces north of Route 9 unless we shift to the offensive." [91]

Westmoreland planned to thin out forces north of Route 9 after suitable defenses were prepared in the Con Thien area to minimize friendly casualties near the DMZ and to inflict maximum casualties on the enemy through air, artillery, and naval gunfire attack. It was in this area that U.S. forces were "butted up" against the DMZ and were, therefore, at a serious tactical disadvantage. "The enemy is permitted to reap full benefits from his sanctuary north of the DMZ secure from our maneuver," the Chiefs informed McNamara. "We must face him on frontal terms. We cannot get behind him to cut him off from his supplies or to overrun his artillery." [92]

To counter this threat, Westmoreland initiated Operation NEUTRALIZE, a massive concentration of air, artillery, and naval gunfire in support of the Marines at Con Thien. This type of operation would become known by its acronym SLAM – for Seeking, Locating, Annihilating, and Monitoring. Between August and October, Momyer would continue to refine the concept, which eventually employed the full spectrum of fires, from B-52 bombers in a tactical role to light artillery. After reconnaissance aircraft and intelligence assets fixed and defined the target, heavy bomber strikes by B-52s typically triggered the attack. Tactical airstrikes and coordinated artillery and naval gunfire then followed. During the attack, reconnaissance elements observed the target. Later, long-range reconnaissance patrols entered the target area to assess bomb damage and locate additional targets for highly accurate tactical aircraft prepared to strike them.

SLAM operations became one of Westmoreland's most valuable and responsive tools. During the forty-nine-day SLAM operation at Con Thien, massed firepower alone would dislodge the entrenched NVA forces, destroy their prepositioned supplies, and break the siege by 4 October. Lessons learned in this operation would prove invaluable later in the year at Khe Sanh.[93]

No Substitute For Victory

Meanwhile, Wheeler returned from convalescent leave to a full slate of activities. "He looked terrible," one aide remembered, "as if he would rather have been anywhere else."[94]

During their extended leave in the country, Betty Wheeler wrote, "I was a quarter of nine getting up this morning. Bus is usually well ahead and has walked to the gate and back (a distance of one mile) by the time I'm down." Ordered by his cardiologist, such walks were Bus's first real exercise in *over five years.*[95]

"Under doctor's orders, I divorced myself from the daily 'flaps', the constantly ringing phones, buzzing buzzers, rushing action officers, not too brief briefers, and reports on reports on reports," Wheeler would state in a speech on 26 October. "I then found I had time to think — to reflect on several of the key issues confronting us these days. I think you'll agree that, in our governmental process, our senior civilian and military policy makers apparently have too little time to think. The top posts within our government are administered on the dead run while short deadlines pry policies and programs off the stove before they're done."[96]

McNamara recalled, "Bus returned to serve the Administration by offering his advice in private meetings and public testimony in a direct but noninflammatory and nonconfrontational way."[97]

In tune with the President's other senior military advisors, Wheeler was convinced that the self-restricted way in which Johnson and McNamara had managed the war would not lead to victory anytime soon. Wheeler knew the Chiefs must become more outspoken in their opposition to the Administration's conduct of the war and more strident in their advocacy of more aggressive military action against North Vietnam. Wheeler anticipated that developments would eventually compel the President to authorize more of the offensive programs the Chiefs had long recommended, and perhaps even justify MULE SHOE. [98]

Wheeler also insisted upon an entirely new role for the Joint Chiefs of Staff. No longer would it serve merely as a planning body for the Secretary of Defense. Instead, it would advise and answer to the President. Wheeler concluded that the relationship between the President and the Chiefs had to change. Instead of having to work through McNamara, the Chiefs needed direct access to their Commander-in-Chief. [99]

Invasion Plans

"Our strategy has achieved success as attested by the fact that the enemy has not won a single tactical victory of significance during the past year," Westmoreland had explained to visiting U.S. officials in September. "His guerrilla ranks have been progressively eroded and a number of his main force units have been destroyed. His main forces are now reluctant to engage us in combat, many have broken into small units, and most are attempting to evade contact." [100]

In recent weeks, however, Communist activity had increased again in the enemy's sanctuary areas, and sizable forces began appearing along South Vietnam's border from the DMZ to III Corps Tactical Zone (CTZ). American military leaders were not overly alarmed. "The war is going along quite steadily in our favor," said Sharp on 13 October. [101]

In contrast, the American home front was nearing a state of collapse. The consensus that the President had so carefully woven in 1964 was in shambles. The nation was now more divided than at any time since the Civil War. Opposition in Congress, as well as inattention and mismanagement resulting in part from the Administration's preoccupation with Vietnam, had brought Johnson's cherished Great Society programs to a standstill. Johnson himself was under siege in the White House. His popularity was steadily waning, and he was the target of vicious personal attacks. His top advisors had to be secreted into public forums to deliver speeches. Despondently, Johnson considered not running for reelection next year.

"How are we going to win?" the President asked plaintively at a top-level meeting in early October. Wheeler had an answer in mind – MULE SHOE – but the circumstances were not yet propitious for suggesting it, and he still needed to get "Johnny" Johnson onboard. [102]

Sharing Wheeler's determination to press the Allies' military advantage, Sharp had directed his major subordinate commanders to develop plans for an amphibious/airmobile/airborne assault to destroy enemy forces in and adjacent to the DMZ. Sharp invited the Joint Staff to send a representative to an invasion planning conference on 20 September. Carlson was selected to attend.

Operation BUTT STROKE, Westmoreland's three-page outline plan, would employ 2 1/3 division equivalents to conduct an amphibious/airborne/airmobile lodgment near Dong Hoi (40 miles north of the DMZ) to destroy the enemy and his logistical installations. Forces to be employed would include the 1st Cavalry Division, the 173rd Airborne Brigade, part of a Marine division, and the South Vietnamese Army (ARVN) Rainbow Division. After establishing the lodgment south of Dong Hoi, the force would sweep south to the DMZ. The plan envisioned a 60-day operation, which could be terminated in 30 days. [103]

Operation COLUBRINE, the 15-page concept developed by the Commander, Fleet Marine Force Pacific (COFMFPAC), would employ 1 1/3 divisions by helicopter/amphibious assault near Xom Lap (6 miles North of the DMZ). Three regimental landing teams (RLTs) would sweep south to the DMZ covered by the fourth RLT on the north. Concurrent with the helicopter/amphibious assault, the III Marine Amphibious Force would launch limited objective attacks to fix and exert pressure on the enemy from south of the DMZ. The plan envisioned a timeframe 10 to 12 days for execution of the operation. [104]

Sharp's planning conference produced an outline plan that incorporated some features of both the BUTT STROKE and COLUBRINE plans. This plan would employ 1 1/3 Marine divisions by helicopter/amphibious assault near Xom Lap, thereafter attacking south. A portion of one RLT would screen the division rear, and one battalion would remain afloat as a reserve. One brigade of the 101st Airborne Division would move by helicopter assault to screen the west flank of the Marine division. The second airborne brigade would stand by for potential commitment if required in I CTZ, and a third brigade would be alerted at base camp in South Vietnam for possible employment. A barrier of air drop munitions would be established in the foothills west of Highway 101. The earliest date the operation could be conducted was April 1968. [105]

Carlson observed several significant deficiencies in Sharp's invasion plan, which he reported to the Joint Staff. On 16 October, Spivy endorsed Carlson's recommendation that Sharp "be provided, at least informally, as a matter of urgency, a copy of the close-hold MULE SHOE study as a background document for use by his planners." Spivy reminded Wheeler that per their previous telephone conversation, Wheeler "wanted to prepare the way first" to ensure that the highly politically sensitive plan would not be leaked and that Sharp understood the plan was for planning purposes only and had not been authorized by the President. Wheeler agreed. Thus, as the most fully developed plan for an invasion of North Vietnam, MULE SHOE would underpin all subsequent U.S. planning for such a contingency operation. [106]

Giap declared in late 1967, "We have adequately prepared ourselves and are ready to deal destructive blows … if they adventurously send infantry troops to the North." Vietnamese General Nguyen Xuan Hoang, Chief of the People's Army Historical Office, stated in 1983, "The landings would have been the most foolhardy. We knew we could easily defeat as many as 100,000 men there." [107]

Rostow and Westmoreland discussed the invasion option on 20 November. Rostow informed the President that Westmoreland wanted to "have the capability to raid North Vietnam in force above the DMZ in May-June of next year – the earliest time that might be technically possible. He is not now recommending such an operation; but he thinks it important that we have such an option if our DMZ position requires it at that time." Rostow suggested to Johnson that preparing for an invasion but not carrying it out was a means for deceiving Hanoi, but that such invasion preliminaries had to be so realistic that "it could be extremely difficult for the President to decide not to carry through." [108]

JCSM 555-67

"The President had taken some guarded steps toward military expansion of the air war in the fall of 1967, undoubtedly as a result of the Stennis hearings and in spite of Secretary McNamara's strong position against any such action," Sharp recalled. "In the military view, however, we were not moving far enough fast enough, and we continued to press our position upon the decision makers, albeit with an increasing sense of futility." [109]

During Wheeler's absence on convalescent leave on 12 September, the President had requested the Chiefs "review thoroughly our military programs in Southeast Asia and to recommend any additional action which, in the opinion of the Chiefs, would shorten the war in South Vietnam." [110]

On 17 October — just a week after Wheeler's return to duty — the Chiefs responded. Wheeler had clearly pushed himself, concerned that the troop deployment plan he had initiated, and which he believed would inevitably force the President to mobilize the nation, could be derailed. To ensure that such a derailment did not occur, Wheeler assumed a formative role in writing Joint Chiefs of Staff Memorandum (JCSM) 555-67. [111]

"The President had asked what could be done to put more pressure on Hanoi, and the Chiefs had responded in their usual decisive, forthright manner," Sharp recalled. "They first outlined their understanding of the objectives of the war, the constraints within which the political leadership wished it to be fought, and the self-imposed operational restrictions that they saw as hindering achievement of the objectives. They then proposed a recommended list of ten measures calculated to convince the enemy we meant business." [112]

"Progress will continue to be slow so long as present limitations on military operations continue in effect," the Chiefs advised. They observed that "the rate of progress has been and continues to be slow, largely because U.S. military power has been restrained in a manner which has reduced significantly impact and effectiveness." Attacks on enemy military targets had been on such a prolonged, graduated basis that the enemy had adjusted psychologically, economically, and militarily to the difficulties and hardships accompanying the war, dispersed their logistic support system, and developed alternate support routes and a significant air defense system. Areas of sanctuary, containing important military targets, had been afforded the enemy. Covert operations in Cambodia and Laos had been restricted. Major importation of supplies into [North Vietnam] by sea had been permitted. [113]

The Chiefs recognized that expansion of U.S. efforts entailed some additional risk, but they believed the likelihood of overt introduction of Soviet or Chinese Communist combat forces into the war was remote. Failure to take additional action to shorten the war also entailed risks as new and more efficient weapons were provided to North Vietnam by China and the Soviet Union. [114]

JCSM 555-67, which bears Wheeler's unmistakable imprint, was one of the most far-reaching and detailed plans for total war ever put forward by the Chiefs. Not only did it reiterate their position on expanding the list of North Vietnamese targets for a 12-month air campaign against North Vietnam, it also argued that the U.S. should mine North Vietnamese harbors and remove bombing restrictions over Hanoi. The Chiefs' memo did not include the centerpiece of Wheeler's plan for beginning to win the war – MULE SHOE – due to "Johnny" Johnson's split opinion from the other Chiefs in June. [115]

The Chiefs' memo was a purposeful attempt by Wheeler to give the President one last chance to change his war strategy. "This was one of the final expositions of the military argument for a strategy that could lead us to a clear victory over North Vietnam," Sharp recalled. "It was an excellent articulation of the [Chiefs'] point of view, with which I, of course, wholeheartedly concurred." [116]

> Wheeler recalled:
> What we try to do is to lay out for the President what the pros and the cons are of adopting any course of action. And

having done that, we then come down and recommend what we think is right. And I might say that the rule that we try to follow is this: If I were the President of the United States, would I follow the advice that is being presented to me? In other words, is it logical? Is it a dangerous course of action? Is it a necessary course of action? So we don't, by any manner or means, advocate the strongest possible military response to a military situation that arises. For example: we never, through the whole course of the campaign against North Vietnam, advocated the use of nuclear weapons. We never advocated the bombing of the dikes in North Vietnam. We advocated a few other things that were too strong for people's stomachs, but not those two anyway, and there were others. In other words, we try to be sensible men. [117]

For Wheeler's purposes, the Chiefs' memo was perfectly timed to coincide with the President's most important year-end conference on the war, a review scheduled to occur during an upcoming Tuesday luncheon at the White House. With McNamara's influence diminished and Johnson under fire from his own party in Congress, the Administration's policymaking apparatus was clearly in chaos and therefore vulnerable, Wheeler believed, to the Chiefs' arguments. [118]

"Days after this joint memorandum from the [Chiefs] went forward, General Wheeler … sent forward his own proposal for expansion of the air war," Sharp recalled. "Among his more significant recommendations was the reduction of the Hanoi and Haiphong prohibited areas to three and 1 ½ miles respectively, thereby opening up an additional 15 vital targets that could be struck on the authority of the field commander." [119]

The 17 October meeting at the White House ran several hours long and once again proved disappointing to Wheeler and the Chiefs. While it sampled opinions on the war from a wider array of experts then had been previously included in such strategy sessions, the review found the President more committed than ever to the unsuccessful graduated response strategy adopted more than 30 months earlier. Once again, Johnson came down on the side of increasing pressures on North Vietnam, but not to the extent recommended by the Chiefs. The bombing target list would be expanded, and troop deployments would be accelerated, but that was all. [120]

This led to another peak in the bombing campaign, with almost 2,000 sorties targeting Haiphong and more than 1,400 against Hanoi – more than 35% of all ROLLING THUNDER sorties. By the end of the year, only four approved targets within the Haiphong exclusion zone would remain untouched, and the President would approve more than two-thirds of all potential targets there.

Sharp would later report that the bombing had reduced Haiphong's cargo handling capacity by more than half. A remarkable 56% of trucks and railway cars destroyed by ROLLING THUNDER in 1967 were destroyed in the Hanoi and Haiphong zones during July and August alone.

"There can be no doubt that the air commanders had thrown their best punch," Prados writes. And yet, Communist infiltration in preparation for the planned offensive in the South increased immensely over the same period." [121]

Antiwar Sentiment

"Everyone is pretty uneasy about the [antiwar] march [on the Pentagon] tomorrow," Betty Wheeler wrote on 20 October. "As Bus's office is on the ground floor and so close to the entrance, he was advised to stay away. Gates have been put on [Fort] Myer. Tomorrow only govt. stickers or 'good reasons' let you in. … MPs [Military Police] are already covering this area and one is posted outside of the house. Isn't it terrible that this is a 'peace march?' I guess we better pray that it will be, but there are so many elements involved." [122]

As the culmination of the Stop the Draft Week, the protest began at the Lincoln Memorial where almost 100,000 protesters, including radicals, liberals, black nationalists, hippies, professors, women's groups, and war veterans, converged. After the rally, nearly 35,000 protesters marched across the Potomac River toward the Pentagon. Violence erupted when the more radical element clashed with soldiers and 236 federal marshals. [123]

Unable to "levitate the nerve center of American imperialism", the protest ended in violence that evening when marshals dispersed the crowd and made 683 arrests. The protest was paralleled by demonstrations in Japan and Western Europe. [124]

Antiwar sentiment had grown against a backdrop of social instability, a foundering economy, and the rising death toll. Urban race riots had threatened social tranquility, and the Administration repeatedly had to employ the Regular Army and National Guard to restore order.

Refusing to cut domestic programs or raise taxes significantly, the Administration had funded much of the war's steep cost with deficit financing, which resulted in inflation, soaring trade deficits, and rocketing interest rates. Even the staunchly anti-Communist *Wall Street Journal* wondered whether, "the U.S. is inflicting more injury on the Communists or on itself." In early August, Johnson had been compelled to ask for a 10% surtax to cover the increasing costs of the war. Polls taken soon thereafter revealed that for the first time most Americans believed that the U.S. had been mistaken to intervene in Vietnam. A substantial majority felt that despite the nation's growing investments, it was not "doing any better". [125]

More than 13,000 Americans had been killed in Vietnam, and the average death rate had grown from 477 per month in 1966 to 816 per month. Draft calls exceeded 30,000 per month. Military and civilian leaders alike understood that American deaths, not antiwar protests, were sapping public support. Public opinion of Johnson's management of the war had now fallen to 28%. [126]

Rusk had noted soon after the Gulf of Tonkin Resolution in 1964 that citizens were "already beginning to ask what we are supporting and why." The President had offered few satisfactory answers. To assert that the U.S. was supporting freedom rang hollow. In 1966, the military government in Saigon crushed the Buddhist movement, which demanded free elections and a civilian government, killing and wounding hundreds of civilians. After a rigged election in 1967, the curtailment of civil liberties became a hallmark of the Saigon regime. [127]

The American public's disaffection that began in 1964-1965 had burgeoned by mid-1967. It included both hawks who wanted to crush North

Vietnam even if it led to war with China and the Soviet Union, and an amorphous flock of doves who wanted the U.S. to quit the war. Relatively few doves engaged in active protests, while a much larger number opposed the war without publicly protesting. The protesters were splintered among pacifists, liberals who disliked the war on ethical and practical grounds, and "New Left" radicals who railed against capitalism and racism. Fractured by disputes, the antiwar movement lacked cohesive leadership and a national organization, so most protests had been small and local. A few had gained national significance, however, such as the Spring Mobilization to End the War, which had attracted hundreds of thousands. [128]

The antiwar protests encouraged Hanoi to hold out for victory. They limited the President's military options and may have thwarted any tendency toward more drastic escalation.

Wheeler was well aware of the domestic situation yet remained undeterred. In vain, he argued, "I would strongly urge the President not to have a [bombing] pause. I urge you to open up a ten-mile circle and also hit the Phuc Yen airfield." [129]

Perhaps most important, the disturbances and divisions triggered by the antiwar movement caused fatigue and anxiety among policymakers and the public, and thus eventually encouraged efforts to find a way out of the war. [130]

State of Equilibrium

In the fall and early winter, the Communists exposed their positions in order to engage U.S. forces in heavy fighting in III Corps Tactical Zone (CTZ) and all along the northern border of I CTZ. Westmoreland's commitment of additional U.S. Army forces to I CTZ created a vacuum that local Viet Cong sought to exploit by reconstituting their forces and reasserting their control over the rural population. Such Viet Cong revival had often preceded resurgence of Communist military activity at the district and village levels. Unable to shift any more U.S. Army units from II and III CTZs to I CTZ, Westmoreland requested the accelerated deployment of the two remaining brigades of the 101st Airborne Division from the United States. Arriving in

December, the brigades would join the growing number of U.S. Army units operating in the northern provinces.

Justifiably, Westmoreland pointed to modest progress in improving South Vietnam's security and to punishing defeats inflicted upon several North Vietnamese regiments and divisions. Yet, these successes had been insufficient to turn the tide of the war. The Communists had matched the buildup of U.S. combat forces. The number of enemy divisions in the South would increase from one in early 1965 to nine in early 1968. Despite heavy bombing of Communist lines of infiltration, the flow of men from the North had continued unabated, even increasing toward the end of the year.

Although Westmoreland had succeeded in averting defeat in 1965 and had gained valuable time for the Saigon government to concentrate its political and military resources on pacification, security in many areas of South Vietnam had improved very little. More and more, success in the South seemed to depend not only on Westmoreland's ability to hold off and weaken enemy main force units, but also on the equally important efforts of the South Vietnamese Army, Regional Forces, Popular Forces, and a variety of paramilitary and police forces to pacify the countryside.

The war seemed to be in a state of equilibrium. Only an extraordinary effort by one side or the other could bring a decision. [131]

McNamara's Final Memo

Meanwhile, antiwar sentiment had crept into the Administration. McNamara was foremost among those members who had begun questioning the war, and the first of three Secretaries of Defense who began as hawks and would morph into doves. [132]

Pressure for abandoning Westmoreland's search and destroy operations had mounted throughout the year. Increasingly disillusioned with high costs and a lack of results, McNamara pressed for a shift to small unit patrols that would be more "cost-effective" and reduce U.S. casualties. [133]

On 1 November, in what would be his last major policy memorandum to the President, McNamara laid bare his opposition to further escalation. He argued that while U.S. forces were making some progress, over the long haul, Washington stood no closer to victory.

"I emphasized that the Joint Chiefs' recommendations for bringing the conflict to a speedy conclusion – geographic expansion of the ground war and intensification of the bombing – gave no reasonable hope of doing so while carrying major risks of widening the war," McNamara recalled. "I therefore concluded the only sensible course involved 'the stabilization of our military operations in the South … along with a demonstration that our air attacks on the North are not blocking negotiations leading to a peaceful settlement.'" [134]

In the meantime, political opposition could easily outrun military achievements. McNamara proposed a study of military operations in the South to find ways to reduce U.S. casualties and transfer much of the responsibility to Saigon while "stabilizing" the war over a 15-month period and reorienting the bombing campaign. [135]

"In appraising alternatives, it is significant to review the list of military actions presented by the Joint Chiefs of Staff on October 17 in response to your request of September 12 for their recommendations of additional actions to bring the conflict to a speedy conclusion," McNamara wrote. "The striking fact is that none of them relate to our conduct of military operations in the South. Six would involve increased operations against North Vietnam – mining the ports and waterways, making greater use of our naval forces to attack North Vietnamese shipping and aircraft and expanding bombing in covert programs. The other four involve extension of our activities in Laos and Cambodia. I do not think adoption of any or all of these proposals would bring us significantly closer to victory in the next 15 months." [136]

The President was ensnared in a trap that he had unknowingly set for himself. His hopes of a quick and painless victory had been frustrated. He was desperately anxious to end the war, but he had been unable to do so by force, and in the absence of a clear-cut military advantage or a stronger political position in South Vietnam, he would not do so by negotiation. [137]

The President had McNamara's memo retyped to conceal the author's identity and then circulated it to senior officials for review and comment.

Clifford and Taylor knocked down McNamara's arguments hard. Rostow did likewise, warning Johnson against "being pushed off the middle ground you now hold" and allowing the Republicans to "move him and crystallize a majority around a stronger policy." Holding the line might lead to greater progress. Not surprisingly, the military was opposed to any program of stabilization and any bombing stand-down. [138]

Rusk knew McNamara had written the memo. He disputed McNamara's predictions but agreed with some of his positions. Significantly, both Rusk and Rostow now agreed with McNamara that no invasion of North Vietnam or Laos should be attempted. [139]

"I strongly oppose U.S. ground operations against North Vietnam, Laos and Cambodia," Rusk wrote to the President. "I would favor increased operations against infiltration routes through Laos, but not with U.S. combat units of significant size." [140]

"I agree strongly with Secretary McNamara that we should not extend ground operations into North Vietnam, Laos and Cambodia and should not go after foreign shipping, irrigation dikes or civilian centers," Rusk continued. "There are large forces in North Vietnam which have not been committed to South Vietnam. If we cannot deal satisfactorily with forces now in South Vietnam, I do not see how we could improve the position by taking on more than 300,000 additional forces in North Vietnam." [141]

"No one knows just where the 'flash point' is which would change the present rules in so far as Peking and Moscow are concerned," Rusk observed. "There is a very high risk that ground action against North Vietnam would cross the 'flash point.'" [142]

Katzenbach's response to McNamara's stabilization proposal was the most remarkable. Like the President, Katzenbach had begun to link North Vietnamese strategy to the antiwar movement in a way that Hanoi had not yet done. "The additional costs we can still impose on North Vietnam without invading [it] way far less in Hanoi's scales than the value of continuing a fight which they believe we will be prepared to abandon relatively soon." There was justification, Katzenbach believed, for "Hanoi's belief ... [that] public and congressional opinion will not permit the United States to keep meeting immense costs." Thus, Katzenbach emphasized, "*the war can be lost in the United States*." [143]

The crucial point in McNamara's argument was that it posed to the President directly and for the first time the proposition that the Vietnam War could be lost at home. Far from politics merely constraining Johnson's range of choices, it could determine the outcome. "Johnson and his predecessors had engaged the nation, but the nature of the war, Johnson's strategic decisions, and the international context made it impossible to win before political factors predominated," Prados asserts. "The antiwar movement was a consequence of those choices, not their antecedent." Katzenbach stated the result clearly: "Time is a crucial element at this stage of our involvement in Vietnam. Can the tortoise of progress in Vietnam stay ahead of the hare of dissent at home?" [144]

The primary influence for change came from the "Wise Men," a group of senior statesmen, including Acheson, U.S. Ambassador Arthur J. Goldberg, former Ambassadors Lodge and C. Douglas Dillon, as well as Bradley and Ridgway, from whom the President had periodically solicited advice. In early November, Johnson asked them for guidance on how to unite the public behind the war. Cognizant that public disillusionment threatened not only success in Vietnam but the internationalist foreign policy the U.S. had pursued since World War II, the Wise Men generally endorsed the President's policies but warned that "endless inconclusive fighting" was "the most serious single cause of domestic disquiet." To address this issue, they suggested adopting a "clear and hold" ground strategy that would stabilize the war at a "politically tolerable level," be less expensive in blood and treasure, shift greater responsibility for the fighting to the South Vietnamese, while saving South Vietnam "without surrender and without risking a wider war." [145]

Johnson would not initiate a change in strategy before the end of the year but did commit himself privately to review the conduct of ground operations with an eye toward reducing U.S. casualties and shifting more responsibility to the South Vietnamese. Once adopted following the Tet Offensive, this new strategy would become known as "Vietnamization." [146]

Although Johnson had begun to consider a change in strategy, he publicly vowed to see the war through to a successful conclusion. He did not reevaluate his policy objectives in Vietnam. If the possibility existed for eventual success, such a step would have been hard for any President to make. Johnson would have found it especially difficult. Hugely ambitious, Johnson had established high goals for his Administration and was unwilling to abandon them even in the face of personal frustration and massive public unrest. Johnson's persistence in the face of declining popularity was primarily a function of pride. Although he had not wanted the war, Johnson had committed his personal prestige to it to a degree that made it impossible for him to back off. He decided to stay the course in 1967 for the same reasons he went to war in the first place – because he saw no alternative that did not require him to admit defeat or failure. [147]

"Let us never forget that, in a democracy such as ours, it is the grave responsibility of the elected Commander-In-Chief to make the final decisions," Wheeler stated in a speech before the Armed Forces Staff College in late October. "He does so after carefully weighing the counsel he has obtained from the Congress and from his various advisors, including the military. I believe that a better understanding of this democratic process would be more helpful to all concerned." [148]

Wheeler added, "I believe that [this is] the proper attitude military men should take when called upon to respond to questions regarding differences of view between statutory civilian officials of our government and the Joint Chiefs of Staff." [149]

On 18 December, the President would write an unprecedented memorandum for record, which was virtually the only contemporaneous, considered, personal judgment by Johnson on the war. Johnson stated: "I see no basis for increasing U.S. forces above the current approved level." This meant there would be no wider war during the Johnson Administration. "As for the movement of U.S. forces across the frontiers of South Vietnam, I am inclined to be extremely reserved." [150]

The steady expansion of the war had spurred strong international and domestic pressures for negotiations, but the military stalemate had produced an equally firm diplomatic impasse. American officials would later count as many as 2,000 attempts to initiate peace talks between 1965 and 1967. Neither side could afford to appear indifferent to such efforts, but neither was yet willing to make the concessions necessary to bring about negotiations. Despite any firm evidence of results, the President had remained confident until mid-year that North Vietnam would eventually submit to U.S. pressure, and he feared that a conciliatory stance would undercut his strategy. To defuse international and domestic criticism, Johnson had repeatedly insisted that he was ready to negotiate, but he refused to make the concessions Hanoi demanded. As each side invested more in the struggle, the likelihood of serious negotiations diminished. [151]

"We failed miserably to integrate and coordinate our diplomatic and military actions as we searched for an end to the war," McNamara later admitted. [152]

Although the President had agreed with essential aspects of McNamara's 1 November memo, Johnson realized that he could not keep McNamara onboard. Their relationship had soured, and it was time to let him go.

"I had come to the conclusion, and had told [the President] point-blank, that we could not achieve our objective in Vietnam through any reasonable military means, and we therefore should seek a lesser political objective through negotiations," McNamara recalled. "President Johnson was not ready to accept that. It was becoming clear to both of us that I would not change my judgment, nor would he change his. Something had to give." McNamara would readily accept Johnson's later appointment to head the World Bank. [153]

Contributing to a joint policy document between the Departments of State and Defense that would govern political and military operations in Southeast Asia for the next four months, the Chiefs informed McNamara on 13 November that the single integrated strategy now being employed against North Vietnam and in the South was sound and would *eventually* lead to the achievement of US objectives in Vietnam. They had reviewed possible additional military measures that might provide more rapid progress but concluded that "there are no new programs which can be undertaken *within current policy guidelines* [author's emphasis] which will result in a rapid or significantly more visible increase in the rate of progress in the near term." [154]

The Chiefs suggested that a high-priority program to modernize and improve the South Vietnamese Armed Forces (RVNAF) as rapidly as possible could provide substantial results in a shorter period. "The sooner this capability is attained by RVNAF, the greater will be the flexibility available to the U.S. during negotiations and the post-hostility period," the Chiefs stated. Such a program, they noted, could not be accomplished within the resources and funds available to the Services without a major detrimental impact on other ongoing military programs, particularly in the equipment modernization of U.S. and Allied forces. Additional funding and production increases would be required. [155]

Westmoreland Returns to DC

Unlike McNamara, the military had not lost hope and gladly supported the Administration's "Success Offensive". Westmoreland returned to the States and expressed exuberant optimism in several highly publicized appearances. "I have never been more encouraged in my four years in Vietnam," he said on 15 November. [156]

Westmoreland's stirringly optimistic address to the National Press Club, telling the reporters that the war was being won, that U.S. forces were on the cusp of victory, posed a dilemma for Wheeler. While he supported Westmoreland's authority to make decisions in Vietnam, the commander's public pronouncements undercut Wheeler's argument for full mobilization. Then, too, while the U.S. had reached the bottom of the manpower barrel, with nearly 525,000 troops serving in South Vietnam, it appeared that Wheeler was just plain wrong about the need for mobilization. To all appearances, the U.S. would not require more troops in Vietnam. It was not losing and was not going to lose. In fact, it soon appeared that Westmoreland was right – the U.S. was starting to win the war. [157]

Owing to Westmoreland's public declarations of success, the hemorrhaging of public opinion ceased. Back in July, 10% of the population thought the U.S. was losing, 34% believed it was winning, and 46% considered the war a stalemate (10% had no opinion). By year's end, the figures would be 8%, 33%, and 51%, respectively (8% still had no opinion). However, in return for increased support, the Administration promised a victory soon. [158]

Many American citizens and the media still trusted the Administration's claims of progress and accepted military pronouncements at face value. Within their trust and optimism were the seeds of dismay and panic that would follow two months later when the Communists unleashed their massive, surprise Tet Offensive. [159]

A growing segment of the U.S. population was angered by the credibility gap, the disparity between what the Administration said and what it actually did. A pervasive mistrust of government had resulted. Rioting in the cities, an exploding crime rate, and unseemly demonstrations in the streets reflected the violence in Vietnam. Increasingly divided against itself, the public's anxiety over the war had not translated into a firm consensus for escalation or withdrawal. But the tired, angry, and frustrated public mood posed a more serious threat to the Administration than did the antiwar movement. Johnson sensed that a change in Vietnam strategy might be necessary. [160]

Wheeler addresses the President during a Tuesday luncheon, the White House Residence, Washington, DC, 22 November 1967. (LBJ Library)

On 24 November, Wheeler commented on Taylor's analysis of potential courses of action in Southeast Asia. Wheeler believed that the option of pulling back would be "tantamount to accepting defeat in a war which, militarily, we are winning." [161]

As for negotiating under the most favorable conditions possible, Wheeler cautioned, "There are substantial military and political dangers inherent in a cease-fire as a prelude to negotiations. In my view, a cease-fire should result from a negotiated political settlement, otherwise we might well afford the enemy opportunity to negate the successes which we have gained at considerable cost in blood and money." [162]

Regarding the option Taylor labeled "sticking it out", Wheeler remarked that the gradual increase in the weight and tempo of the bombing campaign had given the North Vietnamese two years to significantly improve their air defenses and to accommodate to the disruptive and destructive effects of airstrikes. "Unfortunately," Wheeler wrote, "we cannot recapture this lost time; this means that the shock effect of a quick, heavy and sustained air campaign on North Vietnam cannot be achieved at this late date." [163]

"I do not think we can afford to stand on the status quo," Wheeler added. "Our present actions have brought us successes in the military, political and psychological fields. However, the manner in which this policy has been implemented satisfies no one; hawks, doves and moderates all criticize both the policy and the results." He also emphasized that it was militarily disadvantageous to permit the Communists any sanctuaries from which they could operate with complete impunity. [164]

Instead, Wheeler recommended new authorizations for several offensive military actions against North Vietnam, including limited ground operations into Laos to destroy Communist base areas from which attacks against Allied forces were launched and supported. Should Sihanouk continue to permit sanctuary to North Vietnamese Army (NVA) units on Cambodian soil, the U.S. should conduct airstrikes against enemy base areas there. Limited ground actions could become necessary. "When weather and sea conditions permit, we should conduct an amphibious and airborne raid in force against NVA positions and facilities immediately north of the DMZ," Wheeler urged.

The U.S. should also reduce the sanctuaries around Hanoi and Haiphong to three nautical miles and 1 ½ nautical miles respectively and conduct an air campaign designed to isolate Hanoi and Haiphong from the rest of North Vietnam and from each other. [165]

Buttered-Up

Back in October, Wheeler explained to Armed Forces Staff College students the dual nature of his responsibility to the President and to the Congress, which "involves the seeming impossibility of obeying two masters who may agree on the requirement for military strength, but who are likely to disagree as to what constitutes that strength and as to how it should be attained." [166]

President Johnson and the Joint Chiefs of Staff, the White House Cabinet Room, Washington, DC, 4 December 1967. (LBJ Library)

With another round of congressional testimony coming up in early December, the President attempted to butter-up the Chiefs. Urging them to try to reconcile their differences with McNamara before testifying, Johnson pointed out the negative effects from the Stennis hearings in August. "These differences permit [Congress] to propagandize that we have deep divisions between the civilian and military leadership," Johnson said. "I certainly have seen no evidence of that while I have been here. I think you all are superior and stable and dependable." 167 Johnson then admonished the Chiefs:

You must take into account not only what you say but the effects of what you say. You must keep in mind the relation between the military committees of Congress and the Chief Executive. Some committee chairmen think they should run the strategy of the war rather than the President. I base this on all my years in the Congress. We do want the understanding of the committees, but it does not strengthen our system to air our differences. [168]

And then, Johnson flattered them:

I am pleased and proud of your performance, your competence, and your dedication. ... All of you know that you are welcome to visit me anytime you want. ... You can call my secretary and slip into the side door if you have some personal problem or some complaint. There is nobody that stands between you and me if the issue is serious enough to bring it up. [169]

The Administration was going into a very difficult period ahead, Johnson said.

We're going to have a new Secretary of Defense. Most people do not realize how much our wife means to us until she leaves us. Then you learn how difficult it is to do your own cooking. It is the same way with the Secretary. We're going to have to learn to work these things out. It will require all you can – particularly since this is going to be an election year and we are facing some serious financial problems. [170]

Cambodia

On 5 December, the President met with Rusk, McNamara, Wheeler, Helms, Clifford, and Rostow to discuss Westmoreland's request for an aerial attack against Communist sanctuaries in Cambodia. Their dialogue illustrates the positions of the President's senior advisors' and his deferral yet again of another important decision.

Wheeler indicated on a map the area in which intelligence believed that 5,000 enemy troops were "licking their wounds and getting re-equipped and having their manpower replenished" after the Battle of Dak To. The President asked how soon a decision was required. Possibly a week, maybe longer, Wheeler replied. [171]

Johnson asked if this operation would involve any invasion of ground troops. Wheeler replied no, that it would be limited to B-52 strikes along with tactical air.

The President asked if the operation would leak out. Both Rusk and Wheeler said there was no question about it. There would be leaks from South Vietnamese troops, and, of course, Hanoi would definitely announce it.

"The action which General Westmoreland is proposing would be a significant act of war against Cambodia," Rusk pointed out. [172]

This would change the entire character of the war. If Cambodia is attacked, they may ask the Chinese to side with them. Then we will really have a new war on our hands. If we take this action it would be absolutely essential to consult the Congress and our Allies. … It would be a major political burden for us to bear with a minimum military gain toward ending the war. [173]

Rusk continued, "If we could knock out 10% of this force why can't we do the same thing with the enemy divisions which we have clearly indicated in South Vietnam?" [174]

Wheeler said the big difference between the Communist troops in South Vietnam and those in Cambodia was clear. He said that the enemy in South Vietnam dug in well, took cover when B-52s approached, were constantly alert, and they did not expect attacks against them.

The President said, "Aware as I am of the mistakes generals have made in the past, I place great confidence in General Westmoreland. Both him and Ambassador Bunker have recommended this action." [175]

Rusk replied, "This problem is not really different from the one of mining Haiphong. We run the risk of enlarging the war." [176]

"I see this differently from mining Haiphong or bombing the ports," said the President. [177]

McNamara commented:

> This is analogous to a land invasion above the DMZ. This is not the most effective way to do it. This raises a basic issue of our policy, and I have thought that this would be the issue to face us in the coming year for some time. I believe, Mr. President, that it is most unwise to expand the war beyond the South Vietnamese borders. … This action would further divide this nation. This action would further increase our problems in the United Nations. Because of these two points, I would strongly recommend against this proposal. [178]

Wheeler interjected:

> I would not disagree with the importance Secretary Rusk and Secretary McNamara place on this issue. The real question we face is how long we can tolerate these people operating from the sanctuary. I take issue with Bob. Above the DMZ, we can bomb and use artillery against their positions. We cannot use our firepower in Cambodia. The Joint Chiefs do not want to widen the war either. We only wish Cambodia would be neutral – honest to God neutral, too. Anyone else would not permit enemy troops to use their territory for sanctuaries. [179]

"I am scared to death," McNamara said. "I am scared of a policy based on an assumption that by going somewhere else we can win the war. The war cannot be won by killing North Vietnamese. It can only be won by protecting the South Vietnamese so they can build and develop economically for a future political contest with North Vietnam." [180]

Rusk advised, "It may be that our main job is building a security in the center of the country. I have often wondered why we concentrate more on Con Thien and along the borders." [181]

Rostow added, "In the rhythm of things it would take months rather than weeks to rebuild after a defeat such as the one [the Communists] sustained [at Dak To]. We do have some time on our hands." [182]

The President asked whether all the Chiefs agreed with Westmoreland's recommendation. Wheeler replied that it was part of the Chiefs' four-month program for successfully and more quickly concluding the war.

The President then stated:

> As I see it, this act could result in Cambodia declaring war against us and in their inviting the Chinese in. Walt Rostow said he did not think Cambodia would bring the Chinese in. … We should go back to General Westmoreland and tell him we do not see the justification on an immediate decision on this. Ask for more details from him and also ask for more information from Bunker on why he supports this decision. Tell them all the reasons why we don't see this as a good decision. [183]

1967 Recap

"Our military position is greatly improved," Rostow observed on 12 December. The number of U.S. troops in South Vietnam had grown from 385,000 to almost 490,000. The number of maneuver battalions had risen from 265 to 278. In the air, 28 tactical fighter squadrons were now available to provide close air support and assist the interdiction campaign, and the number of B-52 sorties had risen sharply from 725 to 1,200. [184]

"Although the tide of battle is running against Hanoi, they are not yet convinced that they cannot win," Wheeler stated publicly on 18 December. Hanoi was not yet ready to negotiate an end to the war. "Realistically, we must accept that they will not be ready to negotiate nor cease aggression until they believe defeat is inevitable. By defeat, I do not mean military occupation of North Vietnam nor the destruction of the Communist government in Hanoi." Defeat, Wheeler explained, would be Hanoi's recognition and acceptance of the fact that it could not impose its will on the people of the South by force of arms or by political victory in the United States. [185]

"The single most important factor in prolonging the war is Hanoi's calculation that there is a reasonable possibility of a change in U.S. policy before the ultimate collapse of the Viet Cong manpower base and infrastructure," Wheeler stated. "In a very real sense, the major campaign of the war has been and is being fought here in the United States." [186]

"As far as the future is concerned ... I must point out that the North Vietnamese are not yet at the end of their military rope," Wheeler stated presciently. Although North Vietnam and the Viet Cong were feeling a manpower pinch, they still possessed the ability to send additional troops to South. "Thus, there is still some heavy fighting ahead — it is entirely possible that there may be a Communist thrust similar to the desperate effort of the Germans in the Battle of the Bulge in World War II." [187]

The first phase of Hanoi's new strategy had worked perfectly. Westmoreland had responded to North Vietnamese attacks in October and November at Con Thien, across the Laotian border, and towns near Saigon and in the Central Highlands, as well as to the opening of a siege on Khe Sanh by quickly dispatching reinforcements to these areas. While driving back the North Vietnamese and inflicting heavy losses in each case, U.S. forces had become dispersed and left the cities vulnerable. This had enabled Viet Cong units to infiltrate into the cities and towns, accumulating supplies and making final plans. By year's end, the attention of Westmoreland, the President, and much of the American public was riveted on Khe Sanh, which many assumed was an attempt by Hanoi to replicate Dien Bien Phu. [188]

CHAPTER 7

Turning Point
(January – March 1968)

The Tet Offensive would prove the most disastrous defeat North Vietnam suffered in the long war. Paradoxically, it would also be the North's most resounding victory during the years of American military presence.
— Lieutenant Colonel David R. Palmer, 1978 [1]

Solid Progress

On 1 January 1968, General Leonard F. "Chappy" Chapman, Jr. succeeded Greene as Commandant of the Marine Corps. "I thought a great deal
of Chappy," Spivy recalled. "He was a very solid, down to earth kind of guy. He
tended to be very cooperative with the rest of the Chiefs, even though he had
his own views. … He was a good, solid Marine, not a brilliant man, but one
who had a good sense of values." [2]

By this date, the U.S. had been involved in military operations in
Vietnam for over seven years and in major ground combat operations for
two-and-a-half years. The U.S. now had 485,000 troops in South Vietnam.
Westmoreland had employed them aggressively in all parts of the country
to pursue Communist main force units and help shield the population from
enemy attack. American and Allied forces had conducted hundreds of operations both large and small, and 40 of them had achieved a verified body count
of 500 or more enemy soldiers. According to Military Assistance Command
Vietnam (MACV) estimates, 81,000 Communist soldiers had been killed in
1967, giving substance to Westmoreland's belief that the Allies were slowly
winning the war in Vietnam.

Other trends seemed to confirm Westmoreland's optimism. While the American public seemed to be growing weary of recitations of statistics, the Administration continued to put faith in them as a means of making sense of a war that was so difficult to measure. Pacification trends were especially heartening. By 1967, two-thirds of South Vietnamese hamlets were assessed as secure and under control of the Saigon government. Whereas in early 1965, the government was being chased from the countryside and on the verge of collapse. Meanwhile, Communist troop strength in South Vietnam had dropped by one-quarter to 220,000, the result both of attrition on the battlefield and diminished infiltration from the North and recruitment in the South. In 1965 and 1966, some 9,000 North Vietnamese Army (NVA) soldiers traversed the Ho Chi Minh Trail monthly, whereas in 1967 the figure declined to 6,000 a month. Viet Cong recruitment in the villages had fallen to half its previous monthly average of 7,000. This all gave vital breathing space to the Saigon government as it expanded its security programs in the countryside and prepared to assume more responsibility for the main force war from the United States. Westmoreland reported that if all went well, he could initiate a phased withdrawal of U.S. forces in 1970. Not even suspicious signs of enemy movement, concentrations, and an upsurge of terrorism in the cities dampened optimism issuing from Saigon and Washington. [3]

Westmoreland reported that he intended to pursue the enemy throughout South Vietnam, thereby improving conditions for the pacification program to proceed at an ever-increasing pace. He wanted to engage enemy forces as far as possible from populated areas to provide security for the major population centers. Unlike wars of the past, he viewed terrain as of only temporary tactical significance, except for the cities, towns, and other highly populated areas, as well as certain invasion or infiltration corridors.

As 1968 began, MACV intelligence verified massive Communist troop movements toward Saigon, Da Nang, Hue, Khe Sanh, the demilitarized zone (DMZ), and several provincial and district capitals. It also began receiving numerous reports about a major offensive to be undertaken just before or immediately after Tet, the Vietnamese national holiday somewhat akin in significance to Christmas, New Years, and the Fourth of July combined. [4]

As with Johnson's Success Offensive, the Communists promised victory, which would come not against the U.S. but against the South Vietnamese, who would be the Tet Offensive's foremost targets. Through a collapse of military resistance, the North Vietnamese hoped to subvert public confidence in the Saigon government's ability to provide security, thus triggering an urban-based general uprising — a crescendo of popular protest to halt the fighting, overthrow the government, and force a political accommodation. [5]

The offensive sought to weaken U.S. confidence in the South Vietnamese government, discredit Westmoreland's claims of progress, and strengthen American antiwar sentiment both among government officials and the public at large. These unfavorable conditions would bring the U.S. to the negotiating table and hasten its disengagement from Vietnam. The Communists did not anticipate this would be the offensive's most important outcome. [6]

Khe Sanh

The Communist offensive began in mid-January in the remote north-west corner of South Vietnam. Once again, the Marine base at Khe Sanh became the focus of Communist activity in I CTZ. Located astride Route 9, an east-west highway, the Khe Sanh plateau commanded the approaches from the west to Dong Ha and Quang Tri City and to the coastal corridor leading to Hue. If U.S. forces did not occupy the Khe Sanh area, the North Vietnamese would have an unobstructed invasion route into the two northernmost provinces from which they might outflank Allied positions south of the DMZ – positions that blocked North Vietnamese attacks from the north.

Had Westmoreland possessed sufficient combat forces, the Khe Sanh airfield and nearby security base would have been less critical. Westmoreland would have preferred to operate in this area with mobile forces, but at the time, MACV possessed neither adequate combat forces in I CTZ nor the logistical capacity to support them. The weather was a critical factor, as well. Poor visibility due to low clouds and persistent ground fog during the northeast monsoon season (January to March), made helicopter movement hazardous if not impossible much of the time. [7]

North Vietnamese forces appeared to be moving into the Khe Sanh area to stay. Detection of an NVA front headquarters indicated that at least two enemy divisions were massing in the area. Actually, three NVA divisions were on or near the Khe Sanh plateau, while over three more were operating between the DMZ and Hue. [8]

The NVA buildup around Khe Sanh dramatically changed the security situation. The road over which the base had received the bulk of its supplies had been cut in August 1967. Increased enemy anti-aircraft fire seriously threatened aerial resupply by helicopters and fixed-wing aircraft landing at Khe Sanh. The bulk of the 135 tons of supplies required daily had to be air-dropped to the Marine and South Vietnamese Army (ARVN) defenders.

Lacking sufficient forces to counteract the NVA buildup with ground attacks, Westmoreland decided to reinforce with firepower instead of man-power. Increased enemy troop and logistical movements into the area, while menacing to the garrison at Khe Sanh, presented a unique opportunity to employ concentrated U.S. airstrikes against known enemy positions on a sustained basis. Westmoreland directed his staff to plan for a massive aerial bombardment program. Named Operation NIAGARA, the concept called for aerial bombs and artillery rounds to fall in such volume as to suggest the enor-mous waterfall for which the operation was named. Phase One of the opera-tion would consist of intensive intelligence gathering to locate enemy forces. Phase Two would consist of coordinated B-52 tactical airstrikes on a round-the-clock basis against the located targets. [9]

On 21 January, the NVA initiated the Battle for Khe Sanh with a heavy barrage of artillery and rocket fire that destroyed almost all the base's ammu-nition and fuel supplies. Operation NIAGARA commenced on the same day and would run through late March. [10]

The undeniable threat in the Khe Sanh area greatly concerned the President and Westmoreland. Some observers likened the situation to that at Dien Bien Phu, the isolated garrison where the Viet Minh had defeated French forces in 1954. [11]

Wheeler briefs the President and McNamara on the eve of the Tet Offensive, the White House Cabinet Room, Washington, DC, 29 January 1968. (LBJ Library)

"I don't want any goddamn 'Din Bin Phoos,'" Johnson said on the afternoon of 28 January. Near panicked, he demanded that Wheeler order his colleagues to provide assurance that the U.S. forces inside the base would not be overrun and that the Chiefs guarantee a victory in writing. Wheeler returned the following day with the Chiefs and a memo signed by each of them, stating their approval of Westmoreland's plans for Khe Sanh. Wheeler was confident; not only would Khe Sanh hold, he promised, but the drop in Viet Cong activity in South Vietnam had buoyed the Chiefs' flagging spirits. With Khe Sanh well in-hand, Wheeler told the President the time was ripe to increase pressure on North Vietnam. Johnson was unconvinced.[12]

The Joint Chiefs of Staff with the President and McNamara on the eve of the Tet Offensive, the White House Cabinet Room, Washington, DC, 29 January 1968. (LBJ Library)

Wheeler was exhausted by the seemingly interminable debate on U.S. strategy that continued to divide the Administration. "I'm sick of this niggling," he confided to an aide. Wheeler was frustrated by the ambiguity engendered by the U.S. strategy. Khe Sanh might turn out to be a victory, but he was sure it would not be a decisive, war-ending victory. There was also the chilling thought that Khe Sanh would only be a prelude for further North Vietnamese Army actions. While enemy activity in the South had fallen off, there was no sign the North Vietnamese were any more willing to negotiate an end to the war than they had been in 1965. Wheeler remained convinced that mobilization and ground combat operations in North Vietnam were the only ways to escalate the war beyond the point where North Vietnam could continue to bear the cost. All he needed was a spark, an event that would trigger one last debate over the American involvement. For once, the war cooperated. [13]

Wheeler describes the military situation in Vietnam to the President, the White House Cabinet Room, Washington, DC, 29 January 1968. (LBJ Library)

General Offensive-General Uprising

As NVA pressure increased around Khe Sanh, 84,000 other Communist troops were preparing for the Tet Offensive across South Vietnam. Most of their meticulous preparations went undetected, although Westmoreland's intelligence determined something big and unusual was brewing. Growing edgy, Westmoreland pulled thirteen battalions closer to Saigon before the attack, nearly doubling U.S. strength around the capital. However, concern over the critical situation at Khe Sanh and preparations for the Tet holiday festivities preoccupied most Americans and South Vietnamese. Even when Viet Cong forces prematurely attacked Kontum City, Qui Nhon, Da Nang, and other towns in the central and northern provinces on 30 January, the U.S. was unprepared for what followed. [14]

The Tet holiday began on 29 January. As had been observed in previous years, a cease fire went into effect that evening and would run through 31 January. Westmoreland made an exception for I Corps Tactical Zone (I CTZ), which was imperiled by increased Communist activity. The Viet Cong also announced a seven-day truce to run through 3 February. Many South Vietnamese Army (ARVN) soldiers and government officials went on leave to visit their families. Under cover of this subterfuge, the Communists launched attacks of unprecedented scale. [15]

"There is no doubt in my mind that the pattern of enemy actions in the opening months of 1968 arose because of Hanoi's growing awareness that they were losing the military conflict," Wheeler would state publicly six months later. "Giap's objectives were becoming more remote. There is an analogy to a gaming situation here: *never* change a winning game; *always* change a losing effort. I credit Giap for seeing his situation clearly and changing his 'game.'" [16]

On the night of 30 January, North Vietnamese Army (NVA) and Viet Cong forces in I and II CTZs prematurely violated the truce and struck several population centers twenty-four hours before attacks were launched across South Vietnam. [17]

Catching U.S. and ARVN forces largely by surprise, the Communists initially bombarded or attempted to invade 36 of 44 provincial capitals, 5 of 6 autonomous cities (including Hue and Saigon), 64 of 242 district capitals, more than 50 hamlets, and several military installations, including most airfields. [18]

Westmoreland was so preoccupied with Khe Sanh that he initially thought these countrywide attacks were a diversion and that the main assault was still to come against the remote base.

MACV's chief of intelligence acknowledged that even if he had known exactly what the NVA and Viet Cong were about to do, "It was so preposterous that I probably would have been unable to sell it to anybody. Why would the enemy give away its major advantage, which was its ability to be elusive and avoid heavy casualties?" [19]

Once the initial shock and confusion wore off, most Communist attacks were crushed in a matter of days. During those few days, however, the fighting was some of the most violent ever seen in the South. While some attacks succeeded in penetrating into some of South Vietnam's largest cities, including ten provincial capitals that fell under at least partial Communist control, most were beaten back within a few days. By 2 February, Allied forces had cleared almost all towns and cities, except for Saigon and Hue, where heavy urban fighting would endure for weeks. [20]

The situation was particularly grave in northern I CTZ, where the Viet Cong and NVA threatened to sever the Allies' logistical lifeline. Writing to Wheeler on 9 February, Westmoreland observed that logistics would be the key to winning the fight in the northern provinces. [21]

The most tenacious combat occurred in Hue, which was infiltrated by sixteen NVA and Viet Cong battalions. These forces were engaged by the 1st Cavalry and 101st Airborne Divisions, U.S. Marines, and South Vietnamese forces, including the South Vietnamese 1st Infantry Division.

The ancient capital city, Hue had a tradition of Buddhist activism with overtones of neutralism, separatism, and anti-Americanism. North Vietnamese strategists thought that, if anywhere, the General Offensive-General Uprising might gain a political foothold in Hue. Hence, they committed almost seven NVA regiments to the battle, bringing several units down from Khe Sanh, an indication that the stakes were higher in Hue than elsewhere in the South.

Raising the Communist banner above the ancient citadel, the attackers announced the formation of a Revolutionary Government and a New Alliance for National Democrat and Peace Forces in anticipation of splitting off the northern two provinces from the rest of South Vietnam during Phase Two of the general offensive.

During the only extended urban combat of the war, house-to-house and street-to-street fighting caused enormous destruction. The Tet Offensive culminated in late February when the last Communist forces were driven out of Hue. [22]

Ultimately, the Tet Offensive produced no battlefield victories for the Communists, no new territory gained, and within I CTZ alone, they lost the equivalent of three divisions. Many Viet Cong operatives had come out into the open for the first time, which made them vulnerable to retribution. Communist forces attacking in the open were vulnerable to superior American firepower, mobility, and flexibility. The result was extremely high losses of experienced combatants and seasoned political cadres, estimated at more than 30,000 dead or captured, with thousands more wounded. Most devastating, the Viet Cong suffered a major military defeat, seriously weakening the insurgent base in the South. [23]

The South Vietnamese Respond

Although the Communists extended their control in rural areas and temporarily crippled pacification efforts, they misjudged the urban population's revolutionary temper. No urban revolts occurred. Contrary to Hanoi's expectations, the South Vietnamese people did not swing to the Communist banner.

Communist attackers employed Soviet-made rockets against population centers, notably in Hue and Saigon, which to this point had been relatively free from attack. Many South Vietnamese for whom the war had been a mere annoyance were outraged, not the least by news that the Communists executed almost 3,000 civilians at Hue.

Stunned by the attacks, civilian support for the central government of President Nguyen Van Thieu coalesced instead of weakened. Capitalizing on the new feeling, Thieu would enact for the first time a general mobilization. The shift from grudging toleration of the Viet Cong to active resistance provided an opportunity to create new local defense organizations and to attack the Communist infrastructure. Spurred by U.S. advisors, the South Vietnamese would begin to revitalize pacification. [24]

Initially, South Vietnamese Army (ARVN) forces were caught off guard, and many sustained high casualties while bearing the brunt of the assault. However, the ARVN fought surprisingly well in throwing back the enemy throughout the country. Contrary to Communist expectations, not a single ARVN unit defected to their cause, and few desertions occurred. [25]

Despite being surprised, U.S. forces reacted to the Tet Offensive with incredible mobility and firepower, and the U.S. presence remained unshaken. [26]

Khe Sanh

The North Vietnamese Army (NVA) would not launch a major assault against the base during the Tet Offensive, but continued to harass the beleaguered Marines with indirect fire. During the first week of February, the NVA launched three, heavy ground attacks against the base and its outposts. [27]

For weeks after Tet exploded, Wheeler and Westmoreland spoke every day over secure phone and exchanged a flurry of back channel cables with Sharp about operational requirements and opportunities.

"Our situation at Khe Sanh as compared with the French at Dien Bien Phu is different in three significant respects," Westmoreland explained to Wheeler and Sharp on 3 February. Westmoreland had tactical air support and B-52s for all-weather attack of enemy forces by orders of magnitude over that at Dien Bien Phu. He had reinforcing heavy artillery within range of the Khe Sanh area. He had multiple and vastly improved techniques for aerial supply, and Khe Sanh was within helicopter support range for troop reinforcement, logistic support, medevac, and other requirements. [28]

That same day, Wheeler informed Westmoreland of the President's concern that the situation would become so serious "that he would be confronted with a decision to use tactical nuclear weapons to redress the balance – a decision which he does not want to be forced to make." [29]

Westmoreland replied, "The use of tactical nuclear weapons should not be required in the present situation," since he had received permission to use a special artillery ammunition with greatly improved antipersonnel capabilities. However, should the situation in the DMZ change dramatically, "We should be prepared to introduce weapons of greater effectiveness against massed forces. Under such circumstances, I visualize that either tactical nuclear weapons or chemical agents would be active candidates for employment." [30]

PACIFIC GROVE / BLUEBERRY

Wheeler informed Sharp and Westmoreland on 1 February that he had discussed with the President an amphibious feint north of the DMZ. Stressing that such an operation had not been approved, Wheeler suggested they develop a deception plan to create the impression that an amphibious landing north of the DMZ was being planned. Reconnaissance, airstrikes, naval gunfire, and deception measures would be incorporated. Outloading of troops into amphibious shipping was not authorized, nor would amphibious shipping be moved north of an extension of the demarcation line between North and South Vietnam. The U.S. did not want to provide the North Vietnamese any justification to later claim they had defeated an amphibious landing. [31]

Sharp was dubious that the deception operation could achieve the desired results within the limitations imposed on it. He also agreed with Westmoreland's reply on 3 February that "the timing and intricacies involved in the planning and execution of strategic deception operations of the type suggested are not considered responsive to the immediate needs created by the current tactical situation." [32]

Three days later, Wheeler informed Sharp that during the weekly White House luncheon, alternative courses of action to relieve pressures on Khe Sanh were discussed. "One of these actions was the diversionary amphibious operation, which was authorized for planning purposes in a modified version. In view of the interest shown in this operation during this meeting, it would be desirable to continue planning activities." [33]

On 10 February, Sharp informed Wheeler that his staff would proceed with the planning of Operation PACIFIC GROVE, the name given to the amphibious deception operation. Several actions appeared to be feasible and should be included in the concept.

A conference would be convened at U.S. Pacific Command headquarters on 14 February to complete the required planning. Sharp requested that a Joint Staff representative provide a list of possible strategic deception support measures.

Other staff planning conferences and coordination visits should be conducted. Planned movements of units in South Vietnam could enhance the theme of a buildup in northern I CTZ to support an impending amphibious operation in North Vietnam. Advance force operations could be conducted to include reconnaissance and area preparation by air and naval gunfire bombardment. Amphibious shipping could maneuver south of an extension of the demarcation line while utilizing communication deception. [34]

Two days later, Wheeler informed the Chiefs that he had charged Major General William E. DePuy, his Special Assistant for Counterinsurgency and Special Activities (SACSA), to support Sharp on the amphibious deception plan, which the Joint Staff had codenamed Operation BLUEBERRY. [35]

Ultimately, the operation was overtaken by events. Once the Tet Offensive was largely contained, the operational requirement for an amphibious deception was negated. Wheeler remained convinced that offensive ground operations on North Vietnamese territory were the sure way toward victory, and perhaps events might yet warrant them.

Reinforcements

The central issue in back channel cables between Wheeler and Westmoreland now shifted. "Do you need reinforcements?" Wheeler asked him on 8 February. The Pentagon could provide the 82nd Airborne Division and about half of a Marine Corps division, "both loaded with Vietnam veterans. However, if you consider reinforcements imperative, you should not be bound by earlier agreements. … [The] United States government is not prepared to accept defeat in Vietnam. In summary, if you need more troops, ask for them." [36]

Westmoreland responded later that day, "It is only prudent plan for the worst contingency, in which case I will definitely need reinforcements." [37]

In case of a setback in Quang Tri and Thua Thien Provinces, Westmoreland would have the Marines make an amphibious landing near

Quang Tri City to establish a beachhead, put the 82nd Airborne Division ashore through the beachhead, then employ the beachhead as a base for offensive operations in the DMZ-Quang Tri area. Surf conditions would permit the operation to commence in April.

"[Westmoreland] had absolutely no reserve, none," Wheeler recalled. "He had not a single American unit, nor was there a single Vietnamese unit that was not committed. Therefore, if there came a second wave of attacks and if the [South] Vietnamese forces began to disintegrate, he would have been left in a rather precarious position." [38]

The following day, Wheeler suggested that additional forces might be desirable earlier than April. "Please understand that I am not trying to sell you on the deployment of additional forces which in any event I cannot guarantee. However, my sensing is that the critical phase of the war is upon us, and I do not believe you should refrain from asking for what you believe is required under the circumstances." [39]

"[Wheeler's] were encouraging words that confirmed my own convictions," Westmoreland recalled, "yet in the past every troop request had undergone such detailed scrutiny and had evoked such alarm in the press that I may have become less than aggressive in my demands." [40]

Westmoreland began to appreciate Wheeler's reasoning. "It seemed to me that for political reasons or otherwise, the President and the Joint Chiefs of Staff were anxious to send me reinforcements. We did a little sparring back and forth. My first thought was not to ask for any, but the signals from Washington got stronger." [41]

By persuading Westmoreland to request additional troops for Vietnam, Wheeler knew *a priori* that presidential approval of such a request would be harmful to U.S. capabilities throughout the world. Wheeler hoped the rejection would finally compel the President to mobilize the strategic reserve so that the U.S. could meet its worldwide commitments. [42]

Meanwhile, Taylor had asked Wheeler to provide "arguments with which to confute publicly the allegation that the United States is militarily overextended." [43]

"I believe I should reemphasize the concern that the Joint Chiefs of Staff have expressed previously regarding our current restrictive worldwide military posture vis-à-vis our commitments," Wheeler responded. "In addition, we have conveyed our concern to the Secretary of Defense by way of periodic Posture Papers, in response to DPMs, and more frequently and informally through personal contact. There have been no developments which would serve to allay our concern. Recent events have tended to deepen it." [44]

American forces were stretched tightly to prosecute the war in Southeast Asia and maintain minimum essential deployments to Europe and the Western Pacific, Wheeler noted. Any subsequent contingency that required significant U.S. forces could only be met by redeployment of forces from Southeast Asia or by mobilization of reserve forces. [45]

"Needless to say, I would welcome reinforcements at any time they can be made available," Westmoreland replied to Wheeler on 9 February. "It is conceivable that a six-month loan of these [reinforcements] would turn the tide to the point where the enemy might see the light or be so weakened that we could return them," Westmoreland noted. "In summary, I prefer a bird in the hand than two in the bush." [46]

White House Discussons

Back in Washington that same day, the President met with Rusk, McNamara, Clifford, and Rostow. "I want you to lay out for me what we should do in the minimum time to meet a crisis request from Vietnam if one comes," Johnson said.

"I understand the tactical situation around Khe Sanh, but I do not see the strategic situation very clearly," Rusk admitted. "Is there some way we can turn this around and take the offensive ourselves?"

McNamara replied, "The answer from the Joint Chiefs will be to try a false offensive or an actual invasion against North Vietnam above the DMZ. They will say we should develop a feint or invade north of the DMZ."

"This is more of a political decision than a military one," Rusk advised. [47]

General Earle G. Wheeler, the White House Cabinet Room, Washington, DC,
9 February 1968. (LBJ Library)

After Wheeler and the Chiefs joined the meeting, the President stated, "I want a military review of the problems confronting us if the enemy continues more of the same activities as during the past two weeks." Johnson felt the Administration should "anticipate all the surprises and determine what is going to confront us if the Viet Cong attacked the cities, attack Khe Sanh, and pull off a few surprises elsewhere." He had two questions for the Chiefs: "Will we have to put in more men? Can we do it with the [South] Vietnamese as they are now?"

"During the past few days, I have talked with General Westmoreland over the phone and received a number of cables from him," Wheeler replied. "Westmoreland needs reinforcements for several reasons. The reinforcements he has in mind are the 82nd Airborne Division and the six-ninths of a Marine division … to prevent the [South Vietnamese Army] from falling apart; to give himself a reserve to use as quick response units to any initiatives by the enemy in Vietnam; [to reinforce] I Corps [Tactical Zone] permitting amphibious forces to be available at all times; [and to] make available troops for an amphibious landing north of the DMZ if that action is decided upon."

Wheeler added, "The 82nd Airborne and the six-ninths of Marine division can only be deployed if we eliminate the restrictions on frequency of tours and length of tours in Vietnam."

"We should give some very serious thought to the proposal of scrapping the 12-month tour," McNamara replied. "It might have a very bad effect on morale."

"Can we speed up the other infantry battalions we have already promised?" The President asked.

"Johnny" Johnson replied, "We have already curtailed training to the minimum. We must give these units proper training time. They are already squeezed. One battalion is scheduled to go to the last week in March. Three battalions are scheduled to go the last week in April."

"If General Johnson says that is the case then I will accept it," McNamara said. "I would like to look more at this. Perhaps these units could be sent on short training into rear areas."

Johnson retorted, "Mr. Secretary, there are no rear areas in Vietnam anymore."

"All last week I asked two questions," the President said. "The first was did Westmoreland have what he needed? You answered yes. The second question was, can Westmoreland take care of the situation with what he has there now? The answer was yes. Tell me what has happened to change the situation between then and now."

"Since December, the North Vietnamese infantry has increased from 78 battalions to 105 battalions," Wheeler explained. "Estimating there are 600 men per battalion that is approximately 15,000 men. ... This represents a substantial change in the combat ratios of U.S. troops to enemy troops."

"What you're saying is this," the President said. "Since last week we have information we did not know about earlier. This is the additional 15,000 North Vietnamese in the northern part of the country. Because of that we need 15 U.S. battalions?"

"The last report was that there was approximately 15,000 enemy near and around Khe Sanh," Wheeler replied. "As of today, our estimates range between 16,000 and 25,000. ... In addition, Westmoreland is now faced with the problem of the impact of these recent heavy attacks on the [South Vietnamese Army (ARVN)]. We do not know what is going to happen to the ARVN after the second round of attacks. All ARVN units are on maximum alert. But in Hue, the ARVN airborne units are down to 160 men per battalion. Their strength is far below that required."

"There's a very strange contradiction in what we are saying and doing," Clifford observed. "I think we should give some very serious thought to how we explain saying on one hand the enemy did not take a victory and yet we are in need of many more troops and possibly an emergency call-up [of the reserves]."

"The only explanation I can see is that the enemy has changed its tactics," said the President. "They're putting all of their stack in now. We have to be prepared for all that we might face. Our front structure is based on estimates of their front structure. Our intelligence shows that they have changed and added about 15,000 men. In response to that, we must do likewise. That is the only explanation I see."

"The enemy has changed the pattern of the war," Wheeler confirmed. "In the past, there have been instances of terrorism, but this is the first time they have mounted coordinated attacks throughout the country."

The President then changed the subject. "Is there anything new on the *Pueblo*?"

"No," Wheeler replied ominously, "except the North Korean Prime Minister says that North Korea is ready for another war."[48]

In another meeting on 11 February, the President and his senior foreign policy advisors were confused by Westmoreland's cable from two days earlier.

"I want to be completely clear in my mind," the President said. "Is it true that General Westmoreland is not recommending or requesting additional troops now?"

"That is true," Wheeler replied.

Johnson asked, "Is it your judgment not to send additional troops today?"

"Yes, sir," Wheeler replied.

"I am out of tune with this meeting," Taylor spoke up. "I read General Westmoreland's cable differently from you. As I read it, Westmoreland's forces are tied down. He has no reserves except some units of the 101st."

"If General Westmoreland is requesting troops in this cable, he has a poor Colonel doing the drafting for him," Rusk said.

"I interpret it as a man who wanted 600,000 troops last year and was talked down to 525,000," the President said. "Now he is saying he could use the 82nd and the portion of a Marine division because of all the uncertainties which face him. He is concerned about the effective fighting capabilities of the ARVN. I think we should send anything available to get the number up to the 525,000 limit. We should live up to our commitment. 'Just before the battle Mother' the [Chiefs are] now recommending against deploying emergency troop units."

"At this time, yes, sir," Wheeler replied. [49]

The following day, Westmoreland clarified his requirements to Sharp and Wheeler. "I am expressing a firm request for additional troops, not because I fear defeat if I am not reinforced, but because I do not feel that I can fully grasp the initiative from the recently reinforced enemy without them." On the other hand, Westmoreland added, a setback was fully possible if he was not reinforced. [50]

New Ball Game

Once it became apparent that the Communists had dealt themselves a major defeat, Westmoreland, Sharp, Wheeler, and the Chiefs sensed the splendid opportunity to seize the initiative. "I feel that during the past week, although plagued with unpleasantness, we have inflicted the heaviest casualties of the war on the enemy and have also prevented him from taking a single city," Westmoreland had informed Wheeler and Sharp on 4 February. "The next several days may well give us additional opportunities." [51]

Rostow sensed it, as well.

I knew we would defeat the enemy, and after we had, he was going to be down psychologically and was going to be weakened. It was like two boxers in a ring. If you have your opponent on the ropes, that's the time to bore in. It is not the time to throw in the towel. That was the time to really move in and we would have had him by the jugular vein. [52]

Perhaps, Wheeler thought, *here is an opening to recommend MULE SHOE.*

"If the enemy has changed his strategy, we must change ours," Westmoreland wrote on 12 February. "On the assumption that it is our national policy to prohibit the enemy from seizing and permanently occupying the two northern provinces, I intend to hold them at all cost. However, to do so I must reinforce other areas and accept a major risk, unless I can get reinforcements, which I desperately need." [53]

"We are now in a new ball game where we face a determined, highly disciplined enemy, fully mobilized to achieve a quick victory," Westmoreland stated. He is in the process of throwing in all his 'military chips to go for broke.' … We must seize the opportunity to crush him." [54]

"We face a situation of great opportunity as well as heightened risk," Westmoreland concluded. "However, time is of the essence here, too." He did not see how the Communists could long sustain the heavy losses that their new strategy was enabling the U.S. to inflict on them. "Therefore, adequate reinforcements should permit me not only to contain his I Corps [Tactical Zone] offensive but also to capitalize on his losses by seizing the initiative in other areas. Exploiting this opportunity could materially shorten the war." [55]

The Chiefs sent a memorandum to McNamara on 12 February that summarized Westmoreland's view of Tet developments. Although Westmoreland remained optimistic and claimed between 30,000 and 40,000 enemy losses, he admitted uncertainty about new attacks and conceded that three-quarters of the North Vietnamese Army's regular forces had never been engaged. While the public was told that the ARVN was fighting very well, five of its nine airborne battalions were now rated ineffective; the average ARVN battalion had half or fewer of its soldiers present for duty; and desertions had increased. [56]

Although admitting that the situation was still too fluid to articulate firm recommendations, the Chiefs noted several serious problems with fulfilling

Westmoreland's request for reinforcements. For one, the need existed to maintain a minimum capacity to deal with civil disorder in the United States. The deployment of additional forces to Southeast Asia would also strain the U.S. global military posture. The Chiefs, therefore, recommended measures to call-up additional reserve units and bring existing units up to increased combat readiness. [57]

In another meeting between the President and his senior foreign policy advisors that same day, confusion still reigned over Westmoreland's troop request.

"It looks to me like Westmoreland wants to take advantage of an opportunity to exploit the situation," Rusk stated. "I do not read it as a desperate need. He wants to shorten the war with it, and that has a certain attractiveness to all of us."

"I read the Westmoreland cable differently from Dean," said McNamara. "I read that he needs the six battalions in order to avoid defeat at Khe Sanh."

"General Westmoreland makes it clear that he cannot permit the enemy to make gains in other areas," Clifford added. "He does not want to permit a reduction in strength elsewhere. But he has now sent what is clearly an urgent message."

"General Westmoreland has been conservative in his troop requests in the past," Wheeler said. "Now he finds that his campaign plan has been pre-empted by enemy action."

"Westy said he could use troops one day last week," the President said. "Today he comes in with an urgent request for them. … I want to anticipate that more will happen to us than we had planned. … I have a mighty big stake in this. I am more unsure every day."

Johnson then asked, "Do all of you feel that we should send troops?" McNamara, Rusk, Helms, Wheeler, Taylor, and Rostow all replied yes. The President then asked if there were any objections. There were none.

"The Joint Chiefs feel that if you deploy these men there should be a call-up of the reserves," Wheeler stated. "If we send a brigade of the 82nd

Airborne, we should call up two brigades from the Army National Guard. This would total about 30,000 men."

"I want you and Bob McNamara to get together and come in with an agreed recommendation as to whom to call up," the President replied.

"I will call now and get my men drafting the order," an excited Wheeler replied.

After Wheeler left the room, McNamara said, "My position on Vietnam is very clear. I do not think it wise to go to the Congress asking for additional legislation. I do not think the call-up is necessary."

The President replied, "Well, if you cannot agree with the Joint Chiefs on what is needed, then submit to me a minority viewpoint and your separate recommendations." [58]

On 13 February, the Chiefs informed McNamara that the 82nd Airborne Division represented the only readily deployable Army division in the Conus-based active strategic reserve. More ominously, they warned, "The impending reduction of this division by one-third to meet approved deployments establishes an immediate requirement for its prompt reconstitution which is possible only by the call-up reserve units." The Chiefs were essentially saying that it was possible to send additional troops to Vietnam so long as the Administration realized that in doing so they were stripping the country of any internal protection, a chilling prospect for a president faced with nation-wide civil disorders. [59]

The following day, McNamara asked the Chiefs how further troop deployments to Vietnam could be met. "They can't be," Wheeler replied. Without reconstituting the strategic reserve, the U.S. simply could not afford to send more troops to Westmoreland, regardless of how serious the situation became. [60]

"I was … confused when a … message from General Wheeler informed me that he would be unable to fulfill my 'request' because he lacked the troops," Westmoreland recalled. [61]

"I had in the back of my mind a couple of other things," Wheeler recalled. Without mobilization, the U.S. had overcommitted itself. In addition

to Westmoreland's request for substantial reinforcements, North Korea's seizure of the American naval vessel, USS *Pueblo*, a week before the Tet Offensive,
and a new flare-up in Berlin aroused fears that additional troops might have
to be dispatched to these perennial Cold War trouble spots, as well. Available
forces were nearly exhausted, and Wheeler and the Chiefs worried that unless
the U.S. mobilized the reserves, it could not meet its global commitments.[62]

"Admiral Sharp was especially concerned about the possible demand for
withdrawal of Republic of Korea units from South Vietnam," Westmoreland
recalled. "Our planners in Washington shared his concern because of the tense
situation in Korea produced by attempted assassination of South Korean officials, incidents in the DMZ, and by the *Pueblo* incident. In a message dated 1
February 1968, Admiral Sharp had advocated 'contingency planning for the
return of ROK forces from RVN to Korea.'"[63]

"I have argued, am arguing, and will argue," Wheeler would state in
a public speech in August, "for an American military posture which is (1)
Strong, but not belligerent; (2) Too determined to be frightened and too strong
to be defeated; and (3) Unwavering, despite setbacks, disappointments, and
opposition in following the course which we know is the right path to organize
a stable and durable peace."[64]

The Army could only deploy a few more combat units to Vietnam without making deep inroads on forces destined for NATO or South Korea. The
dwindling strategic reserve left the President with fewer options now than
he had in the summer of 1965. Furthermore, Army units in the continental
United States had often been required to enforce Federal civil rights legislation
and to restore public order in the wake of civil disturbances.[65]

On 16 February, Rostow informed Wheeler that, while no decisions
had been made, the President was thinking along the lines of a call up of a
40,000-man reserve unit force; a request to Congress for the funding required
for this call-up plus additional troops for Korea; and no extension of terms
of service. The President reportedly did not understand the need to call-up
individual reservists.

Noting that the Chiefs had advocated a call-up of 46,300 reservists, Wheeler requested Spivy to have the Joint Staff to start work immediately to refine the Chiefs' current paper on minimum and desirable actions to improve the U.S. posture in Southeast Asia. "In particular," Wheeler directed, "I believe that we must lay out clearly and support with facts (tabular if possible) the benefits which would be derived from authority to extend terms of service and call up individual reserves." [66]

Ultimately, the President refused to sanction a major troop levy but did provide Westmoreland with modest reinforcements to bolster the northern provinces. Scraped from the bottom of the strategic reserve barrel, these included the 27th Marine Regimental Landing Team (RLT) deployed to Da Nang on 23 February; the 3rd Brigade, 82nd Airborne Division deployed to Chu Lai on 26 February; plus 13,500 support troops. These deployments raised the total U.S. troop strength authorization to 549,500.

The President also called to active duty a small number of reserve units, totaling some 40,000 men, for duty in Southeast Asia and South Korea — the only use of reserves during the Vietnam War.

For Westmoreland, Johnson's decisions meant that future operations would have to make the best possible use of U.S. forces and that the South Vietnamese Army would have to shoulder a larger share of the war effort. [67]

The U.S. Public Reacts

To Westmoreland, Wheeler, and many other senior military officers, the similarities between the Tet Offensive and the Battle of the Bulge were obvious. Tet was a massive defeat for North Vietnam and the Viet Cong. Hanoi, like Nazi Germany, had now made itself vulnerable to counterattack. [68]

But Westmoreland's ever-optimistic assertions rang hollow back home, as Americans viewed a much different picture on their TV screens. "Tet struck at America — not South Vietnam — with shock and awe," writes Prados. The widespread attacks and the fighting for the U.S. Embassy contradicted all the press releases. Pacification was set back everywhere, as was only too obvious. The infamous photo of the summary execution of a Viet Cong guerrilla by the Saigon chief of police challenged any notion that the Saigon government was one of laws and procedures. The battle for Hue refuted the argument that Hanoi had no staying power. The siege of Khe Sanh negated the talk of light at the end of the tunnel. And all this happened on film, recorded by journalists throughout Vietnam and played back every day on American television screens and in print media.[69]

"The Tet Offensive of 1968 was a tremendous victory for the North Vietnamese in the United States," Wheeler recalled. "Actually, it was a very substantial military defeat for them. They really got themselves creamed, but the way it was played in the press here created in the minds of the American people the same effect that the outcome of the First Battle of Bull Run did. There was more gloom and doom around Washington than somewhat."[70]

Wheeler briefs the President and members of Congress on the unfolding Tet Offensive, the White House Residence, Washington, DC, 31 January 1968. (LBJ Library)

Moral and practical questions and criticisms about the war and the way it was being waged had spread far beyond the traditional peace groups and critics of U.S. foreign policy to include members of the House and Senate, businessmen, clergy, and even some retired military officers. In consequence, public opinion turned decisively against the war. One poll showed 56% in favor of U.S. withdrawal from Vietnam. A month later, a Harris poll recorded the view that Tet represented a U.S. failure to attain its objectives in Vietnam.[71]

On 27 February, CBS News anchorman Walter Cronkite told the nation, "It seems now more certain than ever that the bloody experience of Vietnam will end in a stalemate." Widely considered a bellwether, Cronkite asserted, "To say that we are closer to victory today is to believe, in the face of the evidence, the optimists who have been wrong in the past." The President recognized this pronouncement for what it was. Johnson told associates that when he lost Cronkite, he had lost the country.[72]

Westmoreland recalled:

> In retrospect, I believe that I and officials in Washington should have tried to do more to alert the American public to the coming of a major offensive. Through my reports to the Joint Chiefs, Washington civilian authorities knew all that I knew, yet they too failed to foresee the importance of preparing the American people for it. The order of the day at the White House remained low-key. As a consequence, the offensive seemed to many in direct contradiction to President Johnson's campaign to demonstrate progress in the war, a refutation of my remarks at the [National] Press Club two months earlier. Few bothered to recall that historically a force on the downgrade often tries to recover by means of some spectacular surge.[73]

Johnson's "Success Offensive" had boomeranged, leaving journalists with a sense of betrayal that caused them to question everything thereafter. As South Vietnamese Ambassador Bui Diem put it, "In a sense, the shock effect of the enemy offensive was created in part by Washington itself."[74]

The U.S. Government Reacts

"The term 'fog of war' has been employed by countless writers on military subjects to describe the uncertainties faced by field commanders as to the intentions, strength, location, and capabilities of wily, elusive, and determined enemies," Wheeler explained in a public speech two months earlier. "Historically, success has rewarded those who have best been able to peer through the fog of war and distinguish fact from rumor, fancy, apprehension, wishful thinking, exaggeration, and distortion."[75]

"The Vietnam War is the foggiest war in my own personal experience," Wheeler continued. "Moreover, it is the first war I know of wherein the fog of war is thicker away from the scene of conflict than on the battlefield — or so it seems to me."[76]

Despite the operational victory that the U.S. Military Assistance Command, Vietnam (MACV) proclaimed, the U.S. had suffered a strategic defeat, much in the same way the Sioux victory at Little Big Horn, or Japan's success at Pearl Harbor, presaged strategic defeat. Juxtaposed against the Administration's "Success Offensive", Tet had a cataclysmic political and psychological effect in the U.S., vitiating the illusion of progress and convincing many political elites that the war could not be won at an acceptable cost.[77]

Journalist Ward Just wrote, "Tet was a sobering experience from which American officials in Washington still have not recovered. Could the estimates ever be true again? 'It is very strange,' Ward quoted a U.S. Embassy official in Saigon. 'After Tet, Washington became very pessimistic, and we became very optimistic. Before, it was the other way around.'"[78]

To the extent that the North Vietnamese intended for the Tet Offensive to influence the United States, they succeeded, for it sent instant shockwaves across the nation. Tet left Washington in a state of "troubled confusion and uncertainty."[79]

While Administration officials publicly echoed Westmoreland's statements that the attacks had been repulsed and that there was no need to fear a major setback, Johnson and his advisors were shocked by the sudden mass and magnitude of the offensive. Intelligence estimates were much more pessimistic than was Westmoreland. Many officials feared that Tet was only the opening phase of a larger Communist offensive. Some felt that Khe Sanh was still the primary objective, a fear that seemed to bear out when the besieging North Vietnamese Army forces renewed their attack in early February. Others feared a major offensive in the northern provinces or a second wave of attacks on the cities. An "air of gloom" hung over White House discussions, Taylor later observed. Wheeler likened the mood to that following the Battle of Bull Run in 1861.[80]

Publicly, the President responded with stubborn determination to hold the line at any cost. Conveying a sense of urgency, Johnson insisted that Khe Sanh be held and advised Westmoreland that he would send whatever reinforcements he needed to defend the besieged camp or meet any other threat. In the first few weeks after Tet, the President's main concern seemed to be to "get on with the war as quickly as possible," not only by sending reinforcements, but also by stepping up air attacks against North Vietnam.[81]

On 7 February, the President sent the following quote from British philosopher John Stuart Mill to Wheeler and his other senior foreign policy advisors, perhaps not only to bolster their morale, but his own:

> War is an ugly thing, but not the ugliest thing: the decayed and degraded state of moral and patriotic feeling which thinks nothing is worth a war is worse. ... A man who has nothing which he cares about more than his personal safety is a miserable creature who has no chance of being free, unless made and kept so by the exertions of better men than himself.[82]

Privately, the President's confidence had been punctured, and he was unnerved by the ongoing siege of Khe Sanh, which seemed a parallel of Dien Bien Phu.

Bunker sent a steady stream of upbeat cables to Washington, as did Westmoreland. The CIA's daily reporting from across Vietnam was less optimistic, however. Doubts had been sown.[83]

Some senior civilian Department of Defense officials had begun thinking in terms of de-escalation in Vietnam. In a 13 February letter to Clifford, Under Secretary of the Air Force Townsend W. Hoopes II argued for a reduction in the bombing level. "Reducing the intensity of the war tempo ... could materially improve the [sic] the course of our staying the course for an added number of grinding years without rending our own society."[84]

Wheeler's Assessment

Dismayed by pessimistic intelligence estimates, the President dispatched Wheeler to South Vietnam to assess the situation first-hand. "As you would surmise," Wheeler informed Westmoreland, "the Administration must face up to some hard decisions in the near future regarding the possibility of providing you additional troops, recouping our strategic reserves in [the continental United States], and obtaining the necessary legislative support in terms of money and authorities." Johnson and McNamara had decided to defer consideration of these matters until Wheeler's return. [85]

Departing Washington on 21 February, Wheeler arrived in Saigon two days later with DePuy and Ambassador Phillip C. Habib, the Deputy Assistant Secretary of State for East Asian and Pacific Affairs. "When General Wheeler arrived," Westmoreland recalled, "I found him a tired man, seemingly near the point of exhaustion." [86]

Wheeler and Westmoreland at Tan Son Nhut Air Base, Republic of Vietnam, 23 February 1968. (Office of the Chairman of the Joint Chiefs of Staff)]

On the night of Wheeler's arrival, an enemy rocket exploded near his quarters. Fearing that Wheeler had been deliberately targeted, MACV insisted that he move into a room next to Westmoreland in the Combat Operations Center. For three days, Wheeler conducted a breakneck round of meetings and conversations with Westmoreland, his staff, and senior commanders to gather facts and develop recommendations. [87]

It was obvious to the Chiefs that the Communists had expended much of their combat power and that the strategic initiative was ripe for seizure by the Allies. Once the strategic reserve had been reconstituted and the nation put on a virtual war footing, resources would be available for achieving victory in Vietnam. The Chiefs, therefore, saw Tet not as a repudiation of past efforts in Vietnam but as an opportunity to attain their military objectives by eliminating the detestable restrictions that had hampered previous efforts. [88]

Wheeler explained his logic to Westmoreland: McNamara was leaving the Administration, and the hawk Clark Clifford was replacing him as Secretary of Defense. True, Tet was a victory, an exasperated Wheeler said, but here was a chance to make the victory stick. "General Wheeler came over there and he was actually begging me to ask for more troops," Westmoreland recalled. "Really, just begging me. And he told me the President was ready to call up the reserves, and if that were to happen how many men would I need, how many men would I use." [89]

Academic commentator Duane W. Thorin presciently assessed shortly before Tet that absent seizure of the strategic initiative, U.S. forces in South Vietnam "could win all the battles and still lose the war." Strategic initiative for U.S. ground forces in the South could be gained only if they were authorized to pursue the enemy when he fled across borders for sanctuary, and to occupy or at least to threaten to occupy territory in North Vietnam. Strategic initiative for U.S. air and naval forces required that they be permitted to prevent military supplies from entering North Vietnam, as well as attempting more aggressively to destroy those supplies in storage and in transit to the South. Finally, Thorin argued, strategic initiative required a clear declaration and demonstration that the Hanoi regime would be destroyed or seriously damaged unless it halted its aggression against the South. [90]

Confident they could exploit the Communists' weakened state and buoyed by the President's apparent willingness to send substantial reinforcements, Wheeler and Westmoreland seized the "great opportunity" to revive their proposals to expand the war.

Westmoreland recalled, "I envisaged a new approach to the war that would take timely advantage of the enemy's apparent weakness; for whereas our setback on the battlefield was temporary, the situation for him as it developed during February indicated that the enemy's setbacks were, for him, traumatic."[91]

The North Vietnamese Army and Viet Cong could not afford the heavy losses they had sustained during Tet, and with large numbers of additional U.S. troops, Westmoreland was certain he could gain the upper hand. By taking the offensive at a time when the Communists were overextended, Wheeler and Westmoreland were confident they could shorten the war.[92]

"The American generals believed this to be the golden moment to lean heavily on Hanoi in a strong effort to end the war. ...[They] devised an offensive strategy which they believed would end the war quickly and decisively," Dave Palmer wrote. "They wanted to go for the jugular. It was high time to break out of the attrition straitjacket, to go after the enemy in his sanctuaries."[93]

Wheeler wanted to execute Operation MULE SHOE. There was still time to prepare for and execute an amphibious operation into North Vietnam within the optimal weather and surf window so long as the President authorized it before April.[94]

Westmoreland's and Wheeler's offensive strategy would also apply greater pressure on the Communists throughout South Vietnam. They would expand territorial security by destroying the Communists' guerrilla and main force units and by neutralizing their traditional base areas. They would accelerate the bombing campaign in North Vietnam, to include striking more productive targets, such as the port of Haiphong. They would cut the Ho Chi Minh Trail, the enemy's main infiltration route for men and supplies, and they would raid the Communists' border sanctuaries in Cambodia and Laos.

"Such a campaign, coming rapidly after the defeat of the enemy's maximum effort, the Tet Offensive, had the prospect of destroying his will to win and his desire to prolong the war," Westmoreland recalled. "In any case, it would so weaken the enemy that it would be possible to proceed more rapidly with my plan for withdrawing American troops and turning the war over to the South Vietnamese." [95]

"We reviewed in depth the various contingencies which would influence our future troop requirements in South Vietnam," Westmoreland added, "and we prepared an outline plan for the deployment of additional forces." [96]

Wheeler and Westmoreland settled on the figure of 206,000 troops, a sum large enough to meet any contingency in Vietnam and force mobilization of the reserves. This number was the exact figure that Wheeler had brought with him from Washington, the figure that resulted from the study he had ordered the Joint Staff to complete in answer to his question of just how many troops it would take to "trigger" a reserve call up. Wheeler convinced Westmoreland that 206,000 was exactly the total number of reinforcements he needed. [97]

"There was the question of getting the reserves in the bank," Westmoreland recalled. "The availability was the first thing, and then deployment would be in accordance with what the requirements were and what the strategy would permit. … In other words, the requirements would materialize only if the reappraisal of national policy being conducted in Washington resulted in the approval of new strategic objectives." [98]

Consistent with his "one thing at a time" approach, Wheeler convinced Westmoreland to defer his recommendations on proposed changes in strategy until the President had approved the new troop level. "General Wheeler told me to hold off on long-range requirements," Westmoreland recalled. "As he had explained a number of times in regard to dealing with the Secretary of Defense and the White House, 'We can only handle one problem at a time.'" Keenly aware of Johnson's opposition to widening the war, Wheeler feared that if he presented the case for additional troops based on an optimistic assessment and an offensive strategy, he would be turned down again. Troops, not strategy, offered the "stronger talking point." [99]

Westmoreland observed:

> The Chairman of the Joint Chiefs of Staff has a difficult job living with his civilian bosses, the Secretary of Defense and

the President, striving to convince them in terms they can understand of matters that he views as military necessity and, in General Wheeler's case, within the concept of one thing at a time. One thing at a time was all he could hope to accomplish. Since Vietnam was the visible part of the iceberg, the part he knew was perturbing his civilian bosses, Vietnam rather than the strategic reserve was the context in which to present the request for additional troops. If he could gain authority to raise the troops, exactly what was to be done with them could be decided once the troops were actually available. [100]

"General Wheeler and I saw only a 50-50 chance that President Johnson would accept a more aggressive policy, but that seemed sufficient odds," Westmoreland recalled, "in view of the rewards that might be realized, to justify an effort to promote a change." [101]

"I stopped in Honolulu and conferred with Admiral Sharp and his people," Wheeler recalled. "We went over the whole program. And we began to work the problem then, as to units, call up of reserves, increases in the draft, and all the rest of it." [102]

Westmoreland had not seen the trip report that Wheeler forwarded from Honolulu to McNamara and the White House on 27 February. "Making no mention that I was considering more troops in the hope of exploiting the enemy's defeat, nor making any allusion to the need to rebuild the strategic reserve, General Wheeler, probably as a tactic, emphasized uncertainty, that the enemy 'had the will and the capability to continue' a high level of attacks." [103]

Wheeler emphasized in his report the gravity of the situation in South Vietnam and said nothing about a new strategy, about contingencies that would determine the level of forces required there, or about reconstituting the strategic reserve for possible use independent of Vietnam. Wheeler's omission would have significant, unintended consequences on how Washington and later the American public viewed his report. [104]

Wheeler was fully aware of the unconducive political reality at home. Public approval for the President's conduct of the war had sunk to an all-time low of 26% during Tet. None of the President's civilian advisors favored expansion of the war or another large troop increase. Evidence of growing public discontent with the war confirmed that it would be politically disastrous to escalate the war. [105]

And yet, foremost in Wheeler's mind was the maxim that *wars, once fought, should be fought to achieve victory*. Warfighting doctrine made clear to the President's military advisors that to achieve victory, the U.S. and its Allies must conduct *offensive* ground, air, and naval operations in sufficient *mass* against the *objectives* of the North Vietnamese armed forces in their sanctuaries in North Vietnam, Laos, and Cambodia.

Wheeler's comment that the U.S. must be "prepared to accept some reverses" was calculated to sway the President — who had already made clear that he was not willing to accept defeat — to accept the recommendation for large-scale reinforcements and its implied corollary of mobilization. "By presenting a gloomy assessment, Wheeler hoped to stampede the Administration into providing the troops to rebuild a depleted strategic reserve and meet any contingency in Vietnam," says military historian George Herring. "His proposal reopened in even more vigorous fashion the debate that had raged in Washington throughout 1967." [106]

"I can hardly fault General Wheeler's approach," Westmoreland recalled. "Imbued with the aura of crisis in Washington, he at least partially discounted the sanguine briefings I and my staff had given him. In any event, he saw no possibility at the moment of selling reinforcements in terms of future operations. Who among the civilians would appreciate a policy of exploiting the enemy's defeat, of reinforcing success? Having read their newspapers, who among them would even believe there had been success? Better to exploit their belief in crisis to get the troops, then argue new strategy later. One thing at a time." [107]

In his report to the Administration, Wheeler did not mention the best-case scenario, a stabilization of the situation in Vietnam with few additional forces required. Neither did he mention reconstitution of the strategic reserve,

the possibility of an expanded strategy, or the fact that all three troop increments would be needed in Vietnam only to support an expanded strategy.
Wheeler put the worst-case scenario forward as though it represented the current situation in South Vietnam.

"I emphasized how Westy's forces were badly stretched, that he had
no capability to redress threats except by moving troops around," Wheeler
recalled. "I emphasized the threat in I Corps [Tactical Zone]. More attacks on
the cities were, I said, a possibility. I argued that Westy needed flexibility and
capability. I talked about going on the offensive and taking offensive operations, but I didn't necessarily spell out the strategic options." [108]

Wheeler arrived at rain-soaked Andrews Air Force Base at 6:00 AM on
28 February and proceeded straight to the White House for a special breakfast
meeting with the President and his senior advisors. [109]

Wheeler reported that he had talked to Westmoreland and all the senior
U.S. commanders. He had also talked with Bunker, Thieu, and Ky. There were
several factors that surprised him. "I certainly learned things I did not know
before," Wheeler stated. The margin of victory was very thin in a number of
battles. What the future intensity of the conflict would be was unknown. As for
American forces, they were in good shape. Westmoreland had asked for three
reinforcement packages. The total request came to 205,000 men. [110]

"What are the alternatives?" asked the President.

"The only alternative to this, in our judgment, is a decision to be prepared to give up areas in lieu of more troops," Wheeler replied. "Without the
reserve, we should be prepared to give up the two northern provinces of South
Vietnam. This, of course, would be a political hazard. It also would give the
North Vietnamese a strong position for negotiating. It would, I believe, cause
the collapse of the ARVN."

"What about taking the initiative ourselves?" the President asked. "Is
there anything we can do other than just sitting and waiting for them to attack?"

"As far as new bombing efforts there is nothing new in the cards,"
Wheeler replied. "We could plan an amphibious operation in the North, but
we do not have the capacity to do it at this time." [111]

"General Westmoreland has asked for 105,000 additional men by May 1," McNamara added. "He has asked us to do it in 60 days, but I don't think we can do it in less than 90 to 120 days." McNamara explained the reinforcements would come in two increments from a call up of the reserve. There would be two call ups in the Army, the first for 90,000 and the second for 70,000. There would be about 50 to 60 thousand Marines called and about 20,000 Navy and Air Force. This would total about 250,000 in all. In addition, the U.S. would need to extend tours up to six months and increase the draft call in May. [112]

In his parting shot as Secretary of Defense, McNamara warned the President about the economic costs of further expanding the war. "As I see this total program, it would add $2 ½ billion to the 1968 budget," McNamara stated. "It would increase the 1969 budget by $10 billion. It would increase in 1970 budget by about $15 billion. Of course, we would have to expand production of helicopters, ordnance, airpower, and ground support equipment." [113]

Later that day, Wheeler and the Chiefs were among hundreds of spectators standing in the rain outside the Pentagon's River Entrance as the President presided over a "cold, wet, and miserable" Joint Honors Ceremony for the departing McNamara. "Rain marred the honor ceremony and forced cancellation of the flyover," McNamara recalled. Presenting McNamara with the Medal of Freedom, Johnson said, "For seven years … you have brought a new dimension to defense planning and decision-making." [114]

"For seven years, it had been 'McNamara's war,'" Dave Palmer observed. "His cybernetic strategy of graduated response, and his scarcely concealed disdain for military advice, had inexorably brought the fighting to its present unquantifiable situation." [115]

"The [troop] request may have been doomed from the start in any event, for it ran head-on into another proposed new strategy," Westmoreland recalled. "That was de-escalation, to include a bombing halt, that Secretary McNamara had begun to promote the preceding November. … It was easy, also, for many of the President's advisors to discern the incongruity between my public statements on the enemy's military defeat and General Wheeler's portrait of continuing crisis." [116]

"Unaware of the crisis context in which the Chairman of the Joint Chiefs of Staff had presented the case for reinforcements, unwilling to accept that a crisis existed, and having had no word of any change in national policy, I was in no position to answer the questions in terms of the options that I hoped a change in policy and the reinforcements would enable me to exercise," Westmoreland recalled. "Thus I was unable to make a strong presentation on behalf of the reinforcements." [117]

On 1 March, Westmoreland chimed-in on Wheeler's report, merely reiterating that "additional forces would serve to forestall the danger of local defeats. … With the total additive combat forces requested it will be possible to deal with the invader from the north." [118]

Khe Sanh

Meanwhile, Khe Sanh was heating up again. Enduring an eleven-week period of heavy bombardment, the besieged U.S. Marines and South Vietnamese Army Rangers would resist and throw back all attacks. On 23 February, the base received 1,307 rounds of mortar, rocket, and artillery fire, but North Vietnamese Army (NVA) troops never penetrated beyond the base's outer perimeter. [119]

NIAGARA, the intensive air interdiction operation, continued to provide excellent results around Khe Sanh. For 77 days, U.S. Air Force, Navy, and Marine aircraft provided around-the-clock, close-in support to the defending garrison. Between 22 January and 31 March, tactical aircraft would fly an average of 300 sorties daily, close to one every five minutes, and expend 35,000 tons of bombs and rockets. At the same time, B-52s flew 2,062 sorties, dropped over 75,000 tons of bombs during the siege, and were instrumental in preventing the NVA from massing in large formations. Marine and Army artillery fires supplemented aerial firepower, firing over 100,000 rounds into the area at an average rate of 1,500 rounds per day. [120]

During the early evening hours of 29 February, multiple sensors detected a major movement of NVA troops along Route 9. Massive U.S. firepower from artillery, radar-guided fighter bombers, and B-52 airstrikes pounded the NVA's route of march. The badly depleted NVA 304th Division attempted three assaults against the base over the night of 29 February-1 March, but supporting joint fires prevented the assaults from gaining momentum.

Although the North Vietnamese continued to harass the base, to probe for weaknesses along its perimeter, and to shell it from a distance, they shifted tactics to a less aggressive posture. By mid-March, intelligence indicated that major NVA units were withdrawing away from the Khe Sanh area. [121]

By the time the siege of Khe Sanh ended on 30 March, more than 24,000 fighter-bomber and 2,700 B-52 sorties had pulverized the NVA positions. [122]

"Khe Sanh will stand in history, I am convinced," Westmoreland later wrote, "as a classic example of how to defeat a numerically superior besieging force by coordinated application of firepower." [123]

Meanwhile, once the immediate Tet emergency subsided and the siege of Hue was reduced, Westmoreland had instructed his staff to begin planning for the relief of Khe Sanh. U.S. Army reinforcements would deploy into the area, lines of communication would be opened, and supplies would be reconstituted.

Operation PEGASUS - LAM SON 207 would begin on 1 April with U.S. Army, U.S. Marine, and three ARVN airborne battalions moving along Route 9 from Ca Lu toward Khe Sanh. The 1st Cavalry Division would affect the relief of Khe Sanh one week later. [124]

A-Z Review

Meanwhile back in Washington, Clifford had been sworn-in as Secretary of Defense on 1 March. In part, the President had appointed Clifford to replace the dovish McNamara because he was adamantly pro-war. It would take little time, however, for Clifford to join the doves. [125]

The Chiefs were relieved when McNamara's retirement was announced. In Clifford, they believed they were getting someone who shared their hawkish views and would be much easier to work with than McNamara. Unlike McNamara, Clifford had asked the Chiefs for their opinions, and not only had he been respectful and honest, but he had seemed to value their views, even if he had not always agreed with them. [126]

Secretary of Defense Clark M. Clifford and Wheeler, the White House, Washington, DC, April 1968. (LBJ Library)

A crisis atmosphere already hung over the Administration when Wheeler's trip report struck like a bombshell. "Wheeler's call for an additional 206,000 troops had all the subtlety of a high-megaton blast," author Mark Perry writes. Shocked by Wheeler's pessimistic assessment, which CIA estimates corroborated, the President was stunned by the magnitude of Westmoreland's huge troop request. [127]

From the military's viewpoint, the 206,000-troop request was prudent, reasonable, and would provide for a wide variety of contingencies, whether dangers or opportunities. Few civilians saw it that way. The massive reinforcement would further Americanize the war in Vietnam while bringing the war home to the U.S. with greater impact than ever before. The hundreds of thousands of Reservists, National Guardsmen, potential draftees, and their families would be most immediately affected, but all Americans would feel the effects in higher taxes, more pressure on the dollar, greater inflation, and above all, more domestic turmoil. [128]

Westmoreland, Sharp, Wheeler, and the Chiefs saw no need for a new strategy, but instead foresaw an opportunity to finally pursue the strategy they had for so long advocated. The massive troop request could not have been revealed at a worse time psychologically. In the existing atmosphere, an increased American effort in Vietnam was politically unacceptable to a larger segment of the American public.

The choices Wheeler had presented were unattractive ones. To accept and meet Wheeler's and Westmoreland's request for troops would mean a total U.S. commitment to South Vietnam, a further Americanization of the war, a large call-up of reserve forces, and a need to put the economy on a semi-war footing to meet vastly increased expenditures – all in an election year and at a time of growing domestic dissent, dissatisfaction, and disillusionment about the purposes, conduct, and cost of the war. On the other hand, to deny their request for troops, or to attempt again to cut it to a size that could be sustained by the thinly stretched active forces, would surely signal that an upper limit to the U.S. military commitment in South Vietnam had been reached and that a satisfactory end to the war had been pushed far into the future. [129]

Disinclined to make a hasty decision on a matter fraught with such grave implications, the President gave Clifford three days to conduct a complete reassessment, an "A to Z" review, of the way forward in Vietnam. [130]

"The Clifford Task Force," as it became known, included McNamara, Rusk, Helms, Wheeler, Taylor, Katzenbach, and a few others. With the grim instruction to "give me the lesser of evils," the President undoubtedly expected hawkish advice from Clifford. [131]

This difficult task would engender the most soul-searching debate within the Administration during the whole history of the war as to what course of action to take, historian Herbert Schandler notes. "In the end, it would become one of the most controversial episodes in recent American history." [132]

Clifford seized the opportunity. The magnitude of Westmoreland's troop request was such that it demanded careful scrutiny. Clifford had consistently defended the President's policies in Vietnam, but his newness to the job and his need to clarify many fundamental issues also led him toward a full reassessment. Thus, he immediately began raising at the highest levels questions that had been avoided for years. [133]

When asked by Clifford if a military victory could be won, Deputy Assistant Secretary of State for East Asian and Pacific Affairs Philip C. Habib answered, "Not under the present circumstances."

"What would you do?" Clifford asked.

"Stop bombing and negotiate," Habib replied." [134]

Clifford asked the Chiefs whether 206,000 men would be enough. If not, then how many more would be needed? The Chiefs could not provide definite answers. "The military was utterly unable to provide an acceptable rationale for the troop increase," Clifford concluded. [135]

Clifford asked Wheeler, "What is the plan for victory?"

"There is no plan," Wheeler replied.

"Why not?" Clifford asked.

"Because American forces operate under three restrictions," Wheeler explained. "The President has forbidden them to invade the North, lest China intervene; he has forbidden the mining of Haiphong harbor, lest a Soviet supply ship be sunk; he has also forbidden pursuing the enemy into Laos and Cambodia because that would widen the war, geographically and politically." [136]

Clifford soon came to appreciate that "these and other restrictions which precluded an all-out, no-holds-barred military effort were wisely designed to prevent our being drawn into a larger war." [137]

Clifford asked, "Given the circumstances, how can we win?"

"The United States is improving its posture all the time," Wheeler could only reply. "The enemy cannot afford the attrition being inflicted on him; at some point he will discover there is no purpose in fighting anymore." [138]

There was no consensus as to when this elusive psychological objective would be achieved. Thus, the decision as to when to end the war was left in the hands of the North Vietnamese. [139]

Clifford instructed his civilian deputies within the Department of Defense (DOD) to study the implications of Westmoreland's reinforcement request and to review possible alternatives. They responded with a sharp indictment of prevailing policy. Alain C. Enthoven of Systems Analysis attacked the request for more troops as another "payment on an open-ended commitment" and questioned whether it would shorten the war. North Vietnam had already demonstrated that it could match American increases and that it could limit its losses if it chose. Enthoven and others concluded that even with 206,000 additional troops, the current strategy could "promise no early end to the conflict, nor any success in attriting the enemy or eroding Hanoi's will to fight." Moreover, the costs would be heavy. The provision of substantial additional troops could lead to the "total Americanization of the war," encouraging the South Vietnamese Army's' tendency to do nothing and reinforcing the belief of South Vietnam's "ruling elite that the U.S. will continue to fight while it engages in backroom politics and permits widespread corruption." Expansion of the war would increase U.S. casualties and require new taxes, risking a "domestic crisis of unprecedented proportions." Thus, Clifford's civilian deputies argued that the Administration should maintain existing limits on the war and give Westmoreland no more than a token increase in troops. [140]

The senior DOD civilians went even further. In their final report, they urged a shift from search and destroy, with its goal of "attriting" the enemy, to a strategy of "population security." The bulk of U.S. forces would be deployed along the "demographic frontier," an imaginary line just north of the major population centers, where they would defend against a major North Vietnamese thrust, and, by engaging in limited offensive operations, keep the enemy's main forces off balance. At the same time, the U.S. would force the ARVN to assume greater responsibility for the war and compel the Saigon government to "end its internal bickering, purge corrupt officers and officials, and move to develop efficient and effective forces." The goal of the new approach would be a negotiated settlement rather than military victory. In this regard, the senior DOD civilians urged the scaling down of U.S. objectives to a "peace which will leave the people of South Vietnam free to fashion their own political institutions." The plan closely resembled McNamara's proposals of 1967, but it was stated more emphatically and went further in outlining specific alternatives. [141]

After receiving a series of briefings, Clifford concluded that U.S. policy had failed "because it was based on false premises and false promises." No quick solution was imminent. More troops, guns, planes, and ships would simply increase VC/NVA casualties and cause "significantly higher" U.S. deaths, which were already exceeding the Pacific Theater's monthly KIA rate during World War II. Nor could the President ignore economic problems. The costs of the 206,000-man troop request were huge expenditures, considering the faltering economy. Topping it off, an international gold crisis portended a global depression. Clifford concluded that the U.S. could not win the war in Vietnam and must begin to disengage. [142]

In Clifford's Draft Presidential Memorandum (DPM), he recommended against the military's proposals without resolving the debate on strategy. Clifford's memo kept the strategic issue alive by calling for continued study of possible alternatives. It did not address the issues raised by his senior DOD civilians. Clifford merely recommended the immediate deployment to Vietnam of 22,000 troops, a reserve call-up of unspecified magnitude, and a "highly forceful approach" to Thieu and Ky to get the South Vietnamese to assume greater responsibility for the war. [143]

Clifford's DPM was presented to the President in a meeting of senior Administration officials on 4 March. Clifford pointed out that his memo made a sharp distinction between present needs and the longer-run question of overall strategy and military posture. He felt that his short-range recommendations were urgently needed to meet the immediate situation in Vietnam, as well as other possible contingencies there and elsewhere. But in the longer run, he noted, there were many difficulties. He felt that the President should ponder hard before he took additional measures. [144]

Upset with the senior DOD civilians who had written Clifford's memo, Rostow pointed out to the President the extremely pessimistic nature of some of it. Johnson acknowledged later that he had indeed detected a deep sense of pessimism not only in the report from but from those around the table, as well. [145]

Public Disillusionment

The Administration's inclination to move in new directions was strengthened by mounting evidence of public dissatisfaction with the war. Discussion of Vietnam occurred within an atmosphere of gloom and futility. The media continued to depict events in highly unfavorable and sometimes distorted terms.

Polls revealed a sharp rise in public disillusionment. Support for the war itself had remained steady around 45% between November 1967 and March 1968. Approval of Johnson's conduct of it, which had risen to 40% due to the previous fall's "Success Offensive", plummeted to an all-time low of 26% during Tet. Moreover, by March, 78% of Americans believed the United States was not making any progress in Vietnam. Polls indicated no consensus for either escalation or withdrawal, only a firm conviction that the U.S. was hopelessly bogged down and a growing doubt that Johnson could break the stalemate.

As the Administration mulled Westmoreland's reinforcement request and Clifford's reassessment, the *New York Times* leaked on 10 March that the Administration was considering sending another 206,000 soldiers to Vietnam. Johnson had not revealed his intentions publicly, and the story set off a barrage of protests. The official optimism about a magnificent victory during Tet now seemed as fraudulent as the "Success Offensive". Stunned by the size of Westmoreland's troop request, critics asked why so many were needed and whether more would follow. Skeptics questioned the results of further escalation, warning that the North Vietnamese would be able to match any U.S. increase. [146]

"Ironically, even as the *Times* broke the story, the issue was all but dead," Westmoreland recalled. "Two days earlier, on March 8, General Wheeler had notified me of 'strong resistance in all quarters to putting more ground force units in South Vietnam. ... You should not count on an affirmative decision for such additional forces.'" [147]

"General Wheeler and I assumed that secrecy would be preserved in the analysis of our proposals at the highest levels in Washington," Westmoreland recalled. "We had developed our plans primarily from the military viewpoint, and we anticipated that other, nonmilitary considerations would be brought to bear on our proposals during an intensive period of calm and rational deliberation. This had been the case in the past when I had made similar projections of requirements for Secretary McNamara, normally done on a calendar-year basis." [148]

"I never considered the plan developed by General Wheeler and me to be a demand or a request per se for the deployment of additional forces," Westmoreland explained. "Rather, I considered it a request to prepare troops for deployment consistent with policy determination. Consequently, I was perplexed and puzzled when I read an article in the *New York Times* on 10 March 1968 alleging that I had 'asked for 206,000 more American troops.' This assertion undoubtedly confused the public's views on the situation in South Vietnam and was evidently based on information leaked to the press by a party in the Pentagon who wanted to prejudice the President's reappraisal of our Vietnam War policy." [149]

"The plan submitted to Washington in the wake of the Tet Offensive involving additional forces for the year 1968 was not, as has been alleged, 'an emergency request for battlefield reinforcements,'" Westmoreland explained. "Instead, it was a prudent planning exercise designed to generate the military capability to support future tactical and strategic options. It was a senior military commander's contribution to a policy reappraisal that was underway at the highest levels of government — one that I fervently hoped would be designed to shorten the war." [150]

The possibility of another major troop increase provoked a stormy reaction in Congress, as well. Democrats and Republicans, hawks and doves, demanded an explanation and insisted that Congress share in any decision to expand the war. [151]

"Mr. Clifford and I conferred with congressional leadership at great length," Wheeler recalled. "The matter of the reserve call-up was very, very onerous for any of these gentlemen to accept, because of the political problem of considerable dimensions and heat. And progressively, what was proposed was whittled down." [152]

Rusk was subjected to eleven hours of hearings before a hostile Congress on 11 and 12 March. A week later, 139 members of the House voted for a resolution that called for a complete review of Johnson's Vietnam policy. Discontent in Congress mirrored the general sentiment in the country. A poll that month revealed that 78% of Americans expressed disapproval of Johnson's handling of the war. [153]

CHAPTER 8

DOUBLING DOWN
(MARCH - DECEMBER 1968)

The United States could not win the Vietnam War at a politically acceptable level of commitment. — Major H.R. McMaster, 1997 [1]

The Military Persists

When word of the tone of the Clifford task force deliberations reached the Pacific, Sharp and Westmoreland made eleventh hour bids to buttress their case for a more aggressive strategy. They, Wheeler, and the Chiefs were bitterly opposed to the senior DOD civilians' recommendations. [2]

"I find it difficult to fault our political or military objectives," Westmoreland wrote to Wheeler and Sharp on 2 March. "I just question whether or not we have always directed our best efforts to achieve them." [3]

Recognizing the threat to his request for additional troops — indeed, to his entire strategy — Westmoreland, with Wheeler's full support, warned that rejection of his proposals would deny the U.S. a splendid opportunity to take advantage of an altered, favorable strategic situation. Westmoreland renewed his argument for authorization for U.S. forces to drive into Laos to cut the Ho Chi Minh Trail as soon as the necessary forces were available. [4]

The following day, Westmoreland reported that Communist action in Laos was reaching the critical point and asked for serious consideration of a plan for U.S. forces to intervene through Thailand under the sponsorship of the Southeast Asia Treaty Organization. [5]

"We must stop thinking about the next [Viet Cong] attack and start thinking, all of us, of continuing to carry the attack to the enemy," Westmoreland chided. "We are fully capable of doing it. It is true that our forces have been operating at a fast pace for 30 days and we have suffered heavy casualties. Some may be tired. However, the main thing now is our state of mind. It will be the side that perseveres and carries the fight to the enemy that wins. We're going to do it. Throughout the country we are moving to a general offensive." [6]

Westmoreland hoped the simultaneous major operations he proposed would convince the people of South Vietnam and Washington that "we are not waiting for either the [Viet Cong] to resume the initiative, or for someone to help us. The time is ripe to move out and we will do so." [7]

On 1 March, Sharp renewed his argument for removing restrictions on the air campaign against North Vietnam, "other than those against foreign shipping, hospitals, schools, and population." Phrasing his plea in terms of the overall reevaluation of Vietnam strategy, he stated, "To permit the enemy to fight the war in his way is to permit him to take the strategic offensive while U.S. and [Allied] forces remain on the strategic defensive." The ROLLING THUNDER campaign, Sharp argued, was the only means available to U.S. forces to conduct a strategic offensive "against what we must recognize as a determined enemy." [8]

"It seems to me we are at a crossroads," Sharp stated three days later. "We have the choice of using our military power at full effectiveness with provision of the necessary forces, or we can continue a campaign of gradualism and accept a long drawn-out contest, or we can retreat in defeat from Southeast Asia and leave our Allies to face the Communists alone." [9]

The choice seemed obvious to Sharp. "I suggest that we need to think and act in an aggressive, determined, and offensive manner. ... Now we need to get tough in word and deed, the only policy that the Communists understand." He recommended a combined amphibious and air campaign against North Vietnam be authorized and undertaken "as the weather and the current situation permits." [10]

"With respect to overall strategy in Vietnam, I would make this observation," Wheeler advised the President on 11 March. "We are now engaged in the most crucial phase of the war. The events of the next three or four months could fundamentally alter the nature of this war. In my view, it is not timely to consider fundamental changes in strategy when we are fully committed in what could be the decisive battles of the war." [11]

In a tank session among the Chiefs a week later, "Johnny" Johnson lamented, "We'll find ourselves where we are today – even if we build up forces – one year from today." Wheeler noted "fatal flaws" in the senior DOD civilians' proposed population security strategy. It would lead to increased fighting near the population centers, and hence to more civilian casualties, and it would cede the initiative to the Communists. Besides MULE SHOE, Wheeler also advocated building up the South Vietnamese Army as rapidly as possible and pummeling North Vietnam from the air and sea. McConnell favored hot pursuit into Laos and Cambodia and hitting "any target of military worth in North Vietnam." Moorer favored relaxing bombing restraints in Hanoi and Haiphong and complained that "we have not really gone out to win the war." Chapman favored expanding the sea and air campaigns, as well as "preparing our forces to invade North Vietnam. Unless we can expand our efforts North – we cannot hope to achieve our purpose." Most remarkably, the gravity and opportunity of post-Tet circumstances had overcome "Johnny" Johnson's previous reservations, and now he agreed with Chapman and Wheeler that the U.S. should conduct an amphibious invasion of North Vietnam. [12]

In lock-step with Westmoreland and Sharp, Wheeler and the Chiefs strongly recommended to Clifford expanded authorities to pursue Communist forces into Laos and Cambodia, a substantial extension of targets and authority in and near Hanoi and Haiphong, the mining of Haiphong, naval gunfire up to a Chinese buffer zone, as well as "an Inchon-type landing [to] take and occupy parts of North Vietnam as far as 30 miles north of the demilitarized zone." [13]

Wheeler outlines the situation in Vietnam to the President and his national team, the White House Cabinet Room, Washington, DC, 13 March 1968. (LBJ Library)

The military's recommendations for an aggressive and expanded strategy swam against the tide of opinion in Washington. All their proposals required a political decision to widen the war and increase U.S. forces at a time when most officials who had participated in the discussions with Clifford felt the U.S. commitment had already exceeded the bounds of America's national interest. [14]

Johnson Weighs Options

During the last week of March, debate within the Administration reached a decisive stage and became increasingly sharp and emotional. The President remained noncommittal and alternately blew hot and cold.

Some of the President's advisors insisted the U.S. "hang in there." Rostow had recently proposed asking Congress for a new Southeast Asia Resolution to rally the nation behind the war, and he continued to urge Johnson to stand firm at what could be a critical turning point. Rusk persisted in working for the partial bombing halt he had outlined in early March. He was concerned by the loss of domestic support for the war, but had not despaired of success, nor was he disposed to capitulate to the Administration's critics. Although Hanoi would certainly reject another overture, Rusk felt that a conciliatory gesture would demonstrate to the U.S. public that the Administration was doing everything possible to bring about negotiations. This would buy time to stabilize the home front and shore up South Vietnam. [15]

None of the President's civilian advisors favored an expansion of the war and another large troop increase. Growing popular discontent meant that it would be disastrous to escalate. Acceptance of the military's recommendations would significantly escalate the war and impose heavy new demands on the American people in an election year and at a time when public anxiety about Vietnam was already pronounced.

Rostow advised the President on 21 March, "I feel in my bones that after the Tet Offensive, things can never be quite the same, and that a simple return to the 1966-67 strategy will not wash." [16]

The following day — even before the public protest reached significant proportions — the President rejected the military's proposals to seek victory through an expanded war. He was undoubtedly influenced by public opinion, the economic crisis, and the steadily improving situation in South Vietnam. [17]

Unaware of the President's decision, Westmoreland expressed concern about the situation in Laos to Sharp on 23 March and suggested "a broadening of our strategy to counter the total threat of [North Vietnam] to Southeast Asia." [18]

"I share your concern about the situation in Laos," Sharp replied, but he favored more direct action against North Vietnam instead. Besides, Sharp noted, Chinese intervention and a major expansion of the war could be triggered over a secondary area at a time when the situation in South Vietnam required all available forces, and the U.S. had yet to apply available combat power against the source of the aggression in North Vietnam. [19]

Meanwhile, the uncertainty surrounding the Tet Offensive had abated. The Communists had committed a major share of their forces and had been severely defeated. The intensity of their rocket attacks was steadily diminishing, and Communist forces were withdrawing from their pre-Tet positions and dividing into small groups to avoid destruction or capture. The South Vietnamese government had held firm, South Vietnamese troops had generally fought well, and no public uprising had occurred. Saigon was responding to U.S. pressures. Stability and order had been restored to the cities, and in late March, Thieu announced a massive increase in draft calls that would raise the ARVN's strength by 135,000. Furthermore, U.S. and South Vietnamese forces had fully recovered from the initial shock of the enemy offensive, Westmoreland and Bunker reported, and were ready to mount a major counteroffensive. [20]

Under these circumstances, the President saw no need for a major increase in U.S. forces to continue the war within the existing constraints he had imposed. Johnson did not even authorize the 22,000 troops recommended by Clifford, and merely agreed to deploy 13,500 support troops to augment the emergency reinforcements deployed in February.

At the same time, the President decided he would bring Westmoreland back to Washington to replace "Johnny" Johnson as Chief of Staff of the Army. Abrams would replace Westmoreland, who had come under heavy fire for his predictions of victory and his failure to anticipate the Tet Offensive. The President may have wanted to spare Westmoreland from becoming a scapegoat. He also may have wished to remove Westmoreland from the untenable position of fighting a war under conditions he did not agree with. Whatever the President's rationale, Westmoreland's recall would signify the Administration's determination to maintain the limits it had placed on the war and, tacitly at least, to check its further escalation.

Publicly, however, the President still took a hard line. "We must meet our commitments in Vietnam and the world," he proclaimed. "We shall and we are going to win!" Instinctively, Johnson leaned toward Rusk's position. He was furious with Clifford's desertion and had counted upon his support. Johnson was deeply opposed to abandoning his policy in which he had invested so much, particularly in view of the improved situation in South Vietnam. [21]

On the other hand, Johnson could not ignore the protest building around him, both inside and outside the government. He concluded, gradually and with great reluctance, that some additional conciliatory steps must be taken. [22]

Wheeler made a quick, unannounced trip to the Philippines to review the dire situation with Westmoreland and Abrams and to craft their arguments for an upcoming meeting with the President. With Clifford having turned dove and Johnson's rejection of Westmoreland's reinforcement request, Wheeler knew this would probably be the military's final shot to convince the President to stay the course and not de-escalate.[23]

Wheeler arrived at Clark Field about 9 PM after travelling nearly 24 hours from Washington. He, Westmoreland, and Abrams talked alone into the night.[24]

"General Wheeler … told me that a significant change in our military strategy for the Vietnam War was extremely remote, and that the Administration had decided against a large call-up of the reserves," Westmoreland recalled. "Consequently, since we could not execute the strategic options that General Wheeler and I had discussed in February, the question of deploying major additional forces to South Vietnam became a moot issue."[25]

Wheeler informed Westmoreland, "The President says very bluntly that he does not have the 'horses' to change our strategy." By "horses", Johnson meant votes among his advisors.[26]

"The war, General Wheeler explained … had become a political issue, with the prospect that the enemy might win in Washington as he had in Paris in 1954," Westmoreland recalled. "Under those circumstances, the President had asked General Wheeler to tell me, making a major call-up of reserves and contesting the enemy's geographical widening of the war was politically infeasible. He felt he had no choice over the next few months but to try to calm the protesters lest they precipitate an abject American pullout."[27]

Recently arrived from the Philippines, Wheeler and Abrams urge the President not to change strategy in Vietnam, the White House Cabinet Room, Washington, DC, 25 March 1968. (LBJ Library)

In several emotionally charged meetings with the President in the White House the following day, Wheeler and Abrams pitched their strongest argument. "Our basic strategy is sound," Wheeler insisted. "We can't fight a war on the defensive and win. Westmoreland has tried to go on the tactical offense. In certain places he must defend – such as Cam Ranh Bay. Within our strategy, there are tactical variations." [28]

In another meeting about Vietnam War strategy, Wheeler and Abrams implore the President not to change course, the White House Cabinet Room, Washington, DC, 26 March 1968. (LBJ Library)

"I don't feel we need to change strategy," Abrams added. "We need to be more flexible tactically inside South Vietnam. Khe Sanh is an example." Wheeler argued that denial of Westmoreland's reinforcement request could result in a military defeat, or at least an indefinite continuation of the war. [29]

Wheeler, Abrams, and the President continue their discussion of Vietnam War strategy, the White House Residence, Washington, DC, 26 March 1968. (LBJ Library)

The embattled President sought to deflect the military's criticism of his peace moves. In tones that verged on despondency, Johnson lamented the "abominable" fiscal situation, panic and demoralization in the country, near universal opposition in the press, and his own "overwhelming disapproval" in the polls. "I will go down the drain," he concluded gloomily. [30]

Wheeler and Abrams argue for staying the course in Vietnam to the President and his "Wise Men" advisors, the White House Residence, Washington, DC, 26 March 1968. (LBJ Library)

Trusted advisors from outside the government clinched a decision for Johnson. Acheson had suggested that the President summon his senior advisory group, the Wise Men, back to Washington for another session on Vietnam. The group, which had supported the war during the "Success Offensive", received another series of briefings by diplomatic and military officials on 26 March. The group's gloomy conclusion was that the U.S. "could no longer do the job we set out to do in the time we have left, and we must begin to take steps to disengage." A minority advocated holding the line militarily and even escalating if necessary, but the majority favored immediate steps toward de-escalation. The Wise Men disagreed among themselves about what to do, some proposing a total and unconditional bombing halt, others a shift in the ground strategy. Most agreed, however, that the goal of "an independent, non-Communist South Vietnam" was probably unattainable and that moves should be made toward eventual disengagement. [31]

Because of the gold crisis that month, Westmoreland's request for additional troops was increasingly linked to the nation's mounting economic woes. In this context, some leading "establishment" figures concluded that the war was doing irreparable damage to the nation's overall national security position, and they began to press for disengagement. Acheson, Harriman, and Nitze had served in the Truman Administration and had helped formulate the original containment policy. Now regarding Vietnam as a dangerous diversion from Europe, they advised, "Our leaders ought to be concerned with the areas that count." Fearing that the nation was hopelessly overextended, and that Vietnam was eroding popular support for an internationalist foreign policy, they pressed for a review of Vietnam policy within the larger context of America's global national security concerns. Acheson warned that the gold crisis and America's "broader interest in Europe" required a "decision now to disengage within a limited time." [32]

Clifford had moved significantly beyond his position of late February. He was concerned by the damage that Vietnam was apparently doing to the nation's international financial position. He was alarmed by the growing domestic unrest, particularly the "tremendous erosion of support" among the nation's business and legal elite. At a meeting on 28 March, Clifford delivered an impassioned plea to initiate the process of de-escalation. Working behind the scenes with Acheson and White House aide Harry McPherson, he waged an unrelenting battle for the President's mind. [33]

Although Johnson did not formally approve Clifford's recommendations at this point, he agreed with them and was prepared to act upon them. Johnson also accepted the principle that South Vietnam should do more to defend itself. His civilian advisors agreed that from a long-range standpoint, the key to achieving national policy objectives was South Vietnam's ability to stand on its own, and they had concluded in late 1967 that more should be done to promote self-sufficiency. Some of their strongest arguments against sending massive reinforcements had been that it would encourage the South Vietnamese to do less when they should be doing more, and that it would keep equipment in American hands that might be better employed by the South Vietnamese Army. Thus, in early March, consensus had formed among the President's civilian advisors that Thieu and Ky should be informed bluntly that the U.S. was willing to send limited reinforcements and substantial quantities of equipment, but that continued American assistance would depend upon South Vietnam's ability to put its house in order and assume a greater burden of the fighting. A presidential decision to this effect would constitute a significant shift in U.S. policy — a return, at least in part, to the principle that had governed the U.S. involvement before 1965. [34]

The Speech

Sensing the mood of the country, the President had inwardly determined to shift more of the responsibility for the war onto the South Vietnamese. Keeping his cards close until the very end, a dismayed Johnson revealed a series of major decisions in a televised address on 31 March. [35]

Taking the first steps toward de-escalation and de-Americanization of the war, Johnson announced that the bombing of North Vietnam would henceforth be limited to the area just north of the demilitarized zone where enemy activity directly threatened Allied forces in South Vietnam. He would also send just 13,500 more troops, thus capping the U.S. commitment and confirming the Communists' hopes that the U.S. would de-escalate if its limited war strategy failed. With the U.S. doing less, the President insisted the South Vietnamese must do more, and the war's burden would now begin to shift to them. [36]

"The political objective established by our government to be gained in Southeast Asia is simple and limited — indeed, the most limited war objective of which I have knowledge," Wheeler explained in a public speech three months later. "It is, as the President reminded us on the 31st of March, 'to bring about a recognition in Hanoi that its objective — taking over the South by force — could not be achieved.'" [37]

The President also named Harriman as his personal representative should peace talks materialize, and he made clear that the U.S. was ready to discuss peace, any time, any place. However, nothing in his speech indicated that he had forsaken the goal of a non-Communist South Vietnam. Shifting to gradual de-escalation and a process that would later be labeled "Vietnamization" were ways to buy time for the South to become stronger and, perhaps, survive. Hanoi's strategists had been correct: the decisive moment had arrived in early 1968. The U.S. either had to escalate dramatically or begin to disengage, and now Johnson edged toward disengagement. [38]

Johnson concluded his speech with a bombshell announcement that caught the nation by surprise. He stated emphatically that he would not seek reelection for a second term as President to devote his full attention to resolving the conflict.[39]

Bitter Pill

"[What] struck me at the time – because I was present at some of the drafting sessions on his speech, to include the night before he made it – I could tell that he was in more of a swivet than I had ever seen him before in my life," Wheeler recalled. "He was really very much concerned about something; his manner was completely different than it usually was. He was obviously upset emotionally and, I would say, mentally. As I say, this was not his usual demeanor, and I thought to myself at the time he was just awfully tired. I knew he was tired; he was damn near exhausted, as a matter of fact."[40]

"Every one of the Chiefs was terribly upset," Spivy recalled. "They were mentally and psychologically frustrated because the things that every one of them felt deeply were the right things to do were not being done. They were not able to get the message through to the Administration. Whether or not for good reasons, year after year of that sort of a frustration really soured a lot of them. I don't know of a single one of them who didn't express those kinds of feelings from time to time in the sanctity of the tank. … Harold K. Johnson … became quite upset, even bitter."[41]

"War is not a passive act; it must be dynamic," Wheeler would later explain publicly. "That is, a war cannot be conducted defensively; strategically, it must be prosecuted offensively if the war effort is to be successful."[42]

Hours before the President's speech, Wheeler advised all U.S. commanders in the Pacific of its substance. It was a bitter pill for them all to swallow, knowing how much more difficult the President would make it to win the war.[43]

Wheeler listed several factors pertinent to the President's decision. Since the Tet Offensive, support of the American public and the Congress for the war had decreased at an accelerating rate. Many of the strongest proponents of forceful action in Vietnam had reversed their positions, had moved to neutral ground, or were wavering. If this trend continued unchecked, public support of U.S. objectives in Southeast Asia would be too frail to sustain the effort. Weather over the northern portion of North Vietnam would continue to be unsuitable for air operations during the next 30 days. Therefore, if a cessation of air operations was to be undertaken, now was the best time from the military viewpoint. The President hoped his unilateral initiative to seek peace would reverse the growing dissent and opposition within American society to the war. The initiative would also aid in countering foreign criticism. President Thieu had been consulted and agreed to the cessation.

"The Joint Chiefs of Staff have been apprised of the unilateral initiative to be taken, understand the reasons therefore, and they enjoin all commanders to support the decision of the President," Wheeler wrote. He encouraged commanders to solicit their subordinates' understanding and support. "In particular, every effort should be made to discourage military personnel from expressing criticism to news media representatives. I recognize that this is a delicate matter and one which cannot be approached on the basis of issuing fiats; rather, the attitudes of commanders will probably be most influential and guiding the reaction of their subordinates." [44]

"Again I have been caught completely unaware of an impending major change of policy in the air war," Sharp replied angrily to Wheeler.

> Frankly I simply cannot understand why am not forewarned of the possibility of such important decisions. It should be noted that in nearly four years of this war there has yet to be a leak of an important subject from my headquarters. I further note that President Thieu was consulted so obviously numerous people in Saigon had the info. Despite this [Pacific Command] was kept in the dark. In summation, I have not been kept informed. If this results from decision by higher authority than I suggest revision of this policy be urgently requested. [45]

Clifford had accurately predicted Sharp's negative response and requested that Rusk "discuss fully with you the situation in this country ... and to acquaint you fully with the problems we face here," as Wheeler explained to Sharp. [46]

Shift in Tactics

Johnson's speech is usually cited as a major turning point in U.S. involvement in Vietnam, and it was in some ways. As Dr. Henry A. Kissinger later observed:

> The Tet Offensive marked a watershed of the American effort. Henceforth, no matter how effective our actions, the prevalent strategy could no longer achieve its objectives within a period or with force levels politically acceptable to the American people. ... This made inevitable an eventual commitment to a political solution and marked the beginning of the quest for a negotiated settlement. [47]

On the other hand, the President had not placed a ceiling on U.S. ground forces, nor did he obligate himself to maintain the restrictions on the bombing. Indeed, in explaining the partial bombing halt to the U.S. Embassy in Saigon, the State Department indicated that Hanoi would probably "denounce" it and "thus free our hand after a short period." Nevertheless, the circumstances in which Johnson's decisions were made and the conciliatory tone of his speech had made it difficult, if not impossible, for him to change course. Johnson's speech marked an inglorious end to the triumvirate's policy of gradual escalation. [48]

The President had not changed his policy objectives. The American successes during and after Tet that Wheeler, Sharp, and Westmoreland emphasized, reinforced the convictions of Johnson, Rusk, and Rostow that an independent, non-Communist South Vietnam might still be attainable. By rejecting major troop reinforcements, reducing the bombing, shifting some military responsibility to the Vietnamese, and by withdrawing from the Presidential race, Johnson hoped to salvage his Vietnam policy at least until the end of his term. He was also convinced that history would vindicate him for standing firm.

Thus, Johnson's speech did not represent a change of policy, but merely a shift in tactics to salvage a policy that had come under bitter attack. [49]

The new tactics were even more vaguely defined and contradictory than the old, however. Johnson's decisions marked a shift from the "military theology" of graduated pressure to the pre-1965 concept of saving South Vietnam by denying the Communists victory. Precisely how this objective would be achieved was not articulated. The debate over ground strategy was not resolved, and Abrams was given no strategic guidance. Civilian members of the Administration generally agreed that ground operations should be scaled down to reduce casualties, but it was not clear how they would contribute to the achievement of American policy. The bombing would be concentrated against North Vietnamese staging areas and supply lines, but that tactic had not reduced infiltration significantly in the past, and there was no reason to assume it would be more effective in the future, as Sharp, Wheeler, and the Chiefs well knew. The exigencies of domestic politics required adoption of the concept of Vietnamization, and the South Vietnamese Army's (ARVN) surprising resilience and agility during Tet had raised hopes that it would succeed. Negotiations were also desirable from a domestic political standpoint, but in the absence of concessions that the Administration was unwilling to grant, diplomacy could accomplish nothing. In fact, its failure might intensify the pressures that negotiations were intended to ease.

"Negotiation is not an end in itself," Wheeler would explain publicly. "Negotiation is not a face-saving device for abandoning the objectives we have been fighting for. It is a method for achieving our objectives." In short, Johnson's new tactics would perpetuate the ambiguities and inconsistencies that had marked U.S. policy from the start. [50]

Westmoreland later asserted, "While I could live with the situation and continue to prosecute the war in terms of the old parameters, including gradually turning the war over to the ARVN, failure to provide large numbers of additional U.S. troops and exploit the enemy's losses with bold new moves seriously prolonged the war." [51]

On 10 April, the President officially announced that Abrams would succeed Westmoreland as Commander, U.S. Military Assistance Command,

Vietnam (MACV) in July. This came as no surprise, as Abrams had served as MACV Deputy Commander for a year. Goodpaster would receive his fourth star and replace Abrams as Deputy Commander. Many speculated that the President had delayed Westmoreland's relinquishment of command until the Tet Offensive had been demonstrably defeated and Khe Sanh was no longer under siege. [52]

"There was some sympathy, at least, by Wheeler and others that Westmoreland had a rough row to hoe and deserved better treatment by the Administration than he had gotten over there," Spivy recalled. "I don't believe that Westmoreland would have become Chief except for the insistence of Lyndon Johnson." [53]

"Now is the time to put more, rather than less, pressure on the enemy," Sharp emphasized to his subordinate commanders and Wheeler on 13 April. "In Korea, by going on the defensive as soon as the enemy announced his willingness to talk, we lengthened the war and incurred more casualties than during the offensive phase. We should not be guilty of the same error again. … Victory in Vietnam may not be as distant as many believe. To let it slip our hands now because of pressures for peace would be a grave disservice to our own nation and to the entire free world." [54]

National Security Advisor Walt W. Rostow and Wheeler, Hawaii, 17 April 1968.
(LBJ Library)

On 15 April, the President arrived in Hawaii to confer with Sharp and his senior commanders in the Pacific. Increased world tensions resulting from a budding democratic revolution in Soviet-dominated Czechoslovakia, Communist provocations in Korea, and the Tet Offensive were concerns that finally prompted the President to mobilize a portion of the Army's Ready Reserve. The President limited the mobilization to 24 months and minimized the number of soldiers mobilized to 19,874. Of the 76 Army National Guard and Army Reserve units mobilized, 43 would deploy to Vietnam and 33 would be allocated to the Strategic Army Forces. The effort succeeded in providing temporary augmentation for the strategic reserve and deploying troops to Vietnam much sooner than would have been possible with new recruits. [55]

Wheeler briefs President Johnson and former President Eisenhower aboard Air Force One, 18 April 1968. (LBJ Library)

DELAWARE

Beginning in April, Westmoreland assumed the offensive across South Vietnam. "Having met the challenge of the Tet Offensive and the siege of Khe Sanh," he reported, "we were prepared to exploit fully the dominant military position and high level of experience we had built up over the preceding three years." [56]

After the relief of Khe Sanh, Westmoreland would redistribute his forces within the Khe Sanh and DMZ areas during the good weather period of the next several months. His subordinate commanders would subsequently recommend abandoning the airfield and base at Khe Sanh and instead defending the Khe Sanh plateau with airmobile troops supported from the new airfield and logistic base constructed at Ca Lu. Westmoreland approved the plan, but deferred its execution to his successor, Abrams.

The senior U.S. commanders in northern I CTZ also recommended modifications to the strongpoint barrier system because intensive North Vietnamese artillery and rocket fire had rendered infeasible the construction of the originally planned physical obstacles. Westmoreland approved a modified concept in principle but directed development of a detailed plan for Abrams' final decision. [57]

Meanwhile, the absence of Allied forces from the A Shau Valley for a two-year period had enabled the Communists to construct a secure base of operations from which they could launch and resupply attacks toward Hue. To reduce this threat and take advantage of the short period of good weather in the region, Westmoreland rapidly shifted U.S. and South Vietnamese forces operating on the Khe Sanh plateau to Thua Thien Province.

Operation DELAWARE commenced on 19 April to locate and destroy the enemy's logistics base in the A Shau Valley. American and South Vietnamese forces made contact with the enemy, captured vital maintenance, communications, and supply facilities, and uncovered numerous caches of weapons, ammunition, and heavy anti-aircraft weapons. Westmoreland directed B-52 tactical airstrikes to interdict this area of concern. Communist resistance diminished by early May. American and South Vietnamese forces were extracted from the A Shau Valley between 10-17 May. [58]

Lauded as "one of the most skillfully executed and successful undertakings of the Vietnam War," DELAWARE seriously hindered the Communists' ability to launch major offensive operations out of the A Shau Valley and cost them huge stockpiles of supplies and over 850 killed. [59]

Wheeler stated publicly, "I suggest that the bloody losses suffered by the enemy during Tet, at Khe Sanh, in the A Shau Valley, and in many other less known actions, were, in total, a major defeat which will affect the course of the war." [60]

Negotiations

Despite the accommodating tone of his 31 March speech, the President approached the reality of negotiations with extreme caution. Some Administration officials had expected the North Vietnamese to rebuff the U.S. proposal, but Tet had generated pressures for negotiations in Hanoi, as well as Washington. Three days after Johnson's speech, the Politburo agreed to meet with the U.S. to discuss an unconditional end to the bombing. [61]

Clifford and Harriman were enthusiastic, and Abrams was resigned to negotiations, but others were less amenable. Rusk continued to be reluctant, while Bunker took Thieu's side. The Chiefs were uncomfortable but went along. Rostow seemed to adopt the President's position, but also threw up obstacles. Rostow echoed the Chiefs' recommendations to plan for military action in case diplomacy failed, suggesting bombing Cambodian base areas, resuming ROLLING THUNDER, bombing Hanoi and Haiphong, mining Haiphong, and ground attacks in or north of the DMZ. One reason that the President's deliberations continued for more than a month was his struggle to get everyone in his Administration on board. [62]

Formal talks opened in Paris on 13 May and immediately deadlocked. North Vietnam had agreed to the meetings as part of its broader strategy of fighting while negotiating. It had little interest in substantive negotiations while the military balance of forces was unfavorable, and it viewed the Paris talks as a means of getting the bombing stopped, exacerbating differences between the U.S. and South Vietnam, and intensifying antiwar pressures in the United States. The Administration was willing to stop the bombing, but as in the past, it insisted upon reciprocal de-escalation. Hanoi continued to reject the U.S. demand for reciprocity and refused any terms that limited its ability to support the war in the South while leaving U.S. a free hand there. [63]

"It takes two to make peace," Rusk had observed almost a year earlier, "unless we are prepared to surrender." [64]

During the Guam conference of the previous March, Ky had asked the rhetorical question, "When will Hanoi be ready to negotiate?" He answered himself with a series of questions. "How long can Hanoi enjoy the advantage of restricted bombing of military targets? ... How long can the Viet Cong be permitted to take sanctuary in Cambodia – be allowed to regroup and come back at their will? ... How long can war material be permitted to come into Haiphong harbor?" [65]

In late May, Wheeler and the Chiefs pressed relentlessly for re-escalation, including B-52 strikes against North Vietnamese sanctuaries in Cambodia. Not until 30 July would the exasperated Johnson express his wish to "knock the hell" out of the North Vietnamese. At a press conference the following day, he threatened that if there were no breakthrough in Paris, he might be compelled to undertake additional military measures. [66]

"In debating with the Communists, there is no substitute for the imperative logic of military pressure," Admiral C. Turner Joy, the chief negotiator for the United Nations Command, stated in 1952. "In the end, might is essential to right, not because you or I would have it that way, but because, unless we have armed might in dealing with the Communists, we cannot win our point and, in fact, we may not survive to argue our point." [67]

When the Korean negotiations bogged down once again in the summer of 1953, Eisenhower made it known to Pyongyang that unless negotiations were resumed and concluded promptly, he would order whatever military actions might be necessary to end the war. The Communists promptly returned to the negotiating table and shortly agreed to a cease fire.

North Vietnamese documents captured back in May 1967 revealed that the Hanoi regime had already considered it probable that "a situation where fighting and negotiations are conducted simultaneously." North Vietnamese General Nguyen Van Vinh stated, "In fighting while negotiating, the side which fights more strongly will compel the adversary to accept its conditions." [68]

The President and his senior foreign policy advisors were exhausted. Rusk later admitted that he was "bone tired" and survived on a daily diet of "aspirin, scotch, and four packs of Larks." [69]

While standing firm in Paris, the Administration used every available means to strengthen its position in South Vietnam. Abrams stepped up the pace of military operations. In April and May alone, 3,700 Americans and an estimated 43,000 Communists were killed. The air war in South Vietnam reached a new level of intensity, as well, as B-52s and fighter-bombers relentlessly attacked infiltration routes, lines of communication, and suspected Communist base camps. The number of B-52 missions would triple in 1968, and the bombs dropped on South Vietnam would exceed 1,000,000 tons. In March and April, the U.S. Military Assistance Command, Vietnam (MACV) and the South Vietnamese Army had conducted the largest search and destroy mission of the war, sending more than 100,000 troops against enemy forces in the provinces around Saigon. The scale of U.S. military operations would diminish somewhat in the summer and fall as Abrams shifted to small unit patrols and mobile spoiling attacks, but throughout the rest of the year, the U.S. would maintain intense pressure on Communist forces in South Vietnam. [70]

Mini-Tet

Tet had been only the first in a series of coordinated attacks during the spring and summer. A little more than a month after Johnson's speech, the Communists launched a second offensive with 119 rocket and mortar attacks across South Vietnam. [71]

"It is my view that Hanoi and the [National Liberation Front] are now engaged in a great gamble," Bunker declared at the height of the May attacks. "This is the year of climax. Perhaps most important in terms of their gamble is that they now hope to win because of what they regard as our desperate desire for peace." [72]

Because of their earlier losses during Tet, these attacks were not nearly as fierce or well-coordinated as Tet. The results, however, were essentially the same – heavy losses for the Communists, a broadening of the war into urban areas, and a quantum jump in civilian casualties. Although "Mini-Tet" lacked the intensity of Tet, the two-week period of 5-18 May would prove the war's most costly for U.S. forces, with 1,168 killed in action and 2,479 wounded requiring hospitalization (as opposed to 1,120 dead and 1,909 hospitalized during the worst two weeks of Tet.)[73]

The Communists continued their countrywide attacks in attempt to give the South Vietnamese and the world public an impression of North Vietnamese strength while exaggerating the human and material costs of the war to the Allies. Allied tactical aircraft and American B-52s continued to support ground operations in South Vietnam, with the B-52 effort concentrated primarily on truck parks, storage areas, and troop concentrations. The air effort further compounded the Communists' difficulties in moving supplies and equipment along infiltration routes. Still, they continued to reconstitute and reposition their forces for further attacks.

In late May and early June, the Communists renewed their assaults, particularly on Saigon. American military installations and South Vietnamese government headquarters appeared to be the initial objectives. Once again, the Communists demonstrated a complete disregard for the lives of South Vietnamese civilians. When these attacks were thwarted, the Communists initiated a series of indiscriminate rocket attacks against the civilian populace of Saigon, creating widespread destruction, heavy civilian casualties, and increasing numbers of refugees. These assaults on Saigon were intended to influence the stalled negotiations in Paris, where Hanoi showed no inclination to budge from its position.[74]

Sharp and Westmoreland estimated that by 30 June more than 300,000 North Vietnamese Army troops had infiltrated into South Vietnam. Still, the Communists were not thought to possess the means of achieving a military victory in South Vietnam, although they did retain a dangerous capability to mount serious attacks. There was no indication that the Communists had abandoned their goal of a unified Communist Vietnam. Against the backdrop of the Paris negotiations, a major victory would loom large. The Communists no doubt recalled how well their combined military and political strategy had worked for them in Geneva in 1954.[75]

MULE SHOE Imagined

"I was of the opinion that, to succeed, we should apply the forces necessary to get the job done, which meant taking the war north and invading the Cambodian and Laotian sanctuaries," Army General Michael S. Davison recalled. He thought it possible that China might intervene, but if the U.S. could clear the North Vietnamese out of their sanctuaries, push their forces north of the border, and seek a peace agreement, there might not be a Chinese intervention. "This would not be an effort to invade North Vietnam and take Hanoi but to contain North Vietnamese forces within their own territory."[76]

Assuming away the political impossibility that Clifford had concurred with and the President had approved the Chiefs' suggestion on 18 March to execute Operation MULE SHOE, it would have been conducted in late June by the battle-tested U.S. forces that had recently concluded Operations PEGASUS, NIAGARA, and DELAWARE.

Those operations in northern I Corps Tactical Zone (I CTZ) would have well-prepared the Provisional Corps, Vietnam and III Marine Amphibious Force units to execute the complicated logistics, engineering, and fire support aspects of MULE SHOE, which in turn would have enabled U.S. combat forces to destroy large material stores in the North Vietnamese logistics bases and to defeat considerable NVA forces caught in the trap or attempting to reinforce the engagement area.

Regardless of how tremendous the U.S. operational successes might have been, MULE SHOE would not have provided the entrée for prolonged U.S. combat operations in southern North Vietnam that Wheeler intended. The domestic and international reaction to President Nixon's Cambodian incursion two years later suggests that Johnson similarly would have been under immediate and enormous pressure to curtail the operation prematurely. Wheeler, Sharp, and Westmoreland (whose tours as the Commander-in-Chief, Pacific (CINCPAC) and Commander, U.S. Military Assistance Command, Vietnam (COMUSMACV) would have been extended during MULE SHOE) would have vehemently opposed early withdrawal, but the President would have weighed domestic considerations and evidence of imminent Chinese ground intervention above their military advice.

What actually happened instead, Abrams's abandonment of the Khe Sanh combat base on 5 July signaled the demise of the McNamara Line and further postponement of the military's hopes for large-scale, U.S. cross-border operations. For the remainder of the year, U.S. forces in I CTZ would assist restoration of security around Hue and other coastal areas and work closely with the South Vietnamese Army in support of pacification. North Vietnamese Army and Viet Cong forces, having suffered heavy losses, would generally avoid offensive operations. [77]

Changes of Command

During Westmoreland's final press conference in Saigon on 10 June, a reporter asked him, "General, can the war be won militarily?"

"Not in a classical sense, because ...," Westmoreland paused, "of our national policy of not expanding the war."

But, said Westmoreland, even if the U.S. could not win a "classic" victory, "the enemy can be attrited, the price can be raised ... and is being raised to the point that it could be intolerable to the enemy." [78]

The following day, after nearly four and a half years in Vietnam, Westmoreland relinquished command of MACV to Abrams. Westmoreland would serve as Chief of Staff of the Army until his retirement from the Army on 30 June 1972. [79]

Although Abrams had the aura of a blunt, hard-talking, World War II tank commander, he had spent a year as Westmoreland's deputy, working closely with South Vietnamese commanders. [80]

Spivy recalled:

> Abe ... was first-rate. He was a very solid, sage kind of guy in his own way. He was very impressive when in contact with these other senior people. ... He had a very simple down-to-earth way of figuring through problems to solutions. He was an absolute master, too, at psychology. His approach to

people, and situations, and things was absolutely fascinating. Sometimes it was startling. He really came across. … He was very thoughtful about people around him, not only his own family. … He was very considerate. In spite of his dour and often gruff appearance, he was real quick to get through to his soldiers. God, they knew that he was looking after them and doing his best, too. [81]

Like Westmoreland, Abrams viewed the military situation after Tet as an opportunity to make gains in pacifying rural areas and to reduce the strength of Communist forces in the South. Until the weakened Viet Cong forces could be rebuilt or replaced with North Vietnamese, both guerrilla and regular Communist forces had adopted a defensive posture. Nevertheless, 90,000 North Vietnamese Army troops were in the South or in border sanctuaries waiting to resume the offensive at a propitious time. [82]

Without "clear guidance from the national level," Abrams and his new deputy Goodpaster "worked up [their] own overall strategic plan." They would confront the daunting task of managing the war's de-Americanization while still trying to preserve a viable South Vietnam. In certain ways, their war would remain much the same as under Westmoreland. Some large operations would still occur, and a heavy reliance on firepower would remain standard operating procedure within many units. [83]

On the other hand, Abrams would emphasize a "one war" strategy to reduce the focus on the big unit war. Battles, he stressed, were not that important since the true measure of success was not the body count but population security. Understanding that the Communists made no distinction among the big unit war, pacification, and territorial security, that they operated on the preposition that "this is just one, repeat one, war," Abrams wanted the U.S. to confront them "simultaneously, in all areas of the conflict." Protecting the population, which would enable progress in pacification, would require small patrols and ambushes rather than big units "thrashing around" in the jungles, limiting firepower in populated areas, building effective South Vietnamese forces, and neutralizing the Viet Cong infrastructure. [84]

Abrams would admit that most of this was "completely *undramatic*. It's just a lot of damn *drudgery*.... but that's what we've got to do." [85]

The level of frustration both in Vietnam and domestically at home had never been higher. Even though Abrams' "clear and hold" strategy replaced Westmoreland's "search and destroy" for conducting the war in the countryside, it could not be a winning strategy; by now, it could serve only as a basis for a negotiated "honorable" withdrawal. [86]

Storms in Washington

"Heavy showers this afternoon," Betty Wheeler wrote on 24 June. "Such interesting lights. Green, green grass and leaves. A gray river. The Lincoln Memorial stark white. Gray clouds. Just a few buildings [visible], all else lost in mist." Her weather report was metaphoric for the political storms raging in Washington. [87]

That same day, Wheeler responded to the President's request for an assessment of the present military situation as compared with 31 March. "On balance we have gained ground to date on the enemy," Wheeler wrote.

> His Winter-Spring Campaign was disrupted, his casualty rates are high, and his overall offensive capability appears to be declining. However, the greatly increased war supporting activities in the North have not yet been fully felt in South Vietnam. I would expect the output of the rapidly recuperating North Vietnam to make substantial impacts on us in late summer and fall. [88]

The unfortunate consequence of Johnson's unilateral bombing halt was that it had enhanced the North Vietnamese overall position, Wheeler reported. Hanoi's air defense system had improved significantly with the appearance of more and newer MIG-21s, double the number of fighter pilots, the use of new or long-idle airfields for MIG operations, and the extension of fighter operations south into the panhandle of North Vietnam. Additional surface-to-air missile and antiaircraft artillery defense systems had been moved into the area south of the 20th Parallel. As the enemy was granted more time to recuperate, reinforce and expand his air defense system, airstrikes south of the 19th Parallel were increasingly threatened.

The enemy's war supporting capabilities had also improved. Roads throughout North Vietnam had been restored, improved, and extended. The port of Haiphong was now handling more cargo than ever before. Waterways, roads, and trails converging at the logistics complex of Thanh Hoa near the 20th Parallel were handling a two-fold increase in southbound supplies. Power plants and industrial facilities were being restored. The number of North Vietnamese troops on the move south had reached unprecedented levels over the past several months with about 80,000 detected in transit since 31 March.[89]

Meanwhile, divisions within the U.S. government became even more pronounced during this new phase of the war. The split between the President's civilian and military advisors was deepening, with a growing doubt that the war, even assuming it could still be won, would be worth the expenditure, not only in troops and matériel, but also in national honor.[90]

Convinced that the Communists had suffered a "colossal" defeat and that in any negotiations the U.S. would hold the upper hand, Rusk, Rostow, Bunker, and the military staunchly opposed concessions and sought to apply intensive military pressure. They feared that the North Vietnamese would use negotiations to divide the U.S. from its South Vietnamese ally. They insisted that if the Administration could shore up the home front and improve its military position in Vietnam, Hanoi could be forced to make major concessions.[91]

"I understand full well the complex character of the war in Southeast Asia. Interacting forces are political, military, economic, psychological, and even ethnic in nature," Wheeler would state publicly later that summer. "I wish to make clear that, while I recognize the many important forces at play, I am convinced that the military outcome in Southeast Asia is fundamental to the nature of the settlement which will someday be reached."[92]

Clifford and Harriman, on the other hand, sought to extricate the U.S. from what they considered a hopeless mess. Certain that the war was crippling America's ability to deal with more important problems and undermining its position as the "standard-bearer of moral principle in the world," they sought through Clifford's "winching-down process" mutual de-escalation and disengagement, even at the expense of South Vietnam.[93]

This battle in Washington would rage throughout the remainder of the year. The two factions would fight bitterly over such issues as the U.S. negotiating stance, the scale and purpose of ground operations, and resumption or full curtailment of the bombing. The stakes were high, the participants exhausted, their nerves frayed. The President himself was worn out, increasingly angry and frustrated, more indecisive than usual, and at times petulant and petty. Rusk's and Rostow's hard line still appealed to him. On occasion, he regretted having made his 31 March speech, and he yearned to bomb Hanoi and Haiphong off the map. A man who thrived on consensus, Johnson could not stand the bitter divisions among his advisors. During its final months, his Administration would not address, much less resolve, the fundamental issues of the war or develop a well-considered negotiating position.[94]

Military Transitions

July brought more changes to the top military positions. The month began with Wheeler swearing-in Westmoreland in as the Chief of Staff of the Army on 3 July.[95]

Wheeler was reappointed for what would be the first of two consecutive, one-year terms following enactment of a Joint Resolution of Congress, which provided exceptions to the law that the Chairman of the Joint Chiefs of Staff could be appointed for only two, two-year terms except in time of war declared by Congress.[96]

The President confers with his military commanders and South Vietnamese leaders, U.S Pacific Command headquarters, Hawaii, 19 July 1968. (LBJ Library)

Wheeler chats with a member of the South Vietnamese delegation during a conference break, U.S Pacific Command headquarters, Hawaii, 19 July 1968. (LBJ Library)

On 31 July, Wheeler presided over the U.S. Pacific Command's change of command ceremony in which Sharp was replaced as Commander-in-Chief (CINCPAC) by Admiral John S. McCain, Jr. Sharp had served in that capacity for four years. [97]

(From left) Admiral Thomas H. Moorer, Wheeler, Admiral John S. McCain, Jr., and Sharp during the U.S. Pacific Command change of command ceremony, Hawaii, 31 July 1968. (Office of the Chairman of the Joint Chiefs of Staff)

A Sailor Reports

At the end of their tenures, Sharp and Westmoreland released a report on the progress of the war. The embittered Sharp reflected on the positive contributions that ROLLING THUNDER operations had made prior to the President's unilateral decision of 31 March to halt bombing attacks on the principal populated and food-producing areas of North Vietnam, except in the area north of the demilitarized zone (DMZ).[98]

The bombing halt, Sharp noted, had resulted in the concentration of attack sorties in southern North Vietnam, primarily directed against traffic on roads and trails, to hinder reinforcements and supplies from reaching South Vietnam where they would be brought into battle against Allied forces.[99]

Despite operational restrictions, weather cycles, and a resourceful enemy, ROLLING THUNDER had had a profound effect on North Vietnam. By 1 April, when air operations over the northern areas were halted, Hanoi was faced with numerous and serious problems that had placed unprecedented strain upon the North Vietnamese economy, production, and distribution systems, the life of the people, and the political apparatus. Such conditions may have contributed to Hanoi's willingness to enter negotiations to gain a period of relief, Sharp suggested.

ROLLING THUNDER had induced a significant manpower drain on North Vietnam caused by the need to supply reinforcements for the war in the South and to man air and coastal defenses. Workers had also been required to repair roads and rail lines and reconstruct bridges and ferry crossings damaged or destroyed by the air campaign. Workers had also been needed for site construction and as laborers at the many hastily built radar, antiaircraft artillery, and surface-to-air missile sites.

ROLLING THUNDER had also affected the production and distribution of food in North Vietnam. It had destroyed most of the country's heavy industry and power-generating capability and made transportation much more complicated.

Sharp pointed out that air operations had also caused a decline in the North Vietnamese standard of living. Dislocation of the populace, interdiction of transportation, destruction of goods, and more stringent rationing of all commodities were attributable in varying degrees to ROLLING THUNDER.

The impact of air operations on the morale of the North Vietnamese people was harder to quantify, Sharp admitted, but indicators suggested that morale had slipped because of the economic and sociological problems aggravated by ROLLING THUNDER. This had compelled the authoritarian Hanoi government to redouble its population control efforts.

Sharp also surmised how the war might have played out had no bombing campaign been executed. "The uninhibited flow of men, weapons, and supplies through North Vietnam to confront our forces in South Vietnam could have had only one result for the United States and its Allies," he wrote, "considerably heavier casualties at a smaller cost to the enemy. Since this alternative was unacceptable, the bombing of North Vietnam, as an essential element of the overall strategy, was clearly successful in fulfilling its purposes." [100]

Wheeler shared Sharp's admiration for the airmen who had waged an uphill battle in the air campaign. "I give great credit to the leadership and discipline of our airmen for their dedicated and professional performance over North Vietnam in spite of restrictions and limitations, imposed for nonmilitary reasons, which afforded great advantages to the enemy and cost casualties to our airmen, which otherwise would not have been sustained," Wheeler later wrote. [101]

Sharp also recapped Operation SEA DRAGON in his swan song report. By June, naval surface operations had greatly reduced seaborne infiltration of enemy personnel and supplies from North Vietnam. As in the ground war, Hanoi appeared to be willing to accept high losses and continue its attempts to resupply in certain hard-pressed areas.

During the first three months of 1968, the North Vietnamese had increased pressure along the DMZ and stepped-up logistic movement in the southern portion of North Vietnam. SEA DRAGON ships had been shifted southward to provide increased naval gunfire support to friendly forces near the DMZ. The two remaining destroyers in the southern SEA DRAGON area of operations had destroyed or damaged 34% of the enemy waterborne logistic craft they detected. The number of land targets engaged had remained high, although poor weather hindered adequate assessment of results.

The President's decision of 31 March to limit attacks on North Vietnam to the area below 19 degrees North had reduced the SEA DRAGON area of operations by one-third. [102]

After his retirement, Sharp lectured widely on what had gone wrong in Vietnam. The central lesson, as he, Westmoreland, Wheeler, and the Chiefs saw it was that "We should never commit the armed forces of the United States to combat unless we have decided at the same time to use the nonnuclear power we have available to win in the shortest possible time." [103]

"The blame for the lost war rests, *not* upon the men in uniform, but upon the civilian policymakers in Washington — those who evolved and developed the policies of gradualism, flexible response, off-again on-again bombing, negotiated victory, and, ultimately, one-arm-behind-the-back restraint, and scuttle-and-run," Sharp asserted. "Our Vietnam policies, forged in Washington, forced our military men to the most asinine way to fight a war that could possibly be imagined." [104]

Looking Forward

Persisting in their effort to weaken the South Vietnamese government, the North Vietnamese Army (NVA) and Viet Cong conducted a third offensive in August, which was dubbed "Mini-Mini-Tet." MACV had taken several preemptive actions, however, and while this offensive was only a pale version of the earlier two, 308 American soldiers were killed. Pockets of stiff fighting occurred throughout the South, and Communist forces again infiltrated into Saigon, leading to heavy destruction in several neighborhoods. Thereafter, the Viet Cong and NVA would generally disperse and avoid contact with American forces. [105]

"Our forces have achieved an unbroken string of victories which, in the aggregate, is something new in military history," Wheeler stated publicly on 31 August.

> Can we stay the course? We all hear, from time to time, that we have grown tired of meeting foreign responsibilities in the face of Allied indifference and competing domestic needs. The final answer to this question will emerge over the not-too-distant future. I'm betting that we can and we will stay the course. Certainly, we are somewhat more 'tired' then we were 15 or 20 years ago, but to me the test of true greatness of a man or of a nation is what they can do when they are tired. And I believe that the United States of America is a great nation. [106]

The Tet Offensive begun on 30 January had not been a precise turning *point* because the war remained mired in a stalemate. However, although it had not collapsed, America's "aggressive will" wavered. Reinforced by the two subsequent Communist offensives, Tet represented a turning *curve* that had started the U.S. down the road to withdrawal and defeat. [107]

"The first priority foreign policy objective of our next Administration will be to bring an honorable end to the war in Vietnam," Richard M. Nixon pledged in his Republican presidential nomination acceptance speech in Miami on 8 August. "My fellow Americans, the dark long night for America is about to end." [108]

On 14 September, DePuy submitted a memorandum to Wheeler regarding major strategy and turning points in Vietnam. "The war has not yet run its course and may change its direction again on more than one occasion," DePuy wrote. "At the moment, however, the military problem has been put back in the enemy's court. The political problem on the other hand seems to be squarely in ours." [109]

Six days later, Wheeler informed Clifford of the situation in the demilitarized zone (DMZ) area and current U.S. planning to meet enemy initiatives there and in the extended battle areas in Laos and north of the DMZ during the upcoming northeast monsoon season.

The enemy had maintained considerable threatening forces in the DMZ area with no apparent indications of departure during the coming northeast monsoon. "He is expected to keep pressure on our positions along the DMZ and in northern I CTZ through attacks by fire and intermittent ground assaults against our fire support and logistic bases," Wheeler wrote. "In spite of adverse weather and our air and artillery attacks, he will continue infiltrating troops and supplies across the DMZ." [110]

"[McCain] and I concur in General Abrams' assessment of the continuing threats to friendly forces and to [South Vietnam] from enemy infiltration through the sea and land approaches of [North Vietnam] and Laos," Wheeler continued. "We consider that enemy infiltration of troops and supplies must be held down by continued attacks on the enemy arteries in the [North Vietnamese] and Laotian Panhandles and at sea. ... Impeding the enemy's flow of support to the battlefield, seeking out the enemy to spoil his planned offensives and levying high casualties in all contacts will continue to weaken enemy resolve and staying power." [111]

The Chiefs still regarded Clifford as the one civilian official responsible for changing the President's mind, the man who had pushed Johnson away from mobilization. Still, he had gained their grudging admiration, for he had proven himself more adept at dealing with the military, even when he had disagreed with them, than McNamara ever had. Clifford was honest, straightforward, hard-working, realistic, and respectful, everything the Chiefs considered McNamara was not.

"I knew the Chiefs were extremely disappointed with the way things had turned out," Clifford later said. "That they had wanted to take a stronger stand in Vietnam. So at least in part my job was to help allay that disappointment, to get us working together. I wanted to do this not only because it would be good for the country, but because frankly I was very disturbed about the future. We had an opportunity to extricate ourselves from this terrible war and very little time to do it." [112]

Clifford was convinced that Nixon's election would be a disaster for the country, leading to four more years of war and causing further strains on civilian-military relations. Clifford reiterated these views to Wheeler in September and October, attempting to persuade him from his doctrinal stance on the war toward one that could accommodate a diplomatic solution. Wheeler could not be convinced, although by November he would concede that Nixon's "secret plan to end the war" probably did not mean an acceptance of the Chiefs' long-held position on the imperative for mobilizing the reserves. [113]

On 16 October, Wheeler wrote to Abrams regarding a recent *Newsweek* article that implied Wheeler's criticism of him. "[The reporter] wanted my estimate of you as a commanding general," Wheeler clarified. "I told him something to the effect that you were as fine a commander as the United States Armed Forces has produced in this generation; that you were a fighter who understands what war is all about; and that you were a real pro. I added that I could think of no higher words of praise for a military officer." [114]

"You should know that there is an insidious effort being undertaken in the press to derogate Westy as a commander," Wheeler continued. "I surmise that this effort is based upon the fact that the press is now becoming aware of the fact that, if we have not yet won the war in South Vietnam, we are well on the way to doing so." Wheeler believed that rather than admitting they had been wrong in the past, the press was attempting to rationalize the shift in the thrust of their stories by attributing the change in the situation entirely to Abrams and by denigrating Westmoreland's efforts prior to Abrams' assumption of command. [115]

"I cannot tell you how sickening I find this attitude on the part of [the] press to be," Wheeler continued. "I also want you to know that I am more than pleased at the results you have achieved since you [assumed command]. Moreover, I recognize that you have instituted innovations in tactics and in concepts, and for what you have done I have nothing but praise. On the other hand, I refuse to be a party to the denigration of Westy who, I think you will agree, did an exceedingly fine job under adverse circumstances." Wheeler's objective, he said, was for both officers to receive from the American people and from history the credit that was due to them both and to the forces that Abrams and Westmoreland had commanded so well. [116]

Bombing Halt

Largely in response to domestic pressures, the President made one last effort in late October to get the peace talks "off the dime". On 29 October, Johnson asked Abrams whether, from a military standpoint, he could accept a cessation of attacks against North Vietnam. To appease his military advisors and keep pressure on North Vietnam, Johnson agreed to refocus U.S. air power against North Vietnamese supply lines in Laos. He also stipulated that Abrams would retain the right to retaliate against Communist attacks across the DMZ if he deemed necessary. With Abrams' acquiescence, Johnson announced to the nation on 31 October that he was immediately halting all air, naval, and artillery bombardment of North Vietnam. [117]

The military, both active and retired, had long detested Johnson's bombing halts because they had only served to benefit the Communists, who had consistently and demonstrably taken advantage of the free passes to redouble their infiltration and resupply activities. To the contrary, the military community was still arguing for escalation.

On 27 October, LeMay stated on *Face the Nation*, "[I] would continue the bombing. … I just can't see how the United States, with its great strength, cannot win a victory against a small, backward country like North Vietnam. … I think that if we tell them we are going to win, then set about doing it, we will have a victory in very short order." [118]

Earlier in the month, LeMay had startled a press conference in Pittsburgh, stating:

> I would use anything we could dream up, including nuclear weapons. … We seem to have a phobia about nuclear weapons. … I think there are many times when it would be more efficient to use nuclear weapons. However, the public opinion in this country and throughout the world would throw up their hands in horror when you mention nuclear weapons, just because of the propaganda that's been fed to them. I don't believe the world would end if we exploded a nuclear weapon. [119]

LeMay's frustration was understandable, considering the statistics for ROLLING THUNDER upon its termination on 31 October. The U.S. had dropped 634,000 tons of bombs (approximately 100,000 thousand tons more than it dropped in the Pacific Theater during World War II), inflicted $600 million in damage and killed 52,000 North Vietnamese civilians out of a population of 18 million. Although Hanoi claimed it had shot down more than 3,000 planes, the U.S. had *only* lost 938 aircraft at a cost of about $6 billion. In aircraft losses alone, it had cost $10 to afflict $1 worth of damage. And since 1965, North Vietnam had received more than $2 billion in foreign aid, more than compensating for its losses. [120]

Rostow (left), Wheeler, and Clifford, the White House Cabinet Room, Washington, DC, 29 October 1968. (LBJ Library)

Wheeler, like many senior military officers, was relieved when Nixon won the close election, primarily because they believed that a change in national leadership was at least better than continuing along the same path charted by Johnson. But when Nixon appointed Wisconsin Congressman Melvin R. Laird as his Secretary of Defense, the Chiefs were dubious. They had long experience in dealing with Laird, who had served nearly all his sixteen years in the House as a member of the Subcommittee on Military Preparedness, and they knew he wanted to get the U.S. out of Vietnam as quickly as possible.

Serving as an initial bridge between the military and the new Administration, the recently reassigned Goodpaster would inform Wheeler that Nixon was more willing to listen to the Chiefs than Johnson had been, that he admired the military and Wheeler, and that he hoped that Wheeler would stay on as Chairman.

Wheeler remained skeptical. While he desired good relations between the Chiefs and the new Administration, he was physically worn out by his service during the previous five years and wanted to retire. The inauguration of a new President, he thought, would be an appropriate juncture to initiate a change, a point of view he communicated to the incoming Administration but was diligently ignored. Wheeler was adamant, but he did not have a chance to broach the subject until after Nixon had been inaugurated. [121]

Wheeler uses a secure phone to speak with the Joint Staff from the White House, Washington, DC, 31 October 1968. (LBJ Library)

On 3 November, Hanoi's delegation in Paris announced that it was ready to participate in peace talks. Two days later, however, the North Vietnamese negotiators refused to attend, accusing the U.S. of breaking its promise by continuing reconnaissance flights over North Vietnam. Not surprisingly, the U.S. announced that these flights had revealed intensified North Vietnamese efforts to resupply their forces in the South, particularly along the routes through Laos. [122]

Pacification

For the first time, the U.S. and South Vietnam now firmly committed to controlling the countryside. An essential component of Abrams's strategy for the ground war was pacification, which assumed heightened significance when a three-month Accelerated Pacification Campaign commenced on 1 November to secure as much of the countryside as possible should serious negotiations begin. Proving reasonably effective, the campaign would be extended for three years.

Because the Viet Cong had sustained heavy casualties during Tet, and the South Vietnamese had abandoned hamlets and villages to defend the cities, a vacuum existed in the rural areas. Under the Accelerated Pacification Campaign, the Saigon government would regain considerable control of the countryside while the surviving Viet Cong apparatus suffered, particularly since the U.S. Military Assistance Command, Vietnam (MACV) would shift much of its military effort to directly support pacification.

The combined American-South Vietnamese Phoenix Program targeted the Viet Cong infrastructure for assassination or capture. Other Viet Cong changed sides via the *Chieu Hoi* (Open Arms) Program that offered defectors a monetary reward and lenient treatment. For the most part, these two programs would neutralize low-level operatives. Large numbers of hard-core Viet Cong infrastructure remained unidentified, and thus, the infrastructure would survive intact. In some places, the Viet Cong cadre would conduct a "Phoenix in reverse," assassinating or abducting more than 50,000 village and hamlet officials and Popular Force leaders between 1969 and 1972. Abrams believed it was "far more significant that we neutralize 1,000 of these guerrillas and infrastructure than kill 10,000 North Vietnamese soldiers." [123]

1968 Recap

"In 1968, there was a plate full of problems," Wheeler recalled. "The Pueblo incident; the attempted assassination of Park, South Korea's President; the Tet Offensive in Vietnam; and the touchy Middle East situation. That was quite a year." [124]

"Our strength, military and political, has grown unceasingly while that of the United States' puppets have suffered heavy losses," Giap exclaimed in a speech at an Army Day rally in Hanoi. "The enemy battle order has been upset and they are sinking ever deeper into passive defense and into a strategic position of being attacked and encircled on all battlefields." [125]

"Manifestly, 1968 was the climactic year of the Vietnam War," Dave Palmer observed. It was the turning point that saw the virtual elimination of the Viet Cong as a viable movement, the apex of U.S. involvement in Southeast Asia, the final North Vietnamese attempt to gain a military victory in the face of U.S. ground forces, the uniting of South Vietnam, the emergence of the ARVN as a mature fighting force, and a shift in the entire thrust of the conflict. "Both sides," wrote Palmer, "despairing of winning militarily as things stood, decided to explore other avenues to end the war or to change the balance of power." [126]

The year ended as it had begun, with deadlock on the battlefield and in diplomatic councils. In the aftermath of Tet, both sides had gone on the offensive, seeking a knockout blow against a weakened enemy, and both sides had suffered enormous losses. Despite claims of victory, each side was significantly weakened, and neither emerged with sufficient leverage to force a settlement. Tet had merely hardened the deadlock, and it would take four more years of "fighting while negotiating" before it would finally be broken. [127]

CHAPTER 9

THE INDISPENSABLE MAN
(1969)

The Nixon Administration refused to take what was on the table and gambled the balance could be reversed. In making that choice, by inclination and by will, Nixon would follow the path of force. – Dr. John Prados, 2009 [1]

End Honorably

Once elected, Nixon needed to deliver on his campaign promise to end the Vietnam War. Wheeler and the Chiefs, minus Moorer, were skeptical that the new Administration could alter U.S. policy in South Vietnam to the degree necessary to force a resolution of the war. They believed the issue had already been decided publicly by the electorate's condemnation of President Johnson. Wheeler was not convinced that the new foreign policy team understood the complexity of U.S. involvement in Southeast Asia and that, as a result, the Chiefs and the rest of the military would be forced to suffer through its long learning process. McConnell, in his last year before retirement, agreed that unless the Administration was willing to depart radically from past policies, it was doubtful that any solution short of an all-out commitment (a political impossibility) would end the war. Even Westmoreland was pessimistic about the feasibility of the tougher strategy. Only Moorer was absolutely convinced that the U.S. could still actually win the war with a tougher strategy, although he questioned whether Nixon and Kissinger had any idea just what that entailed. [2]

Priding himself on toughness and vowing that he would not be the first President to lose a war, Nixon determined to preserve a non-Communist South Vietnam and achieve "peace with honor." His Administration had no plan, but took office determined to find new solutions to an old problem in Vietnam. [3]

Nixon and Kissinger recognized that the war must be ended. It had become a divisive force that had torn the country apart and hindered any constructive approach to domestic and foreign policy problems. Nixon also realized that his ability to extricate the nation from Vietnam would decisively affect his political future and his place in history. Nevertheless, he and Kissinger insisted that the war must be ended "honorably." To simply pullout of Vietnam, they believed, would be a callous abandonment of the South Vietnamese who had depended upon U.S. protection and would be unworthy of the actions of a great nation. [4]

Most importantly, Nixon and Kissinger feared the international consequences of a precipitous withdrawal. Even before taking office, they had begun sketching the outlines of a new world order based on U.S. primacy. Their grand design included at least limited accommodations with the Soviet Union and China, and they felt they must extricate the U.S. from the war in a manner that would demonstrate to these old adversaries a resoluteness of purpose and certainty of action in a manner that would uphold U.S. credibility with friends and foes alike. [5]

Survey Says

Nixon directed Kissinger, who would serve as his National Security Advisor, to lead a Vietnam policy review to elicit the differences among Washington agencies, field commanders, the U.S. Embassy in Saigon, and other key players. Kissinger, in turn, hired the defense think tank RAND Corporation to prepare a range of policy options for Nixon's consideration. [6]

Kissinger's review revealed agreement on some matters, but also significant differences of opinion on many aspects of the situation. While some divergence on the facts existed, the sharpest differences were in the interpretation of those facts, the relative weight given them, and the implications drawn. The agencies were generally divided along the lines of relative optimism and relative pessimism. The optimists included McCain, Abrams, Wheeler, the Chiefs, and the U.S. Embassy in Saigon, while the pessimists included the Central

Intelligence Agency (CIA), the Office of the Secretary of Defense (OSD), and the State Department.

There was general agreement that the Communists had not decided to negotiate in Paris out of weakness. They had suffered some reverses, but had not changed their essential objectives, and they possessed sufficient strength to pursue their objectives. The U.S. was not attriting Communist forces faster than they could recruit or infiltrate. The Communists could endure the current rate of attrition almost indefinitely and believed they could persist long enough to obtain a favorable negotiated settlement. Communist forces were capable of defeating the South Vietnamese Armed Forces if the U.S. were to withdraw from the war anytime in the foreseeable future. All the agencies believed the South Vietnamese government was improving but questioned whether it could survive even a peaceful competition with the Communists' National Liberation Front. [7]

Beyond these areas of agreement, the military and the U.S. Embassy in Saigon were relatively optimistic about South Vietnam's prospects. (False data underlay much of the optimism, however, since the U.S. Military Assistance Command, Vietnam (MACV) had suppressed negative analyses from the field.) On the other hand, OSD, the CIA, and elements within the State Department were decidedly more skeptical about the present and pessimistic about the future. They believed that recent pacification improvements were illusory and that Communist forces were far more numerous than the optimists thought. Thus far during the war, the optimists had been consistently wrong. [8]

Regarding U.S. combat operations, fundamental disagreements existed. The military assigned very much greater effectiveness to current and past bombing campaigns in Laos and North Vietnam than did OSD and the CIA. The military also believed that a vigorous bombing campaign could choke-off enough supplies to Hanoi to make it stop fighting, while OSD and the CIA saw North Vietnam continuing the struggle even against unlimited bombing.

All agencies agreed that Chinese and Soviet aid had provided almost all the war material used by Hanoi. However, OSD and the CIA disagreed with the military over whether the flow of aid could be reduced enough to make a difference in South Vietnam. If all imports by sea were denied and land routes through Laos and Cambodia attacked vigorously, the military believed that North Vietnam could not obtain enough supplies to continue. The OSD and CIA disagreed completely, believing that the overland routes from China alone could provide North Vietnam enough material to carry on, even with an unlimited bombing campaign. [9]

Resignation

In a private meeting with Nixon before the new Administration's first National Security Council (NSC) meeting on 21 January, Wheeler tendered his resignation. After exchanging pleasantries, including the traditional pledge of cooperation from the Chiefs, Wheeler said that he wanted to retire, that Nixon deserved a Chairman of his own choosing. Wheeler recited his role in the Johnson Administration to make certain that Nixon understood his position.

Wheeler told Nixon that he had served the nation for five full years, well beyond the usual four-year term for a Chairman of the Joint Chiefs of Staff, only because Johnson had insisted that he serve until the official end of his Administration. Now, Wheeler said, it was time for him to retire; he had served his country well past the time that most Army officers retired. He expected Nixon's thanks for a job well done and agreement that it was time for a new Chairman. Instead, Nixon shook his head in disagreement and surprise. Hadn't Wheeler already been confirmed by Congress? Why would he want to resign? How could he be replaced?

Wheeler later admitted to colleagues that he did not know whether to be complemented or suspicious. Apparently, it had never occurred to Nixon that Wheeler would want to leave, that he would choose retirement over power. It was a notion so foreign to Nixon as to be beyond belief. Wheeler had his reasons, which he repeated in increasingly insistent tones: not only had he served well past the time of other Chairmen, he had actually served longer than any other individual, including Bradley and Radford. To serve any longer, he told Nixon, would set a bad precedent. Again, Nixon disagreed, saying that he not only liked Wheeler personally, but he admired the position he had taken on the war. Wheeler was one military man who had wanted to win the war, Nixon said, adding that he understood just how difficult it had been for him over the last several years. As for precedent, Congress had already settled that matter by extending Wheeler's term another year. They could do so again. [10]

Wheeler's reasoning was not so much that he didn't want to set a precedent. Actually, he was exhausted. "He had suffered a heart attack in 1967 and could not be sure that he was medically fit for the job," Wheeler's son Bim explains. Wheeler needed a change, rest, a chance to recover his health. Then, perhaps, he could continue to serve the nation in some other capacity. He had been looking forward to retirement. Nixon would not listen. He dismissed Wheeler's arguments with a wave of his hand, ready to change the subject. Only when Wheeler continued to press his point, leaning impolitely over the President's desk, did Nixon finally comprehend that Wheeler was serious. Surprised by Wheeler's continued argument, Nixon appealed to his patriotism, telling him that the nation had not passed its "moment of decision" in Vietnam and that his invaluable experience was desperately needed. Promising Wheeler his full cooperation, Nixon said he would take the military's advice on the war more seriously than Johnson had. [11]

Wheeler may have been intrigued by Nixon's offer and implicit promise that the war could and would be, won; that it would end with a military victory, or at the very least Nixon and his appointees intended to see the war through to its conclusion. Undeterred, Wheeler admitted to Nixon that he was dying and had served long enough. "Of course, sir, if you make it a direct order, I will do as you wish." Otherwise, he was leaving. After a short pause, Nixon gave the order. [12]

"He didn't hear a goddamn thing I said!" Bus later exclaimed to Bim. [13]

In requesting Wheeler's reappointment for a sixth year as Chairman, Laird wrote that he and the President believed that retaining Wheeler would be in the best interests of the nation. "General Wheeler's intimate knowledge of our overall military posture and requirements, including operations in Southeast Asia, acquired during his tenure as Chairman of the Joint Chiefs of Staff, makes it prudent and wise to retain his invaluable experience and counsel during the current and impending period of operations and negotiations affecting Southeast Asia." [14]

"Wheeler's integrity and experience proved so indispensable that Nixon extended his term by yet another year," Kissinger recalled. "Tall, elegant, calm, Wheeler by that time was deeply disillusioned. He looked like a wary beagle, his soft dark eyes watchful for the origin of the next blow." [15]

RAND Study

Kissinger distributed the RAND paper during the NSC meeting on 25 January, the Nixon Administration's first conclave on Vietnam policy. RAND offered four policy options for escalation, including two variants on an invasion of North Vietnam, even though this was expected to require an additional 250,000 U.S. troops and added costs of $6-9 billion. A partial pullout option of leveling off at about 100,000 troops was included, while a full U.S. withdrawal was not. [16]

Nixon stated he felt the best course of action would be to hold on and told the group that achieving a cease-fire ought to be dropped as a negotiating goal. Offers of unilateral withdrawal were also to be eliminated. Nixon wanted to "seek ways in which we can change the game." He said, "I visualize that it could take two years to change this thing." Wheeler warned that draft calls would increase. Nixon wanted six months of strong military action combined with "a good public stance which reflects our efforts to seek peace." Candidly, he said that some troops could be brought home after a few months, "as a ploy for more time domestically." [17]

The RAND paper's judgments embodied contradictions. For example, although officials believed that Hanoi was talking because of its military defeat at Tet, the paper contained a clear sense that North Vietnam could maintain its strength in the field over the foreseeable future, and no expectation that Hanoi might offer the concessions to be expected of a defeated power. Second, although Nixon had issued the paper on Inauguration Day, he had never actually decided upon an option. Instead, he went straight to implementation. The use of threat to influence Hanoi became central to his strategy.

Arguments about all the options included claims or beliefs about the antiwar movement, what consequences that respective courses of action would have upon it, and inferences about the movement's impact on subsequent strategic choices. This reflected the new Administration's recognition that Vietnam strategy could no longer be determined in isolation. From the start, Nixon realized he was in a race for victory.[18]

Wishful Thinking

Nixon and Kissinger set as their optimum goal a "fair, negotiated settlement that would preserve the independence of South Vietnam." At a minimum, they insisted upon a settlement that would give South Vietnam a reasonable chance to survive. Although this objective had eluded the U.S. for more than a decade, they believed that they could succeed where previous Administrations had failed. Nixon and Kissinger were confident they could compel Hanoi to accept the terms that it had consistently rejected. The Soviet Union had made clear its keen interest in expanded trade with the U.S. and an agreement on limiting strategic arms. This leverage could be applied to secure Soviet assistance in convincing North Vietnam to agree to a "fair" settlement.[19]

In what was termed "linkage," Nixon would promise the Soviets arms limitation talks, economic cooperation, and other benefits if they exerted pressure on North Vietnam to accept an "honorable" settlement. Nixon would also attempt to establish linkage to China.[20]

Nixon and Kissinger were certain they could end the war within six months to a year. Through French intermediaries, the President would convey a personal message to the North Vietnamese expressing his sincere desire for peace and proposing as a first step mutual withdrawal of U.S. and North Vietnamese troops from South Vietnam and the restoration of the demilitarized zone as a boundary between North and South.

Great power diplomacy would be supplemented by the use of force. Nixon agreed with Wheeler's arguments that military pressure had thus far failed because it had been employed in a limited, indecisive manner. Nixon and Kissinger were prepared to use maximum force, threatening the very survival of North Vietnam, to achieve their policy objective. Nixon was certain that the threat of "massive retaliation" would intimidate Hanoi. He counted upon his image as a hardline anti-Communist to make the threats credible.[21]

Greatest Possible Pressure

Nixon had given Wheeler and the military reason for optimism that the war might now proceed on a more doctrinal and effective course. They were initially encouraged that an anti-Communist President was prepared to do what it took to "win this damn war!"[22]

Prior to his inauguration, Nixon had raised the issue of Cambodia and what could be done to destroy Hanoi's forces there. On 21 January, he asked Wheeler for options to stop supplies passing through Cambodia.[23]

"President Nixon … expressed great interest in the military situation in South Vietnam," Wheeler informed Abrams and McCain's deputy Air Force General Joseph H. Nazzaro the following day. "He believes that our negotiating interests would be best served by maintaining the greatest possible pressure on the enemy." The President had enquired whether there were any additional military actions, within present ground rules, that could be undertaken to exert increased pressures on the North Vietnamese Army (NVA) and Viet Cong. Wheeler sensed flexibility in Nixon's position on invading Cambodia, Laos, or North Vietnam.[24]

Encouraged that the new Administration "was intent on solving the problem in Vietnam, beginning with a full assessment of where we stand on the war," Wheeler quickly issued planning guidance to the Joint Staff.[25]

"It is possible that the [Communists] will employ stalling tactics as part of their negotiating strategy in Paris," Wheeler wrote. "If so, it could be to our advantage to create fear in the Hanoi leadership that the U.S. is getting ready to undertake new and damaging military actions against their territory, installations, or interests." Wheeler envisioned a psychological campaign supported by news leaks, movements of troops, aircraft, amphibious units, and other means, designed to create the belief that "we are fed up with their intransigence, are determined to achieve our stated objectives in Southeast Asia, and are readying the means to bring the war to a military conclusion."[26]

Wheeler requested the Joint Staff study several scenarios in sufficient detail for higher authorities to evaluate. These included combined airborne/amphibious operations against several objective areas in North Vietnam;

punitive expeditions in force against enemy lines of communication and base areas in Laos and Cambodia; renewed and expanded air and naval operations against North Vietnam, to include closing Haiphong and blockading North Vietnam; instigation of mass uprisings in North Vietnam; and any other realistic possible actions. [27]

Wheeler also requested the Joint Staff study the feasibility and utility of quarantining Cambodia against the receipt of supplies and equipment for Communist forces operating in and from Cambodia against South Vietnam. The study should contemplate a wide range of actions, including a naval blockade of Cambodian seaports and blocking the Mekong River to river traffic serving Cambodia. Wheeler wanted the study to be available for the Chiefs' consideration on 31 January. [28]

Before the Chiefs submitted any recommendations on Cambodia to the Secretary or Deputy Secretary of Defense, Wheeler felt the Chiefs' new civilian bosses should receive "a thorough backgrounding on our current activities in Cambodia." [29]

On 30 January, Kissinger discussed with Laird and Wheeler what might be done to signal escalation to Hanoi, such as a buildup of amphibious shipping at a South Vietnamese port to indicate an imminent invasion of North Vietnam. Convinced that attacking North Vietnam's capacity to sustain its forces on its own territory was the most direct and efficient way to proceed, Wheeler suggested ground operations against enemy base areas in southern North Vietnam or in the demilitarized zone (DMZ). Kissinger and Laird countered that ground operations within or above the DMZ were politically unsupportable.

"Wheeler proposed, as an alternative, attacks on the complex of bases that the North Vietnamese had established illegally across the border in Cambodia," Kissinger recalled. Abrams's forces were already fully committed within South Vietnam, however, and the discussion turned to the potential for CIA covert operations in Cambodia and increasing B-52 airstrikes in South Vietnam. To Wheeler's suggestion to renew bombing of the North, Kissinger recalled, "Laird demurred ... emphasizing that the bombing halt had encouraged public expectations that the war was being wound down. Nor did I favor it, because I was eager to give negotiations a chance." [30]

"While my colleagues and I keep ourselves fully informed on the wide spectrum of external and internal problems confronting our country, our role and our duty *under the law*, is to focus upon those concerns which are wholly, or largely, military in nature," Wheeler would later explain. "This point ... may seem to be self-evident. It isn't, unhappily, to some people. Solutions to nonmilitary problems should, and I'm confident will, come from non-military agencies and resources of government." [31]

In focusing on their task of providing military advice to the President, the Chiefs had, over the years, developed a rather stern self-administered test. "This test has only one question," Wheeler said. "If I (the members of the JCS) were the President of the United States, would I be willing to undertake this course of action that my principal military advisors have recommended to me? Applying this 'test' before furnishing military advice is the most surefire inducer of responsibility I know of — and we have every personal and institutional inducement to identify and discard the irresponsible before applying the simple 'test'." [32]

Laird, Nixon, and the Chiefs

A former leader of the House of Representatives, Laird was a smart, shrewd, and consummate politician. One senior military officer called Laird "a political animal to the marrow of his bones. ... He could use one line on the JCS, a somewhat different one with the Service Secretaries, and a third version in dealing with key members of Congress, many of whom were close personal friends." [33]

Among all Secretaries of Defense, Laird remains one of the most respected by senior military officers, not because he agreed with military programs and policies (he often did not), but because he was willing to compromise on the Chiefs' positions and accorded them the respect they deserved.

Like everything else in the Nixon Administration, the relationship between Laird and the Chiefs was unorthodox. Laird had difficulty accepting the Chiefs' belief that they were apolitical. Indeed, he sometimes believed some of them were playing politics to get into good graces with the White House. Any problems in his relationship with them stemmed less from any political behavior on their part than from his views on the situation in Vietnam. He was strongly opposed to any widening of the war and in fact wanted the U.S. to withdraw as quickly as possible.

Relieved to be free of Johnson's micromanagement, Wheeler and the Chiefs were happy to greet Nixon, but soon learned that his unscrupulous actions and his secretive behavior put them in a very difficult situation. The Chiefs would appreciate Nixon's authorization of many of the offensive actions they had advocated ever since the U.S. had gone to war in Vietnam. They also appreciated that he left the operational details of such actions to the military. Ultimately, though, the Chiefs would grow to distrust and dislike Nixon. Frustrated by his Vietnam War policy, they also could not countenance Nixon's lies, his deceitful ways, and his many efforts to get them to violate the chain of command. [34]

COSVN

Meanwhile in South Vietnam, the Communists launched another nationwide offensive that would claim another 1,740 American lives. Moving toward a new strategic approach, their offensive would last six weeks, demonstrating that despite having sustained horrific losses in 1968, the Communist dream of unifying Vietnam under their banner had not faded. Again, the North Vietnamese Army (NVA) and Viet Cong would suffer severely. Morale among the survivors would plummet by mid-1969. Between 1969 and 1971, captured documents would reveal defeatism, desertions, self-inflicted wounds (even suicides), debilitating supply shortages, and insufficient recruiting. [35]

Synchronizing and controlling the nationwide Communist offensive was Hanoi's elusive Central Office for South Vietnam (COSVN). On 9 February, Abrams informed Wheeler that recent intelligence had determined that COSVN was located just across the border in the Fish Hook area of Cambodia. Abrams requested authority to bomb the headquarters with B-52s, and Bunker endorsed the idea. Their request propelled Nixon into his first big Vietnam decision. [36]

Meanwhile, Wheeler's health issues still plagued him. During his annual physical exam, an electrocardiogram detected an arterial blockage that subsequent electrocardiograms would also observe over the next twelve months. [37]

While Wheeler was on medical leave on 13 February, McConnell, as Acting Chairman, sent Laird the Chiefs' recommendations to meet the Administration's request for a program of potential military actions that "might jar the North Vietnamese" into being more amenable at the Paris talks by conveying "that there is a new, firm hand at the helm." Their request included Abrams's recommendation to bomb COSVN. [38]

The Chiefs primarily requested authorizations for Abrams to conduct ground operations in the DMZ south of the demarcation line as necessary to counter enemy activities; to respond to a major enemy attack through or from the DMZ; and to counter attacking enemy forces with artillery, air, and naval gunfire against targets north and south of the demarcation line as necessary.

As for Cambodia, the Chiefs requested authorization for friendly ground forces in contact with Communist forces to pursue the enemy into Cambodia to a depth of 5 kilometers by ground and 10 kilometers by air, following offensive action in South Vietnam by these Communist forces. Pursuit operations would be of short duration, usually not exceeding three to five days, and the friendly forces would return to South Vietnam. The Chiefs also requested authorization for U.S. long-range reconnaissance patrols to be employed north of Route 13 to a depth of 30 kilometers into Cambodia. They recommended the employment of reconnaissance aircraft over Cambodia to a depth of 20 kilometers with no sortie limitation. They sought authorization for artillery and airstrikes against observed enemy forces and installations in Cambodia to a depth of 20 kilometers north of Route 13 and 10 kilometers south of Route 13. These strikes would avoid Cambodian villages, forces, or population. The Chiefs further sought authorization for air and artillery strikes to support the emergency extraction of ground reconnaissance teams from Cambodia to prevent loss of life from enemy actions. [39]

In the event of a large-scale enemy offensive in South Vietnam, the Chiefs requested additional authorization for B-52 strikes on the COSVN headquarters. For planning purposes, they recommended a short duration, concentrated B-52 attack of up to 60 sorties. This weight of effort was not excessive considering the 9 square kilometer size of the target area and the necessity for complete destruction of this key headquarters. The Chiefs noted Bunker's support for the attack. Abrams had advised that there was little chance of involving Cambodian nationals in this attack. [40]

On 18 February, Abrams provided further justification for bombing COSVN, after which Kissinger sent the President a lengthy paper on the pros and cons of such an operation. [41]

Later that month, the Chiefs submitted an additional list of possible military actions to exert increased pressures on the North Vietnamese and Viet Cong. Besides their usual recommendations, the list included options for either the actual or feigned use of each, and it added one for "technical escalation," an apparent euphemism for nuclear weapons. The Chiefs also recommended an invasion of North Vietnam, invasions of Laos or Cambodia, resumed bombing of North Vietnam, and attempted subversion of North Vietnam. Laird forwarded their recommendations to Kissinger. [42]

When Kissinger responded to Laird on 3 March, the political constraints were manifest. "I'm somewhat concerned," Kissinger wrote, "that the 'realities' of the current domestic and international environment do not lend themselves to the acceptance of these risks at this time." Kissinger returned to the proposals he had pressed on Laird and Wheeler a month before — visible signals of a build-up such as planning conferences or "even the staging of amphibious shipping" — that "could be implemented with less risk of international or domestic turbulence." [43]

Wheeler and Secretary of Defense Melvin R. Laird aboard a military aircraft bound for the Far East, March 1969. (Office of the Chairman of the Joint Chiefs of Staff)

(From left) Wheeler, Abrams, U.S. Ambassador to South Vietnam Ellsworth F. Bunker, and Laird confer in Saigon, March 1969. (Office of the Chairman of the Joint Chiefs of Staff)

After a trip with Laird to the Far East on 5-12 March, Wheeler submitted a series of recommendations to Laird. "The most striking and dangerous situations are comprised of the enemy troop and logistic buildups in the DMZ area, in the panhandle of Laos, and in Cambodia," Wheeler wrote. The enemy had been urgently stocking his base areas in the panhandle of Laos in order to be logistically prepared for the onset of the rainy season. "The immense quantities of material and supplies seized or destroyed during the recent operation in the A Shau Valley are, I think, ample proof that enemy base areas situated deeper and further to the north in Laos represent lucrative targets for preemptive action by our ground and air forces." [44]

"By now, I think that all of us recognize the importance to the enemy and the threat to our forces posed by the Cambodian sanctuary base areas," Wheeler continued. "In actuality, it is those base areas from which the threat to Saigon originates and is sustained. They, and their counterparts in Laos and contiguous to the DMZ, are also the prime cause of U.S. casualties." [45]

Enemy base areas provided the human and material means to inflict casualties on U.S. and Allied forces. If these base areas were destroyed or neutralized, friendly casualties would automatically decrease. "The next rocket attacks on Saigon, Hue, or Da Nang must be followed by an appropriate U.S. response," Wheeler urged. "Preferably, our response should take the form of naval and/or air attacks against targets in North Vietnam." [46]

Abrams should be immediately authorized to operate offensively in the southern DMZ in order to preempt enemy buildup in and use of that area, Wheeler recommended. Abrams should also be tasked for plans to attack and destroy, by air and ground raids in force, critical enemy base areas in Laos in order to deplete enemy logistic resources during the rainy season there. Abrams should be also tasked for plans to destroy, by air and ground raids in force, enemy Cambodian sanctuary base areas. [47]

Wheeler also recommended that "mining operations against Haiphong Port be carried out as part of a large-scale sustained air campaign against all military targets in the area." He also advised that it was feasible to block the outer Haiphong Channel with a scuttled U.S. submarine. "However, to be effective, a hydrographic survey of the probable scuttling area must be conducted and supporting operations such as mining and harassing of dredging and salvage operations must be conducted subsequent to the scuttling of the submarine." [48]

Furthermore, Wheeler also requested approval of Abrams's recommendation for B-52 strikes against enemy sanctuary targets in several base areas in Cambodia. [49]

Responding to discussions about the possible conduct of "surgical" strikes on the Haiphong area, Wheeler observed that since the cessation of bombing operations north of the 19th Parallel on 31 March 1968, the defenses in the Haiphong area had been increased to formidable proportions, and in order to effectively suppress them large numbers of aircraft would be required. The disadvantage of conducting attacks over relatively short periods of time, Wheeler explained, was that in addition to strike aircraft, aircraft were required for MIG protection, air defense suppression, and electronic countermeasures, and in the initial phases, until these threats could be appreciably diminished, losses to friendly aircraft would be high. A 3% initial lost rate could be anticipated. Furthermore, suppression of air defenses would have to be a continuous program aimed not only at the air defenses themselves but also at the supply areas feeding them and at the routes for resupply. After having suppressed and destroyed much of the threat in the target area, however, the effectiveness of strike forces would improve, and their loss rate would be lowered.

Retaliatory attacks against a few selected targets by tactical aircraft and naval gunfire ships in the Haiphong area for a short duration were feasible, Wheeler stated. However, the large effort that would be required to suppress air defenses and to protect against the MIG threat was not commensurate with the results likely to be achieved. In view of the large effort required for a selective retaliatory attack in the Haiphong area, the Chiefs recommended instead a sustained bombardment of all war-supporting targets in the area. "This would better serve the purpose of retaliation, be of military significance, and bring into sharp focus the need for productive talks in Paris," Wheeler wrote. [50]

On 4 March, Laird had responded to the Chiefs' earlier recommendation for authority to react to enemy operations in the DMZ area south of the demarcation line with friendly forces appropriate to the enemy threat involved. He requested specific evidence of enemy intentions to launch significant attacks from the southern portion of the DMZ. He also requested alternatives and the Chiefs' judgment of the effectiveness and risks in the alternatives.

Responding on 15 March with a brief review of past operations in the DMZ, Wheeler reported that current intelligence indicated that, during the past four weeks, three North Vietnamese Army (NVA) regiments had used the southern portion of the DMZ for transit, that the enemy had apparently been moving forces toward the eastern part of the DMZ, and that the overall enemy threat in the immediate DMZ area had increased by two regiments. Another full NVA division was at Dong Hoi within short motor march of the DMZ.

"In view of the building enemy threat and [Abrams's] current capability," Wheeler advised, "I consider that provision of authority to conduct ground operations south of the [demarcation line] of not greater than five days duration and not greater than brigade-size would permit [Abrams] to conduct limited combat sweeps to counter enemy activity in the area. [51]

MENU

Nixon and Kissinger realized that domestic politics stood in the way of their preferred option of hammering the North Vietnamese. Laird opposed them, fearing that they would "do the one thing we don't want to happen, they will expand the war." Rather than abandon his course, Nixon tried to contrive conditions under which it could be carried out. The first element, beginning in mid-March, was the President's counterattack on the antiwar movement. The second element involved formalizing Vietnamization, which Laird would do in Saigon on 3 April. A final element centered on the Paris negotiations, where Nixon and Kissinger both perceived that the appearance of U.S. flexibility would help them gain freedom of action. [52]

On 14 March, "the North Vietnamese fired five rockets into Saigon – a further escalation in violation of the understanding," Kissinger recalled. "There were 32 enemy attacks against major South Vietnamese cities in the first two weeks of March." The President wanted to attack the Cambodian sanctuaries with an immediate B-52 strike. Kissinger convinced him to consult with his senior foreign policy advisors first. [53]

Two days later, the President met with Secretary of State William P. Rogers, Laird, Wheeler, and Kissinger. Laird and Wheeler strongly advocated the airstrikes. Rogers objected, not on foreign policy but on domestic grounds, fearing "that we would run into a buzz saw in Congress just when things are calming down." Ultimately, Rogers agreed to a B-52 strike on the base area containing the presumed COSVN headquarters." [54]

After the meeting, Wheeler and the Chiefs attempted to amend the President's orders to include additional attacks on North Vietnamese troop concentrations violating the DMZ. Kissinger recalled, "Laird and I agreed that it was more important to keep Rogers with us, and the proposal was not approved." [55]

As a signal to both Hanoi and Moscow that the U.S. meant business, Kissinger advised Nixon to approve intensive bombing attacks against North Vietnamese sanctuaries in Cambodia. Sharp, Westmoreland, Wheeler, and the Chiefs had repeatedly recommended it, but Johnson had always refused. [56]

Cambodian neutrality had been routinely violated by both the Communists and the United States, the former by maintaining sanctuaries there and the latter by cross-border raiding under Operation DANIEL BOONE (later redesignated SALEM HOUSE). [57]

The bombing of Cambodia would be known as Operation MENU, and its military objective was to limit North Vietnamese capacity to launch an offensive against the South by destroying COSVN and degrading Communist capabilities throughout III and IV Corps Tactical Zones. Nixon's primary motive, however, was to send a message to Hanoi that he was not bound by Johnson's self-imposed restraints and that he would take measures that his predecessor had avoided. Thus, Nixon hoped to drive Hanoi into negotiating on his terms. [58]

"The state of play in Paris is completely sterile," Nixon stated. "I am convinced that the only way to move the negotiations off dead center is to do something on the military front. That is something [Hanoi] will understand." [59]

Kissinger informed Laird on the eve of MENU that Nixon's order to bomb neutral Cambodia was "something he cannot ever avow." Nixon insisted that the operation be kept an absolute secret from the American public, and indeed from much of the government. Only select individuals would be informed. Laird did notify key legislators, but neither the Secretary of the Air Force nor the Vice Chief of Staff of the Air Force were advised of the bombing.[60]

Importantly, the decision to keep the operation secret from the public had a major impact on Laird's dealing with the White House. He had argued against both the operation and the secrecy surrounding it. From then on, his relationship with the White House would become increasingly adversarial.[61]

To preclude an anticipated domestic uproar, Laird instructed Wheeler to maintain strict operational security so that MENU was not divulged to the American public.[62]

Nevertheless, on 25 March, an article appeared in the *Washington Star* under a full-page headline, "Military Asks to Hit Cambodia: Presses Nixon to Knockout Red Sanctuary: Points to Hints by Sihanouk That He Won't Object". The article, datelined Saigon and written by Jack Walsh, a writer for United Press International, leaked detailed and accurate information on proposed airstrikes under consideration.

"Both DoD and State have refused to comment with State disclaiming any planned escalation of our effort," Wheeler advised Abrams that day. "I further understand that you will also decline to comment. I believe this is the best posture for all of us and one I plan to adopt. Needless to say, we all needed this exercise like a hole of the head. I presume you are looking into the possible source of the reporter's information."[63]

In consequence, a cover story was devised, knowledge of the operation was restricted to those with a need-to-know basis only, and elaborate methods of bookkeeping were employed.[64]

The menu bombing commenced on 17 March with BREAKFAST, a strike by almost sixty B-52s against a single Communist base area in the Fish hook region of Cambodia. Each base area was assigned its own codename — LUNCH, DINNER, SUPPER, DESSERT, and SNACK.

In April, Nixon expressed his satisfaction with the bombing to Wheeler. The operation then became a sustained air campaign, averaging 800 sorties a month into the summer, several hundred monthly after that. About 70,500 tons of bombs would fall on Cambodia during 1969, with another 35,300 tons in the first five months of 1970. This would represent almost 15% of the bomb tonnage dropped on North Vietnam during all of ROLLING THUNDER.[65]

Vietnamization

Wheeler reported to Abrams on 27 March that "the Walsh article was taken in stride here, which pleased me no end." Wheeler went on to inform Abrams that "the subject of troop reductions is an exceedingly hot one here. I fear that we will be faced soon with very serious financial problems which will impact directly on this matter and perhaps on our future course in Vietnam. I will keep you informed of such developments and will solicit your help in finding satisfactory solutions."[66]

In a speech in Saigon on 3 April, Laird formalized Vietnamization, the broad policy that would guide the final phase of U.S. involvement in South Vietnam.

The primary goal of Vietnamization was to create a strong, largely self-reliant South Vietnamese Armed Forces, an objective that had been espoused by U.S. advisors since the 1950s. But Vietnamization also meant the withdrawal of half a million U.S. soldiers. Past efforts to strengthen and modernize the South Vietnamese Army (ARVN) had proceeded at a measured pace, without the pressure of diminishing U.S. support, large-scale combat, or the presence of formidable North Vietnamese forces in the South. Vietnamization entailed three overlapping phases: redeployment of U.S. forces and the assumption of their combat role by the South Vietnamese; improvement of the ARVN's combat and support capabilities, especially firepower and mobility; and replacement of MACV by a U.S. advisory group. Vietnamization included the additional dimension of fostering political, social, and economic reforms to create a vibrant South Vietnamese state based on popular participation in national political life. Such reforms, however, depended on progress in the pacification program, which never had a clearly fixed timetable.[67]

Abrams still commanded strong U.S. forces, which reached their peak at 543,000 in March. But he was also under pressure from Washington to minimize casualties, to conduct operations with an eye toward leaving the South Vietnamese in the strongest possible military position when U.S. forces withdrew, and to convince the American people with progress on the battlefield that the tide had turned in the Allies' favor. With these considerations in mind, Abrams pressed the attack, especially against enemy bases near the borders to prevent their use as Communist staging areas for offensive operations. At the same time, to enhance the South Vietnamese government's pacification efforts and improve local security, Abrams called upon his commanders to intensify small-unit operations with extensive patrolling and ambushes, aiming to reduce the Communists' base of support among the rural population. [68]

"I feel obliged to place before [Laird] at this time our considered judgment against adoption of a purely defensive posture in [South Vietnam]," Wheeler had written to McCain and Abrams on 28 March. [69]

Wheeler informed Laird that throughout the course of the war, the Chiefs and commanders at all echelons had conducted a continuing and searching examination of equipment, tactics, techniques, and long-established military doctrines and principles with a view toward improving combat effectiveness and reducing U.S. casualties. "Since this war has been different in many respects from previous wars which the United States has been engaged, no aspect of this problem has been exempted from scrutiny," Wheeler wrote. [70]

"A fundamental desideratum in military operations is to gain and maintain the initiative – that is, freedom of action," Wheeler explained. "This consideration underlies the strenuous and continuous efforts of [Abrams] to gain the initiative in the greatest degree possible in [South Vietnam]." [71]

Wheeler then articulated the offensive warfighting doctrine that had always underpinned the U.S. military's conviction of how to fight the Vietnam War, or any other war for that matter:

> The commander who enjoys the initiative can act when, where, and how he chooses; the enemy can only react. A commander exercises the initiative by continually probing

the enemy, seeking out places, times, and enemy activity patterns which will permit the determination of situations exploitable to his advantage. Such action has the bonus effect of keeping the enemy off balance, unable to mount telling attacks and less able himself to assess the weaknesses of the opposing offensive force. As offensive initiatives unbalance enemy planning and activities, the enemy tends to operate by rote, thus further compounding his vulnerability. The offensive force gathers information, seeks advantageous terrain, gains spirit and confidence, and creates situations which will require the enemy to fight on terms most favorable to the attacker. Using offensive tactics, a commander can attack the enemy's points of weakness with overwhelming strength at times and locations providing the greatest advantage of mass, firepower, and ability to the attacker. [72]

Reflecting the Administration's emphasis on minimizing casualties, Wheeler wrote, "It is my professional judgment, supported fully by that of General Abrams, General Goodpaster, and their commanders and the other members of the Joint Chiefs of Staff, that to change the pattern of our operations in South Vietnam from offensive to defensive would increase, rather than decrease casualties to U.S. and other friendly forces and would place in jeopardy our progress and objectives in Vietnam." [73]

Friendly casualties had resulted largely from enemy troops and munitions coming from sanctuary base areas in Laos and Cambodia along the South Vietnamese borders, Wheeler continued. How long the U.S. must continue to sustain U.S. and Allied casualties from the enemy's unimpeded use of the sanctuaries involved questions of significant international and national importance, he noted. It was the judgment of Abrams and his commanders at all levels, which was shared by the Chiefs, that the destruction of these base areas and their denial as sanctuaries could result in a very significant reduction in U.S. and Allied casualties and was the single most important action that could be taken toward that end. "I recommend that military operations, both ground and air, be undertaken to destroy these enemy sources of friendly dead and wounded," Wheeler wrote.[74]

To the greatest extent possible, Abrams planned to improve the ARVN's performance by enhancing training and conducting combined operations with U.S. combat units. As the ARVN assumed the lion's share of combat, Abrams expected it to shift operations toward the borders and to assume a role like that performed by U.S. forces since 1965. In turn, the Regional Forces and Popular Forces would assume the ARVN's role in area security and pacification support, while the newly organized People's Self-Defense Force assumed the task of village and hamlet defense. Abrams reiterated his "one war" concept, which stressed the close connection between combat and pacification operations, the need for cooperation between U.S. and South Vietnamese forces, and the importance of coordinating all echelons of Saigon's armed forces.

Yet, even in Abrams's emphasis on combined operations, his targeting of Communist base areas, and U.S. support of pacification, his strategy included strong elements of continuity with Westmoreland's. Westmoreland had laid the foundation for a more extensive U.S. role in pacification back in 1967 when he established Civil Operations and Rural (later changed to Revolutionary) Development Support (CORDS). Under CORDS, MACV assumed control of all U.S. activities, military and civilian, in support of pacification.

Abrams had expanded the U.S. Army's contribution to pacification. The U.S. advisory effort at provincial and district levels had grown as the territorial forces gained importance. In 1967, there were 108 American advisors attached to the Regional Forces and Popular Forces; a year later, the number grew to 2,243. Another important step pushed by CORDS had been the PHOENIX Program, which was expanded into virtually every district in South Vietnam, using a combination of conventional forces, militia, police, and psychological and intelligence operations not previously possible on such a large scale.

Despite all efforts, many Americans doubted whether the South Vietnamese Armed Forces (RVNAF) could successfully perform their expanded role under Vietnamization. On paper, Saigon's armed forces were formidable and improving. Thanks to the Thieu government's mobilization law and U.S. aid and assistance, the RVNAF had become among the largest and most heavily equipped in the world. The regular and territorial forces end-strength, which stood at 850,000 in late 1968, would rise to over 1 million in less than two years. The newest weapons in the U.S. arsenal were being given to the South Vietnamese, from M-16 rifles and M-60 machine guns to helicopter gunships, jeeps, and jet fighters. Combat effectiveness was also apparently on the rise. Nonetheless, earlier counterinsurgency efforts had languished under less demanding circumstances, and Saigon's forces continued to be plagued by a high desertion rate, spotty morale, and shortages of high-quality leaders. Like the French before them, U.S. advisors had assumed a major role in providing and coordinating logistical and firepower support, leaving the Vietnamese inexperienced in the conduct of large combined-arms operations. Despite the Viet Cong's weakened condition, the RVNAF also continued to sustain high casualties.

Similarly, pacification had registered gains in rural security and other measures of progress, but such improvements often obscured its failure to establish deep roots. The challenge was that the Communist infrastructure had not been eliminated entirely and still constituted a potent threat to the government. The PHOENIX Program, despite its success in seizing low- and middle-level cadres, rarely caught high-level Communist Party officials, many of whom survived, as they had in the mid-1950s, by taking more stringent security measures. [75]

Nixon had recognized that the success of his Vietnam policy hinged upon his ability to maintain at least the appearance of unity at home. Adopting a public relations strategy to parallel his secret diplomacy, Nixon announced on 14 May what he described as a "comprehensive peace plan," publicly revealing the proposals he had privately made to the North Vietnamese and adding his hope that all "foreign" troops might be removed from South Vietnam within a year after the signing of a peace agreement. Previously, the U.S. had insisted that North Vietnamese troops leave the South six months prior to a U.S. withdrawal. Now, however, Nixon called for "mutually phased withdrawals" of troops from both sides. [76]

Combat Operations

"The [Chiefs] are not repeat not convinced that, if the North Vietnamese see the opportunity to inflict a substantial defeat of the 1st ARVN Division, they will forgo the chance because of political considerations," Wheeler informed McCain and Abrams on 31 May. "On the contrary, the [Chiefs] are of the opinion that the North Vietnamese efforts steadily to erode the 'understanding' regarding the DMZ reached at the time of the total cessation of bombing last spring and their buildup of logistics and combat forces contiguous to the DMZ and in Laos opposite northern I Corps [Tactical Zone] may have been undertaken in anticipation of seizing a favorable opportunity to inflict a defeat upon us." Moreover, the Chiefs considered that a substantial defeat inflicted on ARVN forces, particularly the 1st ARVN Division, would "destroy our concept of Vietnamizing the war and could have psychological consequences as great as, or greater than, the Tet Offensive of 1968." [77]

Since the 1968 Tet Offensive, the Communists had restocked the A Shau Valley with ammunition, rice, and equipment. The logistical buildup had indicated a possible North Vietnamese offensive in early 1969, so a quick succession of U.S. and Allied operations had been launched in the familiar pattern of air assaults, establishment of fire bases, and exploration of the lowlands and surrounding hills to locate Communist forces and supplies. [78]

On 10-20 May, elements of the 101st Airborne Division and the 1st ARVN Division fought to seize Hill 937. Despite losing 56 killed and 420 wounded in one of the war's fiercest and most controversial battles, the U.S. soon abandoned the hard-won "Hamburger Hill", and the North Vietnamese Army (NVA) returned, reinforcing the public perception that the war was not just futile, but absurd.

In consequence, Laird insisted that Abrams make reducing casualties a primary objective. A new mission statement no longer called for the Communists' defeat but instead directed MACV to provide maximum assistance to strengthening the ARVN and to reducing infiltration down the Ho Chi Minh Trail. Abrams's emphasis had to shift from fighting the war to improving the ARVN and to locating and destroying the NVA's logistical system. [79]

Financial austerity measures, which limited ARC LIGHT strikes, artillery fire, tactical air support, and fuel consumption, would impact MACV's conduct of the war. Between 1968 and 1970, the B-52 sortie rate would fall from 1,800 to 1,000 per month, and harassment & interdiction fire would be restricted to reduce munitions consumption. Such reductions, Abrams complained, were "*entirely* a budgetary motivated thing" that had nothing to do with the tactical situation. [80]

Troop Withdrawals

Back on 5 March, Moorer, as Acting Chairman, had informed Laird that plans existed to cover a variety of possible situations under which withdrawal might occur. A reporting system together with a comprehensive, automated database was being developed to support any withdrawal plan. By approximately mid-April 1969, McCain should be able to determine the logistic feasibility of any withdrawal plan. In the meantime, McCain was preparing a conceptual plan for a 'worst' option in which total withdrawal including a Military Assistance and Advisory Group could occur within six months after T-day. This plan should be completed by the end of April for subsequent review by the Joint Staff. [81]

Eight days later, Wheeler forewarned Abrams about significant impending changes in U.S. policy by quoting a portion of Laird's Vietnam trip report:

> I believe it is essential that we decide now to initiate the removal from Southeast Asia of some U.S. military personnel. The qualitative and quantitative improvements of the [South Vietnamese Armed Forces] to date, although perhaps less than desired, should permit us to redeploy from Southeast Asia between 50 to 70 thousand troops during the remainder of this calendar year. I am convinced that this will in no way jeopardize the security of the remaining U.S. and Allied forces and that such a move is necessary to retain U.S. public support for continued efforts in South Vietnam. [82]

To make plain his intention of terminating U.S. involvement in the war, Nixon now initiated planning for the phased withdrawal of U.S. combat troops.

Nixon met with Rogers, Laird, Wheeler, and Kissinger in Honolulu on 7 June. "The meeting was to take the final decision on withdrawal strategy," Kissinger recalled. "It was clear that the military approached the subject with a heavy heart. Deep down they knew that it was a reversal of what they had fought for. However presented, it would make victory impossible and even an honorable outcome problematical. The process of withdrawal was likely to become irreversible," Kissinger realized. "Henceforth, we would be in a race between the decline in our combat capability and the improvement of South Vietnamese forces – a race whose outcome was at best uncertain." [83]

"It was obvious to me that both Wheeler and ... Abrams ... could not have been more unhappy," Kissinger recalled. "Every instinct told them it was improbable that we could prevail by reducing our strength. The more forces were withdrawn, the less likely a tolerable outcome would be achieved." [84]

"It was painful to see General Abrams, the epitome of the combat commander, obviously unhappy, yet nevertheless agreeing to a withdrawal of 25,000 combat troops," Kissinger wrote. "He knew then that he was doomed to a rearguard action, that the purpose of his command would increasingly become logistic redeployment and not success in battle. He could not possibly achieve a victory that had eluded us at full strength while our forces were constantly dwindling." [85]

The following day, Nixon met with Thieu on Midway Island and informed him that the U.S. planned to withdraw 25,000 troops beginning in July. He assured Thieu that the withdrawals "would be timed so as not to undermine South Vietnam's stability or political viability, and that the United States would not be party to the imposition of a coalition government on the Vietnamese." [86]

After Midway, Nixon announced the first increment of 25,000 American combat troops would be withdrawn by 31 August. To emphasize to the Soviets, the North Vietnamese, and conservatives at home that he had not gone soft, Nixon delivered several tough speeches, attacking as "new isolationists" those doves who argued that the war was diverting the nation from more pressing problems at home and stressing his determination to uphold America's international responsibilities. [87]

Peace Talks

Nixon's secret diplomacy and implied military threats failed to wrench concessions from Hanoi, though. "The North Vietnamese considered themselves in a life-and-death struggle; they did not treat negotiations as an enterprise separate from the struggle; they were a form of it," Kissinger explained. "To them, the Paris talks were not a device for settlement but an instrument of political warfare. They were a weapon to exhaust us psychologically, to split us from our South Vietnamese ally, and to divide our public opinion through vague hints of solutions just out of reach because of the foolishness or obduracy of our government." [88]

"Our negotiating delegation in Paris anticipated (wrongly, as it turned out) that Hanoi would raise this issue [of de-escalation] and urged that we would be obliged to reply," Kissinger continued. "The State Department and our Paris team argued that we offer to discuss the curtailment of B-52 strikes, of U.S. offensive operations, and of the use of artillery for interdiction." Both Abrams and the Chiefs strongly disagreed, insisting that such measures would cede the military initiative to the Communists and allow them to rebuild their strength in the populated areas. "That too turned out to be a moot issue, since Hanoi never showed the slightest interest in de-escalation, even as we implemented it unilaterally," Kissinger wrote. "The North Vietnamese were less interested in stopping the fighting than in winning it." [89]

From the North Vietnamese standpoint, Nixon's proposals were no improvement over Johnson's, and to have accepted them would have represented the abandonment of goals for which they had been fighting for nearly quarter century. They continued to demand the total and unconditional withdrawal of all U.S. forces from Vietnam and called for the establishment of a government from which Thieu would be excluded. Hanoi also shifted to a defensive, protracted war strategy, sharply curtailing the level of military activity in the South and withdrawing some troops back across the demilitarized zone. Certain that American public opinion would eventually force Nixon to withdraw from Vietnam, Hanoi prepared to wait him out, no matter what the cost might be.

Home Front

Nixon's peace moves also failed to mollify the opposition at home. When it became obvious that no breakthrough would be forthcoming in Paris, public approval of the President's handling of the war dropped sharply. The organized peace movement, dormant since the Democratic convention of 1968, began to stir again, announcing plans for massive demonstrations in the fall. Congressional doves had remained silent during the Administration's first hundred days, giving the President an opportunity to end the war, but by June they began to speak out anew. Senate doves were not satisfied with Nixon's peace offer and troop withdrawal, and many Democrats rallied behind Clifford's call for the withdrawal of all U.S. forces by the end of 1970. By mid-summer, Nixon's brief honeymoon with the Democrat-controlled Congress had ended.

Never one to avoid a fight, the pugnacious Nixon struck back at his foes. The Administration used all its public relations skills to draw attention to those who supported Nixon's policies and to discredit those who opposed him. Viewing the antiwar movement as an enemy that must be crushed, Nixon launched a systematic campaign to destroy it.

The Administration increased government surveillance of antiwar organizations and their leaders. The FBI, CIA, and the military expanded their surveillance activities, tapping phones and ransacking files of antiwar groups. Like Johnson, Nixon was certain that the Communists were masterminding the movement, and when extensive analysis again failed to establish a direct connection, he disparaged the intelligence rather than re-examine his assumptions. The Administration went well beyond intelligence gathering to infiltration and sabotage. Government agencies spread disinformation to discredit antiwar groups. The Internal Revenue Service and FBI harassed major organizations and their leaders. Agents working inside these organizations helped to disrupt their lawful activity, incited them to violent acts against each other, and engaged in actions to make them look bad. [90]

Vietnamization

Ideally, the withdrawal of U.S. forces would be synchronized with progress in the peace negotiations, a reduced level of Communist activity, and success in Vietnamization and pacification so that South Vietnam could defend itself. Then, even if the Communists refused to negotiate a settlement, a reinvigorated South could confront them with the prospect of perpetual war. However, "[Laird] seemed obsessed with getting out of Vietnam for political reasons as soon as possible," Westmoreland recalled. "He put such emphasis on withdrawal as to be virtually indifferent to what happened on the battlefield." [91]

Virtually everyone understood that, at best, Vietnamization would be a difficult, long-term process. Kissinger believed it would never work. Laird thought it was a farce. Abrams considered it a "slow surrender," nothing but a fig leaf to cover a U.S. retreat. Unless the North Vietnamese Army returned to North Vietnam, MACV concluded, "there is little chance that any improvement in the Republic of Vietnam's Armed Forces or any degree of progress in pacification, no matter how significant, could justify significant reductions in U.S. forces from their present level." [92]

Invigorating the ARVN would have been difficult in peacetime. Doing so in wartime compounded the difficulty. The ARVN had systemic problems, foremost among them being poor leadership. Abrams asserted that the ARVN was "not going to be any better, no matter what we do, no matter what we give them in the way of equipment, and no matter what we do with them in the way of training, unless they've got the kind of leadership that'll take a hold of it and carry it." But solid, aggressive leadership was scarce because Thieu, always fearing a coup, selected commanders based on political loyalty, not combat ability. In late 1970, a senior U.S. official would rate only one South Vietnamese general as "fully competent." [93]

Even if South Vietnam had competent officers, they served in a dysfunctional system. Corruption was rampant. Desertion was a disruption at best, a serious manpower drain at worst. Soldiers endured poor food and housing, low pay, medical malpractice, and inadequate training, all of which led them to resent their government. Another problem was that the Saigon government recruited, trained, and based almost all ARVN units territorially. If the government ordered those troops outside their region, the unit could disintegrate as men deserted to stay close to their families.

With U.S. troop withdrawals under way, the effort to expand and improve South Vietnam's military and security forces commenced. The ARVN would increase from 380,000 in 1968 to 416,000 two years later, primarily through tightening deferments, expanding the draft age, and mandating that soldiers serve for the duration. Both the South Vietnamese Navy and Air Force would approximately double in size between 1968 and 1970. The Territorial Forces would also expand, going from 393,000 men in 1968 to 543,000 in 1970. Regular and territorial forces would receive upgraded equipment, including M-16 rifles and M-79 grenade launchers, and the regulars would benefit from infusions of artillery, tanks, helicopters, aircraft, and ships. In 1971, the National Police would number 114,000 men, while the People's Self Defense Force (PSDF), an unpaid, lightly armed militia, would contain 4,429,000 members, at least on paper.

Captured documents revealed that the Communists were worried about Vietnamization, especially the upgrading of the territorials and the establishment of the PSDF, both of which provided local security. The crucial question, however, was whether quantitative growth equaled qualitative improvements, and that could not be answered until the ARVN and territorials faced a test in major combat.[94]

Wheeler, McCain, and Abrams in South Vietnam, 16 July 1969.
(Office of the Chairman of the Joint Chiefs of Staff)

Publicly, the Administration put a positive spin on the war. In mid-July, Wheeler made another trip to Vietnam accompanied by McCain. The President was there, as well. Addressing the troops of the 1st Infantry Division on 20 July, Nixon said, "I think history will record that this may have been one of America's finest hours, because we took a difficult task and we succeeded." [95]

"We trust that the war in Vietnam can be brought to a successful conclusion," Nixon said in a toast to Philippine President Ferdinand Marcos nine days later. "I happen to be an optimist. ... We can see the exciting possibilities for progress." [96]

Hanoi's New Approach

Whether because of heavy losses sustained during four consecutive offensives, declining morale, or a matter of strategic choice (or a combination of all three), the Communists adopted a new approach. In July, the Central Office for South Vietnam (COSVN) unveiled a protracted war strategy, in which the Viet Cong & North Vietnamese Army (NVA) would wait for U.S. strength to ebb before attempting another major strike. Victory, the Communists now realized, would not come suddenly through a Tet-like offensive, "but in a complicated and tortuous way." Many large NVA units pulled back to base areas in Cambodia and Laos, while those that stayed in the South broke into smaller units and employed commando tactics and indirect attacks with mortars and rockets to conserve strength while still inflicting casualties on U.S. forces.

As combat intensity declined, political *dau tranh* received heightened emphasis. The Communists' attention shifted from urban to rural areas, where the goal was to disrupt a revived pacification effort. Propaganda activities increased, and terrorist incidents, such as assassinations and abductions, would grow from 7,566 in 1967 to 12,056 in 1970. While this strategic shift was underway, another change occurred: Viet Cong casualties were so heavy in 1968 that NVA soldiers had begun replacing Southerners to rebuild the Viet Cong's strength, a task that would eventually achieve considerable success by 1972.[97]

Troop Withdrawals

The Administration intended the departure of U.S. troops to transform the war, reduce casualties, save money, and buy more time by appeasing the antiwar movement. Once initiated, the withdrawals would become irreversible. Laird would "turn dove" as McNamara and Clifford had done and would pressure Nixon to continue the drawdown. Not only would the withdrawals come faster and larger than Abrams advised, but they would also be unilateral (since North Vietnam rejected mutual withdrawals) and total, even though Abrams's planners had assumed the U.S. would leave a residual force, as it had done in Korea. Because of the need to undercut antiwar protests and to revive a flagging economy, Nixon felt that bringing the troops home took precedence over South Vietnam's survival. While the withdrawals scored political points domestically, they would also reduce Hanoi's incentive to negotiate: Why sign an agreement if the U.S. was disengaging anyway, and withdrawing so quickly that, as Kissinger would note, it placed "a burden of credulity on Vietnamization"?[98]

Laird and the military could not agree on how best to proceed. McCain, Abrams, Wheeler, and the Chiefs wanted the withdrawals to be carefully balanced between combat and support forces. They also wanted forces outside of Vietnam, which they considered vital to the country's defense, to be considered support, not combat forces. The Office of the Secretary of Defense, however, considered the forces outside of Vietnam to have been ineffective; withdrawing them would have little adverse impact on the war. Similarly, the Department of Defense (DOD) argued for a more rapid reduction of maneuver forces, such as infantry and armor, than the Chiefs thought advisable. The DOD maintained that this would permit U.S. forces to provide the South Vietnamese with more air, artillery, and logistical support. The Chiefs countered that, if anything, the combat efficiency of the South Vietnamese forces was "declining in relationship to that of U.S. troops in combat."[99]

Kissinger made the situation facing the Chiefs even more difficult when he approached Wheeler suggesting that the National Security Council and the Chiefs work together in "sharing foreign policy and military information outside the government's usual lines of communication." Kissinger informed Wheeler that neither he nor the President thought Laird could be trusted. Days later, the President reiterated Kissinger's point, saying he hoped Wheeler would be "frank" in his appraisal of Laird's views. These overtures put Wheeler in a very difficult position. [100]

Kissinger approached Wheeler again the following month and told him that Nixon wanted a "more open policy" on Vietnam that the Secretary of Defense "doesn't seem to agree with." Kissinger intimated that Wheeler's support "in this matter was certainly appreciated," and that a means had to be found to "communicate the President's concern directly to the men in the field" – a euphemism. Kissinger meant that Nixon wanted to run the war without passing orders through Laird. Wheeler soon realized that the White House also wanted to obtain information on Laird's programs at the Pentagon. [101]

At first, Wheeler assumed this was just another example of bureaucratic infighting, but in time he began to realize that Nixon and Kissinger actually believed that Laird was attempting to sabotage the Administration's policy in Vietnam. Wheeler refused to pick up on these "hints," and the White House eventually dropped the issue but kept looking for another route.

Developing a withdrawal plan proved a difficult challenge for Wheeler and the Chiefs, who knew the war was lost. The writing had been on the wall since 1965 when Johnson first refused to call-up the reserves. Nevertheless, the withdrawal of troops would be hard for the military to take. Going home without victory suggested that the troops had died in vain. Withdrawal was a hard pill to swallow, yet a reality the military could not ignore. The South Vietnamese, who could not expect the U.S. to continue to fight their war forever, would have to save themselves.

Wheeler and the Chiefs were caught between a rock and a hard place. While the President prodded them to use aggressive military force in Vietnam, Laird made it known that if they pushed hard for the use of more military force, their budget would suffer. Laird told the Chiefs that if they wanted new weapons, the U.S. had to withdraw from Vietnam — the sooner the better. Funding for the war could and should go toward purchasing new weapons. The new Administration could not be expected to pay for both the war and purchase new weapons that all the Services desperately required. [102]

The first increment of 25,000 troops departed Vietnam in July and August when two brigades of the 9th Infantry Division pulled out of III and IV Corps Tactical Zones (CTZs) and a regiment of the 3rd Marine Division departed from northern I CTZ. These units were selected because they were considered first-rate and would consequently make the reduction in forces credible to all concerned — not just to the governments in Hanoi and Saigon but also to the American public. [103]

Combat Operations

About a month after the 101st Airborne Division seized "Hamburger Hill", the division left the A Shau Valley, which granted the North Vietnamese free access to use it again. Abrams's plans to return in the summer of 1970 would come to naught when Communist pressure forced the abandonment of two firebases needed for operations there. Their loss would be an ominous sign that Communist forces had re-occupied the A Shau and were seeking to dominate the valleys leading to the coastal plain. Hence, until the 101st Airborne Division redeployed in 1971, it would devote most of its efforts to protecting Hue along with the U.S. Marines and South Vietnamese forces. While combat operations in western I Corps Tactical Zone (I CTZ) had inflicted casualties on the Communists and bought the Allies some time, it remained to be seen whether the South Vietnamese Army (ARVN) could hold the area once U.S. forces departed. [104]

In the Central Highlands, the war of attrition continued. The 4th Infantry Division continued to protect major population centers and keep important interior roads clear. Special Forces continued working with tribal highlanders to detect infiltration and harass Communist secret zones. As in the past, highland camps and outposts were a magnet for enemy attacks, meant to lure reaction forces into an ambush or to divert the Allies from operations elsewhere.

When a new threat from seven North Vietnamese regiments emerged in III CTZ, Abrams went on the offensive. Since late 1968, U.S. forces, including the 1st Cavalry Division, had been engaged in a corps-wide counterattack to locate and destroy Communist force units and prevent enemy main forces from returning.

Closer to Saigon, the 1st and 25th Infantry Divisions continued combat operations to the north and west of the city, but in somewhat reduced operating territory since border coverage was no longer required. Intensifying their operations behind the 1st Cavalry Division's border screen, they focused on pockets of Communist resistance that still threatened the capital. Their operations would quiet this area by the end of the year. Whatever the situation elsewhere in Vietnam, III CTZ was the one place where U.S. commanders had sufficient troops to deal effectively with the threat.

As III CTZ stabilized behind the Allied shield, an uneasy sense of hope took hold in Saigon, although the city was not impregnable. During the Tet celebration in 1969, heavy fighting had broken out near Bien Hoa and Long Binh. Into the early summer, Communist troops had still penetrated close enough to launch an occasional rocket attack or detonate a bomb. Such incidents terrorized civilians, caused military casualties, and raised questions about the Saigon government's ability to protect its citizens. By the autumn, however, the attacks would virtually cease. Saigon seemed to lapse back into a period of tranquility and prosperity in which the main concern seemed to be not the fighting off in the distance but the wartime inflation eating into the purchasing power of the urban population. The trauma visited upon the city during Tet 1968 had become a bad memory on the wane. [105]

Nixon Doctrine

A new defense policy enunciated by Nixon would influence every component of the U.S. and South Vietnamese strategy. The "Nixon Doctrine" hearkened back to the precepts of the New Look, placing greater reliance on nuclear retaliation, encouraging Allies to accept larger shares of their own defense burden, and barring the use of U.S. ground forces in limited wars in Asia, unless vital national interests were at stake. Under this policy, U.S. ground forces in South Vietnam, once withdrawn, were unlikely to return. For Thieu in Saigon, the future was inauspicious. For the time being, large numbers of U.S. forces would continue to bolster his country's war effort, but what would happen when they were withdrawn had yet to be seen. [106]

Fearful that growing domestic opposition might doom his efforts to pressure Hanoi into a settlement, Nixon had also improvised a "go-for-broke" strategy, an all-out attempt to "end the war one way or the other — either by negotiated agreement or by force." Nixon had ordered Kissinger to convene a special, top-secret National Security Council study group to draw up plans for what he described as "savage, punishing blows" against North Vietnam. Known as DUCK HOOK within the White House (and PRUNING KNIFE in the military), the operation would exert maximum political and military shock through massive bombing attacks against its major cities, a blockade of its ports, and possibly even the use of tactical nuclear weapons under certain "controlled" situations. [107]

To give force to his warnings, Nixon leaked word to journalists that he was considering such options, and he emphatically told some members of Congress that he would not be the first U.S. President to lose a war. The Administration also alerted North Vietnam in early August that if no substantive progress toward peace occurred by 1 November, the U.S. would resort to "measures of great consequence and force." [108]

The Chiefs did not consider DUCK HOOK feasible because the 1 November deadline coincided with dismal weather over North Vietnam, aerial refueling capacity to support the proposed blitz was insufficient, and additional aircraft carriers could not arrive in time. [109]

In consequence of Nixon's ultimatum, Hanoi agreed to secret peace talks outside the Paris framework. On 4 August, in the first of a long series of secret meetings, Kissinger met privately with North Vietnamese diplomat Xuan Thuy. Kissinger reiterated Nixon's peace proposals and ultimatum, but Thuy responded with Hanoi's fixed position that the U.S. must withdraw all its troops and abandon Thieu to secure an agreement.

Nixon had inadvertently undermined his threats by announcing the first troop withdrawals and then enunciating the "Nixon Doctrine." [110]

From Nixon's perspective, Hanoi's "cold rebuff" was not only intransigent but also deliberately provocative. Unable to intimidate Hanoi into making even the slightest concession, Nixon had to choose between a major escalation of the war or an embarrassing retreat. He was infuriated by Hanoi's defiance and by his own domestic criticism, which he felt encouraged it. His natural inclination was to strike back, but Laird and Rogers implored him not to take any action that would inflame the opposition at home.

After weeks of careful analysis, Kissinger's study group concluded that airstrikes and a blockade might not force concessions from Hanoi or even significantly limit its capacity to continue the war in the South. Haunted throughout his political career by a near-obsessive fear of defeat and humiliation, Nixon abandoned his plan for "savage, punishing blows" with the greatest reluctance and only after being persuaded that it would not work. Having relied on military pressure to bring a quick and decisive end to the war, he suddenly found himself without a policy. [111]

A New Approach

Nixon and Kissinger did not take escalation off the table, however, and took measures to minimize opposition within the Administration for its eventuality. On 9 September, Kissinger instructed Wheeler to confine all escalation planning strictly within *military* channels — that is, to keep it from Laird whom Nixon and Kissinger distrusted and were convinced would undermine any escalatory efforts.

Three days later, the President convened a strategy planning meeting for which Kissinger had directed a lengthy analysis of four possible courses of action. For the current strategy, as well as those of accelerating negotiations or Vietnamization, the paper advanced detailed criticism; for escalation, there were none. [112]

Unwilling to make concessions and unable to end the war by force, Nixon again improvised, this time falling back on the Vietnamization policy he had inherited from Johnson. The Administration had little choice but to buy time to win the war by quelling dissent and reducing casualties, lessen the U.S. commitment, and prod the Saigon government to greater efforts on its own behalf. To achieve these goals, Nixon had been compelled to embrace the dual policies of Vietnamization (accompanied by U.S. troop withdrawals) and pacification, occasionally undertake unexpected military actions to keep Hanoi off balance, while working assiduously to undermine the antiwar movement. [113]

On 16 September, the President announced the second increment of U.S. troop withdrawals. A total of 45,000 troops would redeploy by mid-December.

"I judge that we are on the right track," Wheeler stated in Saigon on 7 October. Following his return to Washington two days later, he affirmed that "Vietnamization is on schedule and in some places ahead of schedule." [114]

While the President was still pondering escalation in October, the British counterinsurgency expert Sir Robert Thompson advised him that South Vietnam was growing stronger daily and that if the U.S. continued to furnish large-scale military and economic assistance, the government in

Saigon might become strong enough within two years to resist a Communist takeover without external help.

With no other viable options, Nixon uncritically embraced Thompson's conclusions as the foundation for a new approach to extricate the U.S. from the war. Nixon figured that if he could mobilize American public opinion behind him, persuade Hanoi that he would not abandon Thieu, and intensify the buildup of South Vietnamese military strength, the North Vietnamese might conclude that it would be better to negotiate with the U.S. now than with a stronger South Vietnam later, and he could extract from the North Vietnamese the concessions necessary to secure peace with honor. [115]

Time was not running in Nixon's favor, however. The New Mobilization Committee to End the War initiated monthly national moratoriums on 15 October, resulting in a huge antiwar protest. The next one, scheduled for 15 November, promised to be even bigger. Meanwhile, although Hanoi expected the U.S. to unleash its bombers and perhaps even to invade, it refused to buckle. [116]

In a major speech on 3 November, Nixon set out to isolate his critics and mobilize popular backing for his policy. He openly appealed for the support of those he labeled the "great silent majority." The speech was shrewd and, for the most part, a successful political maneuver. Nixon placed his opponents squarely on the defensive. Offering a policy that could achieve an honorable peace with minimal American sacrifice, he appeared to reconcile the contradictory elements of popular attitudes toward the war. He cleverly appealed to the patriotism of his listeners and their reluctance to accept anything resembling defeat. By specifically identifying a "silent majority," he helped mobilize a block of support where none had existed. [117]

Declining Combat Effectiveness

Meanwhile, "Johnny" Johnson's warning to McNamara in July 1965 that the U.S. Army would break because President Johnson decided to embark upon a course of major U.S. combat operations in Vietnam without mobilizing the reserves had come to fruition. Vietnamization and societal factors had exacerbated the Army's already pervasive personnel issues.

American war crimes, such as at My Lai, were born of a sense of frustration that also contributed to a host of morale and discipline problems among enlisted men and officers alike. As U.S. forces were withdrawn by a government eager to escape the war, the lack of a clear military objective contributed to a weakened sense of mission and a slackening of discipline. The "short-timer" syndrome — the reluctance to take risks in combat toward the end of a soldier's one-year tour — was compounded by the "last-casualty syndrome". Knowing that all U.S. troops would soon leave Vietnam, no soldier wanted to be the last one killed. [118]

Meanwhile, in the United States, harsh criticism of the war, the military, and traditional military values had become widespread. Heightened individualism, growing permissiveness, and a weakening of traditional bonds of authority pervaded American society and affected the Army's rank and file. The Army grappled with problems of drug abuse, racial tensions, weakened discipline, and lapses of leadership. While outright refusals to fight were few, incidents of "fragging" (murderous attacks on officers and NCOs) occurred frequently enough to compel commanders to institute a host of new security measures within their bases. All these problems were symptomatic of larger social and political forces and underlined the growing disenchantment with the war among deployed soldiers in Vietnam.

As U.S. troop withdrawals continued, lassitude and war-weariness increasingly pervaded among the remaining units. Declining combat effectiveness reflected a decline in the quality of leadership among both commissioned and noncommissioned officers. Lowered standards, abbreviated training, and accelerated promotions to meet the high demand for noncommissioned and junior officers often resulted in the assignment of squad, platoon, and company leaders with less combat experience than the troops they led. Careerism and ticket-punching in officer assignments, false reporting and inflated body counts, and revelations of scandal and corruption all raised disquieting questions about the professional ethics of Army leadership. Critics indicted the tactics and techniques that the Army had used in Vietnam, noting that air mobility, for example, tended to distance troops from the population they were sent to protect and that commanders aloft in their command-and-control helicopters were at a psychological and physical distance from the soldiers they led. [119]

CHAPTER 10

AT LONG LAST
(JANUARY – JUNE 1970)

Being a product of the JCS system, I may be forgiven for my strong belief in the system. It is not designed to be easy on my colleagues or myself nor should it be. It has, in my view, done its job and all of us committed to the system can take sober satisfaction from this fact. — General Earle G. Wheeler, 1969 [1]

Celebrations

For the fifth and final time, the staff of the Chairman's Dining Room served cake and champagne to celebrate Wheeler's 62nd birthday on 13 January 1970. [2]

Meanwhile, celebrations of another sort seemed in order. By the time the Administration announced that the third increment of U.S. troop withdrawals had commenced in January, Vietnamization was in full swing, and most observers agreed that significant gains had been made. Almost overnight, the South Vietnamese Army (ARVN) had become one of the largest and best equipped in the world. On paper, the ARVN appeared a formidable force, but many of its fundamental weaknesses remained uncorrected. Americans continued to doubt that the ARVN could fill the vacuum left by U.S. troop withdrawals.

Real progress in Vietnamization remained uncertain, however. The biggest question remained the Saigon government itself, which had not yet "succeeded in mobilizing the will and energies of the people against the enemy and in support of national programs." [3]

The situation was not for lack of effort. While hunting down the Viet Cong infrastructure and welcoming defectors, the U.S. and South Vietnam had also implemented civic action campaigns to enhance the Saigon government's image and to improve rural living conditions, which officials assumed would alleviate the insurgency's underlying causes. To date, the U.S. had tallied an impressive number of roads, bridges, schools, playgrounds, and dispensaries built or rebuilt, of wells dug, food distributed, and of health services rendered. [4]

Even land reform, the South Vietnamese government's most successful program for building political strength in the countryside, rested on an uncertain foundation. In 1970, the Thieu Administration would finally address the contentious land reform issue, passing a Land-to-the-Tiller Law to distribute several million acres to hundreds of thousands of tenant farmers. The perception of the Saigon government as merely the protector of the rich and powerful blurred, as at least some previously landless farmers now had a stake in Thieu's regime. [5]

The Land-to-the-Tiller Program would become one of the most advanced undertaken anywhere in the developing world. Thieu gave it unwavering support and placed strong leaders in charge. Land tenancy would drop from 60% to 10% between 1970 and 1973. Even so, the social and economic benefits for the peasantry were understood to be only as durable as U.S. aid and the conventional-force security shield. In that sense, despite the progress made, the entire South Vietnamese enterprise remained in doubt. [6]

Laos

On 13 February, Wheeler and Laird visited the U.S. Pacific Command headquarters to confer with McCain, whom Kissinger described as a "doughty, crusty officer [who] could have passed in demeanor, appearance, pugnacity, and manner of speech for Popeye the Sailor Man. His son had been a prisoner of war in Hanoi for years, but this tragedy left him undaunted. He fought for the victory that his instinct and upbringing demanded and that political reality forbade." [7]

A significant dilemma impeding Vietnamization was the presence of Communist sanctuaries just across the border in Cambodia and in the portion of Laos through which the Ho Chi Minh Trail passed. Fourteen major North

Vietnamese bases were in Cambodia, some of which were only 35 miles from Saigon. The U.S. had bombed the sanctuaries, but they continued to function. Recognizing that the lack of security posed an obstacle to successful pacification, Wheeler and the Chiefs were determined to reduce the North Vietnamese threat by striking at their logistical assets regardless of their location.

Wheeler told Kissinger that B-52 attacks would be preferable in this instance because they were more accurate than fighter-bombers. The President decided to take Wheeler's suggestion but to conduct the operation in secret. Three B-52s attacked Laos on the night of 17-18 February. [8]

Gathering Spring Storms

By the spring of 1970, the contradictions in Nixon's Vietnamization strategy had become all too apparent. The "silent majority" speech had quieted the opposition temporarily, but Nixon realized that his success was only transient. [9]

On 18 March, New York City mail carriers began an unauthorized work stoppage that threatened to halt essential postal services. Nixon declared a national emergency on 23 March, paving the way for a partial mobilization of the Reserves and National Guard. More than 18,000 National Guardsmen and Army Reservists were activated and worked with other regular and reserve forces to get the mail through. The postal workers would soon return to work, and by 3 April the last of the reservists were deactivated. [10]

Nixon announced the phased withdrawal of another 150,000 troops over the next year to "drop a bombshell on the gathering spring storm of anti-war protests." He recognized that this withdrawal, however necessary from the standpoint of domestic politics, would weaken his hand in other areas. "Troop cuts poulticized public sores at home, but they were evaporating Hanoi's need to bargain about our disengagement," Kissinger recalled. "And if Vietnamization was not making good the defensive gaps created by our withdrawals, we hazarded not only the negotiating lever but South Vietnam's independence and the entire basis of our sacrifices." [11]

Abrams had bitterly protested the new troop withdrawals, warning that they would leave South Vietnam vulnerable to Communist military pressure and could be devastating to the Vietnamization program. "I took seriously Abrams's and Wheeler's pleas to maintain troop levels," Kissinger recalled, "especially in the light of North Vietnamese offensives in Laos and Cambodia." [12]

Nixon had rather naïvely hoped that his professed determination to remain in Vietnam indefinitely and the demonstrations of public support that had followed his 3 November speech would persuade the North Vietnamese to negotiate. There had been no breakthrough in Paris, however, and he recognized that the announcement of additional troop withdrawals would probably encourage Hanoi to delay further. Increasingly impatient for results and still certain that he could end the war by a dramatic show of force, Nixon once more began looking for initiatives to "show the enemy that we were still serious about our commitment in Vietnam." [13]

Cambodia

In March, the pro-American Cambodian Prime Minister, General Lon Nol, deposed his country's neutralist head of state, Prince Norodom Sihanouk. Favoring vigorous action against the Communists, Nol ordered the Cambodian Army to attack them in three border provinces and closed Sihanoukville. This port city had been a major Communist supply point from which food and equipment moved along the Sihanoukville Trail to positions adjacent to IV and III Corps Tactical Zones (CTZs). Nol also demanded that Communist forces leave Cambodia and accepted the South Vietnamese government's offer to apply pressure against those located near the border. [14]

In late March, South Vietnamese forces raided Communist bases in the Parrot's Beak region, a strip of Cambodian territory just 33 miles from Saigon. Responding to these threats, as well as to the menu bombings, the Viet Cong and North Vietnamese Army, as well as the indigenous Communist Khmer Rouge movement headed by Pol Pot, counterattacked and soon threatened Cambodia's capital city of Phnom Penh. [15]

The change in government in Cambodia had removed the long-standing concern about violating its neutrality, and attacks on the sanctuaries could now be justified in terms of sustaining a friendly Cambodian government, as well as easing the military threat to South Vietnam. [16]

For six years, Wheeler and his fellow senior officers had persistently recommended U.S. ground offensives against North Vietnamese sanctuaries in Cambodia, Laos, and North Vietnam. Restrictions against such operations by the Johnson and Nixon Administrations had always rankled the military, who regarded the restrictions as a potentially fatal mistake. By harboring Communist forces, command facilities, and logistical depots, the sanctuaries threatened all the progress the Allies had made in the South since 1968.

To the Administration, the military's desire to attack the sanctuaries had the special appeal of gaining more time for Vietnamization and of compensating for the bombing halt over North Vietnam. Most U.S. combat units were slated to leave South Vietnam during 1970 and 1971. Time was a critical factor for the success of Vietnamization and pacification, and neither program could thrive if South Vietnamese forces were distracted by Communist offensives launched from bases in Cambodia or Laos. [17]

The Operation MENU bombings begun a year earlier had been difficult to assess, but clearly had not eliminated the Central Office for South Vietnam (COSVN) or the sanctuaries. (By the time the operation was terminated in May, B-52s would fly 3,875 sorties and drop more than 105,800 tons of bombs on Cambodia.) Consequently, Nixon contemplated a ground invasion to finish the job and to reinforce his madman image. [18]

At Long Last

"I see that, at long last, they're going to let you retire," former President Johnson wrote to Wheeler on 15 April.

> I know perhaps better than anyone else the quality of the service you rendered — the professional judgment, integrity, wisdom, discretion, and loyalty you brought to these difficult years.
>
> I was startled once when General Eisenhower told me he thought Westmoreland's task in Vietnam was more difficult

than his in Europe. On reflection, I believe he was correct. And I would add, your task has been more difficult than George Marshall's during the Second World War.

You faced all the complexities, abroad and at home, with extraordinary steadiness and grace. As President, no man gave me more strength and comfort. I shall always be grateful to you. [19]

One week later, Wheeler was briefly hospitalized at Walter Reed for a thorough pre-retirement physical exam. The physician recommended that he be referred to the Physical Evaluation Board as medically unfit due to his chronic obstructive pulmonary disease and chronic bronchitis and that he be medically retired. [20]

Cambodian Incursion

During a National Security Council meeting on 22 April to discuss Cambodia, three options were considered: status quo, preferred by the State and Defense Departments; Kissinger's recommendation of attacking the sanctuaries with South Vietnamese forces only; and using whatever forces were necessary to neutralize all the base areas, including U.S. combat forces. The latter option was strongly endorsed by Bunker, Abrams, Wheeler, and the Chiefs.

Two days later, the President met with CIA Director Richard Helms and Moorer, serving as Acting Chairman in Wheeler's absence, to discuss the feasibility of a combined U.S.-South Vietnamese operation against the fish hook in parallel with the parrot's beak operation. "Helms and Moorer were both strongly in favor of an attack on the fish hook sanctuary," Kissinger recalled. "They felt it would force the North Vietnamese to abandon their effort to encircle and terrorize Phnom Penh. The destruction of supplies would gain valuable time for Vietnamization." [21]

On 26 April, the President met with Rogers, Laird, Wheeler, Helms, and Kissinger to hear a briefing by Wheeler about the proposed fish hook operation. No decision was announced at that meeting, but "as soon as the meeting was over," Kissinger recalled, "[Nixon] called me over to the family quarters and instructed me to issue a directive authorizing an attack by American forces into the fish hook area."[22]

The President's ultimate decision to send U.S. troops into Cambodia would prove one of the most important and controversial decisions of his Administration and was motivated by a variety of considerations. Swayed by Wheeler's arguments that the operation would buy time for Vietnamization and help sustain a friendly government in Cambodia, Nixon also realized that his decision would have a "shattering effect" at home. His willingness to run this risk for uncertain gains reflected, in part, what he called his "big play philosophy," his belief that since his Administration was "going to get unshirted hell for doing this at all," it might as well "go for all the marbles." Nixon was also still confident that he could make peace by threatening Hanoi. Embarrassed by backing down from his November ultimatum, a move that conveyed precisely the wrong message, Nixon reasoned that widening the war into previously off-limits Cambodia would make it clear that unlike his predecessor, he would not be bound by restraints. The North Vietnamese would then have to decide "whether they want to take us on all over again," and in terms of pressures on them to negotiate, "this was essential."[23]

"Perhaps the most difficult lesson for a national leader to learn is that with respect to the use of military force, his basic choice is to act or to refrain from acting," Kissinger recalled.

> He will not be able to take away the moral curse of using force by employing it halfheartedly or incompetently. There are no rewards for exhibiting one's doubts in vacillation; statesmen get no prizes for failing with restraint. Once committed they must prevail. If they are not prepared to prevail, they should not commit their nation's power. Neither the successive Administrations nor the critics ever fully understood this during the Vietnam War. And therein lay the seeds of many of its tragedies.[24]

Nixon authorized the military's recommendation that 50,000 South Vietnamese Army (ARVN) troops with U.S. air support to attack the Parrot's

Beak. He also approved a more dramatic and much riskier operation. Over vigorous opposition from Laird and Rogers, he approved Abrams's recommendation that 30,000 U.S. troops attack the Fish Hook area 55 miles northwest of Saigon. [25]

On 30 April — just ten days after he had given an optimistic assessment of the prospects for Vietnamization in South Vietnam — Nixon announced to the nation the Allied offensive into Cambodia. He justified his decision by charging Communist forces with a series of recent attacks there. He did not reveal that the Vietnamese Communist attacks were in response to attacks on their sanctuaries first by Lon Nol's troops beginning on 22 March, then by South Vietnamese forces, and finally, to Cambodian Army massacres of Vietnamese civilians beginning on 11 April. [26]

"After full consultation with the National Security Council, Ambassador Bunker, General Abrams, and my other advisors, I have concluded that the actions of the enemy in the last ten days clearly endanger the lives of Americans who are in Vietnam now and would constitute an unacceptable risk to those who will be there after the withdrawal of another 150,000," Nixon stated. "To protect our men who are in Vietnam and to guarantee the continued success of our withdrawal and Vietnamization programs, I have concluded that the time has come for action." [27]

"Cambodia... has sent out a call to the United States, to a number of other nations, for assistance," Nixon stated. "Because if this enemy effort succeeds, Cambodia would become a vast enemy staging area and a springboard for attacks on South Vietnam along 600 miles of frontier, a refuge where enemy troops could return from combat without fear of retaliation." Some of these sanctuaries that served as bases for attacks on both Cambodia and on U.S. and South Vietnamese forces in South Vietnam were as close to Saigon as Baltimore is to Washington, Nixon pointed out on a map. [28]

"This is not an invasion of Cambodia," Nixon asserted. "The areas in which these attacks will be launched are completely occupied and controlled by North Vietnamese forces. Our purpose is not to occupy the areas. Once enemy forces are driven out of the sanctuaries and once their military supplies or destroyed, we will withdraw." [29]

The main assault had already commenced the day prior when three ARVN task forces with a full complement of U.S. advisors and preceded by heavy air and artillery attacks launched Operation TOAN THANG 42, driving into Cambodia's Svay Rieng Province and pushing through Communist resistance.

Two days later, U.S. forces of the 1st Cavalry Division; 25th Infantry Division; 3rd Brigade, 9th Infantry Division; 11th Armored Cavalry Regiment; and the South Vietnamese 3rd Airborne Brigade, attacked into the Fish Hook. The 4th Infantry Division attacked from II Corps Tactical Zone (II CTZ) four days later.

By 2 May, ARVN forces cut off the Parrot's Beak, and U.S. and South Vietnamese troops linked up near Memot in the Fish Hook area, meeting little opposition from Communist forces. Snuol, a large enemy logistical hub, fell three days later. In the weeks that followed, the Allies would cut a broad swath through the Communist sanctuary and uncovered storage sites, training camps, and hospitals far larger and more complex than anyone had anticipated. One site in the Fish Hook dubbed "the city", covered three square kilometers and contained mess halls, a livestock farm, supply issuing and receiving stations, and over 200 caches of weapons and other material, most of it new. [30]

Protests

Testifying about Cambodia to the Department of Defense Subcommittee on Appropriations of the House Appropriations Committee on 4 May, Wheeler explained the driving purpose of Allied operations in Cambodia was to disrupt the supplies that were going to the North Vietnamese and Viet Cong in South Vietnam, not to invade Cambodia. "Our intentions are to withdraw our forces once the enemy supplies are destroyed. We also hope that, as a result of this operation, the enemy will recognize that we intend to protect the Vietnamization Program and that there is no way around serious negotiations." [31]

"I am pleased to report this committee that, to date, these operations have been highly successful in achieving both our short-range and long-range objectives," Wheeler testified. Abrams had informed him that the Communists were caught by complete surprise and that their reaction to Allied operations had been one of apparent bewilderment. They were making a desperate effort to avoid contact, and intelligence indicated that the Communists were having a difficult time responding to both operations. [32]

That same day, student protests against the Cambodian incursion led to tragedy at Kent State University in Ohio. Panicked National Guardsmen opened fire on the antiwar demonstrators, killing four bystanders and wounding a dozen others. [33]

After the killings at Kent State and the Administration's perceived insensitive statement in response, "the momentum of student strikes and protests accelerated immediately," Kissinger recalled. "Campus unrest and violence overtook the Cambodian operation itself as the major issue before the public. Washington took on the character of a besieged city." [34]

Five days later, 100,000 demonstrators converged on Washington, DC to protest the shootings and the Administration's expansion of the war. Police ringed the White House with buses to block the demonstrators from getting too close. Federal troops stood by the national capital region, although none were employed. Early in the morning before the march, Nixon met with protesters briefly at the Lincoln Memorial, but nothing was resolved, and the protest went on as planned. [35]

"The military impact [of ground operations in Cambodia] might have been even greater had we not withdrawn our forces arbitrarily in two months," Kissinger recalled. "The enormous uproar at home was profoundly unnerving." [36]

Cambodia Assessed

"The Cambodian operation to date has been analyzed," said Colonel William C. Moore, U.S. Air Force, in *U.S. News & World Report* on 22 June. "The statistics are impressive," Moore claimed. "They leave no doubt that the enemy has been hurt." The sheer magnitude of the impact on the enemy's capability to fight was hard for many to comprehend, he said. Plans were disrupted, units decimated, communications destroyed. "Their capabilities as soldiers are seriously impaired. ... Not even the jungle can hide the facts. Not even the cleverest propaganda from the leaders in Hanoi can minimize the military debacle they have suffered."[37]

From a military standpoint, the operation had produced significant, if limited, results. The U.S. Military Assistance Command, Vietnam (MACV) claimed to have killed some 2,000 Communist troops, cleared over 1,600 acres of jungle, and destroyed 8,000 bunkers. Allied forces uncovered a "treasure trove" of intelligence and huge caches of food and equipment. By one estimate, they had also seized enough weapons and ammunition to arm 55 battalions of main-force infantry, although some of the weapons were obsolete. The incursion rendered the sanctuaries temporarily unusable and vastly complicated North Vietnamese supply problems, thus buying vital time for Vietnamization. The CIA estimated that the Communists could replace their losses within three months, but other agencies believed the losses would cripple their capabilities to conduct main-force offensives against South Vietnam's III and IV Corps Tactical Zones for at least a year.[38]

Allied forces had not located the Central Office for South Vietnam (COSVN) headquarters, however, and in most cases the Viet Cong and the North Vietnamese Army fled rather than fight. Only relatively small delaying forces offered resistance, while main-force units retreated deeper into Cambodia.

Despite perennial problems with timid leadership, ineffective artillery fire, and faulty communications, the South Vietnamese Army had fought very well in most areas, even aggressively in some places, which seemed promising for Vietnamization.[39]

"The operation in Cambodia has been a tremendous military success," said Republican House Minority Leader, Congressman Gerald R. Ford, on the ABC News program *Issues & Answers* on 22 June. "I believe [it] will be ... successful far beyond the expectations of any of those who planned it."[40]

Nixon claimed the Cambodian Incursion was "the most decisive action in terms of damaging the enemy's ability to wage effective warfare that has occurred in this war to date."[41]

Such assessments days before Wheeler's retirement were bittersweet vindication to him and his fellow senior officers who had for years consistently recommended such ground offensives against Communist sanctuaries as a means for moving the war more rapidly and conclusively toward victory.

"We never used, during the entire course of our military operations in Vietnam or in Southeast Asia, even a fraction of the military power that is available to us," Wheeler recalled. [42]

> Now it happens to be my view that had we done so the war would have been over two years ago. … not by a stalemate, [but] by proving, yes, proving, to the North Vietnamese that they could not possibly take over South Vietnam by force. And I might add that we certainly have proved that. They can't. But you don't win wars like that. No war has ever been won on the defense, at least not in my reading of military history. So what it amounts to is that the North Vietnamese fought from the very outset, and are still fighting a war all-out, and we have fought a war with a fraction of the power that we could bring to bear. [43]

Unfortunately, the Cambodian Incursion was conducted four years too late to achieve the intended effect. Instead, it generated significant, but not unforeseen, negative second- and third-order effects. Abrams admitted that the operation had caused the Communists "some temporary inconvenience" at best. Another U.S. general considered it a disaster that fatally wounded South Vietnam because of the widespread unrest it generated on the American home front. The North Vietnamese agreed. As one high-level Communist leader put it, "Nixon paid dearly for our temporary discomfiture by sustaining major political losses." [44]

Whatever advantages the operation had gained for Vietnamization were more than offset by the domestic reaction to Nixon's expansion of the war, which exceeded his worst expectations. The incursion had "reignited an anti-war movement that had been smoldering that spring." Opposition had been quiescent when it appeared that Nixon was liquidating the war through troop withdrawals, Vietnamization, and pacification. [45]

As frustration mounted that the President was now widening rather than ending the war, renewed demonstrations erupted, and not just in the streets. Secretary of the Army Stanley R. Resor informed Abrams that "there were great delegations of people, some of them very substantial people, coming down to call on their congressmen to do something about getting out [of Vietnam] faster." [46]

To the military's dismay, the violent demonstrations in the U.S. prompted Nixon to limit the U.S. penetration to 30 kilometers and to announce a 30 June deadline for the withdrawal of all U.S. advisors accompanying the South Vietnamese and all U.S. Army ground forces from Cambodia. These restrictions enabled the Communists to stay beyond reach. [47]

"The President was coming dangerously close to the perennial error of our military policy in Vietnam: acting sufficiently strongly to evoke storms of protest but then by hesitation depriving our actions of decisive impact," Kissinger recalled. "The limitations of time and geography placed on our forces' operations helped only marginally to calm the Congress and the media but certainly kept us from obtaining the operations' full benefit." [48]

Nixon's removal of U.S. troops would deprive his opponents of their most pressing issue, and the protests would gradually abate. [49]

Thieu, meanwhile, did not feel bound by the limitations Nixon had imposed. The ARVN penetrated twice as far into Cambodia as U.S. forces and would sustain operations for the next several years, supported by U.S. artillery, B-52 strikes, and tactical air support.

With Sihanoukville no longer available and Operation MARKET TIME frustrating their seaborne supply efforts, the Communists initiated urgent measures to improve and defend the Ho Chi Minh Trail. Greater numbers of trucks provided by China and the Soviet Union moved along a steadily improving road network. Repair facilities proliferated, bomb damage was quickly repaired, a newly constructed pipeline transported fuel, and antiaircraft and surface-to-air missile batteries shifted southward to protect the indispensable trail and pipeline.

At the heart of the Allied interdiction effort was Operation COMMANDO HUNT, which had begun in November 1968 and would run until April 1972. Operation FREEDOM DEAL, a new name for the Cambodian bombing that was now conducted openly, complemented COMMANDO HUNT by attacking the Ho Chi Minh Trail in northeastern Cambodia. ARC LIGHT strikes, fighter-bombers, and night-flying AC-130 Specter gunships struck at reinforcements, trucks, supply caches, and enemy defenses. [50]

The Cambodian Incursion undermined Vietnamization in that while the U.S. was scaling down its role in Vietnam, it had to divert precious resources to support an even more fragile client state in Cambodia. Such support was unsustainable and would ultimately contribute to a holocaust that would kill up to 2 million Cambodians after the "demonic" Pol Pot later assumed power.

Hoping to break the diplomatic deadlock by going into Cambodia, Nixon had merely hardened it. Hanoi did not capitulate to Nixon's madman gambit by offering concessions, but boycotted the formal Paris talks until U.S. troops were withdrawn from Cambodia, and the secret talks lapsed for months. Hanoi continued to bide its time, and the uproar in the U.S. reinforced its conviction that domestic pressures would eventually force a U.S. withdrawal. [51]

The Cambodian Incursion tightened the political trap Nixon had set for himself. The domestic reaction reinforced his determination to achieve "peace with honor" but sharply limited his options for attaining it. Cambodia may have bought some time for Vietnamization, but it also imposed clear-cut, if implicit, limits on the future use of U.S. combat forces and increased pressures for speeding the pace of withdrawal. Divisions within the U.S. increased even beyond the level of 1968, with far-reaching, if still unforeseen, implications for Nixon's future. [52]

The Cambodian Incursion would provoke the most serious congressional challenge to presidential authority since the beginning of the war. Despite a flurry of threats, though, Congress was not yet ready to challenge the President directly or assume responsibility for ending the war. Nixon would escape with his power intact, and the Administration would eventually ride out the storm. Late in the year, however, Congress would pass a bill containing the Cooper-Church Amendment, which prohibited all future U.S. ground (but not air) activity in Cambodia and Laos. The Senate would also repeal the Gulf of Tonkin Resolution, after which Nixon would continue the war by relying upon his authority as Commander-in-Chief. [53]

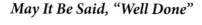

May It Be Said, "Well Done"

Wheeler and Moorer converse during Wheeler's retirement dinner, Bolling Air Force Base, Washington, DC, 26 June 1970. (Office of the Chairman of the Joint Chiefs of Staff)

On 2 July, the day that Wheeler retired from military service, a newspaper article reported, "There are too many people these days who think the Joint Chiefs of Staff are fire breathing monsters trying to control government policy, foreign and domestic. Anyone who has met Gen. Wheeler should know this is not the case." [54]

Wheeler epitomized what the architects of Federal government had in mind when they established a system of military advice under civilian control, the article claimed.

Gen. Wheeler presented and defended the military view in the highest councils of government. But he was willing to break with the other Chiefs when he disagreed. … And when he was overruled by a President or defense secretary – as occurred when Mr. Johnson and former Secretary McNamara spurned the Chiefs' advice to take tougher measures against North Vietnam early in the war – Gen. Wheeler took his orders and followed them to the letter. [55]

Gen. Wheeler has served – and served well through a period that included an unpopular war and saw the public image of the military battered by its critics. This troubled the general but never interfered with his loyal devotion to duty. [56]

CHAPTER 11

EPILOGUE
(JULY 1970 – DECEMBER 1975)

If you undertake to fight a war, you must take a long look down the road and
see where you will be afterwards. You could win a war and lose the peace.
— General Earle G. Wheeler, 1964 [1]

Vietnam

The Vietnam War continued without Wheeler's influence. A month after
his retirement, the U.S. Military Assistance Command, Vietnam (MACV)
determined that the Communists still retained a viable military and political
apparatus throughout South Vietnam. While Allied efforts had caused a gradual erosion of their capability, Abrams's staff debated whether pacification programs were maintaining momentum, whether local South Vietnamese forces
were effective in providing population security, and whether the morale of
province and district chiefs could be sustained. [2]

South Vietnamese Ambassador to the United States Bui Diem presents
two awards to Wheeler, Washington, DC, 16 September 1970.
(Office of the Chairman of the Joint Chiefs of Staff)

Against this backdrop, on 16 September, South Vietnamese Ambassador Bui Diem presented Wheeler the National Order Second Class and the Gallantry Cross with Palm at the South Vietnamese Embassy. Westmoreland and Moorer attended. [3]

"The U.S. has never sought to widen the war," Nixon insisted in public remarks three weeks later. "What we do seek is to widen the peace." [4]

1971

Laos

In January 1971, Nixon authorized another expansion of the war, this time a major ground offensive into Laos to disrupt the Ho Chi Minh Trail and remind Hanoi that he did not play by Johnson's self-imposed rules. Operation LAM SON 719 was conceived in the White House with the objective of buying time for Vietnamization by disrupting Communist supply lines and seizing a key logistics node on the Ho Chi Minh Trail near Tchepone approximately 25 miles west of the South Vietnamese border. Abrams's intelligence had detected a buildup of North Vietnamese Army (NVA) infantry, armor, artillery, and air defenses there and regarded it as a prelude to a North Vietnamese spring offensive in the northern provinces of I Corps Tactical Zone (I CTZ). [5]

The Administration's enthusiasm for the operation exceeded that of the U.S. and South Vietnamese militaries. Abrams vigorously opposed the operation. The heavy jungle area near Tchepone was ill-suited for helicopter warfare, and Hanoi would detect the invasion weeks in advance. Furthermore, because of the Cooper-Church Amendment, for the first time no U.S. troops or advisors could accompany the South Vietnamese Army (ARVN), although the South Vietnamese would receive support from U.S. helicopters, planes, and artillery, and from hard U.S. fighting on the Vietnamese side of the border in I CTZ. Anticipating high casualties, South Vietnamese leaders were reluctant to involve their army once more in extended operations outside the country. [6]

On 26 January, Nixon asked Moorer, who had replaced Wheeler as Chairman, for assurance that the offensive would succeed. "Moorer was emphatic," Kissinger recalled. If the Communists fought, and they probably would, U.S. airpower would isolate the battlefield and inflict heavy losses that would be difficult to replace. If they did not, their supply system would be destroyed. The operation would ensure the success of Vietnamization, increasing our ability to withdraw forces more rapidly. It would also help the Cambodian government and its struggle for survival by cutting off the Communists' supplies. In short, "decisive" results were probable. [7]

A massive, secure communications system had been installed in Wheeler's farmhouse soon after his retirement for him to maintain contact with the authorities in Washington. "He was always up to date," Wheeler's son Bim recalls, "and he ulcerated about Vietnam." Although Wheeler had long advocated cross-border operations to destroy North Vietnamese sanctuaries, he was less sanguine than Moorer about the proposed operation into Laos. An infantryman, Wheeler probably echoed Abrams's concerns about the unfavorable terrain and enemy situation to Moorer. [8]

The following day, Nixon met with Rogers, Laird, Helms, Moorer, Kissinger, and Deputy National Security Advisor Brigadier General Alexander

M. Haig, Jr. "In an extraordinarily effective [and prescient] presentation, Rogers argued that the risks were excessive," Kissinger recalled. The enemy had intelligence of Allied plans. A major battle was certain. "We were asking the South Vietnamese to conduct an operation that we had refused to undertake when we had 500,000 troops in Vietnam because we thought we were not strong enough. If Saigon were set back, we would risk all the gains of the previous year and might shake Thieu's position in the process." [9]

Unmoved, Nixon "simply did not believe that his Secretary of State knew what he was talking about. He had heard similar objections the year before over Cambodia and none of the predicted horrible contingencies had materialized. He accepted Abrams's and Moorer's word as to military feasibility." [10]

Despite its potential pitfalls, Nixon authorized the operation to proceed. This would be the last opportunity for South Vietnamese forces to sever the Ho Chi Minh Trail while U.S. forces were still available to provide support. Thieu agreed to commit 20,000 men to LAM SON 719. Some of the ARVN's best units would participate, including its 1st Division, the 1st Armored Brigade, three ranger battalions, and most of the elite airborne and Marine divisions from the strategic reserve. [11]

On 8 February, Operation LAM SON 719 commenced with South Vietnamese forces leapfrogging into Laos to establish firebases on the flanks of the attack, while a column from their 1st Armored Brigade advanced down Highway 9 toward Tchepone. [12]

"The operation, conceived in doubt and assailed by skepticism, proceeded in confusion," Kissinger recalled. "It soon became apparent that the plans on which we had been so eloquently and frequently briefed reflected staff exercises, not military reality." [13]

"It was a splendid project on paper," Kissinger explained. "Its chief drawback, as events showed, was that it in no way accorded with Vietnamese realities." South Vietnamese forces were not yet proficient enough for such a complex operation. Nor was the South Vietnamese high command sufficiently experienced to handle two major operations at the same time. Finally,

Tchepone was located at the precise point that Hanoi could most easily reinforce. Its strategic location made it possible to bring up troops from both North and South Vietnam. [14]

Because of security leaks, the North Vietnamese were not deceived about South Vietnamese intentions. Within a week, ARVN forces became bogged down by heavy North Vietnamese Army (NVA) resistance, bad weather, and poor command and control. After a bloody, month-long delay, ARVN troops air assaulted on 6 March into the heavily bombed town of Tchepone. This would be the last good news from the front. [15]

The North Vietnamese then counterattacked, striking the rear of the South Vietnamese forces strung out on Highway 9, thus blocking the ARVN's main route of withdrawal. [16]

On 16 March, ten days after Tchepone was taken, Thieu issued the order to withdraw, disregarding Abrams's plea for an expansion of the offensive in order to inflict serious damage to the Ho Chi Minh Trail. Command-and-control problems that had surfaced during the attack were magnified in the withdrawal, despite warnings from the senior U.S. advisor that the maneuver had to be carefully planned and closely coordinated. The South Vietnamese were in a hurry and soon lost control of the operation. While many ARVN units maintained their cohesiveness and fought well, all semblance of order vanished in others. On 24 March, the last ARVN troops fought their way out of Laos but only after paying a heavy price. They left behind 37 of their 62 tanks, 98 of their 162 armored personnel carriers, as well as 96 artillery pieces. The South Vietnamese also lost nearly 1,600 soldiers. [17]

That the ARVN had reached its objective of Tchepone was of little consequence. Its stay there was brief, and the supply caches it uncovered were disappointing since most caches were in the mountains to the east and west instead. South Vietnamese forces failed to sever the Ho Chi Minh Trail. Communist infiltration reportedly increased during LAM SON 719, as the North Vietnamese shifted traffic to roads and trails farther west in Laos. [18]

LAM SON 719 was a test of Vietnamization less ambiguous than the Cambodian Incursion. While the South Vietnamese had fought tenaciously at times, it was often not enough, and some of the elite ARVN units had collapsed. The ARVN's disappointing performance in Laos was attributable in part to its chronic weakness in planning for and coordinating combat support. The South Vietnamese had become overly dependent upon their U.S. advisors.

"The dry-season offensive of 1971 ... clearly did not realize all our hopes," Kissinger concluded, "nor did it fail completely." The operation did disrupt the Communist's Laotian transportation network and was in part responsible for precluding a Communist spring offensive in the northern provinces of I CTZ for another year. Thus, it had bought time for both South Vietnam and the orderly redeployment of U.S. forces. In other regards, it had failed and was an ill omen for the future. [19]

Nixon proclaimed LAM SON 719 a victory. Addressing the nation on 7 April, the President declared, "The disruption of enemy supply lines, the consumption of ammunition and arms in the battle has been even more damaging to the capability of the North Vietnamese to sustain major offensives in South Vietnam than were the operations in Cambodia ten months ago. Consequently, tonight I can report that Vietnamization has succeeded. ... The American involvement in Vietnam is coming to an end." [20]

From the start, Nixon had sought to portray events in Laos in a positive light. The reality, however, was that after two years of Vietnamization, the ARVN had suffered another setback. This did not necessarily mean the program would ultimately fail, but it created profound doubts about its progress and in so doing weakened the U.S. negotiating position. The President understood this, for he privately complained about the ARVN's poor performance. LAM SON 719 also sparked renewed antiwar demonstrations, sowing concern among Republicans about the President's re-electability. [21]

War Weariness

Meanwhile, neither Nixon's withdrawal policy nor his vigorous counterattacks against the opposition could stem the war weariness and general demoralization that pervaded the nation. An antiwar mood increased. Disillusionment with the war reached an all-time high, with 71% of respondents agreeing that the U.S. had made a mistake by sending troops to Vietnam and 58% regarding the war as "immoral." Nixon's public approval rating on Vietnam had dropped to a low of 31%, and opposition to his policies had sharply increased. A near majority considered the pace of troop withdrawals too slow, and a substantial majority approved the removal of all troops by the end of the year, even if the result was a Communist takeover of South Vietnam. Congress reflected the growing public uneasiness, although it continued to stop short of decisive action. [22]

The limited progress of the South Vietnamese pacification program was evidenced by the embarrassing 1971 national election, during which Thieu's government was unwilling to risk an honest plebiscite. Assisted by the U.S. Ambassador and the CIA, Thieu rigged the election rules so that he ran unopposed. [23]

An extended series of antiwar rallies were held in Washington in April and May. Following a peaceful demonstration by Vietnam veterans on 1 May, youthful protesters attempted to keep federal workers from reaching their jobs by snarling commuter traffic. Anticipating the move, the federal government deployed some 3,000 Marines, 8,600 Regular Army troops, as well as 2,000 National Guardsmen who had been sworn in as special police. These forces succeeded in keeping the traffic moving. [24]

Major New Initiative

To resolve his foreign and domestic problems, the President launched in October what he described as a "major new initiative for peace." After two years of continued heavy fighting, intensive secret diplomacy, and political maneuvering, Nixon's position was worse now than when he had taken office. Negotiations with North Vietnam remained deadlocked, and a National Security Council study in late 1970 had grimly concluded that the United States could neither persuade nor force Hanoi to remove its troops from the South. At home, Nixon narrowly headed off restrictions on his war-making powers, but he still faced hostile and even more determined opposition in Congress and a revived antiwar movement, which had seemed moribund just a year before. The situation in South Vietnam remained stable, but by the end of the year, intelligence reported a sharp increase in the infiltration of troops and supplies into Laos, Cambodia, and South Vietnam. This development posed an ominous threat to the northern provinces and Hue, where sizable U.S. forces had been withdrawn.[25]

By November, when the 101st Airborne Division redeployed from South Vietnam, North Vietnam was preparing for its 1972 spring offensive. With the South's combat capacity diminished and nearly all U.S. combat troops gone, the North sensed an opportunity to demonstrate the failure of Vietnamization, hasten the ARVN's collapse, and revive the stalled peace talks. In its broad outlines and goals, a major offensive in 1972 would resemble Tet 1968, except that the North Vietnamese Army, instead of the Viet Cong, would bear the major burden of combat.[26]

Instead of rethinking his Vietnam policy that had not delivered conclusive results, Nixon had clung stubbornly throughout much of 1971 to the approach he had improvised the preceding year. To appease critics at home, he sped up the timetable of American troop withdrawals. Over Abrams's protests, he ordered the removal of 100,000 troops by the end of the year, leaving 175,000 troops in Vietnam, of which only 75,000 were combat forces. To make clear, at the same time, his continued determination to secure a "just" peace and to counter the threat to Vietnamization posed by increased North Vietnamese infiltration and U.S. troop reductions, he increased military pressure against North Vietnam. American aircraft mounted heavy attacks against supply lines and staging areas in Laos and Cambodia. Using North Vietnamese firing upon American "reconnaissance" planes as a pretext, the Administration ordered "protective reaction" airstrikes against bridges, base camps, and trails across the demilitarized zone and in the Hanoi-Haiphong area.[27]

1972

Easter Offensive

American officials very much wanted pacification to succeed in South Vietnam, and many discerned progress. To some extent, enemy observers and Hamlet Evaluation System (HES) evaluations supported that optimism. HES scores indicated that South Vietnam controlled some 90% of the countryside by 1972, but many peasants living in "secure" villages were there only to find shelter from U.S. firepower. The ARVN's mistreatment of the population continued. Many Saigon government officials remained incompetent and corrupt. Further, HES data was still subjective, falsified, or inflated because of command pressure for positive results. Perhaps most important, physical control had not necessarily equated with heartfelt allegiance.

A weakened National Liberation Front had not automatically translated into a stronger, more popular South Vietnamese government. Until Saigon stood alone against its foes, no one knew whether pacification gains were permanent or fragile and reversible. [28]

Despite the Cambodian Incursion and Operations COMMANDO HUNT, FREEDOM DEAL, and LAM SON 719, Hanoi had achieved its supply and reinforcement goals and was prepared to launch a major offensive. Hanoi decided to reverse the protracted war, economy of force strategy that it had followed for the previous few years and to escalate directly to military *dau tranh*'s conventional warfare phase. In a remarkably short time, the North Vietnamese Army (NVA) had transformed itself from a light infantry force into a Soviet-style mechanized army. The reconstituted Viet Cong would support the major thrusts with hundreds of small attacks in urban areas and the Mekong Delta.

Hanoi hoped to achieve a knockout punch to defeat Vietnamization, gain a decisive victory in 1972, and force the United States to negotiate from a weakened position. Since now only 97,000 U.S. troops remained in Vietnam, and only 6,000 of them were combat troops, the 120,000-man NVA invasion force would concentrate against the ARVN, whose elite units had been weakened during the Laotian offensive. Hanoi correctly reasoned that domestic pressures would prevent Nixon from redeploying additional forces back into Vietnam. A crushing success seemed attainable. However, Communist strategists realized they might have to settle for less, such as merely improving their position by creating enclaves inside the South and by weakening pacification.

On 30 March, North Vietnam launched its massive, conventional invasion of the South. Dubbed the Easter Offensive, it was an unqualified success in its first stages. Because Abrams's intelligence had misjudged the timing, size, and location of the offensive, the ARVN and the Nixon Administration were caught by surprise. After all, it seemed foolhardy for the North to attack in 1972, before all U.S. troops would soon be gone. The ARVN quickly neared collapse. [29]

Although stunned by the swiftness and magnitude of the invasion, Nixon refused to allow South Vietnam to fall. Fearing that he could not win reelection if that happened and that a humiliating defeat might hamper relations with China and the Soviet Union, Nixon responded aggressively. He viewed the Communist invasion as an opportunity to revive the end-the-war strategy he had been forced to discard in 1969. Since domestic antiwar sentiment precluded the reintroduction of U.S. ground troops to Vietnam, Nixon ordered the assembly of an aerial armada to give North Vietnam a "bloody nose." American airpower would shatter the invasion, save Vietnamization and pacification, and compel Hanoi to negotiate a favorable settlement. [30]

Meanwhile, Kissinger met secretly with Soviet Premier Leonid Brezhnev, and made explicit for the first time an American willingness to permit North Vietnamese forces to remain in South Vietnam after a cease-fire. Kissinger also stated emphatically that the U.S. held the Soviet Union responsible for the invasion, and he warned that a continuation of the war could severely damage Soviet-American relations and have grave consequences for North Vietnam. His offer and threats were conveyed to the North Vietnamese on 1 May. [31]

LINEBACKER I

When B-52s struck Haiphong for the first time during the war on 16 April 1972, the Administration hoped it sent "a warning that things might get out of hand if the offensive did not stop." [32]

Still confident of victory, Hanoi flatly rejected Kissinger's offer, leaving Nixon a set of difficult choices. Warning of defeat, Abrams urged on 8 May intensified bombing of North Vietnam and the mining of Haiphong Harbor. On the other hand, Laird and Rogers warned that drastic countermeasures could have disastrous domestic consequences. Kissinger expressed concern that the Soviets might cancel Nixon's impending visit to Moscow, undoing months of negotiations on strategic arms limitation and other major issues.

Kissinger later recanted, acknowledging, "There is no doubt in my mind that the resumption of bombing in May 1972 hastened the end of the war." [33]

Enraged by the North Vietnamese challenge and unwilling to accept defeat, the President struck back furiously. Still intent on persuading the Communists of his resolve and his unpredictability, he set out to make clear that he was "absolutely determined to end the war" and would take "whatever steps are necessary to accomplish this goal." Thus, Nixon decided to "go for broke." He would seize the opportunity presented by the Easter Offensive to destroy Hanoi's capacity to make war — something Wheeler and other senior military advisors to the Nixon and Johnson Administrations had consistently recommended all along. "We have the power to destroy [North Vietnamese] warmaking capacity," Nixon wrote on 9 May. "The only question is whether we have the *will* to use that power. What distinguishes me from [President] Johnson is that I have the *will* in spades." [34]

The U.S. assembled from bases across the world the greatest armada of naval and air power amassed during the war. The number of B-52s on Guam rose from 47 to 210; the number of F-4 Phantoms reached 374; and the aircraft carriers in the South China Sea tripled from two to six. [35]

Even as U.S. airpower pounded the NVA in the South, the President announced to a startled nation on 8 May the most drastic escalation since 1965: the mining of Haiphong Harbor (other major ports and inland waterways would also soon be mined), a naval blockade, and Operation LINEBACKER I, a massive, sustained bombing campaign against the North. Urging his military advisors to "recommend action which is very strong, threatening, and effective," Nixon intended "to stop at nothing to bring the enemy to his knees." Yet, in his 8 May speech, Nixon also issued an "ultimatum" that spelled out terms for a U.S. withdrawal. All the U.S. wanted was the return of its prisoners of war and an internationally supervised cease-fire. Once North Vietnam met these conditions, the U.S. would "stop all acts of force throughout Indochina, and at that time we will proceed with a complete withdrawal of all American forces from Vietnam within four months." [36]

LINEBACKER I supported a more limited policy objective than ROLL-ING THUNDER. As often occurs in warfare, the losing side reduced its war aims. Johnson had sought an independent, non-Communist South Vietnam. Nixon's objective was an independent South Vietnam that would not collapse immediately after U.S. withdrawal. Kissinger informed the Soviet Ambassador that if a new war broke out after the U.S. withdrew, "that conflict will no longer be an American affair; it will be an affair of the Vietnamese themselves, because the Americans will have left Vietnam." He relayed a similar message to China, saying all U.S. wanted was for the South to survive for a "decent interval," which he defined as five years. Nixon contemplated using airpower to ensure the South's existence until at least 1977, when his second term would end, thus removing any imputation that he lost the war. [37]

LINEBACKER I vastly exceeded all previous attacks on North Vietnam. In June alone, U.S. aircraft dropped 112,000 tons of bombs. Before the operation culminated on 23 October, 155,548 tons of bombs would fall on North Vietnam. Even more critical was U.S. tactical air support in South Vietnam. American bombers flew round-the-clock missions — B-52 sortie rates reached an unprecedented 3 per hour each 24 hours — pummeling Communist supply lines and encampments. With the crucial assistance of U.S. airpower, the South Vietnamese Army (ARVN) eventually stabilized the lines in front of Saigon and Hue and even mounted a small counteroffensive. [38]

With Hanoi's conventional forces more vulnerable to aerial destruction than their guerrilla operations had been, and with the North Vietnamese Army (NVA) experiencing untold difficulty in waging combined arms warfare for the first time in its history, the Easter Offensive soon stalled. The NVA would not soon launch another offensive after suffering such a disaster. Thus, a few U.S. aircraft had now achieved greater results than ROLLING THUNDER's large strike forces. Moreover, despite fearsome losses of men and equipment, the ARVN survived under the protective umbrella of U.S. airpower.

Although Nixon's ferocious response shocked Communist leaders, and their offensive failed to deliver a knockout punch, the NVA and Viet Cong nonetheless attained advantages that pointed toward ultimate success. Counterbalancing the destruction LINEBACKER I inflicted upon the North was the destruction in South Vietnam, where combat reduced some cities to rubble and created more than 1 million new refugees. The NVA established control over a belt of strategic terrain running from the demilitarized zone along the Laotian and Cambodian borders to the northern Delta, thus strengthening its grip on the Central Highlands, improving the security of its sanctuaries and the Ho Chi Minh Trail, and gaining essential territory for launching subsequent military actions. [39]

The decisive application of U.S. airpower provided encouragement to South Vietnamese leaders facing a future without U.S. ground forces. Nixon's resumption of the bombing of North Vietnam during the Easter Offensive and, for the first time, his mining of North Vietnamese ports, gave confidence to the South Vietnamese that they could count on U.S. air support in the years ahead. So too would the intense B-52 bombing of Hanoi and Haiphong as part of Operation LINEBACKER II in December 1972. [40]

In the political context, "Nixon's gamble succeeded, at least to a point," Herring explains. "Caught up in an extremely delicate diplomatic game, the two major Communist powers responded to the events of 1972 with the greatest care. Because of their continuing rivalry, neither was prepared to sacrifice North Vietnam on the altar of political expediency." [41]

The domestic fallout was manageable. Although a new round of protests and demonstrations erupted, Nixon's public approval rating shot up dramatically; Congress did nothing; and Nixon emerged in a much stronger position than before the North Vietnamese invasion. [42]

In the offensive's aftermath, both Hanoi and Saigon claimed victory, but the balance had not been significantly altered. The South Vietnamese Army (ARVN) had barely escaped defeat, a fact that Hanoi, MACV, and many South Vietnamese understood. To the Communists, the offensive signaled Vietnamization's failure because the South still could not stand on its own. While praising a few ARVN units that fought well, Abrams and other high-ranking Americans admitted Vietnamization's prospects were precarious, and that only a torrent of bombs had averted a catastrophe by compensating for the ARVN's feeble fighting spirit. Even though the Easter Offensive accomplished less than Hanoi's strategists ideally sought, it also revealed that Vietnamization and pacification had not yet created a stouthearted South

Vietnamese nationalism that could match the Communists, and time was swiftly running out. [43]

Negotiated Settlement

The ferocious campaigns of the spring and summer of 1972 merely raised the stalemate to a new level of violence. Both sides endured huge losses — the North Vietnamese suffered an estimated 100,000 casualties, the South Vietnamese lost as many as 30,000 killed, 78,000 wounded, and 14,000 missing in action — but neither emerged appreciably stronger. Frustrated in their hopes of breaking the diplomatic stalemate by military means, each side, by the fall of 1972, found compelling reasons to attempt to break the military deadlock by diplomacy. From late summer onward, the U.S. and North Vietnam began edged toward a compromise. [44]

Even while the Easter Offensive raged across South Vietnam and LINEBACKER I inflicted crippling losses on the North, negotiators in Paris inched toward a truce. The battering inflicted by U.S. airpower convinced the Communists that they must remove the U.S. from the war as soon as possible. Nixon was also anxious to settle, as indications existed that the Congress that would convene in January 1973 would be so dovish that it might legislate an end to the war. Both sides retreated from long-held positions. The Communists' key concession was to drop their demand for Thieu's ouster and the creation of a coalition government in the South. Nixon's most significant concession — the most significant in the entire negotiating process — was agreeing to allow North Vietnamese Army (NVA) troops to remain inside South Vietnam after previously insisting on mutual troop withdrawals. The NVA's presence in the South virtually guaranteed the Communists' ultimate success, even if Thieu remained in power for the time being. The U.S. also failed to insist upon a cease fire that recognized two Vietnams, thereby conceding, as the Geneva Conference had specified in 1954, that the 17th Parallel was not an international boundary.

The U.S. and North Vietnam completed a treaty on 8 October, agreeing to sign it by the end of the month. But the U.S. had negotiated its retreat without fully consulting South Vietnam — with good reason, since Nixon had capitulated on such crucial issues. Thieu would not agree to the settlement. Fearing that his government would not survive if the NVA remained in the South and wanting the 17th Parallel to be recognized as a boundary between sovereign nations, he insisted that the treaty required major changes. To placate his recalcitrant Ally, Nixon assured Thieu "that the United States will react very strongly and rapidly to any violation of the agreement," and warned him that it was essential "your government does not emerge as the obstacle to peace which American public opinion now universally desires." Thieu was not placated, resulting in the paradoxical situation whereby the United States had a deal with its enemy, but its Ally was the obstacle to peace. [45]

LINEBACKER II

The President directed Kissinger, who considered to Thieu's proposed changes "preposterous," to present them to North Vietnam, but the North's chief negotiator, Le Duc Tho, insisted that the U.S. fulfill the 8 October agreement. When negotiations failed to break the deadlock, Nixon tried to get tough, first with his Ally and then against his foe. He sent several messages to Thieu threatening to move forward with the treaty "at whatever cost." [46]

When Thieu did not relent, Nixon threatened the North with another aerial barrage. When the Communists rejected any amendments, he again determined to go for broke. Nixon made very clear to Moorer and the Chiefs his determination to inflict maximum damage on North Vietnam. "I don't want any more of this crap about the fact that we couldn't hit this target or that one," he instructed Moorer. "This is your chance to use military power to win this war, and if you don't, I'll consider you responsible." The Chiefs recommended and on 18 December Nixon quickly authorized Operation LINEBACKER II, an all-out air campaign against North Vietnam's heartland to force a settlement of the war. The eleven-day "Christmas bombing" was the most intensive and devastating aerial offensive of the war. More than 36,000 tons of bombs were dropped, exceeding the tonnage for the entire period between 1969 and 1971. [47]

"For the first time, B-52s were used in large numbers to bring the full weight of air power to bear," General William W. Momyer, commanding the 7th Air Force, recalled. "What airmen had long advocated as the proper employment of airpower was now the President's strategy — concentrated use of all forms of airpower to strike at the vital power centers, causing maximum disruption in the economic, military, and political life of the country." [48]

Like so many previous bombing operations, LINEBACKER II yielded ambiguous results. Extensively relying upon B-52s, it "rearranged much of LINEBACKER I's rubble", crippled North Vietnamese air defenses, and inflicted additional damage, particularly on previously restricted targets in Hanoi and Haiphong. But the U.S. lost 15 B-52s and 13 other aircraft, leaving 31 crewmen as prisoners of war and another 93 missing and presumed dead. Moreover, the operation provoked domestic outrage. Impeachment threats hung in the air, and Congress vowed to cut off war funding contingent upon the withdrawal of all U.S. troops and the return of its prisoners. Nixon knew he had to obtain a deal quickly because the bombing was politically not sustainable. Even though he threatened the North with still more bombing, the public outcry was so great that "we cannot consider this to be a viable option." Internationally, in contrast to their tepid objections to LINEBACKER I, the Soviets and Chinese now reacted angrily, raising fears that detente was at risk. [49]

Nixon used LINEBACKER II in attempt to influence both North and South Vietnam. Rather than risk a third linebacker, the North returned to the conference table determined to get the U.S. out of the war even if it meant accepting a few cosmetic changes to the 8 October agreement. Nixon hoped LINEBACKER II would reassure Thieu that the U.S. would not desert him or allow the Communists to break the agreement with impunity. When Thieu still balked, Nixon insisted he was going to sign an agreement, alone if necessary, in which case, "I shall have to explain publicly that your government obstructs peace." Not wanting an open break with the U.S., Thieu unhappily acquiesced. [50]

Shred It

Meanwhile, as Wheeler kept abreast of developments in Paris and Vietnam from his farm in Martinsburg, West Virginia, Bim continued to press his father to finish his memoirs. Two years had passed since Bus's retirement, and he had, in fact, completed a draft of several hundred pages. In truth, he was disgusted by it all.

"If you believe that as a professional soldier I am in any way proud of my association with the Vietnam War, you are damn wrong!" Bus finally exploded. "I don't want to hear another word about that goddamned war! Do you understand?"

"Yes, sir!" Bim replied, and he never brought up the subject again. [51]

"Wheeler had participated in a series of decisions any one of which he was able to defend, but the cumulative impact of which he could not really justify to himself," Kissinger recalled. "He was a gentleman to the core, a fine officer who helped his country through tragic times and was himself inwardly eaten up by them." [52]

Wheeler had been given an office in the Pentagon for documenting his tenure as Chairman. To his secretary Mary Feeley's great surprise, he entered the office one day and told her to shred his manuscript. Wheeler stated he was at peace with himself and God with what he done. [53]

Wheeler was also exhausted and angered by the war, and thinking about it exhausted and angered him even more, Bim explained. He also recalls his father saying he that "didn't want to hurt the families of those with whom he'd worked and admired." Although filled with personal bitterness, Wheeler kept his own counsel, refusing to engage in recriminations against those who had decided policies that he opposed. [54]

Sharp took a different tact in retirement and was openly critical of Johnson, McNamara, and their senior civilian advisors:

> Our airpower did not fail us; it was the decision makers. And if I am unsurprisingly critical of those decision-makers, I offer no apology. My conscience and professional record both stand clear. Just as I believe unequivocally that the civilian authority is supreme under our Constitution, so I hold it reasonable that, once committed, the political leadership should seek and, in the main, heed the advice of the military professionals in the conduct of military operations. [55]

Wheeler would make own views clear in congressional testimony about Cambodia in July 1973. "This war in Vietnam — there is no question about it — went on and on and on," Wheeler testified. "It should have been wound up within a few months. If we had bombed earlier in the very beginning as President Nixon has done in the last year, the war wouldn't have lasted in my judgment but a few months." [56]

1973

Paris Peace Accords

On 23 January 1973, all parties — South Vietnam, the United States, North Vietnam, and the National Liberation Front — signed the Paris Peace Accords, which were only slightly modified from the 8 October agreement. The Accords called for a cease-fire in place (which left at least 100,000 North Vietnamese Army troops in the South), complete American withdrawal, and prisoner exchanges, although the North betrayed the Viet Cong because the Accords excluded them from the prisoner swap. In a protocol kept secret from the public and Congress, Nixon pledged the U.S. would pay at least $3.25 billion in what were essentially reparations. The President insisted that he had achieved "peace with honor," but even viewed in the best light the Accords left the South in a precarious position. Former Secretary of State Rusk said they were "in effect a surrender." South Vietnamese Vice President Ky described them as a "sellout." The Chief of Naval Operations, Admiral Elmo R. Zumwalt, Jr., asserted that two words that could never describe the outcome of Nixon's Vietnam policy were "peace" and "honor." [57]

Cambodia Bombing Hearings

Wheeler's health had deteriorated. "Bus was a very sick man, not well," Bim recalls. "He knew he was dying. He had horrible emphysema. He couldn't walk half a block without stopping to catch his breath. Testifying (in July) must have been terribly draining on him." [58]

After newspaper accounts of the secret bombing campaign in Cambodia were published in July, the Senate Armed Services Committee convened a hearing into the matter of falsification of reports associated with this operation. "Public revelation of the bombing by former airmen in 1973 caused a furor, no doubt partly because of the intimation of double-dealing in high places," Westmoreland recalled. The issue was controversial because false reporting is an offense under the Uniform Code of Military Justice. [59]

Summoned to testify, Wheeler revealed that he had, on Nixon's personal orders, directed secret and, when made public, highly controversial, bombing missions over Cambodia in 1969-70. [60]

The committee released to the press a memorandum written by Wheeler on 20 November 1969. This memo stated that Nixon "personally ordered" a 41-aircraft force to attack targets inside of Cambodia while other B-52s attacked normally assigned targets in South Vietnam, and that the Cambodia raids were to be kept "totally secret." Airstrikes on the latter targets would resemble normal operations, thereby providing a credible story for replies to press inquiries. This memo, initialed as approved by Laird, referred to a cover story that applied not only to Congress and the public but also to responsible Pentagon officials, who were given misleading military reports. [61]

"In implementation of the President's instructions with regard to security," Wheeler testified in his opening statement, "it was directed that all communications on the subject be very closely held and transmitted by especially secure channels, with distribution limited to named addressees only, on a strict need-to-know basis." [62]

"No false report was approved to the best of my knowledge and belief and no false report was made," Wheeler testified. The aircraft were ordered to targets in South Vietnam by a routine fragmentary order and assigned a mission identifier, he explained. They were diverted by ground control radar stations to a target in Cambodia. Reports of this activity were transmitted by a special channel. Subsequent reports reflecting time on target, flight time, and the munitions expended were listed by the mission identifier. "It must be remembered that if fuel, munitions, spare parts, and maintenance data were to be acquired, it was necessary to reflect the sorties in some reporting system available to the clerks and administrators responsible for providing the administrative and logistic support for the aircraft without divulging to them the nature and scope of the operation," Wheeler testified. The sorties were routinely entered into the Joint Chiefs of Staff automated database by mission identifier reflecting the original fragmentary order target. No special instructions on such matters were issued. The ongoing administrative procedure simply continued its mechanical function. [63]

"Detailed information concerning planning and execution of strikes, together with estimates of results, were, in accordance with instructions, handled through specially secure means," Wheeler continued. "Therefore, the routine reports combined with the special reports gave those who needed to know the information exactly what was taking place while still retaining the ordered security." [64]

The *New York Times*, commenting on "the spirit of Watergate" in an editorial on 5 August, reported that Wheeler "saw nothing wrong with these actions because nobody 'with a need to know' had been deceived." [65]

South Carolina Senator James Strom Thurmond, Sr. asked, "In looking back over it now, do you feel that it was a wise decision to save American lives?"

"I believe so, Senator," Wheeler replied. "As a matter of fact, during our bombing campaign the casualties which had been running about 250 a week dropped to about half that number. And they continued to decline throughout the rest of the year."

"Do you feel there was false reporting there are not?" Thurmond later asked.

Wheeler replied:

> I do not, sir. I do not think this was false reporting. It is quite true that one thing that went into the automated databank was erroneous; that is, the location of certain of the strikes, which were shown as being in South Vietnam when they were actually in the border area of Cambodia. But I assure you, Senator, that no one was ordered to make a false report. I wasn't directed to by the President or by the Secretary of Defense, nor did I direct anybody in the field make a false report.

"Did the military consider that they were false reporting to try to deceive somebody," Thurmond asked, "or were they following a course during a secret military operation that they thought would save American lives?"

Wheeler replied:

> We weren't trying to deceive anybody, Senator We didn't deceive anybody — we didn't deceive Prince Sihanouk; we didn't deceive the enemy, because he knew he was being bombed; and we certainly did not deceive the President or the Secretary of Defense or those others in the chain of command. I would say that the information which was provided to everyone who needed it was valid; even the logistical information was valid information which the logistics people and technicians needed to do their work. [66]

Georgia Senator Samuel A. Nunn, Jr. asked, "General, is it your understanding that falsifying reports is a violation of the Military Code?"

"Oh, yes," Wheeler replied.

"As I understand it," Nunn asked, "your definition of the distinction between accuracy and falsification was whether everyone who had a need to know the accurate information had it — is that your definition?"

"My definition contained the elements of an attempt to deceive," Wheeler replied. "If you are intending to deceive someone in authority, this is falsification, or a false report. If there is no such intent, and that is not accomplished, there can't be falsification or a false report."

Nunn replied, "No matter how erroneous or inaccurate it is, as long as the President of the United States orders it and it comes that way, then it is still an accurate report?"

"The President of the United States didn't order these particular procedures," Wheeler responded. "What he ordered was security, and the procedures that had to be adopted resulted in this affect. But I don't think that the reports were grossly in error by any manner or means. It is certainly true that certain people did not get information because they were not on the list of those who were in a need-to-know category." [67]

Senator Symington commented:

> Mister Chairman, I have listened to what I am sure is a sin-
> cere attempt by General Wheeler to recount what has hap-
> pened, but it reminded me — not by any intention on his
> part — that it is hard for me to believe that the heads of our
> government, civilian and military, have come up with what
> seems to be almost similar to a shell game that I used to watch
> somewhere back in the past as a kid, whereby we put in dif-
> ferent coordinates on strike reports telling that bombs were
> dropped in South Vietnam but actually they were dropped
> in Cambodia, and then we say, this is not falsification, and
> whereby we get a direct communication from the President
> of the United States to the people of the United States say-
> ing that we have respected the neutrality of the Cambodian
> people, and for five long years we have not violated the
> neutrality of the nation of Cambodia, when, as a matter of
> fact, we were violating the neutrality of Cambodia, crossing
> the borders and dropping bombs, as has now been publicly
> admitted. This, of course, is explained away as saying that it
> does not apply because the people with a need to know had
> the correct information. The only people in the world who
> were kept from knowing were the people of the United States
> of America, who were kept from knowing the truth. Now,
> why that was so damned important is beyond my concep-
> tion, unless the diplomacy they were concerned about was
> the antiwar movement in the United States of America.

Symington had hit the nail on the head, yet none of his fellow committee members pressed Wheeler on this point. Rather, they continued to drill
into the procedural details of the military's reporting system.

"In retrospect it is difficult to find any redeeming features of this vast,
surreptitious bombing campaign which, as we know now, represented the first
fateful step toward our full-scale involvement in Cambodia," Symington read

from a prepared statement. "This involvement has now cost hundreds of millions of dollars, scores of American lives, thousands of Asian lives, and untold destruction which we are now told it is planned to have the American taxpayer pay to repair."

"If the Congress or the American people had been given an opportunity to pass judgment on this secret scheme, all of this might have been avoided," Symington continued. "Little wonder the Administration did not want the American people to know what was going on. Security or diplomacy cannot have been the justification because both our Indochina Allies and enemies were fully aware of what we were doing. The Congress should assure that this experience is not repeated." [68]

After eight hours of Wheeler's testimony, the hearing ended. Thurmond said, "I want to thank you, General Wheeler, for coming here and testifying on this occasion. We appreciate your presence, and we hope you will enjoy good health and happiness in the future."

"I want to ask you this question," Thurmond continued. "Is it your opinion as a military man that the bombing that was done over there at the command of the President was helpful in getting a cease-fire during the war?"

"I believe so, sir," Wheeler replied. "Of course, it has been a long war, and a very harrowing one. But I believe that the military operations that were undertaken, and the bombing, and other actions against the North Vietnamese, did eventually bring them to terms, and perhaps not the terms that some people would have liked to have had, the terms at least that permitted us to disengage our forces." [69]

The War Continues

The Paris Peace Accords removed the U.S. from the war and brought its prisoners of war home, but they had not resolved the fundamental issue of whether Vietnam was one nation or two. Consequently, as Nixon and Kissinger anticipated, the Vietnamese Civil War continued with barely a pause. Thieu ordered the South Vietnamese Army (ARVN) to reclaim as much territory as possible, and it succeeded in recovering some areas the North Vietnamese Army (NVA) had "liberated" during the Easter Offensive. The NVA did not yield terrain without exacting a stiff price. The ARVN suffered 25,473 killed in action during 1973, and it would lose another 19,375 over the first eight months of 1974. By then, it would be stretched dangerously thin. Initially, the South seemed to benefit from Projects ENHANCE and ENHANCE PLUS, two gargantuan efforts to beef up the South's arsenal before the cease-fire went into effect, because the terms limited resupply to one-for-one replacements. The Department of Defense engorged the South Vietnamese Armed Forces with equipment, but as military historian Lieutenant General Philip B. Davidson, Jr. observed, the U.S. had provided "airplanes they couldn't fly, ships they couldn't man, and tanks and other equipment they couldn't maintain." [70]

1974

Beginning of the End

South Vietnamese military security had declined due to a combination of new and old factors. Plagued by poor maintenance and shortages of spare parts, much of the advanced equipment provided to the South Vietnamese forces under Vietnamization became inoperable. A rise in fuel prices stemming from a worldwide oil crisis further restricted South Vietnamese use of vehicles and aircraft. Government forces in many areas of the country were on the defensive, confined to protecting key towns and installations. Seeking to preserve its diminishing assets, the South Vietnamese Army (ARVN) became garrison-bound and either reluctant or unable to react to a growing number of guerrilla attacks that eroded rural security. Congressionally mandated reductions in U.S. aid further reduced the delivery of spare parts, fuel, and ammunition. American military activities in Cambodia and Laos, which had continued after the cease-fire in South Vietnam went into effect, ended in 1973 when Congress cut off funding for them. By late 1974, many ARVN soldiers were dispirited, and about 24,000 deserted each month. [71]

After the U.S. departed, the Communists became more confident than ever of ultimate victory. They moved cautiously, however, for fear of provoking another linebacker because they needed time to rebuild their own weakened forces. Encouraged by cuts in U.S. aid to South Vietnam, the convulsions in the U.S. caused by Nixon's misdeeds during the Watergate scandal, continued Soviet support, and growing unrest against Thieu's dictatorship, the Communists began driving the ARVN from territory that South Vietnam had acquired in its immediate post-peace land grab. Hanoi also adopted a two-year plan to unify Vietnam. Limited offensives in late 1974 and into 1975 would create favorable conditions for a climatic "General Offensive-General Uprising" in 1976.

North Vietnamese strategists had often miscalculated during the war, usually to their regret. This time, however, they miscalculated to their advantage. In mid-December, the NVA attacked out of Cambodia into Phuoc Long Province northwest of Saigon and captured it in only three weeks. Despite this blatant violation of the Paris Peace Accords, the U.S. did not react with anything more forceful than diplomatic notes. [72]

1975

The Final Offensive

In early 1975, Hanoi began planning for a new offensive, still uncertain whether the U.S. would resume bombing or once again intervene in the South. Since its forces' seizure of Phuoc Long Province had provoked no U.S. military response, Hanoi decided to proceed with a major offensive in the Central Highlands aimed at Ban Me Thout. Launched on 10 March, the offensive succeeded in capturing the city within a week. The Communists now stood poised to bisect the South by advancing to the South China Sea. They would not have to fight very hard to do so.

Thieu, desiring to husband his military resources, decided to retreat rather than to reinforce the Central Highlands. Without any notice, he ordered the ARVN to abandon the Highlands. Since it had no plans for withdrawing, the retreat degenerated into a rout. The result was panic among his troops and a mass exodus toward the coast.

Neither Nixon, weakened by the Watergate scandal and forced to resign, nor his successor, President Gerald R. Ford, were prepared to challenge Congress by resuming U.S. military activity in Southeast Asia. The will of Congress seemed to reflect the mood of the American public weary of the long and inconclusive war.

What had begun as a limited offensive in the highlands now became an all-out effort to conquer South Vietnam. As NVA forces spilled out of the Central Highlands, they cut off South Vietnamese defenders in the northern provinces from the rest of the country. Other NVA units now crossed the demilitarized zone, quickly overrunning Hue and Da Nang and signaling the collapse of South Vietnamese resistance in the north. The ARVN suffered another debacle despite a few pockets of heroic resistance.

Pleasantly surprised by these unexpectedly easy successes, Hanoi ordered the NVA to discard the two-year plan and complete the South's destruction that year. Substantially rebuilt after the nadir years of 1968-1971, the Viet Cong played vital roles in supporting the North's conventional forces. By mid-April, the NVA was approaching Saigon, delayed only by a ferocious last stand at the strategic crossroads of Xuan Loc by the ARVN's 18th Division against four NVA divisions.

Hurriedly established defensive lines around Saigon delayed the Communist offensive against the capital for a while, but not for long. On 29 April, the Vietnam War's last battle commenced when NVA rockets blasted Tan Son Nhut air base, which had been the Military Assistance Command, Vietnam's headquarters. As South Vietnamese leaders waited in vain for U.S. assistance, Saigon fell to the Communists the following day.

South Vietnam had collapsed after an indecently brief interval. If the war's beginning was ambiguous, its ending was not. The U.S. and the South Vietnam that it tried to create had lost unequivocally. [73]

Defeat

Saigon's fall was a bitter end to the long U.S. effort to sustain South Vietnam. Ranging from advice and support to direct participation in combat and involving nearly 3,000,000 U.S. servicemen, the effort failed to prevent Communist leaders from achieving their goal of unifying a divided nation. South Vietnam's military defeat tended to obscure the crucial inability of this massive military enterprise to compensate for South Vietnamese political shortcomings. Over a span of two decades, a series of regimes had failed to fully and effectively mobilize their nation's political, social, and economic resources to foster a popular base of support. North Vietnamese conventional units ended the war, but insurgency and disaffection among the people of the South had made that outcome possible. [74]

In succession, the Viet Cong and North Vietnamese Army had defeated America's special war, limited war, and Vietnamization-pacification strategies. By 1975, the U.S. could not afford the cost of propping up Thieu's government; the American public no longer had any interest in Vietnam; and the U.S. could not continue to ignore its other domestic and worldwide commitments. Throughout its brief history, South Vietnam had always been too dependent on the U.S. to stand on its own. Its population, like America's, was never willing to pay anything close to the steep price that the North Vietnamese and Viet Cong did in pursuit of what they considered the sacred goals of national unification and independence. [75]

Approximately 260,000 South Vietnamese military personnel had died, and many hundreds of thousands more were wounded during the war. Hanoi declared that 1,100,000 Viet Cong and North Vietnamese Army troops had been killed or died of wounds. Exactly how many more were wounded in action or missing was unknown, but the numbers were substantial. Accurate estimates of enemy casualties run afoul of the difficulty in distinguishing between civilians and combatants, imprecise body counts, and the difficulty of verifying casualties in enemy-controlled areas. An estimated 500,000 North and South Vietnamese civilians lost their lives, and perhaps three times that many were wounded. By comparison, U.S. losses were relatively modest: 47,364 battle deaths, 10,797 non-battle deaths, and 313,616 wounded in action, about half of whom required hospitalization. [76]

The Military Laments

In the immediate aftermath of the fall of Saigon, senior U.S. military officers were quick to blame their civilian leaders for defeat. They argued that if they had only been allowed to see things through, they could have led South

Vietnam to final victory. Like many, Wheeler believed the U.S. had essentially "won the war and then pissed it away with a scurrilous Congress." [77]

Had the dejected and bitter Wheeler completed his autobiography, he would have decried how resourcing Vietnam on the cheap had debilitated the United States' ability to contend with other threats and meet its obligations worldwide. He lamented that the Johnson Administration fought, not to achieve victory or to *win*, but merely to avoid defeat. "If we had done what we should have done, the war would have been over in 1965," Bim recalls his father saying in retirement. [78]

"Why didn't we go into North Vietnam?" Bim asked. "It's so obvious."

"You are exactly right," Bus replied. [79]

"Granting the enemy that unrestricted use of sanctuary lands on South Vietnam's flanks was at least naïve," Dave Palmer wrote, "at worst an egregious strategic blunder." [80]

Sharp railed against Congress for its 1974 "assault on what was left of our support for South Vietnam by cutting funds for the procurement of military supplies for that beleaguered country." [81]

"I am convinced that history will reflect more favorably upon the performance of the military than upon that of the politicians and policymakers," Westmoreland contended. "The American people can be particularly proud that their military leaders scrupulously adhered to a basic tenet of our Constitution prescribing civilian control of the military." [82]

"Despite military advice to the contrary, our political leaders decreased the pressure on the Hanoi regime and enticed the enemy to the conference table," Westmoreland asserted to U.S. Army Command and General Staff College students in 1978. [83]

"However desirable the American system of civilian control of the military," Westmoreland observed, "it was a mistake to permit appointive civilian officials lacking military experience and knowledge of military history and oblivious to the lessons of Communist diplomatic machinations to wield undue influence in the decision-making process. Overall control of the military is one thing; shackling professional military men with restrictions in professional matters imposed by civilians who lack military understanding is another." [84]

"I can also hope," Westmoreland continued, "that in the future the nation's elected officials will recognize that if war is indeed too complex to be left to the generals, it is also too complex to be entrusted to appointed officials who lack military experience, a knowledge of military history, and an ability to persevere in the face of temporary adversity and vocal ferment." [85]

Westmoreland was particularly outspoken on what might have been:

> The war still could have been brought to a favorable end following the defeat of the enemy's Tet Offensive in 1968. The United States had in South Vietnam at that time the finest military force – though not the largest – ever assembled. Had President Johnson changed our strategy and taken advantage of the enemy's weakness to enable me to carry out the operations we had planned over the preceding two years in Laos and Cambodia and north of the DMZ, along with intensified bombing and the mining of Haiphong harbor, the North Vietnamese doubtlessly would have broken. But that was not to be. Press and television had created an aura not of victory but of defeat, which, coupled with the vocal antiwar elements, profoundly influenced timid officials in Washington. It was like two boxers in a ring, one having the other on the ropes, close to a knock-out, when the apparent winner's second inexplicably throws in the towel. [86]

Goodpaster would later argue that if the nation's military had been left to fight without civilian interference and with what he considered adequate resources (including re-instituting the draft), the U.S. could have avoided the humiliating outcome that ensued. The war was lost at home by incremental policy decisions and mismanagement. [87]

Goodpaster also faulted the Johnson Administration's self-imposed warmaking restrictions for skewing a central strategic aspect of war — the enemy's *center of gravity*:

We had adopted a strategy that focused on none of the possible North Vietnamese centers of gravity — their army, their capital, the army of their protector, the community of interest with their allies, or public opinion. ... Instead, by seeing the Viet Cong as a separate entity rather than as an instrument of North Vietnam, we chose a center of gravity which in fact did not exist. The proof that the Viet Cong guerrillas were not a center of gravity was demonstrated during Tet-68, when, even though the enemy had incurred huge losses, the war continued unabated. [88]

Later asked whether the U.S. could have won in Vietnam, Haig replied, "Absolutely, had we taken the war to Hanoi, and I mean both airpower and at least demonstrated credibility that we were prepared to use ground troops." [89]

Younger officers who had served in Vietnam felt the same way. General H. Norman Schwarzkopf, Jr., commander of Allied ground forces during the First Iraq War (1990-1991), was certain the Vietnam War could have been won in 1965:

I am absolutely convinced that we would have won had we bombed the North and mined Haiphong Harbor. ... We never really fought the war strategically. We never took the war to the North. ... We should have bombed using more B-52s and mined Haiphong Harbor. We should have continued to escalate to include cross-border operations into North Vietnam and, if need be, into all of North Vietnam. Why? Because it would have brought the war to a conclusion. It was fruitless to continue to fight only in South Vietnam when the war was really being conducted by the people in Hanoi. ... We fought the North Vietnamese with one hand tied behind our back. [90]

"The key to winning the war in Vietnam," said General Barry R. McCaffrey, a division commander during the First Iraq War, "was to apply an overmatching level of violence in an explosive manner to overload the North Vietnamese decision-making capacity." [91]

This author does not conclude that the military had a panacea that could have won the war had the President and Secretary of Defense given them freer rein. While the expanded offensive operations the military recommended may have increased the likelihood of success, they may also have widened the war and certainly would have raised the death toll, increased spending, inflamed the antiwar movement, and would not have changed the war's ultimate negative outcome for the United States. The increased costs associated with the military's recommendations were too much for the Johnson and Nixon Administrations, and therein lies the reason why many of the military's recommendations were not adopted or adopted in-full. It was not a function that Wheeler and Chiefs failed to effectively articulate their recommendations and state probable military consequences of the President's decisions. They certainly did, as this book has conclusively demonstrated.

Daddis decries the military's "if only" arguments as counterfactual that the military "had solved the riddle of Vietnam, and that civilian political leaders and the public at large simply had to see the war through to its logical conclusion." [92]

Prados contends that military revisionists and neo-orthodox historians have been unable to propose a convincing argument for how the war could have been won:

> 'Decisive' intervention, pacification, and bombing were options that had to be carried out within the context of specific diplomatic, geographic, logistical, and doctrinal conditions; with a given force posture; and subject to the intractable elements and intrinsic difficulties that applied to Vietnam. The perfect strategies revolved around options that were always on the menu and were either tried and found wanting or were never really practical. Divorcing the options from the political and military context to claim feasibility is not acceptable analysis. And in the moment, befuddled by the

Vietnam data problem, faced with contradictory advice from aides whose understanding of the requirements of insurgency warfare was imperfect, while confronting a running clock, Presidents could never achieve a proper strategy. [93]

The specter of defeat in Vietnam would have a cautionary effect on U.S. foreign policy for at least three decades. The "Vietnam syndrome" was a reluctance to commit U.S. combat power abroad, especially in conflicts deemed "unwinnable." [94]

Kissinger reflected:

A President cannot take away the curse of a controversial decision by hesitation in its execution. The use of military force is a difficult decision that must always be made with a prayerful concern for Bismarck's profound dictum: 'Woe to the statesman whose reasons for entering a war do not appear so plausible at its end as at its beginning.' A leader's fundamental choice is whether to approve the use of force. If he decides to do so, his only vindication is to succeed. His doubts provide no justification for failure; restraint in execution is a boon to the other side; there are no awards for those who lose with moderation. Once the decision to use force has been made, the President has no choice but to pursue it with total determination – and to convey the same spirit to all those implementing it. Nations must not undertake military enterprises or major diplomatic initiatives that they are not willing to see through. [95]

"There are certain fundamentals that you can't ignore," said Senator John S. McCain III, a former Navy fighter pilot who had spent several years as a prisoner of war in Hanoi and whose father had commanded Pacific Command. "Obviously, those are that you don't go into a conflict in a half-hearted fashion without a clear strategy for victory." [96]

William C. Martel, Associate Professor of International Security Studies at Tufts University, echoes McCain's point. "Having clear language on victory is necessary because it's the only way we can establish any coherence on what a society – both its policymakers and its public – can expect to achieve when they decide to use military force." [97]

Summers cites a 1974 survey as evidence of how confusion over objectives had a devastating effect on the U.S. Army's ability to conduct the war. "Almost 70% of the Army generals who managed the war were uncertain of its objectives." The survey concluded that this "mirrors a deep-seated strategic failure: the inability of policymakers to frame tangible, obtainable goals." [98]

At the grand strategic level, Daddis assesses, U.S. policymakers had miscalculated the ways in which military and other means could achieve political ends. Any strategy, therefore, at any level, devised by the Americans was likely to be deficient. In the process, policymakers failed to consider the possibility that when interceding in foreign revolutionary wars, even great powers like the U.S. might not be able to leverage their influence.

While U.S. military and civilian leaders disagreed at times over how military force should be used, few questioned, especially in the war's early years, whether the U.S. mission could solve South Vietnam's problems and uphold the larger policy of containment. Whether it was hubris or naïveté, the reluctance to consider the limitations of U.S. power abroad held lasting ramifications for American military strategy in South Vietnam. [99]

Wheeler Passes

The last eight years of Wheeler's military career were marked by relentless, hard work, frequent consumption of alcohol and rich party food, lack of exercise, and constant smoking. This regimen had exacted a devastating toll on his health. "I think [the job] killed him," Spivy said. [100]

On 18 December 1975, Wheeler succumbed to his health conditions and died in Frederick, Maryland from cardiac arrest. [101]

Five years later, Wheeler's son had an emotional lunch in the Army-Navy Country Club with "Johnny" Johnson. Bim told him that he was aware of the tremendous stress the Chiefs were under during the Johnson Administration and that his father had told him and his mother that the Chiefs had considered resigning en masse after McNamara's testimony during the Stennis hearings in August 1967. Yes, it was true, Johnson acknowledged, despite the vow the Chiefs had sworn never to reveal the incident. "Your father died for his country as surely as any GI who was shot between the eyes in the paddies and jungle of Vietnam," Johnson said. [102]

Conclusion

Synthesizing new oral history, never-before-seen personal correspondence, and recently discovered and declassified official documents, this book has refuted the long-accepted, often repeated, but clearly inaccurate portrayal of Wheeler and his colleagues on the Joint Chiefs of Staff as derelict, passive accomplices to civilian mismanagement of the Vietnam War in 1964-1965. This survey of military advice over the broad span of the war has revealed a much different picture. [103]

Indeed, during the subsequent and preponderant five years of Wheeler's tenure as Chairman, he and the Chiefs invariably persisted to provide consistent, doctrinally grounded recommendations and consequences to the unreceptive Johnson Administration — which did not solicit and often dismissed out-of-hand the Chiefs' independent recommendations — and later to the more receptive but politically constrained Nixon Administration.

This book has demonstrated the requirement for senior officers of the U.S. Armed Forces to be assertive. An overly servile attitude toward appointed civilian officials in the Department of Defense and a reluctance to take an independent stance would greatly de-value professional military expertise or the chance that it will be heard and considered by the President. The Joint Chiefs of Staff have a statutory obligation to serve as the principal military advisors to the Secretary of Defense, the National Security Council, and the President. Regardless of a certain President's predisposition toward professional soldiers, the Chiefs have the right to personally advise their Commander-in-Chief and seek to influence him before decisions are made. They must fulfill their advisory role by persistently ensuring their views are given balanced consideration with other agencies, within the Department of Defense, interagency forums, and by the President.

Wheeler and his colleagues embodied this standard. This book has documented 143 recommendations and 70 consequences stated by Wheeler and the Chiefs regarding Vietnam strategy between August 1964 and May 1970. Probably twice this number or more were undocumented. Five silent men? No way.

Inaccurately impugned, Wheeler's reputation should be restored. He was indeed one of the most important and influential Chairmen in Joint Chiefs of Staff history. "Amid personal defeat and national humiliation, Wheeler significantly strengthened the role of the Joint Chiefs of Staff, winning with his silence and loyalty what could never have been won by him resigning instead," Perry asserts. "More than any of his predecessors, Wheeler was willing to push the Chiefs' programs and policies, even to consider mutiny, to win a voice for the military in the back rooms of official Washington. The Joint Chiefs of Staff and, more importantly, Joint Staff officers are, in large part, the product of his service." [104]

This book has demonstrated that national policy objectives in a military conflict must be clear and attainable. Presidents and their national security teams must level with themselves *and* the American people *before* the nation dives headlong into another costly major war. Strategic assessments should begin with the desired endstate and assess whether the amount of American blood and treasure required to accomplish it is truly worth the expenditure. Would the American people continue to support the war over time until its objective is finally accomplished? What other elements of national power, besides the military, might predominate to accomplish the desired endstate instead?

Public opinion is America's enduring center of gravity. Up-front candor would help condition the U.S. public that is already distrustful of government for the huge losses and probable setbacks attendant to large-scale combat operations. "I have nothing to offer but blood, toil, tears, and sweat," said Winston Churchill with brutal candor to the House of Commons on 13 May 1940. "We have before us an ordeal of the most grievous kind. We have before us many, many long months of struggle and of suffering." [105]

Candor and forethought might preclude the future rending of U.S. society like that which resulted, in part, from the opposite manner in which the Vietnam War was fought and lost in Washington.

CHAPTER NOTES

Introduction

1. Wheeler, Gilmore. Email to Mark Viney. 4 Apr. 2011; Wheeler, Gilmore. Interviews with Mark Viney. 25 Feb. and 10 Mar. 2013.

2. The White House. *Presentation of the Defense Distinguished Service Medal to General Earle G. Wheeler, at The White House on Thursday, 9 July 1970 at 1000 Hours.*

3. Wheeler, Gilmore. Interview with Mark Viney. 9 Oct. 2013.

4. Viney, George C. Interviews with Mark A. Viney. 30 Apr. 2007– 17 Dec. 2010.

5. Prados, John. *Vietnam, The History of an Unwinnable War, 1945-1975.* Lawrence, KS: University Press of Kansas, 2009: xiii. Hereafter cited as Prados. *Vietnam*; Achives.gov. Downloaded from the internet on 5 Nov. 2017 at https://www.archives.gov/research/military/vietnam-war/casualty-statistics.html.

6. Viney, George C. Interviews with Mark A. Viney. 30 Apr. 2007– 17 Dec. 2010.

7. Joint Chiefs of Staff. *Addresses by General Earle G. Wheeler, Chairman, Joint Chiefs of Staff, Vol. II, 7 July 1964 to 2 July 1970.* Washington, DC: Joint Staff Historical Office, no date: 206. Hereafter cited as Joint Chiefs of Staff. *Wheeler Addresses.*

8. Birtle, Andrew. Book review in Army History of *Westmoreland's War: Reassessing American Strategy in Vietnam.* Fall 2014.

9. Ibid.

10. Ibid.

11. Palmer, Bruce Jr. *The 25-Year War, America's Role on Vietnam.* New York: Da Capo Press, 1984: 201.

12. Perry, Mark. *Four Stars.* Boston: Houghton Miflin, 1989: 167-169; McMaster, Herbert R. *Dereliction of Duty.* New York: HarperCollins Publishers, 1997:

327-334; New York Times. Downloaded from the internet on 2 May 2018 at https://www.nytimes.com/1989/03/12/books/the-age-of-brass.html.

13. Hastings, Max. *Vietnam*. New York: Harper Perennial, 2018; Rothmann, Harry. *Warriors and Fools: How America's Leaders Lost the Vietnam War and Why It Still Matters*. RCI Publications, 2018.

14. Prados. *Vietnam*. 542.

Chapter 1

1. Scribner, Charles R. *The Eisenhower and Johnson Administrations' Decisionmaking on Vietnamese Intervention: A Study of Contrasts*. Ph. D. diss., University of California Santa Barbara, 1980: 92.

2. United States Army. *General Orders Number 26*. 19 Dec. 1975; Department of the Army. Office of the Chief of Staff of the Army. Photo Album. *General Earle G. Wheeler, Chief of Staff, United States Army, October 1962, Chairman of the Joint Chiefs of Staff, July 1964*. Jul. 1964; Wheeler, Frances R. Letter to Rebecca Howell. 2-3 Jul. 1964.

3. Odom, Louie W. *Challenging Journey: An Autobiography*. Publisher Unknown, 2008: 199.

4. McMaster, 112-115.

5. Ibid, 115-116; Stewart, Richard. Gen. ed. *American Military History, Vol. II, The United States Army in a Global Era, 1917-2003*. Washington, DC: United States Army, Center of Military History, 2005: 271.

6. McMaster, 115-116.

7. Ibid.

8. Scribner, 74-76.

9. McMaster, 126-128.

10. Herring, George C. *America's Longest War, The United States and Vietnam, 1950-1975*. Fourth Edition. Boston: McGraw Hill, 2002: 141-143.

11. McMaster, 126-128.

12. Perry, 139.

13. McMaster, 126-128.

14. Herring, 148-149.

15. McMaster, 126, 158.

16. Scribner, 74-76; Herring, 144.

17. Scribner, 74-76; Millet, Maslowski, and Feis, 517; Stewart, 302.

18. Millet, Maslowski, and Feis, 517; Stewart, 302.

19. Herring, 144-146.

20. Herring, 146.

21. Sharp, U.S. Grant and Westmoreland, William C. *Report on the War in Vietnam (As of 30 June 1968).* Washington, DC: U.S. Government Printing Office, 1968: I; McMaster, 137-138; Scribner, 76-78.

22. *The Senator Gravel Edition: The Pentagon Papers: The Defense Department History of United States Decisionmaking on Vietnam. Volume III.* Boston: Beacon Press, 1971: 206-207; Hereafter cited as *Gravel Pentagon Papers;* McMaster, 138-139.

23. McMaster, 138-139.

24. McMaster, 164.

25. Stewart, 301-302.

26. Ibid.

27. Ibid.

28. McMaster, 138-139.

29. Ibid.

30. McMaster, 140-142.

31. McMaster, 148-149.

32. McMaster, 146-148.

33. Daddis, Gregory A. *Westmoreland's War: Reassessing American Strategy in Vietnam.* Oxford: Oxford University Press, 2014: 71-72.

34. McMaster, 138-139, 142-146, 152-154.

35. Summers, Harry. *On Strategy: A Critical Analysis of the Vietnam War.* Novato, CA: Presidio Press, 1982: 120.

36. Herring, 146.

37. Herring, 146-147.

38. Ibid.

39. McNamara, xx; Scribner, 170-171; Herring, 144.

40. McMaster, 152-154.

41. McMaster, 155-158.

42. Ibid.

43. Ibid.

44. Ibid.

45. McMaster, 159-160.

46. Ibid.

47. McMaster, 160.

48. Scribner, 122-123.

49. Joint Chiefs of Staff. *Wheeler Addresses.* 145.

50. Wheeler, Earle G. *Interview with Dorothy P. McSweeny.* Interview I, 21 Aug. 1969. Transcription. Wheeler Family Records.

51. LinkedIn SlideShare. Downloaded from the internet on 28 Apr. 20 at https://www.slideshare.net/DaveMcGinnis/princples-of-war-relivance-ada435689.

52. United States Army. *Field Manual 100-5 (Field Service Regulations, Operations),* Feb. 1962. Ike Skelton Combined Arms Research Library Digital Library.

53. Ibid.

54. Joint Chiefs of Staff. *Wheeler Addresses.* 201.

55. Great Quotes.com. Downloaded from the internet on 4 Aug. 2018 at http://www.great-quotes.com/quotes/author/Douglas/MacArthur/pg/2.

56. United States Army. *Field Manual 100-5 (Field Service Regulations, Operations),* Feb. 1962. Ike Skelton Combined Arms Research Library Digital Library.

57. Spector, Ronald. *After Tet: The Bloodiest Year in Vietnam.* New York: The Free Press, 1993: 13.

58. McMaster, 161-162.

59. McMaster, 162-163.

60. McMaster, 163.

61. Sorley, Lewis B. *Honorable Warrior: General Harold K. Johnson and the Ethics of Command.* Lawrence, KS: University Press of Kansas, 1998: 175. Hereafter cited as Sorley. *Honorable Warrior,* 221.

62. Ibid.

63. Herspring, Dale R. *The Pentagon and the Presidency, Civil-Military Relations from FDR to George W. Bush.* Lawrence, KS: University Press of Kansas, 2005: 173.

64. McMaster,166-167; New York Times. *George W. Ball Dies at 84: Vietnam's Devil's Advocate.* 28 May 1994.

65. McMaster, 167-168; Perry, 140.

66. McMaster, 167-168.

67. Ibid.

68. Ibid.

69. Ibid.

70. McMaster, 168-173.

71. McMaster, 173-174.

72. Ibid; Herring, 147.

73. McMaster, 173-174; Herspring, 163.

74. McMaster, 173-174.

75. Ibid.

76. Herring, 149-150.

77. McMaster, 179-180.

78. Scribner, 79-80.

79. McMaster, 184-185.

80. McMaster, 187.

81. McMaster, 181; Perry, 146; Named to Honor the Mustin Family. Downloaded from the internet on 5 Dec. 2015 at https://public.navy.mil.

82. Scribner, 79-80.

83. McMaster, 182.

84. Perry, 144; McMaster, 185-186; Great Quotes.com. Downloaded from the internet on 4 Aug. 2018 at http://www.great-quotes.com/quotes/author/Douglas/MacArthur/pg/2.

85. McMaster, 186.

86. McMaster, 182.

87. McMaster, 186-190.

88. Ibid.

89. McMaster, 175-178.

90. National Security Council. *Intelligence Assessment on the Situation in Vietnam by National Security Council Working Group on Vietnam.* 13 Nov. 1964; Porter, Gareth. *Vietnam: The Definitive Documentation of Human Decisions, Volume 2.* Stanfordville, NY: Earl M. Coleman Enterprises, Inc., 1979: 326-327, 331.

91. Ibid.

92. McMaster, 189-190; Herring, 150.

93. McMaster, 191.

94. McMaster, 191-192.

95. Ibid.

96. Ibid.

97. McMaster, 192; Scribner, 81.

98. McMaster, 192-193, 244.

99. McMaster, 193.

100. Stewart, 302; Sharp and Westmoreland, 3; Millet, Maslowski, and Feis, 517; Herring, 150; Lamy, Perry L. *Barrel Roll: An Air Campaign in Support of National Policy.* Maxwell Air Force Base, AL: Air University Press, 1996.

101. McMaster, 194.

102. Herring, 151.

103. McMaster, 195-196.

104. McMaster, 200.

105. Scribner, 81.

106. Herring, 148.

Chapter 2

1. Warontherocks.com. Downloaded from the internet on 26 Jan. 2016 at http://warontherocks.com/2014/07/iraq-and-longing-for-vietnam/.

2. McMaster, 197.

3. Ibid.

4. Herring, 147-148; Millet, Maslowski, and Feis, 522.

5. Herring, 149; Jordan, 143.

6. McMaster, 179.

7. McMaster, 224-225.

8. Joint Chiefs of Staff. Office of the Chairman of the Joint Chiefs of Staff. *Photo Album for General Earle G. Wheeler, Chairman, 1964-1965.* Jul. 1970; McMaster, 222-223.

9. McMaster, 222-223.

10. McMaster, 222-224.

11. Ibid.

12. Herring, 151-152; Stewart, 302.

13. Stewart, 302; Jordan, 143; Herring, 153; Scribner, 81.

14. Wheeler, Frances R. Letter to Rebecca Howell. 9 Feb. 1965.

15. Ibid; Scribner, 81-82.

16. Millet, Maslowski, and Feis, 517-518; Herring, 153; *Gravel Pentagon Papers, Volume IV,* 18.

17. *Gravel Pentagon Papers, Volume IV,* 18; Millet, Maslowski, and Feis, 518; Herring, 179.

18. Scribner, 161.

19. *Gravel Pentagon Papers, Volume IV,* 18; Millet, Maslowski, and Feis, 517-518; Herring, 153.

20. *Gravel Pentagon Papers, Volume IV,* 18; Scribner, 161.

21. Herring, 154.

22. McMaster, 233.

23. Sharp and Westmoreland, 127.

24. McMaster, 233-234.

25. Herring, 155; Scribner, 83-84.

26. McMaster, 244.

27. Wheeler, Frances R. Letter to Rebecca Howell. 1 Mar. 1965.

28. Millet, Maslowski, and Feis, 522.

29. Perry, 148.

30. Millet, Maslowski, and Feis, 522.

31. Ibid.

32. Herring, 155-156.

33. Ibid; Scribner, 83-84.

34. Scribner, 84-85.

35. Ibid.

36. Ibid.

37. Herring, 156-157.

38. Perry, 148.

39. Perry, 149-150; McMaster, 246-247.

40. Stewart, 303; McMaster, 246-247.

41. Herspring, 166; McMaster, 248-249.

42. McMaster, 248-249.

43. Stewart, 303-304.

44. Joint Chiefs of Staff. Office of the Chairman of the Joint Chiefs of Staff. *Photo Album for General Earle G. Wheeler, Chairman, 1964-1965.* Jul. 1970; Wheeler, Frances R. Letter to Rebecca Howell. 19 Mar. 1965.

45. McMaster, 253-254.

46. Ibid.

47. McMaster, 254.

48. Ibid.

49. Sharp and Westmoreland, 108; Millet, Maslowski, and Feis, 534-535.

50. Millet, Maslowski, and Feis, 534-535.

51. Sharp and Westmoreland, 108; Millet, Maslowski, and Feis, 534-535.

52. Millet, Maslowski, and Feis, 534-536.

53. Ibid.

54. McMaster, 255-256.

55. McMaster, 256; Scribner, 101.

56. McMaster, 256-257.

57. Ibid.

58. Ibid.

59. Ibid.

60. Wheeler, Frances R. Letter to Rebecca Howell. 6 Apr. 1965.

61. Herring, 158-160.

62. McMaster, 260.

63. McMaster, 263.

64. McMaster, 264-273.

65. Ibid.

66. Ibid.

67. Ibid.

68. Ibid.

69. Ibid.

70. Ibid.

71. Herspring, 168.

72. McMaster, 273-274.

73. Wheeler, Earle G. Interview with Dorothy P. McSweeny. Interview I, 21 Aug. 1969: 15.

74. McMaster, 271-272.

75. McNamara, 182.

76. McMaster, 272.

77. McMaster, 275-279.

78. Ibid.

79. Ibid.

80. Joint Chiefs of Staff. Office of the Chairman of the Joint Chiefs of Staff. *Photo Album for General Earle G. Wheeler, Chairman, 1964-1965.* Jul. 1970; Herring, 157.

81. Herring, 157-158; Scribner, 101-102.

82. McMaster, 280-281.

83. Ibid.

84. Sharp and Westmoreland, 16-17.

85. Stewart, 304; Sorley, *Honorable Warrior.* 145.

86. Wheeler, Frances R. Letter to Rebecca Howell. 28 Apr. 1965.

87. Wheeler, Frances R. Letter to Rebecca Howell. 2 May 1[965]

88. Stewart, 269.

89. Stewart, 304.

90. Herring, 160-161.

91. Herspring, 168.

92. McMaster, 288-289.

93. Perry, 152.

94. Wheeler, Frances R. Letter to Rebecca Howell. 19 May 1965.

95. Scribner, 86-87.

96. Scribner, 170-172.

97. Joint Chiefs of Staff. Office of the Chairman of the Joint Chiefs of Staff. *Photo Album for General Earle G. Wheeler, Chairman, 1964-1965.* Jul. 1970; Scribner, 173.

98. Wheeler, Earle G. Interview with Dorothy P. McSweeny. Interview I, 21 Aug. 1969: 20.

99. McMaster, 285-287.

100. Herring, 161-163; Scribner, 103-104.

101. Wheeler, Earle G. Interview with Dorothy P. McSweeny. Interview I, 21 Aug. 1969: 17.

102. Scribner, 86, 119.

103. McNamara, xvii.

104. McNamara, 108.

105. United States Marine Corps. 38; Scribner, 85-86.

106. Scribner, 86-87; Johnson, Lady Bird. *A White House Diary*. Austin, TX: University of Texas Press, 2007.

107. Scribner, 86-87; Herring, 161-163.

108. Wheeler, Earle G. Interview with Dorothy P. McSweeny. Interview I, 21 Aug. 1969: 18.

109. Scribner, 174.

110. McMaster, 290; Scribner, 85-86; Herring, 163.

111. McMaster, 290-292.

112. McMaster, 292; Scribner, 85-86; Herring, 163.

113. Schandler, Herbert Y. *The Unmaking of a President: Lyndon Johnson and Vietnam*. Princeton: Princeton University Press, 1977: 309.

114. McMaster, 292-293.

115. Westmoreland, 144-145.

116. Herring, 163; Stewart, 302; Scribner, 85-86.

117. Scribner, 105-106; Herring, 163; Stewart, 302.

118. Scribner, 103-104.

119. Scribner, 105-106; Herring, 163; Stewart, 302.

120. McNamara, 33.

121. McMaster, 292-293.

122. Scribner, 103-104.

123. Army History. Book review of *Westmoreland's War: Reassessing American Strategy in Vietnam*. Fall 2014.

124. Schandler, 62.

125. Wheeler, Frances R. Letter to Rebecca Howell. 15 Jun. 1965; Joint Chiefs of Staff. Office of the Chairman of the Joint Chiefs of Staff. *Photo Album for General Earle G. Wheeler, Chairman, 1964-1965*. Jul. 1970; United States Marine Corps, 38-39.

126. Scribner, 103-104.

127. *Gravel Pentagon Papers, Volume IV.* 18; Scribner, 86-87, 104-105. When the "search and destroy" catch phrase later acquired a negative connotation in the press, Westmoreland objected to its use, noting that his strategy also contained "clearing" and "securing" operations, but these two pacification-oriented operations never received the prominence in execution that "search and destroy" operations did.

128. Stewart, 306.

129. McMaster, 294-295.

130. McMaster, 295-296.

131. Ibid.

132. Ibid.

133. Ibid.

134. Sharp and Westmoreland, 131.

135. Ibid.

136. Scribner, 183-184; McMaster, 304. According to McMaster, the Chiefs believed the war would require up to three times as many troops than the President was considering. "Johnny" Johnson estimated that it would take 600,000 to 700,000 troops and five years of fighting. "Wally" Greene's figure went as high as 700,000.

137. Scribner, 183-184.

138. Davidson, Phillip B. *Secrets of the Vietnam War.* Novato, CA: Presidio Press, 1990: 185-186; McMaster, 297.

139. McMaster, 297.

140. McNamara, 190.

141. McMaster, 297.

142. McMaster, 297-298; Daddis, 75.

143. McMaster, 298-299.

144. Ibid.

145. McNamara, 190-191.

146. Sharp and Westmoreland, 103; Millet, Maslowski, and Feis, 530.

147. Millet, Maslowski, and Feis, 530.

Chapter 3

1. Thorin, Duane. *The Need for Civilian Authority Over the Military*. Bryn Mawr, PA: Intercollegiate Studies Institute, Inc., 1968: 17.

2. Porter, 383-385; Tucker, Spencer C. *The Encyclopedia of the Vietnam War: A Political, Social, and Military History*. 2nd Edition. Santa Barbara, CA: ABC-CLIO, Inc., 2011.

3. Porter, 383-385.

4. Scribner, 106; McMaster, 298-299.

5. Petitt, Clyde E. *The Experts*. Seacaucus, NJ: Lyle Stuart, Inc., 1975: 224; McMaster, 300-301.

6. McMaster, 305.

7. McMaster, 305-307.

8. Jordan, 117, 182.

9. McMaster, 306; Jordan, 117, 182.

10. McMaster, 307.

11. United States Marine Corps. 108.

12. McMaster, 304-305.

13. Ibid.

14. McMaster, 305.

15. McMaster, 301-302.

16. Ibid.

17. McMaster, 307.

18. McMaster, 305, 308.

19. McMaster, 310-311.

20. Ibid.

21. Sharp and Westmoreland, 109.

22. McMaster, 309.

23. McMaster, 313.

24. McMaster, 314.

25. Ibid.

26. Ibid.

27. McMaster, 314-315.

28. Wheeler, Earle G. Interview with Dorothy P. McSweeny. Interview I, 21 Aug. 1969: 19-20; Herring, 165; Scribner, 182.

29. Wheeler, Earle G. Interview with Dorothy P. McSweeny. Interview I, 21 Aug. 1969: 19-20.

30. Perry, 153.

31. Scribner, 182-183.

32. Scribner, 183-184.

33. Scribner, 184-185.

34. McMaster, 316.

35. Herring, 166; McMaster, 313.

36. McMaster, 313.

37. McMaster, 316-317; Perry, 153.

38. Herspring, 170.

39. Wheeler, Earle G. Interview with Dorothy P. McSweeny. Interview I, 21 Aug. 1969: 19.

40. Millet, Maslowski, and Feis, 525-526.

41. Ibid.

42. Viney, George C. Interviews with Mark A. Viney. 30 Apr. 2007 – 17 Dec. 2010; Joint Chiefs of Staff. *Wheeler Addresses*; Millet, Maslowski, and Feis, 525-526.

43. McMaster, 317-318.

44. Perry, 155.

45. McMaster, 238-239.

46. Scribner, 20-21.

47. Herring, 168-169.

48. Herring, 167-168; Scribner, 190.

49. Herring, 165; Millet, Maslowski, and Feis, 522.

50. Wheeler, Frances R. Letter to Rebecca Howell. 14 Jul. 1965; Sharp and Westmoreland, 109; Herring, 164; McMaster, 313.

51. Sharp and Westmoreland, 109; Scribner, 180.

52. Scribner, 190-191.

53. Scribner, 20-21,192, 202.

54. McMaster, 318-320; Millet, Maslowski, and Feis, 525-526.

55. Ibid.

56. Sorley, *Honorable Warrior.* 189.

57. Palmer, 176.

58. McMaster, 321.

59. Scribner, 59-60; Stewart, 305.

60. Herring, 167-169, 171-173.

61. McMaster, 322.

62. Millet, Maslowski, and Feis, 523-524.

63. Ibid.

64. Joint Chiefs of Staff. Office of the Chairman of the Joint Chiefs of Staff. *Photo Album for General Earle G. Wheeler, Chairman, 1965-1966.* Jul. 1970.

65. Petitt, 233.

66. Wheeler, Frances R. Letter to Rebecca Howell. 9 Aug. 1965.

67. Stewart, 307.

68. Millet, Maslowski, and Feis, 528-529, 532; Stewart, 304-305.

69. Palmer, Dave R. *Summons of the Trumpet: A History of the Vietnam War From a Military Man's Viewpoint.* New York: Ballantine Books, 1978: 110.

70. Stewart, 309-310.

71. Joint Chiefs of Staff. *A Study Group Report on the Feasibility of a Limited Lodgement Operation into Southern North Vietnam.* 31 May 1967: I-1. Hereafter cited as Joint Chiefs of Staff, *Feasibility Study.*

72. Prados. *Vietnam.* 208.

73. Millet, Maslowski, and Feis, 524-526; Stewart, 306.

74. Millet, Maslowski, and Feis, 524-526.

75. McNamara, 213.

76. Ibid.

77. Prados. *Vietnam.* 146-147, 571.

78. Cooper, Charles G. *Cheers and Tears, A Marine's Story of Combat in Peace and War.* Victoria, BC: Trafford Publishing, 2002: 1-5.

79. Ibid.

80. Ibid.

81. Ibid.

82. Ibid.

83. Ibid.

84. Ibid.

85. Ibid.

86. Ibid.

87. Ibid.

88. Ibid.

89. Herspring, 150, 172.

90. Joint Chiefs of Staff. *Wheeler Addresses.* 167.

91. Scribner, 19.

92. Summers, 87-88.

93. Summers, 102.

94. Summers, 124.

95. Summers, 128-129.

96. Ibid.

97. Webb, Willard J. and Cole, Ronald H. *The Chairmen of the Joint Chiefs of Staff.* Washington, DC: Historical Division, Joint Chiefs of Staff, 1989: 75-76.

98. Joint Chiefs of Staff. *Wheeler Addresses.* 211; Gilmore S. Wheeler, Interview with Mark Viney, 8 Nov. 2010: 1.

99. Dorland, Gilbert N. *Legacy of Discord: Voices of the Vietnam Era.* Washington, DC: Brassey's, 2001: 44.

100. United States. Congress. House. Committee on Foreign Affairs. Subcommittee on Asian and Pacific Affairs. *U.S. Policy and Programs in Cambodia: Hearings Before the Subcommittee on Asian and Pacific Affairs of the Committee on Foreign Affairs, House of Representatives, Ninety-third Congress, First Session.* Washington, DC: U.S. Government Printing Office, 1973: 189. Hereafter cited as Congress. *Cambodia Hearings;* Joint Chiefs of Staff. *Wheeler Addresses;* Johnson, Harold K. Interview, 33. Gilmore S. Wheeler, Interview with Mark Viney, 8 Nov. 2010: 1.

101. Joint Chiefs of Staff. *Wheeler Addresses;* Johnson, Harold K. Interview. 33; Gilmore S. Wheeler, Interview with Mark Viney, 8 Nov. 2010: 1.

102. McMaster, 241-242.

103. Sharp and Westmoreland, 22; Prados. *Vietnam.* 159; Spector, 15.

104. Prados. *Vietnam.* 146-147; *Gravel Pentagon Papers, Volume IV,* 32-36.

105. McNamara, 227.

106. Wheeler, Earle G. Interview with Dorothy P. McSweeny. Interview I, 21 Aug. 1969: 24-25.

107. Herring, 154-155, 173.

108. Wheeler, Earle G. Interview with Dorothy P. McSweeny. Interview I, 21 Aug. 1969: 25.

Chapter 4

1. Petitt, 251-252.

2. Palmer, Bruce. 111.

3. Sharp and Westmoreland, 113-114.

4. Prados. *Vietnam.* 179-180.

5. Sharp and Westmoreland, 115-116.

6. Pearson, 6.

7. Sharp and Westmoreland, 23-24.

8. Prados. *Vietnam.* 179-180.

9. Prados. *Vietnam.* 159; Millet, Maslowski, and Feis, 518.

10. McNamara, 252.

11. Ibid.

12. Thorin, 12-13.

13. Palmer, Bruce. 177.

14. Westmoreland, 413.

15. Petitt, 261-262.

16. Petitt, 273.

17. Ibid.

18. Westmoreland, 229.

19. Herring, 159, 214.

20. Wheeler, Frances R. Letter to Rebecca Howell. 7 Feb. 1966; C-Span. Downloaded from the internet on 31 Jan. 2017 at https://www.c-span.org/video/?404455-1/general-james-gavin-testimony-1966-fulbright-vietnam-hearings.

21. Hull, John E. *Letter to Robert S. McNamara*. 14 Dec. 1966; U.S. News & World Report. *A General Tells How US Can Win in Vietnam*. 14 Dec. 1966; Petitt, 281; Arlington National Cemetery. Downloaded from the internet on 19 Apr. 2018 at http://www.arlingtoncemetery.net/jehull.htm.

22. Petitt, 265.

23. Sharp and Westmoreland, 24.

24. Palmer, Bruce. 113.

25. Prados. *Vietnam*. 179.

26. Palmer, Bruce. 115, 150.

27. Stewart, 322.

28. Pearson, Willard. *The War in the Northern Provinces 1966-1968*. Washington, DC: Department of the Army, 1975: v.

29. Sharp and Westmoreland, 123-124; Pearson, 7-8; Stewart, 320; Prados. *Vietnam*. 179.

30. Pearson, 7-9.

31. Ibid.

32. Westmoreland, 409.

33. Schandler, 306-307; Prados. *Vietnam*. 159-160.

34. McNamara, 235; Prados. *Vietnam*. 159-160.

35. Porter; Prados. *Vietnam.* 159-160.

36. Porter.

37. McNamara, 261-262.

38. Ibid.

39. McNamara, 264.

40. Wheeler, Frances R. Letter to Rebecca Howell. 30 Apr. 1966; Casey, George W. Conversation with Mark A. Viney. 25 Apr. 2018.

41. Wheeler, Frances R. Letter to Rebecca Howell. 30 Apr. 1966.

42. Petitt, 212; Perry, 169; New York Times. *The Cold Warrior Who Never Apologized.* 8 Sep. 2017; Scribner, 121.

43. Petitt, 212; Perry, 169; McMaster, 89, 362; New York Times. *The Cold Warrior Who Never Apologized.* 8 Sep. 2017.

44. Wheeler, Earle G. Interview with Dorothy P. McSweeny. Interview I, 21 Aug. 1969: 6-7.

45. Wheeler, Earle G. Interview with Dorothy P. McSweeny. Interview I, 21 Aug. 1969: 15.

46. Sharp and Westmoreland, 125.

47. United States Military Assistance Command, Vietnam. *Back Channel Message from General Westmoreland, COMUSMACV, Saigon, to General Wheeler, CJCS, Washington, and Admiral Sharp, CINCPAC, Hawaii.* 9 May 1966.

48. United States Pacific Command. *Back Channel Message from Admiral Sharp, CINCPAC, Hawaii, to General Westmoreland, COMUSMACV, Saigon, and General Wheeler, CJCS, Washington.* 9 May 1966.

49. Ibid.

50. Petitt, 281; Millet, Maslowski, and Feis, 518.

51. Millet, Maslowski, and Feis, 518-519.

52. Ibid.

53. Petitt, 293.

54. Palmer, Bruce. 176; Millet, Maslowski, and Feis, 520.

55. Millet, Maslowski, and Feis, 520.

56. Petitt, 284.

57. Palmer, Bruce. 191-192.

58. Millet, Maslowski, and Feis, 520-521.

59. Spector, 13.

60. Joint Chiefs of Staff. *Front Channel Message from Rear Admiral H. J. Truman III, National Military Command Center, Washington, to Admiral Sharp, CINCPAC, Hawaii.* 30 Jul. 1966; Stewart, 315.

61. Sharp and Westmoreland, 124, 127; Stewart, 317-318.

62. Perry, 158- 159.

63. Pearson, 9-10.

64. Pearson, 11-12.

65. Thorin, 13; Joint Chiefs of Staff. *Feasibility Study.* I-1. The outline plan used in this study was contained in CINCPAC letter to the JCS 3010, Serial 000197, dated 12 May 1966. The operation was also included in CINCPAC OPLAN 32-65 and SEATO (Southeast Asia Treaty Organization) MPO Plans 4/66 and 6/66.

66. Thorin, 13.

67. Thorin, 26-27.

68. Petitt, 292-293.

69. Perry, 159.

70. Ibid.

71. Spector, 17; Millet, Maslowski, and Feis, 519-520.

72. Millet, Maslowski, and Feis, 519-520.

73. Sharp and Westmoreland, 30.

74. Sharp and Westmoreland, 123-124.

75. Pearson, 21.

76. Joint Chiefs of Staff. *Front Channel Message from Lieutenant General Berton E. Spivy, Director, Joint Staff, Washington, to Admiral Sharp, CINCPAC, Hawaii.* 8 Sep. 1966.

77. Ibid.

78. Ibid.

79. Sharp and Westmoreland, 49.

80. United States Marine Corps. 128.

81. Ibid, 58; Sharp and Westmoreland, 128; History.com. Downloaded from the internet on 2 Feb. 2017 at http://www.history.com/this-day-in-history/manila-conference-attendees-issue-declaration-of-peace.

82. Pearson, 11-12.

83. Herring, 179-181.

84. Stewart, 325.

85. Stewart, 306.

86. Sharp and Westmoreland, 7, 127.

87. Sharp and Westmoreland, 7-8.

88. Sharp and Westmoreland, 124, 145.

Chapter 5

1. United States Army, *Field Manual 6-0 (Commander and Staff Organizations and Operations)*, 5 May 2014.

2. Joint Chiefs of Staff. *Wheeler Addresses.* 147.

3. Joint Chiefs of Staff. *Wheeler Addresses.* 147-148.

4. Joint Chiefs of Staff. *Wheeler Addresses.* 136.

5. United States Air Force, 1.

6. Millet, Maslowski, and Feis, 536.

7. Herring, 213.

8. United States Air Force, Office of Air Force History. *The Air Force in Vietnam, The Search for Military Alternatives 1967.* Dec. 1969: 2.

9. Palmer, Bruce, 151.

10. Herring, 213-214.

11. Sharp and Westmoreland, 126.

12. Ibid.

13. Sharp and Westmoreland, 135.

14. Herring, 213-214.

15. Joint Chiefs of Staff. *Wheeler Addresses.* 147.

16. Herring, 214; Palmer, Bruce, 151.

17. Herring, 214-216.

18. Ibid.

19. United States Air Force. 9; Joint Chiefs of Staff. *Earle G. Wheeler Papers, Chairman, Joint Chiefs of Staff, Calendar of Events, 1 Jan – 31 Dec 1967.* Hereafter cited as Joint Chiefs of Staff, *Wheeler Calendar.* Sorley, Lewis B. *A Better War: The Unexamined Victories and the Final Tragedy of America's Last Years in Vietnam.* New York: Harcourt Brace & Co., 1999: 5. Hereafter cited as Sorley, *A Better War.*

20. Sorley. *A Better War.* 5.

21. Sharp and Westmoreland, 131-133, 156.

22. United States Military Assistance Command, Vietnam. *Back Channel Message from General Westmoreland, COMUSMACV, Saigon, to General Wheeler, CJCS, Washington, and Admiral Sharp, CINCPAC, Hawaii.* 6 Feb. 1967.

23. United States Military Assistance Command, Vietnam. *Back Channel Message from General Westmoreland, COMUSMACV, Saigon, to General Wheeler, CJCS, Washington, and Admiral Sharp, CINCPAC, Hawaii.* 17 Feb. 1967.

24. Sharp and Westmoreland, 134.

25. United States Military Assistance Command, Vietnam. *Back Channel Message from General Westmoreland, COMUSMACV, Saigon, to General Wheeler, CJCS, Washington, and Admiral Sharp, CINCPAC, Hawaii.* 3 Mar. 1967.

26. Ibid.

27. Herring, 178-179, 184.

28. Herring, 186, 188-189.

29. Prados. *Vietnam.* 180-181.

30. Prados. *Vietnam.* 181-182.

31. Wheeler, Frances R. Letter to Rebecca Howell. 24 Jan. 1967; Petitt, 309.

32. Petitt, 311.

33. Joint Chiefs of Staff. Office of the Chairman of the Joint Chiefs of Staff. *Photo Album for General Earle G. Wheeler, Chairman, 1966-1967*. Jul. 1970; Petitt, 316.

34. Prados. *Vietnam*. 181-182.

35. Prados. *Vietnam*. 182.

36. Westmoreland, 115; *Gravel Pentagon Papers*, Volume IV, 126; Millet, Maslowski, and Feis, 519; Prados, John. *The Blood Road, The Ho Chi Minh Trail and the Vietnam War*. New York: John Wiley & Sons, Inc., 1998: 212-213. Hereafter cited as Prados. *Blood Road*.

37. McNamara, 246; Herring, 282; Prados. *Vietnam*. 182-183; Millet, Maslowski, and Feis, 519.

38. United States Marine Corps, 81-82.

39. United States Military Assistance Command, Vietnam. *MACV Practice Nine Requirements Plan*. 26 Jan. 1967.

40. Joint Chiefs of Staff. *CM-2134-67, PRACTICE NINE Requirements Plan, dated 26 Jan 1967*, 22 Feb. 1967; Prados. *Vietnam*. 183.

41. Joint Chiefs of Staff. *Memorandum for the Secretary of Defense, Subject: MACV Practice Nine Requirements Plan, JCSM-97-67*. 22 Feb. 1967.

42. Joint Chiefs of Staff. *Memorandum for the Secretary of Defense, Subject: Practice Nine Requirements Plan, dated 26 January 1967, CM-2134-67*. 22 Feb. 1967.

43. Joint Chiefs of Staff. *Feasibility Study*. I-1. Prados, John. Emails to Mark Viney (2), 24 Feb. 2010; Viney, Mark A. *Determined to Persist*. Monograph. 29 Nov. 2012: 27.

44. Summers, Harry. *On Strategy: A Critical Analysis of the Vietnam War*. Novato, CA: Presidio Press, 1982. 128.

45. Viney, Mark A. *Determined to Persist, 2*.

46. Viney, George C. Interviews with Mark A. Viney. 30 Apr. 2007 – 17 Dec. 2010. Viney had been awarded the Silver Star and Purple Heart while commanding the 3rd Brigade, 82nd Airborne Division in urban combat in the Dominican Republic two years earlier. Viney also had in-country credibility from his tour in South Vietnam in 1963-64 as the Deputy Commander of the

5th Special Forces Group. Incredibly, during Viney's tour in the Joint Staff J-3 Pacific Division, which would conclude in April 1968, none of his fellow staff officers had served in Vietnam.

47. Viney, Mark A. *Determined to Persist*. 2.

48. Joint Chiefs of Staff. *Feasibility Study*. I-5, I-6; Viney, George C. Interviews with Mark A. Viney. 30 Apr. 2007 – 17 Dec. 2010: 6-7, 46; Karen Loving, Email to Mark A. Viney, 9 Sep. 2008; Viney, Mark A. *Determined to Persist*. 7. Loving is the daughter of the late Marine Colonel Evans C. Carlson. Carlson was an intellectual, a fighter pilot, and the son of famed Brigadier General Evans F. Carlson, who earned three Navy Crosses as the commander of "Carlson's Raiders" in World War II.

49. McNamara, 264-265; Prados. *Vietnam*. 183.

50. McNamara, 264-265.

51. Joint Chiefs of Staff. *Memorandum for the Secretary of Defense, Subject: Recommendations for Providing Practice Nine Forces, JCSM-162-67*. 23 Mar. 1967.

52. Prados. *Vietnam*. 183-185.

53. Ibid.

54. Ibid.

55. Ibid.

56. Wheeler, Frances R. Letter to Rebecca Howell. 15 Mar. 1967; Joint Chiefs of Staff. Office of the Chairman of the Joint Chiefs of Staff. *Photo Album for General Earle G. Wheeler, Chairman, 1966-1967*. Jul. 1970.

57. Wheeler, Frances R. Letter to Rebecca Howell. 18 Mar. 1967.

58. Prados. *Vietnam*. 184.

59. Joint Chiefs of Staff. *Feasibility Study*. I-2; Viney, George C. Interviews with Mark A. Viney. 30 Apr. 2007 – 17 Dec. 2010; Wheeler, Gilmore S. Interview with Mark A. Viney, 9 Jun. 2010: 1; Viney, Mark A. *Determined to Persist*. 7-8. Viney and Carlson named the operation MULE SHOE in honor of what they understood was Wheeler's hometown, the tiny, west Texas cattle ranching town of Muleshoe. Actually, Wheeler had been made an Honorary Farrier of

that municipality and had apparently mentioned his "citizenship" tongue-in-cheek to members of the Joint Staff.

60. United States Military Assistance Command, Vietnam. *Front Channel Message from General Westmoreland, COMUSMACV, Saigon, to General Wheeler, CJCS, Washington, and Admiral Sharp, CINCPAC, Hawaii.* 5 Apr. 1967.

61. Sharp and Westmoreland, 145, 155; Pearson, 21-24. In Congressional hearings in 1970, the array of sensors developed for the anti-infiltration barrier system would be credited with having saved many lives by providing early warnings of attack, increasing enemy personnel and equipment losses, as well as by providing the Army with effective, round-the-clock combat surveillance. The sensors would be credited with having contributed to the difficult, important task of finding the enemy and tracking his movements.

62. Ibid.

63. Joint Chiefs of Staff. *Wheeler Calendar;* Department of the Army. *General H.K. Johnson Daily Calendars.* Military History Institute Collection, H.K. Johnson Papers, Series I, Subseries I, Box 157, Book 3. Hereafter cited as Department of the Army. *Johnson Calendars.*

64. Joint Chiefs of Staff. *Memorandum for the Director, Joint Staff, Subject: Operations Against North Vietnam, CM-2233-67.* 13 Apr. 1967: 1.

65. Joint Chiefs of Staff. *Memorandum for the Director, Joint Staff, Subject: Operations Against North Vietnam, CM-2233-67.* 13 Apr. 1967: 1-3.

66. Joint Chiefs of Staff. *Memorandum for the Director, Joint Staff, Subject: Operations Against North Vietnam, CM-2233-67.* 13 Apr. 1967: 2-3; Viney, Mark A. *Determined to Persist.* 44.

67. Joint Chiefs of Staff. *Memorandum for the Director, Joint Staff, Subject: Operations Against North Vietnam, CM-2233-67.* 13 Apr. 1967: 3; Cranc, Conrad C. Conversation with Mark Viney. 5 Nov. 2010; Joint Chiefs of Staff. *Memorandum for the Chairman, Joint Chiefs of Staff, Subject: CINCPAC Planning for Ground Operations North of the DMZ, DJSM-1270-67.* 16 Oct. 1967: 2. These documents indicate that Wheeler had not informed CINCPAC and COMUSMACV of Operation MULE SHOE prior to this date.

68. Joint Chiefs of Staff. *Feasibility Study.* C-1, I-3; Viney, Mark A. *Determined to Persist.* 18-19.

69. Prados. *Vietnam.* 183-185.

70. Ibid.

71. Joint Chiefs of Staff. Office of the Chairman of the Joint Chiefs of Staff. *Memorandum for the Director, Joint Staff, Subject: U.S. Military Posture, CM-2255-67,* 20 Apr. 1967.

72. Ibid.

73. Ibid.

74. Ibid.

75. Sharp and Westmoreland, 134; Stewart, 327; Prados. *Vietnam.* 180.

76. United States Military Assistance Command, Vietnam. *Back Channel Message from General Westmoreland, COMUSMACV, Saigon, to General Wheeler, CJCS, Washington, and Admiral Sharp, CINCPAC, Hawaii.* 12 Apr. 1967.

77. Sharp and Westmoreland, 134; Stewart, 327; Prados. *Vietnam.* 180.

78. Pearson, 18.

79. Stewart, 327; Prados. *Vietnam.* 180.

80. Sharp and Westmoreland, 134.

81. Stewart, 327; Prados. *Vietnam.* 180.

82. Stewart, 330.

83. United States Air Force. 13-14; *Gravel Pentagon Papers. Volume V.* 73-75; Herspring, 174.

84. Spivy, 728.

85. United States Air Force. 13-14; *Gravel Pentagon Papers. Volume V.* 73-75; Herspring, 174.

86. McNamara, 234.

87. Prados. *Vietnam.* 186.

88. Millet , Maslowski, and Feis, 534; Prados. *Vietnam.* 186; New York Times. Downloaded from the internet on 19 Jun. 2017 at

http://www.mobile.nytimes.com/johnson-westmoreland-and-the-selling-of-vietnam.html.

89. Prados. *Vietnam.* 186.

90. Joint Chiefs of Staff. *Wheeler Calendar;* Lyndon Baines Johnson Library & Museum. *President's Daily Diary.* 27 Apr. 1967: 2,10; *Gravel Pentagon Papers. Volume II.* 83; Prados. *Vietnam.* 186.

91. Prados. *Vietnam.* 186-187; Petitt, 322-323. Barrett, David M. Gen. ed. *Lyndon B. Johnson's Vietnam Papers: A Documentary Collection.* College Station, TX: Texas A&M University Press, 1998: 414.

92. *Gravel Pentagon Papers. Volume V.* 83; Prados. *Vietnam.* 186-187.

93. Ibid.

94. Joint Chiefs of Staff. *Wheeler Calendar;* Lyndon Baines Johnson Library & Museum. *President's Daily Diary.* 27 Apr. 1967: 2, 10; *Gravel Pentagon Papers, Volume V.* 83; Prados. *Vietnam.* 187-188.

95. Prados. *Vietnam.* 187-188.

96. *Gravel Pentagon Papers, Volume V.* 83; Joint Chiefs of Staff. *Wheeler Calendar;* Lyndon Baines Johnson Library & Museum. *President's Daily Diary.* 27 Apr. 1967: 2, 10; Joint Chiefs of Staff. *Feasibility Study.* Appendix E; Prados. *Vietnam.* 188. The Special National Intelligence Estimate completed by DIA as Appendix E to the feasibility study determined there was a high risk of Chinese intervention if the U.S. invaded North Vietnam and that Communist leaders in North Vietnam and China would not believe U.S. assertions that the invasion was limited and not intended to overthrow the Hanoi regime.

97. Prados. *Vietnam.* 188-189.

98. Joint Chiefs of Staff. *Wheeler Addresses.* 280.

99. *Gravel Pentagon Papers, Volume V.* 83; Viney, Mark A. *Determined to Persist.* 21-22, 43.

100. Rostow, 513; Prados. *Vietnam.* 188-189.

101. Prados. *Blood Road.* 210.

102. Sharp and Westmoreland, 166-167.

103. Prados. *Vietnam.* 188.

104. Daddis, 86-87.

105. Sharp and Westmoreland, 154; Prados. *Vietnam.* 180.

106. United States Military Assistance Command, Vietnam. *Front Channel Message from General Westmoreland, COMUSMACV, Saigon, to General Wheeler, CJCS, Washington.* 8 May 1967.

107. Sharp and Westmoreland, 154; Prados. *Vietnam.* 180.

108. United States Pacific Command. *Two Back Channel Messages from Admiral Sharp, CINCPAC, Hawaii, to Joint Chiefs of Staff, Washington.* 16 May 1967.

109. Ibid.

110. Joint Chiefs of Staff. *Memorandum for the Chairman, Joint Chiefs of Staff, Subject: Operation HICKORY. 16 May 67.*

111. Ibid.

112. Joint Chiefs of Staff. *Back Channel Message from General Wheeler, CJCS, Washington, to Admiral Sharp, CINCPAC, Hawaii.* 16 May 1967.

113. United States Military Assistance Command, Vietnam. *General Westmoreland's History Notes.* 1-20 May 1967; Sharp and Westmoreland, 9, 132, 154.

114. Sharp and Westmoreland, 167-168.

115. Ibid.

116. Department of Defense. *United States Vietnam Relations, 1945-1967 (aka The Pentagon Papers)* Volume IV. Washington, DC: United States Government Printing Office, 1971: 159. Hereafter cited as Department of Defense. *Pentagon Papers.*

117. Prados. *Vietnam.* 189.

118. Rhynedance, George H. *McNamara vs. The JCS, Vietnam's Operation Rolling Thunder: A Failure in Civil-Military Relations.* Carlisle, PA: United States Army War College, 2000: 8; Prados. *Vietnam.* 189-190.

119. Sharp and Westmoreland, 170.

120. The White House. *Memorandum from Walt W. Rostow to Cyrus Vance, Richard Helms, William P. Bundy.* 22 May 1967; Sharp and Westmoreland, 169;

Prados. *Vietnam.* 190; Berman, Larry. *Lyndon Johnson's War: The Road the Stalemate in Vietnam.* New York: Norton, 1989: 47-48.

121. McNamara, 270-271.

122. Millet, Maslowski, and Feis, 538-539.

123. Porter, 470-472; Herring, 215.

124. McNamara, 266; Prados. *Vietnam.* 206.

125. Prados. *Vietnam.* 207.

126. Herring, 214-215.

127. Prados. *Vietnam.* 207.

128. Department of Defense. *Pentagon Papers.* Volume IV. 177.

129. Ibid.

130. Ibid; McNamara, 275.

131. Joint Chiefs of Staff. *Memorandum for the Secretary of Defense, Subject: Worldwide U.S. Military Posture, JCSM-288-67.* 20 May. 1967; Department of Defense. *Pentagon Papers.* Volume IV. 178-179; Barrett, 431; Porter, 470-472; Herring, 138.

132. Ibid.

133. Porter, 470-472; Herring, 138.

134. Ibid.

135. Sharp and Westmoreland, 175; Porter, 470-472; Herring, 138.

136. Ibid.

137. Ibid.

138. Sharp and Westmoreland, 175.

139. Department of Defense. *Pentagon Papers.* Volume IV. 490-491.

140. Berman, 47.

141. Department of Defense. *Pentagon Papers.* Volume IV. 490-491.

142. Ibid.

143. The White House. *Memorandum from Walt W. Rostow to Cyrus Vance, Richard Helms, William P. Bundy.* 22 May 1967.

144. Ibid.

145. Ibid.

146. Herring, 172; Millet, Maslowski, and Feis, 509.

147. Herring, 172.

148. Herring, 216-217.

149. McNamara, 277.

150. McNamara, 280.

151. Herring, 216-217.

152. Ibid.

153. Prados. *Vietnam.* 207-208; Herring, 216-217.

154. Prados. *Vietnam.* 207-208.

155. Herring, 217-218; Prados. *Vietnam.* 190.

156. Palmer, Dave R. 155, 159.

157. Joint Chiefs of Staff. *Feasibility Study.* I-5; Viney, Mark A. *Determined to Persist.* 14-16, 45.

158. Joint Chiefs of Staff. *Feasibility Study.* I-4, ii.

159. Joint Chiefs of Staff. *Feasibility Study.* 5; Viney, Mark A. *Determined to Persist.* 46. Viney insists that while the study assigned command and control of the operation to CINCPAC, it should have been delegated to COMUSMACV since MULE SHOE primarily would have been a ground fight once U.S. forces entered the area of operations.

160. Ibid.

161. Ibid.

162. Joint Chiefs of Staff. *Feasibility Study.* 6, II-2, II-3.

163. Prados. *Vietnam.* 188-189.

164. Joint Chiefs of Staff. *Feasibility Study.* 6, 9-11, II-2, II-3, IV-1 thru IV-70.

165. Joint Chiefs of Staff. *Feasibility Study.* 8-9, 19; Herring, 164.

166. Viney, George C. *Interview with Mark A. Viney.* 30 Apr. 2007.

167. Joint Chiefs of Staff. *Feasibility Study.* ii, 6-9, 11-12, 15, 18-19, II-3 thru 6, II-8, II-11, II-17 thru 18, III-35, IV-4, IV-15, IV-18, IV-44, F-7, X-2.

168. McNamara, 277.

169. McNamara, 273.

170. Wheeler, Frances R. Letter to Rebecca Howell. 7 Jun. 1967.

171. Petitt, 326.

172. Sharp and Westmoreland, 164.

173. Department of Defense. *Pentagon Papers.* Volume IV. 193.

Chapter 6

1. Joint Chiefs of Staff. *Wheeler Addresses.* 171.

2. Wheeler, Frances R. Letter to Rebecca Howell. 16 Jun. 1967.

3. Joint Chiefs of Staff. *Feasibility Study;* Joint Chiefs of Staff. *Wheeler Calendar;* Viney, George C. Interviews with Mark A. Viney. 30 Apr. 2007 – 17 Dec. 2010. The 158-page MULE SHOE study features 7 maps, numerous diagrams and charts, a 7-page Special Intelligence Estimate, as well as a 14-page Cover and Deception Appendix.

4. Joint Chiefs of Staff. *Wheeler Calendar;* Department of the Army. *Johnson Calendars;* Palmer, Bruce. 21; Viney, Mark A. *Determined to Persist.* 17, 19-20, 30-31, 42; Hallenbeck, Ralph J. Letter to Mark Viney. 19 Sep. 2008. Hallenbeck served as the Deputy Secretary for the Joint Chiefs of Staff from June 1966 to July 1968 and retired as a Brigadier General. None of his shorthand transcripts of JCS tank sessions are known extant. Hallenbeck reviewed and corroborated Viney's account of the 23 June 1967 meeting.

5. Westmoreland, 201; Viney, George C. Interviews with Mark A. Viney. 30 Apr. 2007 – 17 Dec. 2010: 19-20; Viney, Mark A. *Determined to Persist.* 29.

6. Joint Chiefs of Staff. *Feasibility Study.* III-33, V-7, V-8, V-37 through V-44; Viney, George C. Interviews with Mark A. Viney. 30 Apr. 2007 – 17 Dec. 2010: 17.

7. United States Air Force, 63.

8. Viney, George C. Interviews with Mark A. Viney. 30 Apr. 2007 – 17 Dec. 2010: 20, 44-45.

9. Sorley. *Honorable Warrior.* 283.

10. Spivy, 746-747.

11. Viney, Mark A. *Determined to Persist*. 30.

12. Department of State. Office of the Historian. Downloaded from the internet on 17 Dec. 2017 at https://history.state.gov/historicaldocuments/frus1964-68v04/d216.

13. Department of the Army. *Backchannel Message from Johnson CSA Washington to Wheeler CJCS MACV*. 8 Jul. 1967: 1-4; Hallenbeck, Ralph J. Letter to Mark Viney. 19 Sep. 2008; Viney, George C. Interviews with Mark A. Viney. 30 Apr. 2007 – 17 Dec. 2010: 17, 20-21, 41; Viney, Mark A. *Determined to Persist*. 30-31.

14. Viney, George C. Interviews with Mark A. Viney. 30 Apr. 2007 – 17 Dec. 2010: 17, 20-21, 41; Viney, Mark A. *Determined to Persist*. 30-31.

15. Viney, George C. Interviews with Mark A. Viney. 30 Apr. 2007 – 17 Dec. 2010: 17, 20-21, 41; Viney, Mark A. *Determined to Persist*. 30-31; Stewart, 305-306.

16. Joint Chiefs of Staff. *Wheeler Calendar;* Department of the Army. *Johnson Calendars;* Viney, Mark A. *Determined to Persist*. 31.

17. Spivy, 738, 749.

18. Viney, Mark A. *Determined to Persist*. 31-32.

19. Thorin, 15-16.

20. Ibid.

21. Stewart, 327-328.

22. United States Military Assistance Command, Vietnam. *Background Briefing Presented by General Westmoreland*. 29 Jun.1967.

23. Joint Chiefs of Staff. *Impact of the NVA/VC Build-up at the DMZ, 1966-1967*. 11 Jul. 1967.

24. Prados. *Vietnam*. 212.

25. Joint Chiefs of Staff. Office of the Chairman of the Joint Chiefs of Staff. *Photo Album for General Earle G. Wheeler, Chairman, 1967-1968*. Jul. 1970; Berman, 54.

26. Herspring, 175.

27. Joint Chiefs of Staff. Office of the Chairman of the Joint Chiefs of Staff. *Photo Album for General Earle G. Wheeler, Chairman, 1967-1968.* Jul. 1970; United States Army. Walter Reed General Hospital. *Clinical Record.* 22 Apr. 1970; Wheeler, Gilmore. Email to Mark Viney. 10 Jul. 2017; Berman, 54.

28. Joint Chiefs of Staff. Office of the Chairman of the Joint Chiefs of Staff. *Photo Album for General Earle G. Wheeler, Chairman, 1967-1968.* Jul. 1970; Herring, 218.

29. McNamara, 283; Prados. *Vietnam.* 211.

30. Petitt, 329.

31. Prados. *Vietnam.* 208.

32. Spivy, 737.

33. Stewart, 329.

34. Prados. *Vietnam.* 195.

35. Millet, Maslowski, and Feis, 539.

36. Sharp and Westmoreland, 4; Buzzanco, Robert. *Military Dissent and Politics in the Vietnam Era.* Cambridge; New York: Cambridge University Press, 1996: 299.

37. McNamara, 284.

38. Prados. *Vietnam.* 209; Perry, 163-166; Schandler, 55.

39. Perry, 160-161.

40. McNamara, 284-285.

41. McNamara, 284; Prados. *Vietnam.* 209; Perry, 161, 163-166; Schandler, 55.

42. Petitt, 346.

43. Joint Chiefs of Staff. *Front Channel Message from Captain H. B. Sweitzer, Military Assistant (L & L), Office of the Chairman of the Joint Chiefs of Staff, Washington, to Admiral Sharp, CINCPAC, Hawaii.* 11 Aug. 1967.

44. Ibid.

45. Joint Chiefs of Staff. *Front Channel Message from Captain H. B. Sweitzer, Military Assistant (L & L) to the Chairman, Office of the Chairman of the Joint Chiefs of Staff, Washington, to Admiral Sharp, CINCPAC, Hawaii.* 15 Aug. 1967.

46. Ibid.

47. Ibid.

48. Ibid.

49. Odom, 221.

50. Prados. *Vietnam.* 209; Petitt, 346; Herspring, 175; Perry, 161.

51. Ibid.

52. Sharp and Westmoreland, 4.

53. McNamara, 286.

54. Prados. *Vietnam.* 209; Perry, 161.

55. Herspring, 175-176; Perry, 162.

56. McNamara, 289; Prados. *Vietnam.* 209.

57. Oberdorfer, Don. *Tet!* Garden City, NY: Doubleday & Company, Inc. 1971: 96-97.

58. Ibid.

59. Perry, 162; Herspring, 175-176.

60. Perry, 165.

61. Johnson, Harold K. Interview with Rupert F. Glover, United States Army Military History Institute, Senior Officer Debriefing Program, Volume I, Section VI, 1 Dec. 1972: 37; Gilmore S. Wheeler, Interview with Mark Viney, 9 Jun. 2010: 1; Perry, 163-166.

62. Association of the U.S. Army. Army Magazine. *Historically Speaking, Earl G. Wheeler at 100.*

63. Perry, 163.

64. Scribner, 174 – 175.

65. Herspring, 177.

66. McNamara, 284.

67. Herspring, 177.

68. United States Military Assistance Command, Vietnam. *Back Channel Message from General Westmoreland, COMUSMACV, Saigon, to General Wheeler, CJCS, Washington, and Admiral Sharp, CINCPAC, Hawaii.* 26 Aug. 1967.

69. McNamara, 291.

70. Gilmore S. Wheeler, Interviews with Mark Viney, 8 Nov. 2010 and 20 Apr 16.

71. Wheeler, Earle G. Letter to Lyndon B. Johnson, 5 Sep. 1967.

72. United States Pacific Command. *Back Channel Message from Admiral Sharp, CINCPAC, Hawaii, to General Wheeler, CJCS, Washington.* 7 Sep. 1967.

73. United States Army. Walter Reed General Hospital. *Clinical Record.* 22 Apr. 1970; Wheeler, Earle G. Interview with Dorothy P. McSweeny. Interview II, 7 May 1970; Wheeler, Gilmore. Email to Mark Viney. 10 Jul. 2017.

74. Ibid.

75. Wheeler, Gilmore. Interview with Mark Viney. 25 Feb. 2013.

76. Spivy, 744; Stewart, Bill. Interview with Mark A. Viney. 7 Nov. 2013.

77. Millet, Maslowski, and Feis, 539; Prados. *Vietnam.* 209.

78. McNamara, 295.

79. Millet, Maslowski, and Feis, 539; Prados. *Vietnam.* 209.

80. Millet, Maslowski, and Feis, 538.

81. Millet, Maslowski, and Feis, 539; Prados. *Vietnam.* 209.

82. Petitt, 331-332.

83. Ibid.

84. Ibid.

85. Joint Chiefs of Staff. *Wheeler Addresses.* 168.

86. Barrett, 476.

87. Pearson, 18-20.

88. Sharp and Westmoreland, 143, 155.

89. United States Military Assistance Command, Vietnam. *Back Channel Message from General Westmoreland, COMUSMACV, Saigon, to General Johnson, Acting CJCS, Washington, and Admiral Sharp, CINCPAC, Hawaii.* 27 Sep. 1967.

90. Ibid.

91. Ibid.

92. Joint Chiefs of Staff. *Memorandum for the Deputy Secretary of Defense, Subject: Situation in the DMZ Area and Program 5 Accelerated Deployments, CM-2668-67.* 28 Sep. 1967.

93. Sharp and Westmoreland, 143, 155.

94. Perry, 177.

95. Wheeler, Frances R. Letter to Rebecca Howell. 2 Oct. 1967; Wheeler, Gilmore. Email to Mark Viney. 21 Nov. 2013.

96. Joint Chiefs of Staff. *Wheeler Addresses.* 165.

97. McNamara, 291.

98. Herring, 135-138, 147-151, 168; Perry, 167-168.

99. Joint Chiefs of Staff. *Wheeler Addresses.* 139; Herring, 135-138, 147-151, 168; Perry, 167-168; Herspring, 176.

100. United States Military Assistance Command, Vietnam. *Back Channel Message from General Westmoreland, COMUSMACV, Saigon, to General Wheeler, CJCS, Washington, and Admiral Sharp, CINCPAC, Hawaii.* 28 Oct. 1967.

101. Stewart, 320; Petitt, 334-335.

102. Herring, 219.

103. Joint Chiefs of Staff. *Memorandum for the Chairman, Joint Chiefs of Staff, Subject: CINCPAC Planning for Ground Operations North of the DMZ (S), DJSM-1270-67.* 16 Oct. 1967; United States Military Assistance Command, Vietnam. *COMUSMACV Outline Plan BUTT STROKE.* 20 Sep. 1967.

104. Joint Chiefs of Staff. *Memorandum for the Chairman, Joint Chiefs of Staff, Subject: CINCPAC Planning for Ground Operations North of the DMZ (S), DJSM-1270-67.* 16 Oct. 1967; United States Pacific Command. Commander, Fleet Marine Force Pacific. *Outline Plan for Operation COLUBRINE.* 20 Sep. 1967.

105. Joint Chiefs of Staff. *Memorandum for the J-30, Subject: CINCPACFLT Planning Conference; Report of,* 20 Sep. 1967.

106. Joint Chiefs of Staff. *Memorandum for the Chairman, Joint Chiefs of Staff, Subject: CINCPAC Planning for Ground Operations North of the DMZ (S), DJSM-1270-67.* 16 Oct. 1967; Joint Chiefs of Staff, *Register of Personnel*

Handling Classified Document, Subject: CINCPAC Planning for Ground Operations North of the DMZ, 16 Oct. 1967.

107. Prados. *Vietnam.* 209.

108. Joint Chiefs of Staff. *Memorandum for the Chairman, Joint Chiefs of Staff, Subject: CINCPAC Planning for Ground Operations North of the DMZ (S), DJSM-1270-67.* 16 Oct. 1967; United States Pacific Command. Commander, Fleet Marine Force Pacific. *Outline Plan for Operation COLUBRINE.* 20 Sep. 1967.

109. Sharp and Westmoreland, 204.

110. Barrett, 497-498.

111. Perry, 177.

112. Sharp and Westmoreland, 202-203; Perry, 202-203.

113. Barrett, 497-498.

114. Department of Defense. *Pentagon Papers.* Volume IV. 536.

115. Sharp and Westmoreland, 202-203; Perry, 177.

116. Sharp and Westmoreland, 202-203; Perry, 177-178, 202-203.

117. Wheeler, Earle G. Interview with Dorothy P. McSweeny. Interview I, 21 Aug. 1969: 16-17.

118. Perry, 177-178.

119. Sharp and Westmoreland, 230.

120. Perry, 178.

121. Prados. *Vietnam.* 208-209.

122. Wheeler, Frances R. Letter to Rebecca Howell. 20 Oct. 1967.

123. Sharp and Westmoreland, 51; Stewart, 272; History.com. Downloaded from the internet on 5 Jul. 2017 at http://www.history.com/this-day-in-history/100000-people-march-on-the-pentagon.

124. Sharp and Westmoreland, 51; Stewart, 272; History.com. Downloaded from the internet on 5 Jul. 2017 at http://www.history.com/this-day-in-history/100000-people-march-on-the-pentagon.

125. Herring, 211; Millet, Maslowski, and Feis, 537.

126. Ibid.

127. Millet, Maslowski, and Feis, 537-538.

128. Ibid.

129. Herring, 209-210; Barrett, 508.

130. Ibid.

131. Stewart, 329-330.

132. Millet, Maslowski, and Feis, 538-539.

133. Herring, 221.

134. McNamara, 308; Herring, 221; Prados. *Vietnam.* 213.

135. Ibid.

136. Barrett, 518-519.

137. Herring, 204-205.

138. Prados. *Vietnam.* 213.

139. Prados. *Vietnam.* 213.

140. Barrett, 457.

141. Ibid.

142. Ibid.

143. Prados. *Vietnam.* 213-215.

144. Ibid.

145. Herring, 221-223.

146. Ibid.

147. Ibid.

148. Joint Chiefs of Staff. *Wheeler Addresses.* 168.

149. Ibid.

150. Prados. *Vietnam.* 215.

151. Herring, 201-202.

152. McNamara, 299.

153. McNamara, 313; Herring, 216; Prados. *Vietnam.* 215.

154. Joint Chiefs of Staff. Office of the Chairman of the Joint Chiefs of Staff. *Memorandum for General H. K. Johnson, CSA, General J. P. McConnell, CSAF,*

Admiral T. L. Moorer, CNO, General W. M. Greene, Jr., CMC, CM-2754-67. 13 Nov. 1967.

155. Ibid.

156. Petitt, 338; Millet, Maslowski, and Feis, 539; Petitt, 339.

157. Perry, 178-179.

158. Millet, Maslowski, and Feis, 539.

159. Petitt, 341.

160. Herring, 213, 221.

161. Joint Chiefs of Staff. Office of the Chairman of the Joint Chiefs of Staff. *Memorandum for the Under Secretary of State, Subject: General Maxwell D. Taylor's Analysis of Courses of Action in SEA, CM-2782-67*. 24 Nov. 1967.

162. Ibid.

163. Ibid.

164. Ibid.

165. Ibid.

166. Joint Chiefs of Staff. *Wheeler Addresses*. 167.

167. Barrett, 559-565.

168. Ibid.

169. Ibid.

170. Ibid.

171. Ibid.

172. Ibid.

173. Ibid.

174. Ibid.

175. Ibid.

176. Ibid.

177. Ibid.

178. Ibid.

179. Ibid.

180. Ibid.

181. Ibid.

182. Ibid.

183. Ibid.

184. Sharp and Westmoreland, 52; Petitt, 343-344; Stewart, 306.

185. Joint Chiefs of Staff. *Wheeler Addresses.* 176-177.

186. Ibid.

187. Ibid.

188. Herring, 226-228.

Chapter 7

1. Palmer, Dave R. 201.

2. United States Marine Corps. 120; Marines. Downloaded from the internet on 11 Jul. 2017 at http://marines.mil/News/Messages/Messages-Display/Article/886772/death-of-general-leonard-f-chapman-jr-former-commandant-of-the-marine-corps/; Spivy, 738.

3. Stewart, 333-335.

4. Sharp and Westmoreland, 174-175; Pearson, 28.

5. Stewart, 335; Millet, Maslowski, and Feis, 540.

6. Sharp and Westmoreland, 194; Millet, Maslowski, and Feis, 540-541; Stewart, 335.

7. Sharp and Westmoreland, 162; Stewart, 335-336.

8. Sharp and Westmoreland, 29-30, 32, 174; Pearson, 28.

9. Sharp and Westmoreland, 163.

10. Ibid; Pearson, 30-34; Millet, Maslowski, and Feis, 539.

11. Sharp and Westmoreland, 30-34; Pearson, 28; Stewart, 335-336.

12. Perry, 180.

13. Perry, 180-181.

14. Stewart, 336.

15. Stewart, 336; Millet, Maslowski, and Feis, 540.

16. Joint Chiefs of Staff. *Wheeler Addresses.* 203.

17. Stewart, 336; Millet, Maslowski, and Feis, 540.

18. Pearson, 37-39; Sharp and Westmoreland, 158-160, 183; Stewart, 336; Millet, Maslowski, and Feis, 540.

19. Millet, Maslowski, and Feis, 540.

20. Pearson, 37-39; Sharp and Westmoreland, 158-160, 183; Stewart, 336.

21. Stewart, 338.

22. Ibid, 338-339; Herring, 225-226.

23. Pearson, 44-45, 68; Sharp and Westmoreland, 184; United States Marine Corps, 101.

24. Herring, 225-226; Millet, Maslowski, and Feis, 541; Stewart, 339.

25. Ibid.

26. Herring, 225-226; Millet, Maslowski, and Feis, 541.

27. Pearson, 34-36.

28. United States Military Assistance Command, Vietnam. *Back Channel Message from General Westmoreland, COMUSMACV, Saigon, to General Wheeler, CJCS, Washington, and Admiral Sharp, CINCPAC, Hawaii*. 3 Feb. 1967.

29. Schandler, 89-91.

30. Ibid.

31. Joint Chiefs of Staff. *Back Channel Message from General Wheeler, CJCS, Washington, to Admiral Sharp, CINCPAC, Hawaii, and General Westmoreland, COMUSMACV, Saigon*. 1 Feb. 1968.

32. United States Pacific Command. *Back Channel Message from Admiral Sharp, CINCPAC, Hawaii, to General Westmoreland, COMUSMACV, Saigon, and General Wheeler, CJCS, Washington*. 2 Feb. 1968; United States Military Assistance Command, Vietnam. *Back Channel Message from General Westmoreland, COMUSMACV, Saigon, to General Wheeler, CJCS, Washington, and Admiral Sharp, CINCPAC, Hawaii*. 3 Feb. 1968.; United States Pacific Command. *Back Channel Message from Admiral Sharp, CINCPAC, Hawaii, to General Westmoreland, COMUSMACV, Saigon, and General Wheeler, CJCS, Washington*. 4 Feb. 1968.

33. Joint Chiefs of Staff. *Back Channel Message from General Wheeler, CJCS, Washington, to Admiral Sharp, CINCPAC, Hawaii, and General Westmoreland, COMUSMACV, Saigon.* 6 Feb. 1968; United States Pacific Command. *Back Channel Message from Admiral Sharp, CINCPAC, Hawaii, to General Westmoreland, COMUSMACV, Saigon, and General Wheeler, CJCS, Washington.* 8 Feb. 1968.

34. United States Pacific Command. *Two Back Channel Messages from Admiral Sharp, CINCPAC, Hawaii, to General Westmoreland, COMUSMACV, Saigon, and General Wheeler, CJCS, Washington.* 10 Feb. 1968.

35. Joint Chiefs of Staff. Office of the Chairman of the Joint Chiefs of Staff. *Memorandum for the Chief of Staff, Army; Chief of Naval Operations; Chief of Staff, Air Force; Commandant Marine Corps; Director, Defense Intelligence Agency; Director, National Security Agency, Subject: Deception, CM-3004-68.* 12 Feb. 1968; Joint Chiefs of Staff. Office of the Special Assistant for Counterinsurgency and Special Activities. *Memorandum for Record, Subject: Code-Word Designator – Access Plan, Top-Secret – Sensitive.* Not dated (Feb. 1968).

36. Petitt, 351.

37. United States Military Assistance Command, Vietnam. *Back Channel Message from General Westmoreland, COMUSMACV, Saigon, to General Wheeler, CJCS, Washington, and Admiral Sharp, CINCPAC, Hawaii.* 8 Feb. 1968.

38. Wheeler, Earle G. Interview with Dorothy P. McSweeny. Interview II, 7 May 1970: 5.

39. Schandler, 97.

40. Westmoreland, 351-352.

41. Schandler, 97.

42. Berman, 165.

43. Joint Chiefs of Staff. Office of the Chairman of the Joint Chiefs of Staff. *Memorandum for General Maxwell D. Taylor, Subject: Military Posture.* 8 Feb. 1968.

44. Ibid.

45. Ibid.

46. Petitt, 352; Schandler, 97.

47. Barrett, 601-605.

48. Ibid.

49. Ibid.

50. United States Military Assistance Command, Vietnam. *Back Channel Message from General Westmoreland, COMUSMACV, Saigon, to General Wheeler, CJCS, Washington, and Admiral Sharp, CINCPAC, Hawaii.* 12 Feb. 1968.

51. United States Military Assistance Command, Vietnam. *Back Channel Message from General Westmoreland, COMUSMACV, Saigon, to General Wheeler, CJCS, Washington, and Admiral Sharp, CINCPAC, Hawaii.* 4 Feb. 1968; Palmer, Dave R. 205; Prados. *Vietnam.* 242.

52. Schandler, 345.

53. United States Military Assistance Command, Vietnam. *Back Channel Message from General Westmoreland, COMUSMACV, Saigon, to General Wheeler, CJCS, Washington, and Admiral Sharp, CINCPAC, Hawaii.* 12 Feb. 1968; Schandler, 107.

54. Ibid.

55. Ibid.

56. Prados. *Vietnam.* 246-247.

57. Porter, 497-498.

58. Barrett, 605-611.

59. Perry, 185.

60. Ibid.

61. Westmoreland, 357.

62. Wheeler, Earle G. Interview with Dorothy P. McSweeny. Interview II, 7 May 1970: 5; Herring, 234.

63. Westmoreland, 13.

64. Joint Chiefs of Staff. *Wheeler Addresses.* 216.

65. Sharp and Westmoreland, 164; Stewart, 339.

66. Joint Chiefs of Staff. Office of the Chairman of the Joint Chiefs of Staff. *Memorandum for the Chief of Staff, U.S. Army; Chief of Staff, U.S. Air Force; Chief of Naval Operations; Commandant, U.S. Marine Corps; Director, Joint Staff, Subject: Force Posture, CM-2976-68.* 16 Feb. 1968.

67. United States Marine Corps. 101-102; Stewart, 339-340.

68. Prados. *Vietnam.* 241-242.

69. Stewart, 339; Prados. *Vietnam.* 241.

70. Wheeler, Earle G. Interview with Dorothy P. McSweeny. Interview I, 21 Aug. 1969: 28-29.

71. Prados. *Vietnam.* 241; Spector, 6-7.

72. Prados. *Vietnam.* 241.

73. Westmoreland, 321.

74. Prados. *Vietnam.* 242.

75. Joint Chiefs of Staff. *Wheeler Addresses.* 175.

76. Ibid.

77. Millet, Maslowski, and Feis, 541.

78. Petitt, 347.

79. Herring, 233-234.

80. Herring, 233-234.

81. Ibid.

82. Johnson, Lyndon B. Note to Earle G. Wheeler. 7 Feb. 1968.

83. Prados. *Vietnam.* 246-247.

84. Petitt, 353.

85. Schandler, 105; Porter, 501-504.

86. Westmoreland, 354.

87. United States Military Assistance Command, Vietnam. *Back Channel Message from General Westmoreland, COMUSMACV, Saigon, to General Wheeler, CJCS, Washington, and Admiral Sharp, CINCPAC, Hawaii.* 20 Feb. 1968; Office of the Chairman of the Joint Chiefs of Staff. *Photo Album for General Earle G. Wheeler, Chairman, 1967-1968.* Jul. 1970; Porter, 501-504; Schandler, 108; Perry, 186.

88. Schandler, 305.

89. Perry, 187. Herring suggests that Wheeler may have been much less optimistic than Westmoreland about the immediate prospects in Vietnam. Millet suggests otherwise that Wheeler may not have believed the situation was as dire as he would report because, in part, he was using Westmoreland's reinforcement request as a ploy to rebuild the strategic reserve. Perry believes Wheeler wasn't just trying to find out whether Westmoreland needed more troops; he was telling him he needed more troops.

90. Thorin, 18.

91. Department of the Army. Office of the Chief of Staff of the Army. *The Origins of the Post-Tet 1968 Plans for Additional American Forces in RVN.* 9 Nov. 1970: 19-20; Millet, Maslowski, and Feis, 541-542; Schandler, 106.

92. Ibid.

93. Palmer, Dave R. 205.

94. Joint Chiefs of Staff. *Feasibility Study.* x; Prados. *Vietnam.* 247.

95. Westmoreland, 19-20.

96. Schandler, 110.

97. Herring, 235; Perry, 188.

98. Schandler, 111.

99. Westmoreland, 353; Herring, 235, 356.

100. Ibid.

101. Westmoreland, 356.

102. Wheeler, Earle G. Interview with Dorothy P. McSweeny. Interview II, 7 May 1970: 7.

103. Westmoreland, 356.

104. Schandler, 111.

105. Herring, 243, 245.

106. Herring, 235.

107. Westmoreland, 356-357.

108. Schandler, 115-116.

109. Perry, 189.

110. Barrett, 629-634.

111. Ibid.

112. Ibid.

113. Ibid.

114. Joint Chiefs of Staff. Office of the Chairman of the Joint Chiefs of Staff. *Photo Album for General Earle G. Wheeler, Chairman, 1967-1968.* Jul. 1970; Petitt, 354; Schandler, 118.

115. Palmer, Dave R. 204.

116. Westmoreland, 357.

117. Ibid.

118. Petitt, 355.

119. Sharp, 164.

120. Sharp and Westmoreland, 171.

121. Pearson, 76-78.

122. Millet, Maslowski, and Feis, 539.

123. Westmoreland, 337.

124. Sharp and Westmoreland, 165-166.

125. United States Marine Corps, 109; Millet, Maslowski, and Feis, 542.

126. Herspring, 178; Berman, 178.

127. Perry, 189; Prados. *Vietnam.* 247; Millet, Maslowski, and Feis, 542; Stewart, 339.

128. Spector, 6.

129. Schandler, 120, 327-328.

130. Herring, 236; Prados. *Vietnam.* 247; Millet, Maslowski, and Feis, 542.

131. Wheeler, Earle G. Interview with Dorothy P. McSweeny. Interview II, 7 May 1970: 7; Herring, 236; Prados. *Vietnam.* 247; Millet, Maslowski, and Feis, 542.

132. Schandler, 120.

133. Herring, 236.

134. Jordan, 119.

135. Herspring, 178.

136. Perry, 190-191.

137. Berman, 178.

138. Perry, 190-191.

139. Schandler, 311.

140. Herring, 236-237.

141. Ibid.

142. Millet, Maslowski, and Feis, 542; Prados. *Vietnam.* 261-262; Perry, 191.

143. Herring, 238; Schandler, 167.

144. Jordan, 119; Schandler, 177.

145. Schandler, 177.

146. Herring, 241-242; Prados. *Vietnam.* 248; Millet, Maslowski, and Feis, 542.

147. Westmoreland, 24-25, 358.

148. Ibid.

149. Westmoreland, 25, 28.

150. Ibid.

151. Herring, 242.

152. Wheeler, Earle G. Interview with Dorothy P. McSweeny. Interview II, 7 May 1970: 8.

153. History.com. Downloaded from the internet on 2 Sep. 2010 at http://www.history.com/this-day-in-history.do?action=tdihArticleCategory&id=1967.

Chapter 8

1. McMaster, xv.

2. Schandler, 166; Herring, 237-238.

3. United States Military Assistance Command, Vietnam. *Back Channel Message from General Westmoreland, COMUSMACV, Saigon, to General Wheeler, CJCS, Washington, and Admiral Sharp, CINCPAC, Hawaii.* 2 Mar. 1968.

4. Herring, 237-238; Schandler, 166.

5. Schandler, 166.

6. United States Military Assistance Command, Vietnam. *Back Channel Message from General Westmoreland, COMUSMACV, Saigon, to General Wheeler, CJCS, Washington, and Admiral Sharp, CINCPAC, Hawaii.* 3 Mar. 1968.

7. Ibid.

8. Schandler, 166.

9. Herring, 237-238; Schandler, 166-167.

10. Ibid.

11. Barrett, 661.

12. Berman, 188; Herring, 237-238.

13. Herring, 238; Schandler, 169.

14. Schandler, 166-167.

15. Herring, 248-249.

16. Barrett, 699.

17. Herring, 247.

18. United States Pacific Command. *Back Channel Message from Admiral Sharp, CINCPAC, Hawaii, to General Westmoreland, COMUSMACV, Saigon, and General Wheeler, CJCS, Washington.* 23 Mar. 1968.

19. Ibid.

20. Sharp and Westmoreland, 164-165; Herring, 239, 245, 247.

21. Herring, 247-249.

22. Ibid.

23. Wheeler, Frances R. Letter to Rebecca Howell. 20 Mar. 1968.

24. Oberdorfer, 307.

25. Westmoreland, 27, 358-359.

26. Ibid.

27. Ibid.

28. Herring, 249; Barrett, 710.

29. Ibid.

30. Ibid.

31. Herring, 249-250; Millet, Maslowski, and Feis, 542.

32. Herring, 239-240, 246-249.

33. Ibid.

34. Ibid.

35. Prados. *Vietnam.* 249; Millet, Maslowski, and Feis, 542-543.

36. Sharp and Westmoreland, 9-10; Herring, 250; Millet, Maslowski, and Feis, 542-543.

37. Joint Chiefs of Staff. *Wheeler Addresses.* 201.

38. Herring, 250; Millet, Maslowski, and Feis, 542-543.

39. Herring, 250; Stewart, 339-340.

40. Wheeler, Earle G. Interview with Dorothy P. McSweeny. Interview II, 7 May 1970: 14.

41. Spivy, 745.

42. Joint Chiefs of Staff. *Wheeler Addresses.* 201.

43. Porter, 511-512.

44. Ibid.

45. United States Pacific Command. *Back Channel Message from Admiral Sharp, CINCPAC, Hawaii, to General Wheeler, CJCS, Washington.* 1 Apr. 1968.

46. Porter, 511-512.

47. Herring, 251; Schandler, 350.

48. Herring, 251.

49. Ibid.

50. Joint Chiefs of Staff. *Wheeler Addresses.* 179; Herring, 251-252.

51. Westmoreland, 359.

52. United States Marine Corps, 108; Jordan, 117.

53. Spivy, 739.

54. United States Pacific Command. *Back Channel Message from Admiral Sharp, CINCPAC, Hawaii, to General Westmoreland, COMUSMACV, Saigon, and General Wheeler, CJCS, Washington.* 13 Apr. 1968.

55. Joint Chiefs of Staff. Office of the Chairman of the Joint Chiefs of Staff. *Photo Album for General Earle G. Wheeler, Chairman, 1967-1968.* Jul. 1970; Stewart, 280.

56. Sharp and Westmoreland, 166.

57. Sharp and Westmoreland, 165-166.

58. Sharp and Westmoreland, 165, 187; Pearson, 89-92.

59. Pearson, 89-92. One such 37-mm anti-aircraft gun seized by the 101st Airborne Division was captured by the author's father, Lieutenant George S. Viney, leading the Reconnaissance Platoon of the 2nd Battalion, 327th Parachute Infantry Regiment.

60. Joint Chiefs of Staff. *Wheeler Addresses.* 203.

61. Herring, 254.

62. Prados. *Vietnam.* 267-268.

63. Herring, 255-256.

64. The White House. *Remarks of the President and General Westmoreland at a luncheon at the White House, The East Room.* 20 Apr. 1967.

65. Thorin, 22.

66. Herring, 256.

67. Thorin, 20.

68. Thorin, 20-21.

69. McNamara, 260.

70. Herring, 257, 267.

71. Sharp and Westmoreland, 187-188; United States Marine Corps, 106; Millet, Maslowski, and Feis, 543.

72. Spector, 157.

73. Sharp and Westmoreland, 187-188; United States Marine Corps, 106; Millet, Maslowski, and Feis, 543.

74. Sharp and Westmoreland, 187-188.

75. Sharp and Westmoreland, 3, 10.

76. Dorland, 20.

77. Stewart, 340-341.

78. United States Marine Corps, 111.

79. Sharp and Westmoreland, 188; Bell. *Commanding Generals.*

80. Stewart, 341.

81. Spivy, 740-741.

82. Stewart, 341.

83. Jordan, 121; Millet, Maslowski, and Feis, 546-547.

84. Ibid.

85. Ibid.

86. Jordan, 122.

87. Wheeler, Frances R. Letter to Rebecca Howell. 24 Jun. 1968.

88. Joint Chiefs of Staff. Office of the Chairman of the Joint Chiefs of Staff. *Memorandum for the President, Subject: Military Posture Comparisons in Vietnam (U), CM-3423-68.* 24 Jun. 1968.

89. Ibid.

90. Herring, 252; Jordan, 122.

91. Herring, 252-253.

92. Joint Chiefs of Staff. *Wheeler Addresses.* 213.

93. Herring, 253.

94. Ibid.

95. Bell. *Commanding Generals.*

96. Department of Defense. *Ceremony Program, In Honor of General Earle G. Wheeler, Chairman, Joint Chiefs of Staff, Andrews Air Force Base, Maryland.* 2 Jul. 1970.

97. Joint Chiefs of Staff. Office of the Chairman of the Joint Chiefs of Staff. *Photo Album for General Earle G. Wheeler, Chairman, 1968-1969.* Jul. 1970; Sharp and Westmoreland, xv.

98. Sharp and Westmoreland, 9-10; United States Pacific Command. Downloaded from the internet on 19 Jul. 2017 at http:www.pacom.mil/About-USPACOM/USPACOM-Previous-Commanders/.

99. Sharp and Westmoreland, 9-10.

100. Sharp and Westmoreland, 53-54.

101. Joint Chiefs of Staff. *Back Channel Message from General Wheeler, CJCS, Washington, to Admiral McCain, CINCPAC, Hawaii, and General Abrams, COMUSMACV, Saigon.* 28 Mar. 1969.

102. Sharp and Westmoreland, 52.

103. New York Times. Downloaded from the internet on 19 Jul. 2017 at https://mobile.nytimes.com/2001/12/18/us/ulysses-s-grant-sharp-jr-vietnam-war-admiral-95.html.

104. Sharp and Westmoreland, xiii.

105. Millet, Maslowski, and Feis, 543; Stewart, 340.

106. Joint Chiefs of Staff. *Wheeler Addresses.* 216; Petitt, 363.

107. Millet, Maslowski, and Feis, 543.

108. Petitt, 362.

109. Joint Chiefs of Staff. Office of the Special Assistant for Counterinsurgency and Special Activities. *Memorandum for General Wheeler, Subject: Major Strategy and Turning Points in Vietnam (U).* 14 Sep. 1968.

110. Joint Chiefs of Staff. Office of the Chairman of the Joint Chiefs of Staff. *Memorandum for the Secretary of Defense, Subject: Northeast Monsoon Campaign Planning, CM-3662-68.* 20 Sep. 1968.

111. Ibid.

112. Perry, 198.

113. Perry, 198-199.

114. Joint Chiefs of Staff. *Back Channel Message from General Wheeler, CJCS, Washington, to General Abrams, COMUSMACV, Saigon, and Admiral McCain, CINCPAC, Hawaii.* 16 Oct.1968.

115. Ibid.

116. Ibid.

117. Herring, 262.

118. Petitt, 365-366.

119. Ibid.

120. Millet, Maslowski, and Feis, 521-522.

121. Perry, 199-201.

122. United States Marine Corps, 117.

123. Millet, Maslowski, and Feis, 550; Herring, 257-258, 260.

124. Odom, 221.

125. Spector, 311.

126. Palmer, Dave R. 210.

127. Herring, 267-268.

Chapter 9

1. Prados. *Vietnam*. 299.

2. Perry, 205-206.

3. Millet, Maslowski, and Feis, 544; Herring, 271.

4. Herring, 273-274.

5. Ibid.

6. Prados. *Vietnam*. 288.

7. Porter, 522-523; Millet, Maslowski, and Feis, 544.

8. Millet, Maslowski, and Feis, 544-545.

9. Porter, 522-523.

10. Perry, 201-202.

11. Wheeler, Gilmore S. Interview with Mark A. Viney. 14 Mar. 2013; Perry, 203.

12. Perry, 204.

13. Wheeler, Gilmore S. Interview with Mark A. Viney. 14 Mar. 2013.

14. Department of Defense. Brochure. *In Honor of General Earle G. Wheeler, Chairman, Joint Chiefs of Staff, Andrews Air Force Base, Maryland, 2 July 1970*: Jul. 70.

15. Kissinger, Henry A. *White House Years*. Boston: Little, Brown, 1979: 34.

16. Prados. *Vietnam*. 288-289.

17. Kissinger, 239; Prados. *Vietnam*. 290.

18. Prados. *Vietnam*. 288-289.

19. Herring, 274-275.

20. Millet, Maslowski, and Feis, 545.

21. Herring, 274-276.

22. Herspring, 190.

23. Prados. *Vietnam.* 290, 292.

24. Joint Chiefs of Staff. *Backchannel Message from General Wheeler, CJCS, Washington, to General Nazarro, Acting CINCPAC, Hawaii, and General Abrams, COMUSMACV,* Saigon. 22 Jan. 1969: 1-2.

25. Joint Chiefs of Staff. Office of the Chairman of the Joint Chiefs of Staff. *Memorandum for the Director, Joint Staff, Subject: Pressure on North Vietnam, CM-3877-69.* 22 Jan. 1969: 1; Herspring, 192.

26. Ibid.

27. Ibid.

28. Joint Chiefs of Staff. Office of the Chairman of the Joint Chiefs of Staff. *Memorandum for the Director, Joint Staff, Subject: Cambodia, CM-3879-69.* 22 Jan. 1969.

29. Joint Chiefs of Staff. Office of the Chairman of the Joint Chiefs of Staff. *Memorandum for the Director, Joint Staff, Subject: Operating Authorities, CM-3880-69.* 22 Jan. 1969.

30. Kissinger, 239-241; Herspring, 192-202; Prados. *Vietnam.* 292, 302.

31. Joint Chiefs of Staff. *Wheeler Addresses.* 280.

32. Ibid.

33. Herspring, 188-189, 414- 415.

34. Ibid.

35. Millet, Maslowski, and Feis, 543-544.

36. Kissinger, 241; Prados. *Vietnam.* 292-293.

37. United States Army. Walter Reed General Hospital. *Clinical Record.* 22 Apr. 1970.

38. Joint Chiefs of Staff. Office of the Chairman of the Joint Chiefs of Staff. *Memorandum for the Secretary of Defense, Subject: Increased Authorities for Southeast Asia (U), CM-3941-69.* 13 Feb. 1969; Department of Defense. *Ceremony Program, In Honor of General Earle G. Wheeler, Chairman, Joint Chiefs of Staff, Andrews Air Force Base, Maryland.* 13 Feb. 1969.

39. Joint Chiefs of Staff. Office of the Chairman of the Joint Chiefs of Staff. *Memorandum for the Secretary of Defense, Subject: Increased authorities for Southeast Asia (U), CM-3941-69.* 13 Feb. 1969.

40. Joint Chiefs of Staff. Office of the Chairman of the Joint Chiefs of Staff. *Memorandum for the Secretary of Defense, Subject: Increased Authorities for Southeast Asia (U), CM-3941-69.* 13 Feb. 1969.

41. Prados. *Vietnam.* 292-293.

42. Prados. *Vietnam.* 302-303.

43. Ibid.

44. Joint Chiefs of Staff. Office of the Chairman of the Joint Chiefs of Staff. *Memorandum for the Secretary of Defense, Subject: Observations and Recommendations Concerning the Military Situation in Southeast Asia. CM-4001-69.* 12 Mar. 1969.

45. Ibid.

46. Ibid.

47. Ibid.

48. Joint Chiefs of Staff. Office of the Chairman of the Joint Chiefs of Staff. *Memorandum for the Secretary of Defense, Subject: Mining Plans for Haiphong (S). CM-4006-69.* 13 Mar. 1969; Joint Chiefs of Staff. Office of the Chairman of the Joint Chiefs of Staff. *Memorandum for the Secretary of Defense, Subject: Sinking Blocking Craft, Haiphong Channel (TS), CM-4000-69.* 13 Mar. 1969; Joint Chiefs of Staff. Office of the Chairman of the Joint Chiefs of Staff. *Memorandum for the Secretary of Defense, Subject: Authority for B-52 Strikes against Targets in Cambodia (TS), CM-4003-69.* 13 Mar. 1969.

49. Joint Chiefs of Staff. Office of the Chairman of the Joint Chiefs of Staff. *Memorandum for the Secretary of Defense, Subject: "Surgical" Strikes and/or Naval Bombardment in the Haiphong Area (S) CM-3994-69.* 14 Mar. 1969.

50. Ibid.

51. Joint Chiefs of Staff. Office of the Chairman of the Joint Chiefs of Staff. *Memorandum for the Secretary of Defense, Subject: Vietnam Demilitarized Zone (DMZ) (U) CM-4010-69.* 15 Mar. 1969.

52. Prados. *Vietnam.* 303; Herspring, 193; Politico. Downloaded from the internet on 26 Jul. 2017 at http://www.politico.com/story/2013/04/this-day-in-politics-089554.

53. Kissinger, 245-247.

54. Ibid.

55. Ibid.

56. Prados. *Vietnam.* 293; Herring, 276.

57. Millet, 551-552.

58. Herring, 276; Millet, Maslowski, and Feis, 551-552.

59. Prados. *Vietnam.* 294-295.

60. Prados. *Vietnam.* 294; Herring, 276; Millet, Maslowski, and Feis, 551-552.

61. Herspring, 195.

62. Herring, 276.

63. Joint Chiefs of Staff. *Back Channel Message from General Wheeler, CJCS, Washington, to General Abrams, COMUSMACV, Saigon, and Admiral McCain, CINCPAC, Hawaii.* 25 Mar. 1969.

64. Congress. *Cambodia Hearings*; Herring, 276.

65. Prados. *Vietnam.* 295.

66. Joint Chiefs of Staff. *Back Channel Message from General Wheeler, CJCS, Washington, to General Abrams, COMUSMACV, Saigon, and Admiral McCain, CINCPAC, Hawaii.* 27 Mar. 1969.

67. Stewart, 341; Politico. Downloaded from the internet on 26 Jul. 2017 at http://www.politico.com/story/2013/04/this-day-in-politics-089554.

68. Stewart, 342.

69. Joint Chiefs of Staff. *Back Channel Message from General Wheeler, CJCS, Washington, to Admiral McCain, CINCPAC, Hawaii, and General Abrams, COMUSMACV, Saigon.* 28 Mar. 1969.

70. Stewart, 342-344.

71. Ibid.

72. Ibid.

73. Ibid.

74. Ibid.

75. Ibid.

76. Herring, 277; Herspring, 197.

77. Joint Chiefs of Staff. *Back Channel Message from General Wheeler, CJCS, Washington, to Admiral McCain, CINCPAC, Hawaii, and General Abrams, COMUSMACV, Saigon.* 31 May 1969.

78. Stewart, 345-348.

79. Joint Chiefs of Staff. Office of the Chairman of the Joint Chiefs of Staff. *Photo Album for General Earle G. Wheeler, Chairman, 1968-1969.* Jul. 1970; Millet, Maslowski, and Feis, 547.

80. Millet, Maslowski, and Feis, 547.

81. Joint Chiefs of Staff. Office of the Chairman of the Joint Chiefs of Staff. *Memorandum for the Secretary of Defense, Subject: Post-Hostilities Planning for Vietnam (U). CM-3980-69.* 5 Mar. 1969.

82. Joint Chiefs of Staff. *Back Channel Message from General Wheeler, CJCS, Washington, to General Abrams, COMUSMACV, Saigon.* 13 Mar.1969.

83. Kissinger, 272.

84. Kissinger, 35; Herring, 277.

85. Kissinger, 272-273.

86. Herspring, 197.

87. Herring, 277; Millet, Maslowski, and Feis, 547.

88. Kissinger, 261-263.

89. Ibid.

90. Herring, 279.

91. Westmoreland, 387; Millet, Maslowski, and Feis, 548.

92. Millet, Maslowski, and Feis, 548-550.

93. Ibid.

94. Ibid.

95. Petitt, 376.

96. Petitt, 376.

97. Millet, Maslowski, and Feis, 544.

98. Millet, Maslowski, and Feis, 547-548.

99. Herspring, 195-196.

100. Herspring, 196.

101. Ibid.

102. Herspring, 196-197.

103. Stewart, 345-348.

104. Stewart, 348-349.

105. Ibid.

106. Stewart, 345; Millet, Maslowski, and Feis, 547-548.

107. Millet, Maslowski, and Feis, 546.

108. Ibid.

109. Ibid.

110. Ibid.

111. Herring, 280-281.

112. Prados. *Vietnam.* 307.

113. Millet, Maslowski, and Feis, 546; Herring, 281-282.

114. Petitt, 380.

115. Herring, 281-282.

116. Millet, Maslowski, and Feis, 546.

117. Herring, 282.

118. Stewart, 349.

119. Stewart, 349-350.

Chapter 10

1. Joint Chiefs of Staff. Office of the Chairman of the Joint Chiefs of Staff. *Memorandum for General Wheeler, Subject: Proposed Response by CJCS.* 7 Jan. 1969.

2. Joint Chiefs of Staff. Office of the Chairman of the Joint Chiefs of Staff. *Photo Album for General Earle G. Wheeler, Chairman, 1969-1970.* Jul. 1970.

3. Herring, 285-287.

4. Millet, Maslowski, and Feis, 550.

5. Ibid; Stewart, 344-345.

6. Stewart, 344-345.

7. Joint Chiefs of Staff. Office of the Chairman of the Joint Chiefs of Staff. *Photo Album for General Earle G. Wheeler, Chairman, 1969-1970.* Jul. 1970; Kissinger, 480.

8. Herspring, 199-200.

9. Herring, 287-288.

10. Stewart, 281.

11. Kissinger, 290.

12. Kissinger, 479.

13. Herring, 290.

14. Millet, Maslowski, and Feis, 552; Stewart, 350-351.

15. Millet, 552.

16. Herring, 290.

17. Stewart, 350.

18. Stewart, 350-351; Herring, 276; Prados. *Vietnam.* 295; Millet, Maslowski, and Feis, 552.

19. Johnson, Lyndon B. Letter to Earle G. Wheeler. 15 Apr. 1970.

20. United States Army. Walter Reed General Hospital. *Clinical Record, Earle G. Wheeler.* 22 Apr. 1970.

21. Kissinger, 489-490, 495.

22. Kissinger, 495: 499; Herspring, 201.

23. Herring, 290-291.

24. Kissinger, 498.

25. Herring, 290; Millet, Maslowski, and Feis, 552.

26. Porter, 545-547; Petitt, 397.

27. Porter, 545-547.

28. Ibid.

29. Ibid.

30. Stewart, 351.

31. Joint Chiefs of Staff. Office of the Chairman of the Joint Chiefs of Staff. *Statement by General Earle G. Wheeler, USA, Chairman of the Joint Chiefs of Staff, Before the Department of Defense Subcommittee on Appropriations, House Appropriations Committee.* 4 May 1970.

32. Ibid.

33. Stewart, 272.

34. Kissinger, 511.

35. Stewart, 272; Ed Gallucci Photography. Downloaded from the internet on 22 Aug. 2017 at http://www.edgalluciphotography.com/march-washington-d-c-may-10-1970/.

36. Kissinger, 507.

37. Petitt, 400.

38. Millet, Maslowski, and Feis, 552-553; Stewart, 351-353; Herring, 292.

39. Ibid.

40. Petitt, 400.

41. Millet, Maslowski, and Feis, 553.

42. Wheeler, Earle G. Interview with Dorothy P. McSweeny. Interview I, 21 Aug. 1969: 30.

43. Ibid.

44. Millet, Maslowski, and Feis, 553.

45. Herring, 292-293; Stewart, 352-353.

46. Millet, Maslowski, and Feis, 553.

47. Stewart, 352-353; Millet, Maslowski, and Feis, 553.

48. Kissinger, 507.

49. Herring, 295-296.

50. Millet, Maslowski, and Feis, 553-554.

51. Herring, 292-293; Millet, Maslowski, and Feis, 553.

52. Herring, 295-296.

53. Herring, 292-293, 295-296; Millet, Maslowski, and Feis, 553-554.

54. Department of Defense. Brochure. *In Honor of General Earle G. Wheeler, Chairman, Joint Chiefs of Staff, Andrews Air Force Base, Maryland, 2 July 1970*: Jul. 70; Joint Chiefs of Staff. Office of the Chairman of the Joint Chiefs of Staff. *Photo Album for General Earle G. Wheeler, Chairman, 1970.* Jul. 1970; Wheeler, Gilmore S. *Untitled Monograph*; Source unknown. *Chiefs Chairman Gen. Wheeler Retires Today.* 2 Jul. 1970.

55. Source unknown. *Chiefs Chairman Gen. Wheeler Retires Today.* 2 Jul. 1970.

56. Ibid.

Chapter 11

1. New York Herald-Tribune. *Gen. Wheeler, New U.S. Top Military Man.* 19 Aug. 1964: 22.

2. Warontherocks.com. *Iraq and Longing for Vietnam.* Downloaded 15 Jul. 2014.

3. Joint Chiefs of Staff. Office of the Chairman of the Joint Chiefs of Staff. *Photo Album for General Earle G. Wheeler, Chairman, 1970.* Jul. 1970.

4. Petitt, 402.

5. Herring, 297; Millet, Maslowski, and Feis, 554; Stewart, 353.

6. Herring, 297; Millet, Maslowski, and Feis, 554; Stewart, 353.

7. Kissinger, 999-1000.

8. Wheeler, Gilmore. Interviews with Mark Viney. 25 Feb. and 10 Mar. 2013.

9. Kissinger, 999-1000.

10. Ibid.

11. Millet, Maslowski, and Feis, 555; Stewart, 353-355.

12. Stewart, 353-355.

13. Kissinger, 102.

14. Kissinger, 992.

15. Stewart, 355; Millet, Maslowski, and Feis, 555.

16. Stewart, 355-356.

17. Stewart, 356-358; Millet, Maslowski, and Feis, 555.

18. Stewart, 357-358.

19. Kissinger, 1009; Stewart, 358; Millet, Maslowski, and Feis, 555-556.

20. Petitt, 409.

21. Millet, Maslowski, and Feis, 555-556.

22. Herring, 300.

23. Millet, Maslowski, and Feis, 551.

24. Stewart, 272-273.

25. Herring, 296-297.

26. Stewart, 359.

27. Herring, 297.

28. Millet, Maslowski, and Feis, 551.

29. Millet, Maslowski, and Feis, 556; Herring, 304.

30. Herring, 304-305; Millet, Maslowski, and Feis, 557.

31. Herring, 305-307.

32. Millet, Maslowski, and Feis, 557.

33. Kissinger, 983; Herring, 307.

34. Summers, 156; Herring, 307; Millet, Maslowski, and Feis, 557.

35. Herring, 307; Millet, Maslowski, and Feis, 557.

36. Millet, Maslowski, and Feis, 557-558.

37. Ibid.

38. Herring, 309; Millet, Maslowski, and Feis, 557-558.

39. Millet, Maslowski, and Feis, 557-558.

40. Stewart, 362.

41. Herring, 307-308.

42. Ibid.

43. Stewart, 362; Millet, Maslowski, and Feis, 558.

44. Herring, 309-310.

45. Millet, Maslowski, and Feis, 562-563.

46. Ibid.

47. Millet, Maslowski, and Feis, 563; Herring, 316; Summers, 156-157.

48. Summers, 156-157.

49. Millet, Maslowski, and Feis, 563-564.

50. Ibid.

51. Wheeler, Gilmore S. Interview with Mark A. Viney. 9 Oct. 2013.

52. Kissinger, 34-35.

53. Stewart, Bill. Interviews with Mark A. Viney. 20 Oct. and 7 Nov. 2013; Wheeler, Gilmore S. Interview with Mark A. Viney. 9 Oct. 2013.

54. Wheeler, Gilmore. Email to Mark Viney. 4 Apr. 2011; Wheeler, Gilmore. Interviews with Mark Viney. 25 Feb. and 10 Mar. 2013; Perry, 211.

55. Sharp and Westmoreland, xvii.

56. Congress. *Cambodia Hearings.* 157.

57. Millet, Maslowski, and Feis, 564.

58. Wheeler, Gilmore. Interviews with Mark Viney. 3 Jul. 2014 and 20 Apr. 2016.

59. Westmoreland, 389; Millet, Maslowski, and Feis, 551-552; Prados. *Vietnam,* 294.

60. Arlington National Cemetery. Downloaded from the internet on 13 Feb. 2013 from htp://www.arlingtoncemetery.net/ewheeler.htm.

61. Congress. *Cambodia Hearings.*132-133.

62. Ibid.

63. Ibid.

64. Ibid.

65. The New York Times. *Gen. Earle Wheeler Dies; Ex-Head of Joint Chiefs.* 19 Dec. 1975.

66. Congress. *Cambodia Hearings,* 137.

67. Congress. *Cambodia Hearings,* 139-140.

68. Congress. *Cambodia Hearings,* 160, 163-164.

69. Congress. *Cambodia Hearings,* 180, 189.

70. Millet, Maslowski, and Feis, 564.

71. Stewart, 363; Millet, Maslowski, and Feis, 564.

72. Millet, Maslowski, and Feis, 564-565.

73. Millet, Maslowski, and Feis, 565.

74. Stewart, 364, 565.

75. Millet, Maslowski, and Feis, 565-566.

76. Millet, Maslowski, and Feis, 566; Stewart, 365-366.

77. Wheeler, Gilmore. Interview with Mark Viney. 25 Feb. 2013; Warontherocks.com. *Iraq and Longing for Vietnam*. Downloaded on 26 Jan. 2016.

78. Gilmore S. Wheeler, Interview with Mark Viney, Carlisle, PA, 9 Jun. 2010: 1.

79. Ibid.

80. Palmer, Dave R. 111.

81. Warontherocks.com. *Iraq and Longing for Vietnam*. Downloaded on 26 Jan. 2016.

82. Westmoreland, 425.

83. Warontherocks.com. *Iraq and Longing for Vietnam*. Downloaded on 26 Jan. 2016.

84. Westmoreland, 121.

85. Westmoreland, 410.

86. Westmoreland, 413.

87. Jordan, 117, 118, 144, 182.

88. Jordan, 119.

89. Dorland, 42.

90. Dorland, 204-205.

91. Dorland, 158.

92. Warontherocks.com. *Iraq and Longing for Vietnam*. Downloaded on 26 Jan. 2016.

93. Prados. *Vietnam*. 542, 545-546.

94. Warontherocks.com. *Iraq and Longing for Vietnam*. Downloaded on 26 Jan. 2016.

95. Kissinger, 996-997.

96. Dorland, 172.

97. Boston Globe. *What Victory Means Now*. 27 Jan. 2013.

98. Summers, 105.

99. Daddis, 178-179.

100. Veterans Administration. Veterans Benefits Office. *Letter to Earle G. Wheeler.* 10 Jul. 1970; Spivy, 744; Wheeler, Gilmore S. Interview with Mark A. Viney. 3 Jul. 2014.

101. State of Maryland. Department of Health and Mental Hygiene. *Medical Examiner's Certificate of Death.* 30 Dec. 1975; Charleston Gazette. *Former Joint Chiefs Head, Wheeler, Dies.* 19 Dec. 1975; The Charlotte Observer. *Gen. Earle Wheeler, Ex-Military Chief.* 19 Dec. 1975; The Martinsburg Journal. *Gen. Wheeler Dies; County Resident Former JCS Head.* 19 Dec. 1975; Arlington National Cemetery. Downloaded from the internet on 13 Feb. 2013 from http:// www.arlingtoncemetery.net/ewheeler.htm; Wheeler, Gilmore. Interview with Mark Viney. 10 Mar. 2013.

102. Wheeler, Gilmore. Email to Mark Viney. 4 Apr. 2011.

103. Scribner, 253-255.

104. Perry, 168, 210-211.

105. Winstonchurchill.org. Downloaded from the internet on 2 Nov. 2017 at https://www.winstonchurchill.org/resources/speeches/1940-the-finst-hour/ blood-toil-tears-sweat.

BIBLIOGRAPHY

Books

Anderson, David L., ed. *Shadow on the White House: Presidents and the Vietnam War, 1945-1975*. Lawrence, KS: University Press of Kansas, 1993.

Armstrong, David A. Editor. *The Joint Chiefs of Staff and the First Indochina War, 1947-1954*. Washington, DC: Office of Joint History, 2004.

Barrett, David M. Gen. ed. *Lyndon B. Johnson's Vietnam Papers: A Documentary Collection*. College Station, TX: Texas A&M University Press, 1998.

Bell, William G. *Commanding Generals and Chiefs of Staff, 1775-1991, Portraits & Biographical Sketches of the United States Army's Senior Officer*. Washington DC: United States Army Center of Military History, 1992.

Bell, William G. *Secretaries of War and Secretaries of the Army, Portraits & Biographical Sketches*. Washington DC: United States Army Center of Military History, 1982.

Berman, Larry. *Lyndon Johnson's War: The Road the Stalemate in Vietnam*. New York: Norton, 1989.

Bowman, John S. *The Vietnam War: An Almanac*. New York: World Almanac Publications, 1985.

Buzzanco, Robert. *Masters of War: Military Dissent and Politics in the Vietnam Era*. Cambridge; New York: Cambridge University Press, 1996.

Cable, Larry. *Unholy Grail: The U.S. and the Wars in Vietnam, 1965-8*. New York: Routledge, 1991.

Chomsky, Noam, ed. *The Pentagon Papers: The Defense Department History of United States Decisionmaking on Vietnam*. The Senator Gravel Edition. 5 vols. Boston: Beacon Press, 1971-1972.

Collins, J. Lawton. *War in Peacetime, The History and Lessons of Korea*. Boston: Houghton Miflin, 1969.

Collins, J. Lawton. *Lightning Joe: An Autobiography*. Baton Rouge, LA: Louisiana State University Press, 1979.

Cooper, Charles G. *Cheers and Tears, A Marine's Story of Combat in Peace and War*. Victoria, BC: Trafford Publishing, 2002.

Daddis, Gregory A. *Westmoreland's War: Reassessing American Strategy in Vietnam*. Oxford: Oxford University Press, 2014.

Dorland, Gilbert N. *Legacy of Discord: Voices of the Vietnam Era*. Washington, DC: Brassey's, 2001.

Doyle, Edward & Samuel Lipsman. *The Vietnam Experience: America Takes Over, 1965-67*. Boston: Boston Publishing Co., 1982.

Davidson, Phillip B. *Secrets of the Vietnam War*. Novato, CA: Presidio Press, 1990.

Dugan, Clark and Weiss, Stephen. *Nineteen Sixty-Eight*. Boston: Boston Publishing Co., 1983.

Dunnigan, James F. & Albert A. Nofi. *Dirty Little Secrets of the Vietnam War*. New York: St. Martin's Press, 1999.

Gardner, Lloyd C. *Pay Any Price: Lyndon Johnson and the Wars for Vietnam*. Chicago: Ivan R. Dee, Inc., 1995.

Griess, Thomas E. Editor. *Definitions and Doctrine of the Military Art, Past and Present*. Wayne, New Jersey: Avery Publishing Group, Inc., 1985.

Johnson, Lady Bird. *A White House Diary*. Austin, TX: University of Texas Press, 2007.

Jordan, Robert S. *An Unsung Soldier, The Life of Gen. Andrew J. Goodpaster*. Annapolis: Naval Institute Press, 2013.

Hastings, Max. *Vietnam*. New York: Harper Perennial, 2018.

Herring, George C. *America's Longest War, The United States and Vietnam, 1950-1975*. Fourth Edition. Boston: McGraw Hill, 2002.

Herspring, Dale R. *The Pentagon and the Presidency, Civil-Military Relations from FDR to George W. Bush*. Lawrence, KS: University Press of Kansas, 2005.

Imparato, Edward T. *General MacArthur, Speeches and Reports, 1908-1964*. Paducah, Kentucky: Turner Publishing, 2000.

Kissinger, Henry A. *White House Years*. Boston: Little, Brown, 1979.

Kozak, Warren. *The Life and Wars of General Curtis LeMay*. Washington, DC: Regnery Publishing, Inc., 2011.

Lamy, Perry L. *Barrel Roll: An Air Campaign in Support of National Policy*. Maxwell Air Force Base, AL: Air University Press, 1996.

Le Duan. *Ta Nhat Dinh Thang, Dich Nhat Dinh Thua (We Will Certainly Win, the Enemy Will Certainly Lose)*. South Vietnam: Tien Phong, 1966.

LeMay, Curtis E. and Kantor, MacKinlay. *Mission With LeMay: My Story*. Garden City, NY: Doubleday & Company, Inc., 1965.

McMaster, Herbert R. *Dereliction of Duty*. New York: HarperCollins Publishers, 1997.

McNamara, Robert S. *In Retrospect: The Tragedy and Lessons of Vietnam*. New York: Times Books, 1995.

Millet, Allan R., Maslowski, Peter, and Feis, William B. *For the Common Defense, A Military History of the United States from 1607 to 2012*. New York: Free Press, 2012.

Oberdorfer, Don. *Tet!* Garden City, NY: Doubleday & Company, Inc. 1971.

Odom, Louie W. *Challenging Journey: An Autobiography*. Publisher Unknown, 2008.

Palmer, Dave R. *Summons of the Trumpet: A History of the Vietnam War From a Military Man's Viewpoint*. New York: Ballantine Books, 1978.

Palmer, Bruce Jr. *The 25-Year War, America's Role on Vietnam*. New York: Da Capo Press, 1984.

Pearson, Willard. *The War in the Northern Provinces 1966-1968*. Washington, DC: Department of the Army, 1975.

Perry, Mark. *Four Stars*. Boston: Houghton Miflin, 1989.

Petitt, Clyde E. *The Experts*. Seacaucus, NJ: Lyle Stuart, Inc., 1975.

Porter, Gareth. *Vietnam: The Definitive Documentation of Human Decisions, Volume 2*. Stanfordville, NY: Earl M. Coleman Enterprises, Inc., 1979.

Prados, John. *The Blood Road, The Ho Chi Minh Trail and the Vietnam War*. New York: John Wiley & Sons, Inc., 1998.

Prados, John. *Vietnam, The History of an Unwinnable War, 1945-1975*. Lawrence, KS: University Press of Kansas, 2009.

Robinson, Norborne T.N. *The Vietnam Victory Option*. Middleburg, VA: The Gram Press, 1993.

Rostow, Walt W. *The Diffusion of Power: An Essay in Recent History*. New York: The Macmillan Company, 1972.

Rothmann, Harry. *Warriors and Fools: How America's Leaders Lost the Vietnam War and Why It Still Matters*. RCI Publications, 2018.

Schandler, Herbert Y. *The Unmaking of a President: Lyndon Johnson and Vietnam*. Princeton: Princeton University Press, 1977.

Schlesinger, Arthur M. Jr. *The Cycles of American History*. Boston: Houghton Mifflin Harcourt, 1999.

Sharp, U.S. Grant and Westmoreland, William C. *Report on the War in Vietnam (As of 30 June 1968)*. Washington, DC: U.S. Government Printing Office, 1968.

Sorley, Lewis B. *A Better War: The Unexamined Victories and the Final Tragedy of America's Last Years in Vietnam*. New York: Harcourt Brace & Co., 1999.

Sorley, Lewis B. *Honorable Warrior: General Harold K. Johnson and the Ethics of Command*. Lawrence, KS: University Press of Kansas, 1998.

Spector, Ronald. *After Tet: The Bloodiest Year in Vietnam*. New York: The Free Press, 1993.

Stewart, Richard. Gen. ed. *American Military History, Vol. II, The United States Army in a Global Era, 1917-2003*. Washington, DC: United States Army, Center of Military History, 2005.

Summers, Harry. *On Strategy: A Critical Analysis of the Vietnam War*. Novato, CA: Presidio Press, 1982.

The Senator Gravel Edition: The Pentagon Papers: The Defense Department History of United States Decisionmaking on Vietnam, Volumes III-V. Boston: Beacon Press, 1971.

Thorin, Duane. *The Need for Civilian Authority Over the Military*. Bryn Mawr, PA: Intercollegiate Studies Institute, Inc., 1968. This paper was published in February 1968 and does not reflect an influence from the Tet Offensive, which the Communists initiated on 30-31 January 1968.

Tucker, Spencer C. *The Encyclopedia of the Vietnam War: A Political, Social, and Military History*. 2nd Edition. Santa Barbara, CA: ABC-CLIO, Inc., 2011.

Watson, George M. *Secretaries and Chiefs of Staff of the United States Air Force*. Washington, DC: Air Force History and Museums Program, 2001.

Webb, Willard J. and Cole, Ronald H. *The Chairmen of the Joint Chiefs of Staff*. Washington, DC: Historical Division, Joint Chiefs of Staff, 1989.

Werner, Jayne S. & Luu Doan Huynh, eds. *The Vietnam War: Vietnamese and American Perspectives*. Armonk, NY: Sharpe, Inc., 1993.

Westmoreland, William C. *A Soldier Reports*. Garden City, NY: Doubleday & Company, Inc., 1976.

Interviews, Speeches & Lectures

Casey, George W. *Speech to U.S. Army War College*. 23 Sep. 2008. Author's Records.

Casey, George W. *Conversation with Mark A. Viney*. 25 Apr. 2018. Author's Records.

Clodfelter, Mark. *Lecture: The Air Wars in Vietnam*. Pentagon Library. 3 Mar. 16. Author's Records.

Covello, Hank. *Interview with Mark A. Viney.* 7 Jun. 2013. Handwritten notes. Author's Records.

Johnson, Harold K. *Interview with Rupert F. Glover,* United States Army Military History Institute, Senior Officer Oral History Program, Volume III, 1978. Transcription.

Spivy, Berton E. *Interview with James Durham and Nelson Wood,* United States Army Military History Institute, Senior Officer Debriefing Program, Volume I, Section VI, 1 Dec. 1972. Transcription.

Stewart, Bill. *Interview with Mark A. Viney.* 20 Oct. 2013. Handwritten notes. Author's Records.

Stewart, Bill. *Interview with Mark A. Viney.* 7 Nov. 2013. Handwritten notes. Author's Records.

Viney, George C. *Interviews with Mark A. Viney.* 30 Apr. 2007 – 17 Dec. 2010. Transcription and handwritten notes. Author's Records.

Wheeler, Earle G. *Interview with Dorothy P. McSweeny.* Interview I, 21 Aug. 1969. Transcription. Wheeler Family Records.

Wheeler, Earle G. *Interview with Dorothy P. McSweeny.* Interview II, 7 May 1970. Transcription. Wheeler Family Records.

Frances R. Wheeler. *Interviews with Gilmore S. Wheeler,* 2003-2004. Audio files on 9 disks. Wheeler Family Records.

Wheeler, Gilmore S. *Interview with Mark A. Viney.* 16 Feb. 2010. Handwritten notes. Author's Records.

Wheeler, Gilmore S. *Interview with Mark A. Viney.* 9 Jun. 2010. Handwritten notes. Author's Records.

Wheeler, Gilmore S. *Interview with Mark A. Viney.* 8 Nov. 2010. Handwritten notes. Author's Records.

Wheeler, Gilmore S. *Interview with Mark A. Viney.* 25 Feb. 2013. Handwritten notes. Author's Records.

Wheeler, Gilmore S. *Interview with Mark A. Viney.* 10 Mar. 2013. Handwritten notes. Author's Records.

Wheeler, Gilmore S. *Interview with Mark A. Viney.* 14 Mar. 2013. Handwritten notes. Author's Records.

Wheeler, Gilmore S. *Interview with Mark A. Viney.* 24 Apr. 2013. Handwritten notes. Author's Records.

Wheeler, Gilmore S. *Interview with Mark A. Viney.* 14 May 2013. Handwritten notes. Author's Records.

Wheeler, Gilmore S. *Interview with Mark A. Viney.* 9 Oct. 2013. Handwritten notes. Author's Records.

Wheeler, Gilmore S. *Interview with Mark A. Viney.* 3 Jul. 2014. Handwritten notes. Author's Records.

Wheeler, Gilmore S. *Interview with Mark A. Viney.* 28 Aug. 2014. Handwritten notes. Author's Records.

Official Documents

Central Intelligence Agency. *Memorandum, Subject: Reactions to a Further US Buildup in South Vietnam (U).* 10 Jun. 1965. Found in Joint Chiefs of Staff, Chairman (GEN) Earle G. Wheeler, Official Records, Joint Chiefs of Staff, 3 July 64 – 2 July 70, National Archives at College Park, MD. Hereafter cited as Wheeler NARA Records.

Central Intelligence Agency. *Special National Intelligence Estimate, SNIE 10-1-66, Possible Effects of a Proposed US Course of Action on DRV Capability to Support the Insurgency in South Vietnam (U).* 4 Feb. 1966. Wheeler NARA Records.

Department of Defense. Brochure. *In Honor of General Earle G. Wheeler, Chairman, Joint Chiefs of Staff, Andrews Air Force Base, Maryland, 2 July 1970*: Jul. 70. Wheeler Family Records.

Department of Defense. *DD Form 214, General Earle G. Wheeler.* 3 Jul. 1970. Wheeler Family Records.

Department of Defense. Office of the Secretary of Defense. *Memorandum: For the President (U).* 30 Jul. 1965. Wheeler NARA Records.

Department of Defense. *United States Vietnam Relations, 1945-1967 (aka The Pentagon Papers)* (12 books; Washington, DC: United States Government Printing Office, 1971. Pentagon Library.

Department of State. *Memorandum of Conversation with Soviet Ambassador Anatoliy Dobrynin by Deputy Under Secretary Foy D. Kohler (U).* 12 Apr. 1967. Wheeler NARA Records.

Department of the Army. *Backchannel Message from Johnson CSA Washington to Wheeler CJCS MACV (U).* 8 Jul. 1967. Wheeler NARA Records.

Department of the Army. *Biography of Colonel George Catron Viney.* 20 Jun. 1974. Author's Records.

Department of the Army. *DA Form 66.* 15 Feb. 1969. Wheeler Family Records.

Department of the Army. *General H.K. Johnson Daily Calendars.* Military History Institute Collection, H.K. Johnson Papers, Series I, Subseries I, Box 157, Book 3.

Department of the Army. Office of the Chief of Staff of the Army. Photo Album. *General Earle G. Wheeler, Chief of Staff, United States Army, October 1962, Chairman of the Joint Chiefs of Staff, July 1964.* Jul. 1964. Wheeler Family Records.

Department of the Army. Office of the Chief of Staff of the Army. *The Origins of the Post-Tet 1968 Plans for Additional American Forces in RVN (U).* 9 Nov. 1970. Wheeler NARA Records.

Department of the Army. *Resume of Service Career of John Rutherford McGiffert II, Lieutenant General.* 1 April 1977. Author's Records.

Department of the Army. U.S. Army Physical Review Council. *Memorandum, Subject: Review of Proceedings of the Physical Valuation Board.* 28 May 1970. Wheeler Family Records.

Department of Defense. *Ceremony Program, In Honor of General Earle G. Wheeler, Chairman, Joint Chiefs of Staff, Andrews Air Force Base, Maryland.* 13 Feb. 1969. Wheeler Family Records.

Department of Defense. Office of the Secretary of Defense. *Memorandum for the President, Subject: Increased Authorities for Southeast Asia (U).* 2 Jul. 1970. Wheeler NARA Records.

Federal Bureau of Investigation. *Case File, Earle G. Wheeler (U)*. 15 Jul. 1971. Redacted. Wheeler Family Records.

Joint Chiefs of Staff. *Addresses by General Earle G. Wheeler, Chairman, Joint Chiefs of Staff, Vol. II, 7 July 1964 to 2 July 1970*. Washington, DC: Joint Staff Historical Office, no date. Pentagon Library.

Joint Chiefs of Staff. *A Study Group Report on Intensification of the Military Operations in Vietnam Concept and Appraisal (U)*. 14 Jul. 1965. Wheeler NARA Records.

Joint Chiefs of Staff. *A Study Group Report on the Feasibility of a Limited Lodgement Operation into Southern North Vietnam (U)*. 31 May 1967. Wheeler NARA Records. Wheeler's copy #1 of this document is believed to be the only copy of 150 printed still extant.

Joint Chiefs of Staff. *Back Channel Message from General Wheeler, CJCS, Washington, to Admiral McCain, CINCPAC, Hawaii, and General Abrams, COMUSMACV, Saigon (U)*. 28 Mar. 1969. Wheeler NARA Records.

Joint Chiefs of Staff. *Back Channel Message from General Wheeler, CJCS, Washington, to Admiral McCain, CINCPAC, Hawaii, and General Abrams, COMUSMACV, Saigon (U)*. 31 May 1969. Wheeler NARA Records.

Joint Chiefs of Staff. *Back Channel Message from General Wheeler, CJCS, Washington, to Admiral Sharp, CINCPAC, Hawaii (U)*. 16 May 1967. Wheeler NARA Records.

Joint Chiefs of Staff. *Back Channel Message from General Wheeler, CJCS, Washington, to Admiral Sharp, CINCPAC, Hawaii, and General Westmoreland, COMUSMACV, Saigon (U)*. 1 Feb. 1968. Wheeler NARA Records.

Joint Chiefs of Staff. *Back Channel Message from General Wheeler, CJCS, Washington, to Admiral Sharp, CINCPAC, Hawaii, and General Westmoreland, COMUSMACV, Saigon (U)*. 6 Feb. 1968. Wheeler NARA Records.

Joint Chiefs of Staff. *Back Channel Message from General Wheeler, CJCS, Washington, to General Abrams, COMUSMACV, Saigon (U)*. 13 Mar.1969. Wheeler NARA Records.

Joint Chiefs of Staff. *Back Channel Message from General Wheeler, CJCS, Washington, to General Abrams, COMUSMACV, Saigon, and Admiral McCain, CINCPAC, Hawaii (U)*. 16 Oct.1968. Wheeler NARA Records.

Joint Chiefs of Staff. *Back Channel Message from General Wheeler, CJCS, Washington, to General Abrams, COMUSMACV, Saigon, and Admiral McCain, CINCPAC, Hawaii (U)*. 25 Mar. 1969. Wheeler NARA Records.

Joint Chiefs of Staff. *Back Channel Message from General Wheeler, CJCS, Washington, to General Abrams, COMUSMACV, Saigon, and Admiral McCain, CINCPAC, Hawaii (U)*. 27 Mar. 1969. Wheeler NARA Records.

Joint Chiefs of Staff. *Back Channel Message from General Wheeler, CJCS, Washington, to General Nazarro, Acting CINCPAC, Hawaii, and General Abrams, COMUSMACV, Saigon (U)*. 22 Jan. 1969. Wheeler NARA Records.

Joint Chiefs of Staff. *Earle G. Wheeler Papers, Chairman, Joint Chiefs of Staff, Calendar of Events, 1 Jan – 31 Dec 1967*. Wheeler NARA Records.

Joint Chiefs of Staff. *Front Channel Message from Captain H. B. Sweitzer, Military Assistant (L & L) to the Chairman, Office of the Chairman of the Joint Chiefs of Staff, Washington, to Admiral Sharp, CINCPAC, Hawaii*. 11 Aug. 1967. Wheeler NARA Records.

Joint Chiefs of Staff. *Front Channel Message from Captain H. B. Sweitzer, Military Assistant (L & L) to the Chairman, Office of the Chairman of the Joint Chiefs of Staff, Washington, to Admiral Sharp, CINCPAC, Hawaii (U)*. 15 Aug. 1967. Wheeler NARA Records.

Joint Chiefs of Staff. *Front Channel Message from Lieutenant General Berton E. Spivy, Director, Joint Staff, Washington, to Admiral Sharp, CINCPAC, Hawaii (U)*. 8 Sep. 1966. Wheeler NARA Records.

Joint Chiefs of Staff. *Front Channel Message from Major General John P. Mize, Vice Director, Joint Staff, Washington, to Admiral Sharp, CINCPAC, Hawaii (U)*. 9 Feb. 1967. Wheeler NARA Records.

Joint Chiefs of Staff. *Front Channel Message from Rear Admiral H. J. Truman III, National Military Command Center, Washington, to Admiral Sharp, CINCPAC, Hawaii (U).* 30 Jul. 1967. Wheeler NARA Records.

Joint Chiefs of Staff. *Impact of the NVA/VC Build-up at the DMZ, 1966-1967 (U).* 11 Jul. 1967. Wheeler NARA Records.

Joint Chiefs of Staff. *Memorandum for the Chairman, Joint Chiefs of Staff, Subject: Ad Hoc Study Group, Report of, DJSM-672-67 (U).* 31 May 1967. Wheeler NARA Records.

Joint Chiefs of Staff. *Memorandum for the Chairman, Joint Chiefs of Staff, Subject: CINCPAC Planning for Ground Operations North of the DMZ, DJSM-1270-67 (U).* 16 Oct. 1967. Wheeler NARA Records.

Joint Chiefs of Staff. *Memorandum for the Chairman, Joint Chiefs of Staff, Subject: Low-Level B-52 Strikes in DMZ Area, DJSM-422-67 (U).* 7 Apr. 1967. Wheeler NARA Records.

Joint Chiefs of Staff. *Memorandum for the Chairman, Joint Chiefs of Staff, Subject: Operation HICKORY (U).* 16 May 67. Wheeler NARA Records.

Joint Chiefs of Staff. *Memorandum for the Chairman, Joint Chiefs of Staff, Subject: U.S. Objectives in Vietnam, DJSM-556-67 (U).* 5 May 1967. Wheeler NARA Records.

Joint Chiefs of Staff. *Memorandum for the J-30, Subject: CINCPACFLT Planning Conference; Report of (U),* 20 Sep. 1967. Wheeler NARA Records.

Joint Chiefs of Staff. *Memorandum for the Secretary of Defense, JCSM-307-67 (U).* 1 Jun. 1967. Wheeler NARA Records.

Joint Chiefs of Staff. *Memorandum for the Secretary of Defense, JCSM-91-68 (U).* 12 Feb. 1968. Wheeler NARA Records.

Joint Chiefs of Staff. *Memorandum for the Secretary of Defense, Subject: MACV Practice Nine Requirements Plan, JCSM-97-67 (U).* 22 Feb. 1967. Wheeler NARA Records.

Joint Chiefs of Staff. *Memorandum for the Secretary of Defense, Subject: Recommendations for Providing Practice Nine Forces, JCSM-162-67 (U).* 23 Mar. 1967. Wheeler NARA Records.

Joint Chiefs of Staff. *Memorandum for the Secretary of Defense, Subject: Worldwide U.S. Military Posture, JCSM-288-67 (U)*. 20 May 1967. Wheeler NARA Records.

Joint Chiefs of Staff. Office of the Chairman of the Joint Chiefs of Staff. *Memorandum for Admiral David L. McDonald, CNO, General H. K. Johnson, CSA, General J. P. McConnell, CSAF, General Wallace M. Greene, CMC, CM-2434-67 (U)*. 13 Jun. 1967. Wheeler NARA Records.

Joint Chiefs of Staff. Office of the Chairman of the Joint Chiefs of Staff. *Memorandum for Admiral David L. McDonald, CNO, General H. K. Johnson, CSA, General J. P. McConnell, CSAF, General Wallace M. Greene, CMC, CM-2461-67 (U)*. 20 Jun. 1967. Wheeler NARA Records.

Joint Chiefs of Staff. Office of the Chairman of the Joint Chiefs of Staff. *Memorandum for Admiral David L. McDonald, CNO, General H. K. Johnson, CSA, General J. P. McConnell, CSAF, General Wallace M. Greene, CMC, CM-2373-67 (U)*. 23 May. 1967. Wheeler NARA Records.

Joint Chiefs of Staff. Office of the Chairman of the Joint Chiefs of Staff. *Memorandum for All Pacific Commanders (U)*. 30 Mar. 1968. Wheeler NARA Records.

Joint Chiefs of Staff. Office of the Chairman of the Joint Chiefs of Staff. *Memorandum for General Bradley, Subject: Vietnam Trip, CM-2547-67 (U)*. 1 Aug. 1967. Wheeler NARA Records.

Joint Chiefs of Staff. Office of the Chairman of the Joint Chiefs of Staff. *Memorandum for the Deputy Secretary of Defense, Subject: Situation in the DMZ Area and Program 5 Accelerated Deployments, CM-2668-67 (U)*. 28 Sep. 1967. Wheeler NARA Records.

Joint Chiefs of Staff. Office of the Chairman of the Joint Chiefs of Staff. *Memorandum for the Director, Joint Staff, Subject: Cambodia, CM-3879-69 (U)*. 22 Jan. 1969. Wheeler NARA Records.

Joint Chiefs of Staff. Office of the Chairman of the Joint Chiefs of Staff. *Memorandum for the Director, Joint Staff, Subject: Operating Authorities, CM-3880-69 (U)*. 22 Jan. 1969. Wheeler NARA Records.

Joint Chiefs of Staff. Office of the Chairman of the Joint Chiefs of Staff. *Memorandum for the Director, Joint Staff, Subject: Policies for the Conduct of Operations in SEA over the Next Four Months, CM-2752-67 (U)*. 10 Nov. 1967. Wheeler NARA Records.

Joint Chiefs of Staff. Office of the Chairman of the Joint Chiefs of Staff. *Memorandum for the Director, Joint Staff, Subject: Pressure on North Vietnam, CM-3877-69 (U)*. 22 Jan. 1969. Wheeler NARA Records.

Joint Chiefs of Staff. Office of the Chairman of the Joint Chiefs of Staff. *Memorandum for the Director, Joint Staff, Subject: U.S. Military Posture, CM-2255-67 (U)*, 20 Apr. 1967. Wheeler NARA Records.

Joint Chiefs of Staff. Office of the Chairman of the Joint Chiefs of Staff. *Memorandum for General Maxwell D. Taylor, Subject: Military Posture (U)*. 8 Feb. 1968. Wheeler NARA Records.

Joint Chiefs of Staff. Office of the Chairman of the Joint Chiefs of Staff. *Memorandum for General Wheeler, Subject: Proposed Response by CJCS (U)*. 7 Jan. 1969. Wheeler NARA Records.

Joint Chiefs of Staff. Office of the Chairman of the Joint Chiefs of Staff. *Memorandum for the Chief of Staff, Army; Chief of Naval Operations; Chief of Staff, Air Force; Commandant Marine Corps; Director, Defense Intelligence Agency; Director, National Security Agency, Subject: Deception, CM-3004-68 (U)*. 12 Feb. 1968. Wheeler NARA Records.

Joint Chiefs of Staff. Office of the Chairman of the Joint Chiefs of Staff. *Memorandum for the Chief of Staff, U.S. Army; Chief of Staff, U.S. Air Force; Chief of Naval Operations; Commandant, U.S. Marine Corps; Director, Joint Staff, Subject: Force Posture, CM-2976-68 (U)*. 16 Feb. 1968. Wheeler NARA Records.

Joint Chiefs of Staff. Office of the Chairman of the Joint Chiefs of Staff. *Memorandum for General H. K. Johnson, CSA, General J. P. McConnell, CSAF, Admiral T. L. Moorer, CNO, General W. M. Greene, Jr., CMC, CM-2754-67 (U)*. 13 Nov. 1967. Wheeler NARA Records.

Joint Chiefs of Staff. Office of the Chairman of the Joint Chiefs of Staff. *Memorandum for the President, Subject: Khe Sanh, CM-2944-68 (U)*. 3 Feb. 1968. Wheeler NARA Records.

Joint Chiefs of Staff. Office of the Chairman of the Joint Chiefs of Staff. *Memorandum for the President, Subject: Military Posture Comparisons in Vietnam (U), CM-3423-68*. 24 Jun. 1968. Wheeler NARA Records.

Joint Chiefs of Staff. Office of the Chairman of the Joint Chiefs of Staff. *Memorandum for the Secretary of Defense, Subject: Additional Authorities Recommended for Operations in Laos, CM-3894-69 (U)*. 28 Jan. 1969. Wheeler NARA Records.

Joint Chiefs of Staff. Office of the Chairman of the Joint Chiefs of Staff. *Memorandum for the Secretary of Defense, Subject: Additional Authorities Recommended for Operations in South Vietnam Border Areas, CM-3895-69 (U)*. 29 Jan. 1969. Wheeler NARA Records.

Joint Chiefs of Staff. Office of the Chairman of the Joint Chiefs of Staff. *Memorandum for the Secretary of Defense, Subject: Authority for B-52 Strikes against Targets in Cambodia (U), CM-4003-69*. 13 Mar. 1969. Wheeler NARA Records.

Joint Chiefs of Staff. Office of the Chairman of the Joint Chiefs of Staff. *Memorandum for the Secretary of Defense, Subject: Increased Authorities for Southeast Asia, CM-3941-69 (U)*. 13 Feb. 1969. Wheeler NARA Records.

Joint Chiefs of Staff. Office of the Chairman of the Joint Chiefs of Staff. *Memorandum for the Secretary of Defense, Subject: Mining Plans for Haiphong (U). CM-4006-69*. 13 Mar. 1969. Wheeler NARA Records.

Joint Chiefs of Staff. Office of the Chairman of the Joint Chiefs of Staff. *Memorandum for the Secretary of Defense, Subject: Northeast Monsoon Campaign Planning, CM-3662-68 (U)*. 20 Sep. 1968. Wheeler NARA Records.

Joint Chiefs of Staff. Office of the Chairman of the Joint Chiefs of Staff. *Memorandum for the Secretary of Defense, Subject: Observations and*

Recommendations Concerning the Military Situation in Southeast Asia. CM-4001-69 (U). 12 Mar. 1969. Wheeler NARA Records.

Joint Chiefs of Staff. Office of the Chairman of the Joint Chiefs of Staff. *Memorandum for the Secretary of Defense, Subject: Observations on Stennis Hearings, 16 August, CM-2595-67 (U).* 16 Aug. 1967. Wheeler NARA Records.

Joint Chiefs of Staff. Office of the Chairman of the Joint Chiefs of Staff. *Memorandum for the Secretary of Defense, Subject: Post-Hostilities Planning for Vietnam, CM-3980-69 (U).* 5 Mar. 1969. Wheeler NARA Records.

Joint Chiefs of Staff. Office of the Chairman of the Joint Chiefs of Staff. *Memorandum for the Secretary of Defense, Subject: Practice Nine Requirements Plan, dated 26 January 1967, CM-2134-67 (U).* 22 Feb. 1967. Wheeler NARA Records.

Joint Chiefs of Staff. Office of the Chairman of the Joint Chiefs of Staff. *Memorandum for the Secretary of Defense, Subject: Sinking Blocking Craft, Haiphong Channel, CM-4000-69 (U).* 13 Mar. 1969. Wheeler NARA Records.

Joint Chiefs of Staff. Office of the Chairman of the Joint Chiefs of Staff. *Memorandum for the Secretary of Defense, Subject: "Surgical" Strikes and/or Naval Bombardment in the Haiphong Area, CM-3994-69 (U).* 14 Mar. 1969. Wheeler NARA Records.

Joint Chiefs of Staff. Office of the Chairman of the Joint Chiefs of Staff. *Memorandum for the Secretary of Defense, Subject: Vietnam Demilitarized Zone (DMZ), CM-4010-69 (U).* 15 Mar. 1969. Wheeler NARA Records.

Joint Chiefs of Staff. Office of the Chairman of the Joint Chiefs of Staff. *Memorandum for the Under Secretary of State, Subject: General Maxwell D. Taylor's Analysis of Courses of Action in SEA, CM-2782-67 (U).* 24 Nov. 1967. Wheeler NARA Records.

Joint Chiefs of Staff. Office of the Chairman of the Joint Chiefs of Staff. *Memorandum, Subject: PRACTICE NINE Requirements Plan, CM-2134-67 (U)*. 22 Feb. 1967. Wheeler NARA Records.

Joint Chiefs of Staff. Office of the Chairman of the Joint Chiefs of Staff. *Photo Album for General Earle G. Wheeler, Chairman, 1964-1965*. Jul. 1970. Wheeler Family Records.

Joint Chiefs of Staff. Office of the Chairman of the Joint Chiefs of Staff. *Photo Album for General Earle G. Wheeler, Chairman, 1965-1966*. Jul. 1970. Wheeler Family Records.

Joint Chiefs of Staff. Office of the Chairman of the Joint Chiefs of Staff. *Photo Album for General Earle G. Wheeler, Chairman, 1966-1967*. Jul. 1970. Wheeler Family Records.

Joint Chiefs of Staff. Office of the Chairman of the Joint Chiefs of Staff. *Photo Album for General Earle G. Wheeler, Chairman, 1967-1968*. Jul. 1970. Wheeler Family Records.

Joint Chiefs of Staff. Office of the Chairman of the Joint Chiefs of Staff. *Photo Album for General Earle G. Wheeler, Chairman, 1968-1969*. Jul. 1970. Wheeler Family Records.

Joint Chiefs of Staff. Office of the Chairman of the Joint Chiefs of Staff. *Photo Album for General Earle G. Wheeler, Chairman, 1969-1970*. Jul. 1970. Wheeler Family Records.

Joint Chiefs of Staff. Office of the Chairman of the Joint Chiefs of Staff. *Photo Album for General Earle G. Wheeler, Chairman, 1970*. Jul. 1970. Wheeler Family Records.

Joint Chiefs of Staff. Office of the Chairman of the Joint Chiefs of Staff. *Report of the Chairman, Joint Chiefs of Staff, Gen. Earle G. Wheeler, on the Situation in Vietnam (U)*. 27 Feb. 1968. Wheeler NARA Records.

Joint Chiefs of Staff. Office of the Chairman of the Joint Chiefs of Staff. *Statement by General Earle G. Wheeler, USA, Chairman of the Joint Chiefs of Staff, Before the Department of Defense Subcommittee on Appropriations, House Appropriations Committee (U)*. 4 May 1970. Pentagon Library.

Joint Chiefs of Staff. Office of the Special Assistant for Counterinsurgency and Special Activities. *Memorandum for General Wheeler, Subject: Major Strategy and Turning Points in Vietnam (U)*. 14 Sep. 1968. Wheeler NARA Records.

Joint Chiefs of Staff. Office of the Special Assistant for Counterinsurgency and Special Activities. *Memorandum for Record, Subject: Code-Word Designator – Access Plan (U)*. Not dated (Feb. 1968). Wheeler NARA Records.

Joint Staff. The National Military Command Center. *Memorandum for the Chairman, Joint Chiefs of Staff, Subject: Casualties, Weapons Seized and Aircraft Losses in South Vietnam (U)*. 10 Feb. 1968. Wheeler NARA Records.

Lyndon Baines Johnson Library & Museum. *President's Daily Diary*. 27 Apr. 1967.

Monsanto Co. *Biographical Sketch of Gen. Earle G. Wheeler, U.S. Army (Retired)*. Sep. 1970. Wheeler Family Records.

National Security Council. *Intelligence Assessment on the Situation in Vietnam by National Security Council Working Group on Vietnam (U)*. 13 Nov. 1964. Wheeler NARA Records.

National Security Council. *National Security Study Memorandum No. 1 (U)*. 21 Jan. 1969. Wheeler NARA Records.

Office of Joint History. Office of the Chairman of the Joint Chiefs of Staff. *The Joint Chiefs of Staff and The War in Vietnam 1971–1973*. Washington, DC: 2007.

Office of Joint History. Office of the Chairman of the Joint Chiefs of Staff. *The Joint Chiefs of Staff and The War in Vietnam 1969–1970*. Washington, DC: 2002.

Office of Joint History. Office of the Chairman of the Joint Chiefs of Staff. *The Joint Chiefs of Staff and The War in Vietnam 1960–1968 Part 1*. Washington, DC: 2011.

Office of Joint History. Office of the Chairman of the Joint Chiefs of Staff. *The Joint Chiefs of Staff and The War in Vietnam 1960–1968 Part 2.* Washington, DC: 2012.

State of Maryland. Department of Health and Mental Hygiene. *Medical Examiner's Certificate of Death, Earle G. Wheeler.* 30 Dec. 1975. Wheeler Family Records.

The White House. *Address by President Nixon on Cambodia.* 30 Apr. 1970. Wheeler NARA Records.

The White House. *Memorandum from Walt W. Rostow to Cyrus Vance, Richard Helms, William P. Bundy (U).* 22 May 1967. Wheeler NARA Records.

The White House. *Memorandum of Conversation (U).* 9 Sep. 1967. Wheeler NARA Records.

The White House. *Presentation of the Defense Distinguished Service Medal to General Earle G. Wheeler, at The White House on Thursday, 9 July 1970 at 1000 Hours.* Wheeler Family Records.

The White House. *Remarks of the President and General Westmoreland at a Luncheon at the White House, The East Room (U).* 20 Apr. 1967. Wheeler NARA Records.

United States Air Force, Office of Air Force History. *The Air Force in Vietnam, The Search for Military Alternatives 1967 (U).* Dec. 1969. Wheeler NARA Records.

United States Army. *Field Manual 100-5 (Field Service Regulations, Operations),* Feb. 1962. Ike Skelton Combined Arms Research Library Digital Library.

United States Army. *Field Manual 6-0 (Commander and Staff Organizations and Operations),* 5 May 2014. Army Publishing Directorate. Pentagon Library.

United States Army. *General Orders Number 26.* 19 Dec. 1975. Wheeler Family Records.

United States Army. Office, Chief of Information. *Biography: Gen. Berton E. Spivy, Jr.* Apr. 1965. Pentagon Library.

United States Army. Office, Chief of Information. *Biography: Gen. Earle G. Wheeler*. No date. Wheeler Family Records.

United States Army. The Adjutant General. *Memorandum, Subject: Permanent Disability Retirement*. 4 Jul. 1970. Wheeler Family Records.

United States Army. Walter Reed General Hospital. *Clinical Record, Earle G. Wheeler*. 22 Apr. 1970. Wheeler Family Records.

United States. Congress. House. Committee on Foreign Affairs. Subcommittee on Asian and Pacific Affairs. *U.S. Policy and Programs in Cambodia: Hearings Before the Subcommittee on Asian and Pacific Affairs of the Committee on Foreign Affairs, House of Representatives, Ninety-third Congress, First Session (U)*. Washington, DC: U.S. Government Printing Office, 1973. Pentagon Library.

United States Marine Corps. *The Marines in Vietnam: 1954-1973: An Anthology and Annotated Bibliography*. Washington, DC: U.S. Government Printing Office, 1974.

United States Military Assistance Command, Vietnam. *Back Channel Message from General Westmoreland, COMUSMACV, Saigon, to General Johnson, Acting CJCS, Washington, and Admiral Sharp, CINCPAC, Hawaii (U)*. 27 Sep. 1967. Wheeler NARA Records.

United States Military Assistance Command, Vietnam. *Back Channel Message from General Westmoreland, COMUSMACV, Saigon, to General Wheeler, CJCS, Washington, and Admiral Sharp, CINCPAC, Hawaii (U)*. 8 Feb. 1968. Wheeler NARA Records.

United States Military Assistance Command, Vietnam. *Back Channel Message from General Westmoreland, COMUSMACV, Saigon, to General Wheeler, CJCS, Washington, and Admiral Sharp, CINCPAC, Hawaii (U)*. 4 Feb. 1968. Wheeler NARA Records.

United States Military Assistance Command, Vietnam. *Back Channel Message from General Westmoreland, COMUSMACV, Saigon, to General Wheeler, CJCS, Washington, and Admiral Sharp, CINCPAC, Hawaii (U)*. 4 Jun. 1967. Wheeler NARA Records.

United States Military Assistance Command, Vietnam. *Back Channel Message from General Westmoreland, COMUSMACV, Saigon, to General Wheeler, CJCS, Washington, and Admiral Sharp, CINCPAC, Hawaii (U).* 9 May 1966. Wheeler NARA Records.

United States Military Assistance Command, Vietnam. *Back Channel Message from General Westmoreland, COMUSMACV, Saigon, to General Wheeler, CJCS, Washington, and Admiral Sharp, CINCPAC, Hawaii (U).* 17 Feb. 1967. Wheeler NARA Records.

United States Military Assistance Command, Vietnam. *Back Channel Message from General Westmoreland, COMUSMACV, Saigon, to General Wheeler, CJCS, Washington, and Admiral Sharp, CINCPAC, Hawaii (U).* 6 Feb. 1967. Wheeler NARA Records.

United States Military Assistance Command, Vietnam. *Back Channel Message from General Westmoreland, COMUSMACV, Saigon, to General Wheeler, CJCS, Washington, and Admiral Sharp, CINCPAC, Hawaii (U).* 3 Feb. 1968. Wheeler NARA Records.

United States Military Assistance Command, Vietnam. *Back Channel Message from General Westmoreland, COMUSMACV, Saigon, to General Wheeler, CJCS, Washington, and Admiral Sharp, CINCPAC, Hawaii (U).* 3 Feb. 1967. Wheeler NARA Records.

United States Military Assistance Command, Vietnam. *Back Channel Message from General Westmoreland, COMUSMACV, Saigon, to General Wheeler, CJCS, Washington, and Admiral Sharp, CINCPAC, Hawaii (U).* 3 Mar. 1968. Wheeler NARA Records.

United States Military Assistance Command, Vietnam. *Back Channel Message from General Westmoreland, COMUSMACV, Saigon, to General Wheeler, CJCS, Washington, and Admiral Sharp, CINCPAC, Hawaii (U).* 3 Mar. 1967. Wheeler NARA Records.

United States Military Assistance Command, Vietnam. *Back Channel Message from General Westmoreland, COMUSMACV, Saigon, to General Wheeler, CJCS, Washington, and Admiral Sharp, CINCPAC, Hawaii (U).* 12 Apr. 1967. Wheeler NARA Records.

United States Military Assistance Command, Vietnam. *Back Channel Message from General Westmoreland, COMUSMACV, Saigon, to General Wheeler, CJCS, Washington, and Admiral Sharp, CINCPAC, Hawaii (U).* 12 Feb. 1968. Wheeler NARA Records.

United States Military Assistance Command, Vietnam. *Back Channel Message from General Westmoreland, COMUSMACV, Saigon, to General Wheeler, CJCS, Washington, and Admiral Sharp, CINCPAC, Hawaii (U).* 20 Feb. 1968. Wheeler NARA Records.

United States Military Assistance Command, Vietnam. *Back Channel Message from General Westmoreland, COMUSMACV, Saigon, to General Wheeler, CJCS, Washington, and Admiral Sharp, CINCPAC, Hawaii (U).* 28 Oct. 1967. Wheeler NARA Records.

United States Military Assistance Command, Vietnam. *Back Channel Message from General Westmoreland, COMUSMACV, Saigon, to General Wheeler, CJCS, Washington, and Admiral Sharp, CINCPAC, Hawaii (U).* 28 Oct. 1967. Wheeler NARA Records.

United States Military Assistance Command, Vietnam. *Back Channel Message from General Westmoreland, COMUSMACV, Saigon, to General Wheeler, CJCS, Washington, and Admiral Sharp, CINCPAC, Hawaii (U).* 26 Aug. 1967. Wheeler NARA Records.

United States Military Assistance Command, Vietnam. *Back Channel Message from General Westmoreland, COMUSMACV, Saigon, to General Wheeler, CJCS, Washington, and Admiral Sharp, CINCPAC, Hawaii (U).* 2 Mar. 1968. Wheeler NARA Records.

United States Military Assistance Command, Vietnam. *Back Channel Message from General Westmoreland, COMUSMACV, Saigon, to General Wheeler, CJCS, Washington (U).* 4 Nov.1967. Wheeler NARA Records.

United States Military Assistance Command, Vietnam. *Back Channel Message from General Wheeler, CJCS, Saigon, to General Johnson, Acting CJCS, Washington (U).* 25 Feb.1968. Wheeler NARA Records.

United States Military Assistance Command, Vietnam. *Back Channel Message from General Wheeler, CJCS, Saigon, to General Johnson, COFSA,*

Washington, and Admiral Sharp, CINCPAC, Honolulu (U). 25 Feb.1968. Wheeler NARA Records.

United States Military Assistance Command, Vietnam. *Background Briefing Presented by General Westmoreland (U).* 29 Jun.1967. Wheeler NARA Records.

United States Military Assistance Command, Vietnam. *COMUSMACV Outline Plan BUTT STROKE (U).* 20 Sep. 1967. Wheeler NARA Records.

United States Military Assistance Command, Vietnam. *Front Channel Message from General Westmoreland, COMUSMACV, Saigon, to General Wheeler, CJCS, Washington (U).* 8 May 1967. Wheeler NARA Records.

United States Military Assistance Command, Vietnam. *Front Channel Message from General Westmoreland, COMUSMACV, Saigon, to General Wheeler, CJCS, Washington, and Admiral Sharp, CINCPAC, Hawaii (U).* 5 Apr. 1967. Wheeler NARA Records.

United States Military Assistance Command, Vietnam. *General Westmoreland's History Notes (U).* 1 Jun. – 5 Jul. 1967. Wheeler NARA Records.

United States Military Assistance Command, Vietnam. *General Westmoreland's History Notes (U).* 1-20 May 1967. Wheeler NARA Records.

United States Military Assistance Command, Vietnam. *General Westmoreland's History Notes (U).* 10-30 Apr. 1967. Wheeler NARA Records.

United States Military Assistance Command, Vietnam. *MACV Practice Nine Requirements Plan (U).* 26 Jan. 1967. Wheeler NARA Records.

United States Pacific Command and United States Military Assistance Command, Vietnam. *Report on the War in Vietnam (U).* Jun. 1968. Wheeler NARA Records.

United States Pacific Command. *Back Channel Message from Admiral Sharp, CINCPAC, Hawaii, to Admiral Moorer, Acting CJCS, Washington, and*

Admiral Johnson, CINCPACFLT, Hawaii (U). 3 Sep. 1967. Wheeler NARA Records.

United States Pacific Command. *Back Channel Message from Admiral Sharp, CINCPAC, Hawaii, to General Westmoreland, COMUSMACV, Saigon, and General Wheeler, CJCS, Washington (U)*. 8 Feb. 1968. Wheeler NARA Records.

United States Pacific Command. *Back Channel Message from Admiral Sharp, CINCPAC, Hawaii, to General Westmoreland, COMUSMACV, Saigon, and General Wheeler, CJCS, Washington (U)*. 4 Feb. 1968. Wheeler NARA Records.

United States Pacific Command. *Back Channel Message from Admiral Sharp, CINCPAC, Hawaii, to General Westmoreland, COMUSMACV, Saigon, and General Wheeler, CJCS, Washington (U)*. 9 May 1966. Wheeler NARA Records.

United States Pacific Command. *Back Channel Message from Admiral Sharp, CINCPAC, Hawaii, to General Westmoreland, COMUSMACV, Saigon, and General Wheeler, CJCS, Washington (U)*. 23 Mar. 1968. Wheeler NARA Records.

United States Pacific Command. *Back Channel Message from Admiral Sharp, CINCPAC, Hawaii, to General Westmoreland, COMUSMACV, Saigon, and General Wheeler, CJCS, Washington (U)*. 2 Feb. 1968. Wheeler NARA Records.

United States Pacific Command. *Back Channel Message from Admiral Sharp, CINCPAC, Hawaii, to General Westmoreland, COMUSMACV, Saigon, and General Wheeler, CJCS, Washington (U)*. 13 Apr. 1968. Wheeler NARA Records.

United States Pacific Command. *Back Channel Message from Admiral Sharp, CINCPAC, Hawaii, to General Wheeler, CJCS, Washington (U)*. 1 Apr. 1968. Wheeler NARA Records.

United States Pacific Command. *Back Channel Message from Admiral Sharp, CINCPAC, Hawaii, to General Wheeler, CJCS, Washington (U)*. 7 Sep. 1967. Wheeler NARA Records.

United States Pacific Command. Commander, Fleet Marine Force Pacific. *Outline Plan for Operation COLUBRINE (U).* 20 Sep. 1967. Wheeler NARA Records.

United States Pacific Command. *Two Back Channel Messages from Admiral Sharp, CINCPAC, Hawaii, to General Westmoreland, COMUSMACV, Saigon, and General Wheeler, CJCS, Washington (U).* 10 Feb. 1968. Wheeler NARA Records.

United States Pacific Command. *Two Back Channel Messages from Admiral Sharp, CINCPAC, Hawaii, to Joint Chiefs of Staff, Washington (U).* 16 May 1967. Wheeler NARA Records.

Veterans Administration. Veterans Benefits Office. *Letter to Earle G. Wheeler.* 10 Jul. 1970. Wheeler Family Records.

Online Media

Archives.gov. Downloaded from the internet on 5 Nov. 2017 at https://www.archives.gov/research/military/vietnam-war/casualty-statistics.html.

Arlington National Cemetery. Downloaded from the internet on 20 Oct. 2013 and 22 Oct. 2015 at http://www.arlingtoncemetery.net/bespivy.htm.

Arlington National Cemetery. Downloaded from the internet on 13 Feb. 2013 at http://www.arlingtoncemetery.net/ewheeler.htm.

Arlington National Cemetery. Downloaded from the internet on 19 Apr. 2018 at http://www.arlingtoncemetery.net/jehull.htm.

Army Historical Foundation. Downloaded from the internet on 13 Feb. 2013 at https://armyhistory.org/09/general-earle-g-wheeler/.

C-Span. Downloaded from the internet on 31 Jan. 2017 at https://www.c-span.org/video/?404455-1/general-james-gavin-testimony-1966-fulbright-vietnam-hearings.

Department of State. Office of the Historian. Downloaded from the internet on 17 Dec. 2017 at https://history.state.gov/historicaldocuments/frus1964-68v04/d216.

Ed Gallucci Photography. Downloaded from the internet on 22 Aug. 2017 at http://www.edgallucciphotography.com/march-washington-d-c-may-10-1970/.

Extended Remarks. Downloaded from the internet on 2 Sep. 2010 at http://extendedremarks.blogspot.com/2006/12/vietnam-1965-day-it-became-longest-war.html.

Great Quotes.com. Downloaded from the internet on 4 Aug. 2018 at http://www.great-quotes.com/quotes/author/Douglas/MacArthur/pg/2.

History.com. Downloaded from the internet on 2 Feb. 2017 at http://www.history.com/this-day-in-history/manila-conference-attendees-issue-declaration-of-peace.

History.com. Downloaded from the internet on 5 Jul. 2017 at http://www.history.com/this-day-in-history/100000-people-march-on-the-pentagon.

History.com. Downloaded from the internet on 2 Sep. 2010 at http://www.history.com/this-day-in-history.do?action=tdihArticleCategory&id=1967.

LinkedIn SlideShare. Downloaded from the internet on 28 Apr. 20 at https://www.slideshare.net/DaveMcGinnis/princples-of-war-relivance-ada435689.

Marines. Downloaded from the internet on 11 Jul. 2017 at http://marines.mil/News/Messages/Messages-Display/Article/886772/death-of-general-leonard-f-chapman-jr-former-commandant-of-the-marine-corps/.

Named to Honor the Mustin Family. Downloaded from the internet on 5 Dec. 2015 at https://public.navy.mil.

New York Times. Downloaded from the internet on 19 Jun. 2017 at http://www.mobile.nytimes.com/johnson-westmoreland-and-the-selling-of-vietnam.html.

New York Times. Downloaded from the internet on 7 Jan. 2014 at http://www.nytimes.com/1990/02/25/obituaries/lieut-gen-james-gavin-82-dies-champion-and-critic-of-military.html.

New York Times. Downloaded from the internet on 22 Aug. 2017 at http://www.nytimes.com/1974/07/27/archives/

arthur-watson-of-ibm-exenvoy-dies-on-international-role-known-as. html.

New York Times. Downloaded from the internet on 2 May 2018 at https:// www.nytimes.com/1989/03/12/books/the-age-of-brass.html.

New York Times. Downloaded from the internet on 19 Jul. 2017 at https:// mobile.nytimes.com/2001/12/18/us/ulysses-s-grant-sharp-jr-vietnam-war-admiral-95.html.

Politico. Downloaded from the internet on 26 Jul. 2017 at http://www.politico.com/story/2013/04/this-day-in-politics-089554.

Real Clear Defense. Downloaded from the internet on 11 Jul. 2015 at http:// www.realcleardefense.com/articles/2015/07/11/chairman_of_the_joint_chiefs_is_a_commander_of_nothing_108209.html.

75th Ranger Regiment Association. Downloaded from the internet on 16 Dec. 2017 at http://www.75thrra.com/history/n75_hx.html.

Supreme Headquarters Allied Powers Europe. Downloaded from the internet on 2 Jul. 2017 at https://shape.nato.int/page1463252.

The Forgotten General. Downloaded from the internet on 13 Feb. 2013 at http://theforgottengeneral.com/wp-content/uploads/2010/12/JCS-Biography.pdf.

United States Air Force. Downloaded from the internet on 4 Aug. 2018 at http:www.af.mil/About-Us/Biographies/Display/Article/106325/general-john-paul-mcconnell/.

United States Army. Office of the Administrative Assistant to the Secretary of the Army. The institute of Heraldry. Downloaded from the internet on 16 Dec. 2017 at http://www.tioh. hqda.pentagon.mil/Catalog/Heraldry.aspx?Heraldry-Id=15493&CategoryId=9148&grp=2&menu=Uniformed%20 Services&ps=24&p=0.

United States Central Command. Downloaded from the internet on 4 Aug. 2018 at http://www.centcom.mil/ABOUT-US/LEADERSHIP/Article/904768/george-b-crist/.

United States European Command. Downloaded from the internet on 23 Jul. 2017 at www.eucom.mil/media-library/article/20939/the-man-who-moved-eucom-gen-david-a-burchinal.

United States Pacific Command. Downloaded from the internet on 19 Jul. 2017 at http:www.pacom.mil/About-USPACOM/USPACOM-Previous-Commanders/.

Warontherocks.com. Downloaded from the internet on 26 Jan. 2016 at http://warontherocks.com/2014/07/iraq-and-longing-for-vietnam/.

Washington Post. Downloaded from the internet on 4 Jul. 2017 at https://www.washingtonpost.com/archive/local/1997/12/20/admiral-aviator-david-mcdonald-dies-at-91/344cf55b-13b1-4515-829e-9abab41df-d90/?utm_term=.81a3a7bd548d.

Washington Post. Downloaded from the internet on 2 Sep. 2010 at https://www.washingtonpost.com/wp-srv/style/longterm/books/chap1/abet-terwar.htm.

West Point Association of Graduates. Downloaded from the internet on 15 Dec. 2017 at http://apps.westpointaog.org/Memorials/Article/9579/.

Winstonchurchill.org. Downloaded from the internet on 2 Nov. 2017 at https://www.winstonchurchill.org/resources/speeches/1940-the-finst-hour/blood-toil-tears-sweat.

Wunderground.com. Downloaded from the internet on 30 Oct. 2017 at https://www.wunderground.com/history/airport/KDCA/1975/12/22/DailyHistory.html?&reqdb.zip=&reqdb.magic=&reqdb.wmo=.

Periodicals

Army. *Historically Speaking, Earle G. Wheeler at 100.* Feb 2010.

Army History. Book review of *Westmoreland's War: Reassessing American Strategy in Vietnam.* Fall 2014.

Army Times. *Calls for Brass to Resign Add to Debate Over Mideast Policy.* 30 Sep. 2014.

Baltimore Sun. *A Military Man is Chosen and Chief Knows Him Well.* 24 Jun. 1964. Wheeler Family Records.

Baltimore Sun. *Two Generals.* 28 Jun. 1964. Wheeler Family Records.

Boston Globe. *What Victory Means Now.* 27 Jan. 2[013]

Journal Register. *New JCS Chairman.* 27 Jun. 1964. Wheeler Family Records.

Lawton Constitution. *Land Warfare Emphasis.* 2 Jul. 1964. Wheeler Family Records.

Los Angeles Times. *Nicholas Katzenbach Dies at 90; Attorney General Under Johnson.* 10 May 2012.

Los Angeles Times. *Wheeler, Johnson Take Up New Posts.* 7 Jul. 1964. Wheeler Family Records.

Martinsburg Journal. *Editorial: Gen. Earle G. Wheeler.* 22 Dec. 1975. Wheeler Family Records.

National Observer. *General Wheeler's Rising Stars, It's 3-for-3 for the Army As Taylor 'Protégé" Gets Top Job.* 29 Jun. 1964. Wheeler Family Records.

Newsweek. *Merit Will Be Rewarded.* 3 Jul. 1964. Wheeler Family Records.

New York Herald Tribune. *Gen. Wheeler Aims for Harmony.* 7 Jul. 1964. Wheeler Family Records.

New York Herald Tribune. *Gen. Wheeler, New U.S. Top Military Man.* 19 Aug. 1964. Wheeler Family Records.

New York News. *Staff Chief.* 9 Jul. 1964. Wheeler Family Records.

New York Times. *David Lamar McDonald, 91, Former Senior Naval Officer.* 23 Dec. 1997.

New York Times. *Gen. Earle Wheeler Dies; Ex-Head of Joint Chiefs.* 19 Dec. 1975. Wheeler Family Records.

New York Times. *George W. Ball Dies at 84: Vietnam's Devil's Advocate.* 28 May 1994.

New York Times. *Johnson and the General.* 28 Apr. 1967. Wheeler Family Records.

New York Times. *New Military Top Man.* 8 Jul. 1964. Wheeler Family Records.

New York Times. *Rotation Ended For Joint Chiefs.* 24 Jun. 1964. Wheeler Family Records.

New York Times. *'Staff Man' in Chief.* 24 Jun. 1964. Wheeler Family Records.

New York Times. *The Cold Warrior Who Never Apologized.* 8 Sep. 2017.

Observer-Reporter. *Retired General Dies at 76.* 21 Aug. 1990.

Pentagram News. *Gens. Wheeler, Johnson Send Messages.* 9 Jul. 1964. Wheeler Family Records.

Philadelphia Inquirer. *Change of Guard Over S. Vietnam.* 24 Jun. 1964. Wheeler Family Records.

Reuters. *After Seeing Iraq up Close, Top US General Wary on Syria.* 12 Sep. 2013.

Source unknown. *Chiefs Chairman Gen. Wheeler Retires Today.* 2 Jul. 1970. Wheeler Family Records.

Time. *Three Top Soldiers.* 6 Jul. 1964. Wheeler Family Records.

U.S. News & World Report. *A General Tells How US Can Win in Vietnam.* 14 Dec. 1966. Wheeler Family Records.

U.S. News & World Report. *Pentagon Shift – Generals Who Moved Up.* 6 Jul. 1964. Wheeler Family Records.

Washington Post. *Ex-Air Force Gen. John McConnell Dies.* 22 Nov. 1986.

Washington Post. *Gen. Earle Wheeler Dies; Headed Joint Chiefs.* 19 Dec. 1975. Wheeler Family Records.

Washington Post. *Gen. Henry W. Buse, Official of Olympic Panel, Dies at 76.* 22 Oct. 1988.

Washington Post. *Pentagon Shift Shatters JCS Rotation Precedent.* 24 Jun. 1964. Wheeler Family Records.

Washington Post. *Taylor Marked Wheeler Early for High Military Responsibility.* 24 Jun. 1964. Wheeler Family Records.

Washington Star. *General Wheeler Honored.* 7 Jul. 1964. Wheeler Family Records.

Washington Star. *Wheeler Aims to Ease Civilian-Military Gap.* 28 Jun. 1964. Wheeler Family Records.

Wall Street Journal. *Military Chieftain.* 26 Jun. 1964. Wheeler Family Records.

Records Collections

Department of the Army, H.K. Johnson Papers, U.S. Army Military History Institute (USAMHI), Carlisle, PA.

Department of the Army, William C. Westmoreland Collection, Series II, Official Papers - COMUSMACV, U.S. Army Military History Institute (USAMHI), Carlisle, PA. This collection contains 21 boxes of unclassified documents and 76 boxes of unclassified documents.

Joint Chiefs of Staff, Chairman (GEN) Earle G. Wheeler, Official Records, Joint Chiefs of Staff, 3 July 64 – 2 July 70, National Archives, College Park, MD. This collection contains 219 boxes of mostly still-classified documents.

Wheeler Family Records, Martinsburg, WV. This unarchived collection contains Wheeler's official personnel records and vast family correspondence spanning the duration of Wheeler's military career.

Theses

Buzzanco, Robert. *Masters of War? Military Criticism, Strategy, and Civil-Military Relations During the Vietnam War*, Ph.D diss., Ohio State University, 1993.

Morris, Michael F. *Paths Not Taken: MACV's Quest for Military Victory, 1965-1969*. Quantico, VA: Marine Corps University, 2017.

Rhynedance, George H. *McNamara vs. The JCS, Vietnam's Operation Rolling Thunder: A Failure in Civil-Military Relations*. Carlisle, PA: United States Army War College, 2000.

Scribner, Charles R. *The Eisenhower and Johnson Administrations' Decisionmaking on Vietnamese Intervention: A Study of Contrasts*. Ph. D. diss., University of California Santa Barbara, 1980.

Unofficial Correspondence

Cosmas, Graham A. *Email to Randy Rakers*. 5 Jan. 2010. Author's Records.

Crane, Conrad C. *Conversation with Mark Viney*. 5 Nov. 2010. Author's Records.

Hallenbeck, Ralph J. *Letter to Mark Viney*. 19 Sep. 2008. Author's Records.

Hallenbeck, Ralph J. *Letter to Mark Viney*. 15 Oct. 2008. Author's Records.

COLONEL MARK A. VINEY

Hull, John E. *Letter to Robert S. McNamara.* 14 Dec. 1966. Wheeler
    NARA Records.

Johnson, Lady B. *Letter to Betty Wheeler.* 21 Dec. 1974. Wheeler
    Family Records.

Johnson, Lyndon B. *Letter to Earle G. Wheeler.* 15 Apr. 1970. Wheeler
    Family Records.

Johnson, Lyndon B. *Note to Earl¹e G. Wheeler.* 7 Feb. 1968. Wheeler
    Family Records

Kohn, Richard H. *Email to Karen Loving.* 18 Oct. 2008. Author's Records.

Loving, Karen. *Email to Mark A. Viney,* 9 Sep. 2008. Author's Records.

Loving, Karen. *Email to Mark A. Viney,* 21 Oct. 2008. Author's Records.

Nixon, Richard M. *Letter to Earle G. Wheeler.* 18 Jun. 1969. Wheeler
    Family Records.

Nixon, Richard M. *Letter to Earle G. Wheeler.* 9 Jul. 1970. Wheeler
    Family Records.

Odom, Louie W. *Letter to Gilmore S. Wheeler.* 19 Mar. 2013. Wheeler
    Family Records.

Prados, John. *Emails to Mark Viney (2),* 24 Feb. 2010. Author's Records.

Villard, Erik B. *Email to Randy Rakers.* 27 Feb. 2007. Author's Records.

Viney, George C. *Letter to Ralph J. Hallenbeck.* 15 Jul. 09. Author's Records.

Wheeler, Earle G. *Letter to Harold K. Johnson.* 6 May. 1967. Wheeler
    Family Records.

Wheeler, Earle G. *Letter to Lyndon B. Johnson,* 5 Sep. 1967. Wheeler
    Family Records.

Wheeler, Earle G. *Letter to Walter R. Howell.* 20 Jul. 1964. Wheeler
    Family Records.

Wheeler, Frances R. *Letter to Rebecca Howell.* 22 Jun. 1964. Wheeler
    Family Records.

Wheeler, Frances R. *Letter to Rebecca Howell.* 25 Jun. 1964. Wheeler
    Family Records.

Wheeler, Frances R. *Letter to Rebecca Howell.* 2-3 Jul. 1964. Wheeler Family Records.

Wheeler, Frances R. *Letter to Rebecca Howell.* 9 Jul. 1964. Wheeler Family Records.

Wheeler, Frances R. *Letter to Rebecca Howell.* 20 Jul. 1964. Wheeler Family Records.

Wheeler, Frances R. *Letter to Rebecca Howell.* 4 Aug. 1964. Wheeler Family Records.

Wheeler, Frances R. *Letter to Rebecca Howell.* 15 Oct. 1964. Wheeler Family Records.

Wheeler, Frances R. *Letter to Rebecca Howell.* 9 Feb. 1965. Wheeler Family Records.

Wheeler, Frances R. *Letter to Rebecca Howell.* 1 Mar. 1965. Wheeler Family Records.

Wheeler, Frances R. *Letter to Rebecca Howell.* 19 Mar. 1965. Wheeler Family Records.

Wheeler, Frances R. *Letter to Rebecca Howell.* 6 Apr. 1965. Wheeler Family Records.

Wheeler, Frances R. *Letter to Rebecca Howell.* 28 Apr. 1965. Wheeler Family Records.

Wheeler, Frances R. *Letter to Rebecca Howell.* 14 Jul. 1965. Wheeler Family Records.

Wheeler, Frances R. *Letter to Rebecca Howell.* 9 Aug. 1965. Wheeler Family Records.

Wheeler, Frances R. *Letter to Rebecca Howell.* 7 Feb. 1966. Wheeler Family Records.

Wheeler, Frances R. *Letter to Rebecca Howell.* 30 Apr. 1966. Wheeler Family Records.

Wheeler, Frances R. *Letter to Rebecca Howell.* 19 Jun. 1966. Wheeler Family Records.

Wheeler, Frances R. *Letter to Rebecca Howell.* 24 Jan. 1967. Wheeler Family Records.

Wheeler, Frances R. *Letter to Rebecca Howell.* 7 Jun. 1967. Wheeler Family Records.

Wheeler, Frances R. *Letter to Rebecca Howell.* 16 Jun. 1967. Wheeler Family Records.

Wheeler, Frances R. *Letter to Rebecca Howell.* 2 Oct. 1967. Wheeler Family Records.

Wheeler, Frances R. *Letter to Rebecca Howell.* 20 Oct. 1967. Wheeler Family Records.

Wheeler, Frances R. *Letter to Rebecca Howell.* 24 Jun. 1968. Wheeler Family Records.

Wheeler, Frances R. *Letter to Rebecca Howell.* Date unspecified (early Jun. 1970). Wheeler Family Records.

Wheeler, Gilmore S. *Email to Mark Viney.* 5 May. 2013. Author's Records.

Wheeler, Gilmore S. *Email to Mark Viney.* 1 Nov. 2013. Author's Records.

Wheeler, Gilmore S. *Email to Mark Viney.* 9 Jun. 2013. Author's Records.

Wheeler, Gilmore. *Email to Mark Viney.* 10 Jul. 2017. Author's Records.

Wheeler, Gilmore S. *Email to Mark Viney.* 3 Jul. 2014. Author's Records.

Wheeler, Gilmore S. *Email to Mark Viney.* 30 Dec. 2013. Author's Records.

Wheeler, Gilmore S. *Email to Mark Viney.* 31 Jan. 2014. Author's Records.

Wheeler, Gilmore S. *Email to Mark Viney.* 29 Jan. 2014. Author's Records.

Wheeler, Gilmore S. *Email to Mark Viney.* 29 Jul. 2013. Author's Records.

Wheeler, Gilmore S. *Email to Mark Viney.* 29 Mar. 2014. Author's Records.

Wheeler, Gilmore S. *Email to Mark Viney.* 21 Nov. 2013. Author's Records.

Wheeler, Gilmore S. *Email to Mark Viney.* 26 Apr. 2014. Author's Records.

Wheeler, Gilmore S. *Email to Mark Viney.* 23 Sep. 2015. Author's Records.

Wheeler, Gilmore S. *Email to Mark Viney.* 22 Mar. 2013. Author's Records.

Wheeler, Gilmore S. *Email to Mark Viney.* 2 Feb. 2018. Author's Records.

Unpublished Works

Viney, Mark A. *Determined to Persist.* Monograph. 29 Nov. 2012.
Author's Records.

Wheeler, Earle G. *Professional Resume.* 1971. Wheeler Family Records.

Wheeler, Gilmore S. *Untitled Monograph.* 1 Oct. 2010. Wheeler
Family Records.

Index